The Archaeological Northeast

The Archaeological Northeast

Edited by
Mary Ann Levine
Kenneth E. Sassaman
Michael S. Nassaney

Foreword by Alice B. Kehoe

Native Peoples of the Americas
Laurie Weinstein, General Editor

BERGIN & GARVEY
Westport, Connecticut • London

Library of Congress Cataloging-in-Publication Data

The archaeological Northeast / edited by Mary Ann Levine, Kenneth
E. Sassaman, Michael S. Nassaney ; foreword by Alice B. Kehoe.
    p. cm.—(Native peoples of the Americas, 1521–5091)
    Includes bibliographical references and index.
    ISBN 0–89789–517–7 (alk. paper).—ISBN 0–89789–733–1 (pbk.)
    1. Indians of North America—New England—Antiquities. 2. New
England—Antiquities. I. Levine, Mary Ann. II. Sassaman, Kenneth E.
III. Nassaney, Michael S. IV. Series.
    E78.N5   A68   1999
    974′.01—dc21   98–41384

British Library Cataloguing in Publication Data is available.

Library of Congress Catalog Card Number: 98–41384
ISBN: 0–89789–733–1 (pbk.)

First published in 1999

Bergin & Garvey, 88 Post Road West, Westport, CT 06881
An imprint of Greenwood Publishing Group, Inc.
www.greenwood.com

Printed in the United States of America

The paper used in this book complies with the
Permanent Paper Standard issued by the National
Information Standards Organization (Z39.48–1984).

10 9 8 7 6 5 4 3 2 1

Dedicated to Dena F. Dincauze
Professor of Anthropology
University of Massachusetts–Amherst

Contents

Series Foreword

The Archaeological Northeast, edited by Mary Ann Levine, Kenneth E. Sassa-man, and Michael S. Nassaney, is one of the first books in Bergin and Garvey's new series Native Peoples of the Americas. This series will cover indigenous people in North, Middle, and South America. Each volume will explore the history and cultural survival of native peoples by telling their unique stories. Some volumes will focus on competing ethnicities and the struggle for resources; other volumes will illuminate the archaeology and ethnohistory of particular regions; and still others will explore gender relations, warfare, and native cosmologies and ethnobotanies. Yet despite the particular foci or theoretical frameworks of the editor and his or her contributors, all volumes will reveal the rich cultural tapestry of the American continents. Together they will chronicle a common historical theme: despite the invasion of foreign explorers, traders, militia, missionaries, and colonists beginning in the late sixteenth century; despite rapid native depopulation because of disease and overt Anglo policies of ethnocide; despite the penetration of a capitalist market system into tribal economies, native peoples have survived.

The Archaeological Northeast specifically looks at the broad development of native peoples up until and including the Contact period, when European cultures invaded New England during the sixteenth and seventeenth centuries. The editors have also included a chapter specifically about historical archaeology at a seventeenth century colonial site. This volume will prove to be a very timely and useful contribution to New England studies. Few books, since Dean Snow's landmark 1980 publication, *The Archaeology of New England*, have looked at the culture history of the whole region of New England. Further, this volume is thorough in its analyses of the complexity of Northeastern prehistory. Each of the contributors looks at some of the unique problems faced by those wishing to understand New England's past. Environments can change overnight in some areas, as on Cape Cod (Chapter 3) because of wind and water erosion and sea-level rise since the last glaciation. Environments were impacted not only by such natural actions, but they were also impacted by native peoples, with "low-level technologies." The author of Chapter 2 makes us consider what effects of cutting thousands of saplings to build the famous Boylston Street Fish Weir (5300 to 3700 B.P.) would have had on the immediate environment. Other contributors look at some of the long-standing biases in New England archaeology and consider how such biases prevent us from accurately interpreting culture history, whether those biases are about the origins of raw copper (Chapter 12), soapstone technologies and the introduction of broad-bladed points (Chapter 5), or about land use in Vermont's Green Mountains (Chapter 7). This volume is also significant for the variety of approaches it brings to the study of New England's past. Such approaches include faunal analyses (Chapter 11), analyses of native ceramics (Chapter 6), copper (Chapter 12), soapstone (Chapter 5), and lithics (Chapter 4), the problematics of accurately radiocarbon dating shell deposits (Chapter 13), and the integration of deeds, collections, archival research, and excavation in the interpretation of colonial sites (Chapter 15). The editors have also included several chapters that provide theoretical frameworks for retelling this region's past. New, critical perspectives are brought to bear on the Paleoindian colonization of New England (Chapter 1), culture history in western Connecticut (Chapter 8) and western Massachusetts (Chapter 14), Algonquian settlement and farming (Chapter 9), and seventeenth-century Mohegan politics (Chapter 10).

I think readers will agree that this volume's editors have created an important, insightful work on Northeastern archaeology. What makes their volume especially remarkable is that all of the contributors were in some way influenced by the work and advice of one eminent scholar—Dena F. Dincauze.

Laurie Weinstein
General Editor
Native Peoples of the Americas

Foreword

A sea change crept like a tidal flow through American archaeology around 1960. The efficient cause was the 1950s establishment of radiocarbon dating as the standard method for constructing age estimates in prehistoric archaeology. No longer would American archaeologists consider their principal goal the construction of chronologies through stratigraphic sequences and artifact comparisons. Relaxation of this demand—premature relaxation, as Elizabeth A. Little indicates in Chapter 13—opened the field for competing approaches. Settlement pattern studies took the foreground at Harvard in the late 1950s, serving Gordon Willey's goal of making "the archaeologist in effect a cultural anthropologist" (Willey and Phillips 1958:6). Grahame Clark's (1954) environmental contextualization was another contestant. Clark had made his name working with paleoecologists in the 1930s and climaxed his efforts with the monograph on the early Holocene site of Star Carr. It turned out that neither the Bowditch Professor at Harvard nor the Disney Professor at Cambridge, respectively the doyens of Americanist and Old World prehistoric archaeology, set the mode: the upstart Lewis Binford crafted a coup d'état with his New Archaeology promising the discovery of universal laws of human social existence.

Some of the generation of American prehistorians growing up around 1960 rode on Binford's bandwagon, the wind in their faces and dust behind. Others remained skeptical of our ability to discover universal laws, and kept a lower profile carrying out what was then called salvage archaeology, now cultural resource management (CRM). After wetting their feet in Midwest archaeology, the stomping ground of their mentors' University of Michigan, New Archaeologists were drawn to the "richer," more glamorous regions such as the Southwest and Mesoamerica. New England was held to be worked out, its several centuries of Euroamerican farming and industrialization supposedly destroying practically all its prehistoric sites. Any archaeologist serious about a career was advised to forget the region. Any archaeologist who did work in the region was, ipso facto, not a serious contender in the discipline.

The career of Dena Ferran Dincauze illustrates the gratifying reversal of this dictum through three decades of intelligent work. Dincauze had been formed through classes with Richard and Nathalie Woodbury when she was an undergraduate at Barnard College, taking some courses across the street at Columbia University. Following Barnard, she spent a Fulbright year at Cambridge University, earning a Diploma in prehistoric archaeology in 1957. There, Grahame Clark's mode was not yet disputed. Returning to her home state of Massachusetts, Dincauze matriculated in the doctoral program at Harvard. Her options constrained by responsibility for homemaking and eventually two small children, Dincauze proposed dissertation research cooperating with southern New England avocational archaeologists. Colleagues at Harvard considered this foolish, for nothing would be found in situ. Dincauze, however, persevered. With only a small grant for domestic help, she accommodated research to family schedules. Furthermore, Dincauze did respect the avocational archaeologists she had met as she grew up in Concord. Their knowledge of artifacts and sensitivity to topography impressed her and their generosity empowered her. With her characteristic stance of steel encased in silk, Dincauze undertook an investigation of looted cremation cemeteries she knew of in eastern Massachusetts. Her dissertation committee was supportive but not enthusiastic until the work was completed.

Dincauze's two Peabody Museum monographs, the 1968 *Cremation Cemeteries in Eastern Massachusetts* (her dissertation) and the 1976 *The Neville Site*, revolutionized New England archaeology. She demonstrated that the region retained significant prehistoric sites, and, especially at Neville, that data could be recovered to construct a solid prehistory. Her skill in environmental interpretation linked the archaeological data with Quaternary natural science research, strengthening reconstructions and not incidentally, countering with sound accomplishment the New Archaeologists' disdain of work presented without the "window dressing" (as Ernst Mayr terms it [1982:850–852]) of explicit formal logic and elaborate statistics. Dincauze's work was reinforced when she was able to join her mentor, Richard Woodbury, in the expanding Department of Anthropology at the University of Massachusetts at Amherst in 1973. Woodbury's quiet manner almost matched Dincauze's, and the two constituted a rock of empirically grounded methodology.

The growth of CRM archaeology, fostered by federal and state mandates, oriented much of UMass's fieldwork and brought in funds. Simultaneously, Dincauze's long-standing collegial relationships with avocational archaeologists fit into the state university's obligation to taxpayers. With the Woodburys, she fulfilled civic responsibilities to state, municipality, and profession. Dick Woodbury, Nat Woodbury, and Dena Dincauze held a series of major offices in the Society for American Archaeology (SAA), with both Dick and Dena serving in time as editor of the society's journal and then elected to the highest office, president. Their fellow professionals' recognition, via the ballot, of the worth of these strong empiricists is testimony to the continuing current within SAA of its original goals of culture-history correlations and heritage steward-ship. Dincauze's 1977 and 1980 publications assessing southern New England's prehistoric resources came out of the dogged, uncompromising fieldwork UMass–Amherst had carried out under her direction for a decade.

Southern New England lacks ruins in its landscapes. An interesting chicken-and-egg question is, did that condition foster Dincauze's deep interest in environmental correlates of its archaeology, or was it that the condition drew her to continue to work in the region, once released from home and child demands? The intellectual challenges of New England archaeology are formidable, worthy of so penetrating and relentless a mind as Dincauze's. Cognoscenti appreciate the recalcitrance of New England's data—no ancient texts, little iconography, often ephemeral features. Multidisciplinary work such as Dincauze's projects struggles with alternative hypotheses on a range of fronts. That a region crossed off in mid-century as no longer viable for archaeology, is now so productive owes a great deal to the perseverance of a native daughter.

Alice B. Kehoe

Preface

This volume is the first comprehensive anthology of essays on the archaeology of the Northeast to be published in nearly a generation. It is particularly timely, for despite the many substantive advances made in archaeology over the past generation, the Northeast remains the most persistently misunderstood of all the archaeological regions of North America. There has long been a misconception, stemming from a number of related phenomena, that the prehistoric Northeast was a marginal cultural outlier. For example, in contrast to the Southeast and the Southwest, the Northeast lacks highly visible archaeological sites to capture the popular imagination. As the aboriginal peoples of the Northeast chose neither to build regional ceremonial centers replete with large earthen platform mounds nor to construct masonry pueblo architecture, archaeological sites in the Northeast are much more subtle than those found elsewhere on the continent. Furthermore, the Northeast has a unique and complex environmental history that sets it apart from much of the rest of the continent. Nearly all of the region was shaped and reshaped by episodic advances and retreats of ice sheets during the last glaciation. The highly acidic soils characteristic of much of the forested Northeast have destroyed many of the kinds of organic artifacts found in other areas. The result is a sometimes evasive, particularly complicated, and always fragmentary archaeological record. Just because archaeological investigations in the Northeast are challenging, however, it is misguided to dismiss the entire region as an outlier. Rather, as the chapters in this volume demonstrate, the Northeast is a region that inspires the development of innovative research designs and thoughtful and relevant questions. When such are applied to the archaeological Northeast, we begin to understand better the past of this most interesting of regions in its own terms, not in comparison to something else.

In the last thirty years, few people have addressed the challenges of the Northeast as formidably, and contributed to our understanding of the prehistory of Northeastern North America as thoroughly, as Dena F. Dincauze. Her contributions to the study of archaeology in the Northeast have served to revise the commonly—and wrongly—held notion that New England and other areas in the Northeast were "cultural backwaters." Throughout her career, Dincauze has challenged such poorly supported assumptions, not through the use of inflammatory rhetoric but rather through extensive and exhaustive scholarship on every time period of Northeastern prehistory. She has consistently called for the "centering" of the Northeast, that is, to question those historical, thematic, theoretical, and methodological biases that have traditionally shaped the misunderstanding of the Northeast as a cultural and archaeological outlier. This volume, created by her intellectual progeny, serves to demonstrate the depth and breadth of her influence on the development of scholarship on the archaeological Northeast. Each of the authors in this volume has been a graduate student of Dena Dincauze; collectively, we have chosen to acknowledge and celebrate Dena as a mentor by dedicating this volume to her. It is our hope that we, as her students, in accepting Dena's many challenges, have taken appropriate steps toward bringing the Northeast out of the periphery and into the center, where it belongs.

This volume demonstrates the chronological breadth of Dena's influence, as individual papers cover topics ranging from the first colonization of the Northeast by Paleoindians through the establishment of early industrial New England. The organization of the volume similarly reflects the thematic diversity of Dena's influence. A crucial theme in her work, and the subject of the first section of this book, is the importance of understanding ancient environments and landscapes. In her research on the Bull Brook phase, Mary Lou Curran demonstrates the necessity of refining chronologies and phase definitions for the earliest cultures of the Northeast. The region is a particularly important locus for such late Pleistocene research; in part due to the relatively high latitude and the glacial terrain of the Northeast, Paleoindian cultures here had unique expressions not found elsewhere on the continent. The considerable cultural diversity that existed among Paleoindians in the Northeast requires refinements like those presented in Curran's work. As is evident from George P. Nicholas's chapter, human-land relations are dynamic, interdependent, and a defining theme of Northeastern archaeology. Although scales of impact remain difficult to judge, the range of impacts and the duration of prehistoric occupation significantly contributed to the landscape we see today. The importance of human-environmental interaction is further demonstrated in Frederick J. Dunford's consideration of the postglacial occupation of Cape Cod, particularly the relevance of postglacial sea-level rise to site distribution.

As is the case with many areas of North America, prehistorians in the Northeast far too often rely on established ideas about artifact typologies as well as long-held assumptions about indigenous technologies. The chapters in the second section of this volume demonstrate that assumptions about these phenomena should periodically be rethought. In his consideration of Middle Archaic lithic technology, John R. Cross argues that lithic types are inhibiting constructs if viewed in a normative sense; when technological factors are emphasized over stylistic elements we not only see greater variation within types, but we can relate this variation directly to ecological, economic, and social dimensions of human experience. As Kenneth E. Sassaman illustrates, unilineal sequences such as changes in vessel technology dominate our archaeological reconstructions of culture history, so much so that chronologies are rarely questioned. Diffusionist arguments for the introduction of innovations, such as soapstone vessels or pottery in the Northeast, can be seriously flawed if the chronology is misunderstood. A revised chronology for soapstone vessels in the Southeast undermines claims for its origins in this region and thus as a donor source for the Northeast. Elizabeth S. Chilton's technological perspective on pottery, like Cross's examination of lithics, exposes variation that is hidden by culture-historical types. In contrasting Algonquian ceramic variation with Iroquoian ceramic homogeneity, Chilton suggests that Algonquian ceramic technologies reflect social variation, a conclusion that might not otherwise have been reached.

The chapters in the third part of this volume demonstrate the significance of questioning certain deeply entrenched assumptions about the archaeological Northeast. Too often, unsubstantiated speculations have evolved into fact without requisite scientific testing; we thus must be conscious of where specific ideas about the past originated, and whether such ideas pass critical scrutiny. David M. Lacy challenges the received wisdom that the uplands of Vermont were a marginal habitat for indigenous people and thus lack archaeological sites. Through the implementation of a survey strategy specifically designed to test for archaeological sites across a range of elevations, he is able to overcome ancient bias and suggest that the indigenous people of Vermont did in fact utilize the Green Mountains. Similarly, Elena Filios's paper reports on the biases imposed upon the archaeological record of the third millennium by exposing what is lost by privileging natural variables over social variables. From this perspective, her analysis of the Flynn site sheds new light on hunter-gatherer mobility in southern New England. Robert J. Hasenstab critiques the supposition that large Late Woodland villages are absent in New England. By considering such issues as ethnographic bias, poor archaeological preservation, and the shortcomings of commonly applied methods, Hasenstab suggests that large Algonquian villages near to, if not at the scale of Iroquoian villages, may have existed on the New England landscape, but have not yet been identified archaeologically. As Eric S. Johnson's chapter demonstrates, entrenched assumptions about the indigenous peoples of the Northeast are especially pronounced in Contact period studies. Johnson contends that traditional interpretations of the political landscape of seventeenth-century southern New England have obscured the significance of community in indigenous politics and masked the variety of ways native peoples responded to contact with Europeans.

The contributions to the fourth section of this volume all illustrate the importance of applying a multidisciplinary perspective to the study of the Northeast. In chronicling the century-long history of zooarchaeology in New England,

Catherine C. Carlson documents the many ways that the analysis of faunal materials has enriched our understanding of the ancient past. Mary Ann Levine tracks down evidence for geological deposits of native copper throughout the Northeast, both to critique the long-held assumption that indigenous peoples in the Archaic and Woodland periods procured native copper only in the Great Lakes, and to demonstrate the indispensability of knowledge created by sister disciplines, in this case geology. In a third paper in this section, Elizabeth A. Little reasons that archaeologists seeking accurate temporal assessments of coastal sites must understand the unique qualities of radiocarbon dates derived from shell; archaeologists must thus command information not only from physics and statistics, but paleoceanography as well.

The chapters in the concluding section of the volume illustrate the rich contributions cultural resource management (CRM) has made to Northeastern archaeology. In considering the long culture history of Turners Falls, Massachusetts, Michael S. Nassaney discusses a number of important sites excavated as part of CRM projects. Without CRM, many of these sites—all with far-reaching implications beyond the Northeast—may well have been destroyed before archaeologists had the opportunity to investigate them. Mitchell T. Mulholland demonstrates that when done well, CRM archaeology can address questions of relevance not only to archaeologists but also to the general public—in this case, refining our understanding of the construction sequence of one of the Northeast's most significant historic house sites.

While many issues concerning Northeastern archaeology have been addressed in this volume, and this collection goes far to correct the misconception of the Northeast as being a marginal place, many questions remain to be addressed. Nevertheless, we collectively believe that the research presented in this volume demonstrates that this misconception is little more that an artifact of now obsolete research designs. By moving the Northeast to the center of our investigations, it is the hope of all the contributors to this volume that we can, in the tradition of Dena F. Dincauze, continue to revise those misunderstandings that serve to obfuscate rather than illuminate the archaeological Northeast.

Mary Ann Levine
Kenneth E. Sassaman
Michael S. Nassaney

Acknowledgments

Institutional support for the production of this volume was provided by Franklin and Marshall College, University of Florida, Western Michigan University, and South Carolina Institute of Archaeology and Anthropology. Ralph Faulkingham, Chair of the Department of Anthropology at the University of Massachusetts, generously provided a comprehensive list of Dena Dincauze's graduate students so that we could invite them to contribute to this collection of essays. Our thanks also go to Dena for providing a copy of the photograph that graces the frontispiece of this book. Typesetting and copy production were masterfully accomplished by Mary Brohammer through funding provided by the University of Florida. We also extend our gratitude to Laurie Weinstein, General Editor for the Native Peoples of the Americas series, for her unwavering encouragement of our efforts. Finally, we owe a debt of gratitude to Greenwood acquisitions editor Jane Garry, and production editor Meg Fergusson, for their patience and guidance throughout the editorial process.

Part I

Ancient People, Ancient Landscapes

Exploration, Colonization, and Settling In: The Bull Brook Phase, Antecedents, and Descendants

Mary Lou Curran

Interest in the peopling of the New World has heightened in recent years with the discovery of sites in South America that are as old as or older than the earliest dated sites in North America (Dillehay 1996; Flegenheimer and Zarate 1997; Roosevelt et al. 1996; Sandweiss et al. 1998). This emerging evidence is being subjected to intense scrutiny in the hopes of addressing the following questions: Who were the first people to set foot in the Americas, when did the first immigrants arrive, and by what route or routes did they enter this pristine landscape and spread throughout the Americas?

There are now two points-of-view regarding New World origins. Until recently, most researchers believed that the first arrivals to the Americas were terrestrially adapted big-game hunters who originated in western Beringia (Siberia), crossing over the Bering Sea land bridge into Alaska when sea levels were lower than today. Much of the land bridge was exposed above sea level until after 11,000 years B.P. (Elias 1997:123). More recently, arguments have been presented for the possibility of immigrants who originated in the maritime regions of Japan or northern China (Erlandson and Moss 1996; Mandryk et al. 1998). Stone tool technologies in either case were derived from Upper Paleolithic traditions, with the Arctic industries of Siberia distinguished from East Asian industries by a microblade core technology. Early sites in Alaska have produced evidence of both industries, arguably contemporaneous at about 11,500 radiocarbon years B.P. (Goebel et al. 1996; Holmes 1996). By about 10,600 B.P., the microblade industry known as the Denali complex was clearly dominant in Alaska (West 1996:547).

Irrespective of continental origins for humans, by the time Paleoindians reached the northeastern United States at about 10,900 B.P., the dominant stone tool technology was a local variant of the fluted point tradition known as Clovis. Archaeologists had long-assumed that the first entrants into the New World were producers of Clovis fluted points. However, the paucity of fluted point finds in Alaska suggests that the origins of this industry may lie elsewhere, perhaps in the eastern United States. In turn, the connection between New England and presumed western points-of-entry remains uncertain. Given the growing body of evidence for diverse human adaptations and apparent multiple episodes of migration for the period 12,000 to 10,500 B.P., improved knowledge about the colonization of the Northeast depends on fine-grained assemblage analyses and innovative thinking.

PALEOINDIAN COLONIZATION OF THE NORTHEAST

The oldest firm evidence for human occupation of the Northeast is found in the sites and assemblages of the Paleoindian Bull Brook phase (Grimes et al. 1984). The type site for this phase, Bull Brook in Massachusetts, along with several others, are of sufficient size and density to suggest they were locations of relatively large-scale and/or long-term habitation. Dincauze (1993c) has recently proposed a model for Paleoindian sites in the Northeast that places these large sites at the center of the colonization process in this region. She suggested that "these large sites are each the remains of unique circumstances, representing the first human groups considering settlement in their respective area" (1993c:51). Dincauze further suggested that these relatively rare sites may have been "marshalling areas . . . camps from whence [new immigrants] . . . scouted good habitats before dispersing into them . . . gathering, arranging, and allocating resources and information" (Dincauze 1993c:51; cf. Anderson's [1990] "staging areas"). She has presented a seriation of large sites based on "inferred direction of movement and geographical distance from the continental center" (1993c:53). It is now evident that the Dedic site should be added to this large-site grouping (Gramly 1998; Ulrich 1979a).

While no one has challenged the designation of Bull Brook as a large site (although its internal structure has not yet been thoroughly explicated) the other sites designated as large by Dincauze are quite variable in form and content. They all deserve closer scrutiny, given the attendent implications for identifying exploratory, colonizing, and "settling in" sites and their short-term or long-term, small group to large group social correlates.

In defining the Bull Brook phase, Grimes et al. (1984) identified four sites as its component members: the Bull Brook and Bull Brook II sites, Ipswich, Massachusetts; Wapanucket #8, Middleboro, Massachusetts; and the Whipple site in southwestern New Hampshire. They argued further that this constellation of sites embodied the archaeological equivalent of a mating network. Grimes subsequently assigned a fifth site to the phase, Dedic in Massachusetts (Curran and Grimes 1989:73).

Much new fluted point site evidence has accumulated over the past fifteen years since the proposal of a Bull Brook phase. In addition to the recently published report on the Dedic (Sugarloaf) site (Gramly 1998), there are new data on many new fluted point sites in New England and adjacent locations (Curran

1996:3). Pollock's (1987; Pollock et al. 1995) lithological study of the Munsungun Lake formation in northern Maine has been followed more recently by
a descriptive study of the range of the raw materials used in making stone tools
at fifteen fluted point sites in New England (Pollock et al. n.d.), including
thirteen Maine sites, the Whipple site (New Hampshire) and Bull Brook (Massachusetts), a data set unavailable to Dincauze when she was developing her
"marshalling sites" model. These data have been compared, lithologically, to
two fluted point quarry sites at Munsungun-Chase Lakes as well as the original
Munsungun Lake formation outcrops (Pollock et al. n.d.). Similarly, Pollock
and others (1996) have explored the relationship between Mt. Jasper rhyolite and
fluted point sites of New England. In addition, I have recently reviewed the
problems of dating fluted point sites in the Northeast, the changing views relative to the temporal relationships among fluted point sites, and the need to
evaluate the implications of a newly confirmed radiocarbon "plateau" (or date
compression) ca. 10,600–10,200 B.P. (Curran 1996).

Dincauze (1993c:56) has noted that

considerable diversity in Paleoindian settlement patterns and economic strategies should
be discernible in the Northeast in both spatial and temporal dimensions and at several
scales. The spatial concepts of site, range, region, and frontier should be employed
analytically with more imagination than has been the case. We should try to overcome
the constraints of thinking only in secular time or radiocarbon centuries; temporal units
such as seasons (Curran and Grimes 1989; Spiess 1984) and generations (Dincauze n.d.)
should be employed in interpretation because they were the spans of time experienced
by the Paleoindians themselves.

Thorough analysis of Paleoindian sites both large and small is thus in order
if one is to fully evaluate both Grimes et al.'s and Dincauze's constructs. The
relatively new and sizable database should allow one to see emergent patterns
that may reify the proposals of Dincauze and Grimes et al. and/or suggest alternative scenarios for developing cases of strong inference. In this chapter two
data sets, one metric and one lithologic, are presented in order to improve our
understanding of the bases for the models of Dincauze and Grimes et al.; at the
same time they suggest avenues deserving of more thorough explication that will
lead to model refinements and modifications. Here I will indicate how the newly
derived data sets may allow us to restructure our thinking in terms of Paleoindian site chronologies, Paleoindian population distributions and their social
correlates. However, much more detailed analysis of recently acquired materials
and reanalysis of existing collections is necessary to validate this restructuring.

FINDING A PLACE FOR BULL BROOK
IN NEW ENGLAND'S FLUTED POINT CHRONOLOGY

At a relatively early stage of Eastern North American Paleoindian research
the Bull Brook site became a touchstone for explanations of Paleoindian lifeways

in the Northeast (Byers 1954, 1959; Eldridge and Vaccaro 1952). While North-eastern sites of later periods were often viewed as "marginal, culturally retarded outlier[s]" to sites elsewhere in the United States (Dincauze 1993a:33), Bull Brook became not only the dominant representative of the early occupation history of the Northeast but also a strong referrent for pan-American Paleoindian studies. The sheer size of the collection automatically assures its importance as a data base for any technological analyses, yet its place within Grimes et al.'s Bull Brook phase is poorly understood. Dincauze (1993c) has suggested that it may represent the "first arrival" site in New England.

In the following sections metric and lithological data sets will be explored for temporal indicators that may then be used to develop more fully a colonization model. Since colonization involves both an immigration process and subsequent population expansion of a resident population, particular attention will be paid to indicators of directional movement. One must be able to distinguish movement that is only seasonal and short term in nature from a longer-term movement that is indicative of "settling in," that is, the development of a population "center" or core, from which the new residents may disperse over time, as the size of the local population grows.

At a minimum, one would like to find indicators for three stages of population expansion: exploration, colonization, and "settling in" (cf. Wilson and Spiess 1990). In effect, one is attempting to identify the *frontiers* of exploration, the "first arrival" sites, and the general resource extraction range for the resident group or population. Data sets from beyond New England will be employed as needed to help "anchor" the New England database. Range determination allows one to address more completely the colonization model and at the same time permits evaluation of the mating network construct proposed by Grimes et al. (1984).

Fluted Point Site Ages in the Northeast

The ideal chronological evidence would be a stratigraphic record supported by radiocarbon-dated evidence. As will become obvious below, there is a serious lack of reliable, datable materials well associated with fluted point assemblages, but there is at least minimal evidence that permits establishment of general parameters for Paleoindian occupation of New England.

Grimes et al. based their estimate for the age of the Bull Brook phase on a weighted mean of 10,680 ± 400 years B.P. provided by the University of Arizona radiocarbon laboratory for a carbon sample from a Whipple site hearth feature (Curran 1984:13; Grimes et al. 1984:172). The radiocarbon dates obtained from Bull Brook and Whipple indicate mixed populations of charcoal and thus serious limitations in dating diffuse charcoal features, in spite of advances such as direct ion counting. The Bull Brook style points thus remain essentially undated in New England (Curran 1996:6), although numerous researchers have considered the probability of the temporal precedence of Bull Brook phase sites within New England.

Deller and Ellis (1986:17) suggest an age range of roughly between 11,000 and 10,700 B.P. for the "Bull Brook like" Gainey points of the Great Lakes. A feature at the "Gainey-phase" PaleoCrossing site, Ohio, dated 10,980 ± 75 B.P. (Brose 1994:65), provides the only radiocarbon referent in the general region, well to the south of the sites in Deller and Ellis's study, including the Gainey "type" site in Michigan. Relative to the position of other northeastern sites, the latitude of PaleoCrossing places it intermediate between the Wapanucket site (Massachusetts) and the Shoop site (Pennsylvania) (see Table 1.1). Recently radiocarbon dated material from the Shawnee-Minisink site (Pennsylvania) (McNett et al. 1977), somewhat north of Shoop, has also produced an age ca. 10,900 B.P. (Vance Haynes, personal communication 1998). The metrics of a single fluted point from Shawnee-Minisink places it within the upper Shoop/lower Bull Brook cluster (see below).

If we presume a *southern* population origin and if latitudinal gradient alone were a determinant of northward population expansion, one would expect a modest delay between the time of occupation at the PaleoCrossing site ca. 11,000 B.P. (and Nobles Pond [Seeman et al. 1994]) in Ohio and occupation at Bull Brook (i.e., sometime after 11,000 B.P.). Such comparison presumes that each site is positioned at or near its local population center (or core), rather than in an outlying location.

In New England a strong cluster of radiocarbon dates ca. 10,700–10,500 B.P. have been identified for the sites at Debert, Nova Scotia, and Vail, Maine. In noting the differences in basal concavity depths and the absence of sites elsewhere with similarly dominant forms (Ellis and Deller 1997; MacDonald 1968; Ritchie 1957; Spiess and Wilson 1987), numerous researchers have posited a time-transgressive northeastward population movement into the far Northeast. For the Debert data set Levine (1990:49) has suggested that the period from 10,701 to 10,600 years B.P. "may be designated as the period of maximum overlap" (Curran 1996:5). MacDonald (1968) arrived at a similar age range. The dates with the strongest context at Vail appear to date to approximately the same time period. At both Vail and Debert, however, charcoal sample dates suggest the presence of two populations of charcoal within each site, albeit only a small sample for the earlier dates.

There is a weaker cluster of radiocarbon dates in New England at 10,200 B.P. (from the sites Templeton, Michaud, and Neponset) (Curran 1996:8). These three "Neponset phase"[1] sites all contain smaller, flared ear/waisted point forms that are technologically and, at least in part, metrically similar to the Parkhill phase Barnes points of southern Ontario. These point forms appear as ephemeral components or find spots at several presumably temporally discrete "early" sites (Bull Brook; Spiller); they also occur within more clearly mixed multicomponent sites (Wapanucket; Reagen). This study, however, will focus only on those sites with the earliest point forms (large, partially fluted, parallel-sided).

Table 1.1

Assemblage and Site Characteristics for Fluted Point Sites in the Northeast

Site (sample size)	Approx. Lat.	MBD (mm)	Dominant Lithic	Distance to Source (km)	Site Size (ac)	No. of Loci	Site Type	Reference
Shoop, PA (21)	40.40	3.9	Onondaga chert, NY	≤320	20+	16+	Base or winter range	Cox 1972
Nobles Pond, OH (13)	41.00	4.6	Upper Mercer chert, OH	75	22	11+	Base or winter range	Gramly and Summers 1986
Arc, NY (6)	43.00	4.0	Local	–	–	–	Lithic reduction; habitation	Tankersley et al. 1997
Gainey, MI	43.00	4.5	Upper Mercer, OH	380	3	6+	"Summer" range*	Ellis 1989
So. Ontario Group	–	5.5	Local(?)	–	–	–	"Summer" range	Ellis and Deller 1997
Udora, Ontario (7)**	44.20	7.4	Local/Onondaga	–	–	11	"Summer" range	Storck and Tomenchuk 1990
Dedic/Sugarloaf, MA (3)	42.30	5.0	Gray, black cherts	120 or 530	4	11+	Early entry or winter range	Gramly 1998
Hanneman, MA (2)	42.40	4.0	"Southern" jasper	–	0.5+	5	Exploration	Hasenstab 1986
Bull Brook I, MA (25) (32)	42.50	5.7 (5.5)	Gray, black cherts	250 or 400	20	42	Central place/winter range	Grimes 1979 (Spiess et al. 1998)
Whipple, NH (8)	42.50	7.0	Gray, black cherts	–	1	3	"Summer" range	Curran 1984
Spiller, ME	43.50	8.2	Red chert	–	–	–	–	Hamilton and Pollock 1996
Dam, ME (2)	44.00	5.0	Gray, black cherts	–	–	1-2	Exploration	Spiess et al. 1998
Vail, ME (42)	44.80	8.9	Weathered	–	3	8	"Summer" range	Gramly 1982
Debert, Nova Scotia (22)	45.20	10.9	Chalcedony	70	20	11	"Summer" range	MacDonald 1986

MBD = Mean Basal Depth

* "Summer" range includes spring, summer, fall.

** Udora is multicomponent, but only Gainey forms were measured.

The recent recognition of large discrepancies and oscillations between radio-carbon ages and reconstructed (recalibrated) calendar years has important impli-cations for understanding the relationship among fluted point sites in New England (Curran 1996; Taylor et al. 1992). A date compression (radiocarbon "plateau") between 10,600 and 10,200 B.P. (uncalibrated) or after ca. 10,500–10,100 B.P. has been related to changes in atmospheric radiocarbon, ascribed to climatic changes of the Younger Dryas. Radiocarbon dates that appear virtually contemporaneous may not have been so. A period of approximately 1400/1500 calendrical years corresponds to only 400 radiocarbon years at this time (Curran 1996). Recognition of this anomaly greatly increases the difficulty of understand-ing the significance of the range of dates produced from the Vail site, but more particularly Debert.

The observed anomaly potentially (although not necessarily) increases the time interval between sites of this age and presumed temporal descendants (the Neponset phase, for example). At the same time one must give serious consid-eration to the possibility that the subtle variation noted within currently "homogenized" (and presumably single-component) site data may actually repre-sent temporal distance. MacDonald (1968) diligently, but unsuccessfully, sought patterning within the Debert site loci and features that might be construed as evidence of temporal and/or social group differences.

In the absence of such distinctions for the period ca. 10,600–10,200 B.P., one is faced with accepting the existence of very long-lasting regional point styles or as yet unrecognized gaps in the archaeological record. The existence of a longer time span would "ease the fit" of the Great Lakes fluted point sequences that Ellis and Deller (1997) propose prior to the drainage of Lake Algonquin at 10,400 B.P.

As a further interpretative complication, accelerator mass spectrometry (AMS) dated lakebed sediments and a brief German tree-ring sequence indicate a large jump in carbon-14 ages from ca. 11,400 to ca. 10,900 B.P. and a second "jump" (or reversal) in radiocarbon ages from 10,900 to 10,600 B.P. (Curran 1996). Taylor and others (1992) recognized the imprecision of the currently available radiocarbon dates for Clovis and Folsom in the American West, where there are also numerous overlapping radiocarbon dates and yet stratigraphic context clearly supports temporal separation.

The radiocarbon dates from Vail and Debert thus overlap with and fall within the period of date compression, as well as occur during a period of "jumps" or reversals in radiocarbon ages. It is thus not currently possible, nor may it ever be, to seriate the Vail and Debert sites based solely on radiocarbon-dated materials. That is to say, it is equally possible that the sites are temporally proximate or temporally distant, using these data. The Vail and Debert site dates may include radiocarbon reversals and jumps that have gone unrecognized, since site features are in an unstratified context. The more pessimistic researchers suggest that the radiocarbon confusion may never be fully understood or corrected. Patterns within and between fluted point assemblages may provide the stronger chronological evidence.

Metric Seriation of Fluted Points in the Northeast

Over a long period of time researchers have unsuccessfully sought metric means to determine temporal and spatial relationships between fluted point industries across the continent. Perhaps best known was Krieger's Naco evidence, employed to challenge Witthoft's (1952) attempt to distinguish Shoop points both by size and technology. Krieger argued that the Clovis points used in a single mammoth kill exhibited a wide range in size and technology (MacDonald 1968:77) and thus rejected Witthoft's efforts. Others, such as MacDonald, noted the distinctiveness of Debert points, both in terms of size and basal depth. Influenced by the Naco example, however, MacDonald dismissed the differences as uninformative relative to site chronologies. At the same time he recognized the limitations of attempting site correlations based on small data sets spread over a large area (MacDonald 1968:77).

More recently, however, as larger samples have become available, differences within and between site assemblages have become more obvious, encouraging researchers to again attempt to define, metrically, as well as technologically, the patterns they have long suspected. Ellis and Deller (1997) successfully incorporated a series of four metric variables in their characterization of the differences between three major fluted point forms of southern Ontario. The observed differences, including point diminution, were linked by them to changes in resource acquisition strategies associated with biotic changes over time.

Two of the metric variables from Ellis and Deller's grouping appear to be generally unaffected by attrition and rejuvenation: depth of basal concavity and basal width, the latter an indicator of overall point size, as well. It is useful to explore the extent to which these variables may inform temporal relationships *within* the earliest of the phases identified by both Grimes (1979) and Ellis and Deller (1997), where no major technological shift has been observed.

Figure 1.1 is a bivariate plot of values for depth of basal concavity and basal width taken from 118 fluted projectile points from five sites. With the exception of Whipple, these sites have been described by Dincauze (1993c) as large "marshalling camps" (Shoop, Bull Brook, Vail, and Debert) (cf. Table 1.1). The Whipple site data are included here to permit comparison with the Bull Brook site, since both sites are part of Grimes et al.'s (1984) Bull Brook phase mating network construct. The summary metrics for the southern Ontario Great Lakes "Gainey" sites and find spots (G2 in Figure 1.1) are included as well. Incorporation of both the Shoop site data set and the Great Lakes sample provides a south-north "anchor" beyond New England, necessary if one is to be able to evaluate the manner in which New England was colonized (including probable point of entry).

Figure 1.1
Bivariate Plot of Depth of Basal Concavity and Basal Width of Fluted Points from
Five Sites in New England. Included is a value (G2) for the average of these variables
for "Gainey" fluted points from southern Ontario.

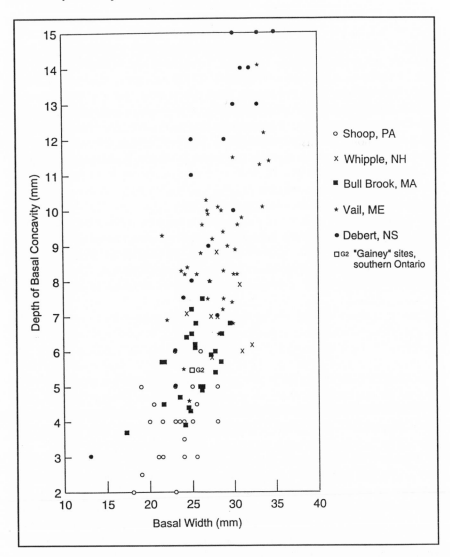

When considering the metric clusters of Bull Brook, Vail, and Debert, the
patterning is remarkably consistent. Basal concavity depths (and, to a lesser
extent, widths) increase in the direction of the more northerly sites, a pattern
that appears to be reiterated in the Great Lakes region, based on metrics summarized by Ellis and Deller (1997:5) and measurements of fluted points from

the Udora site, near Toronto (Storck and Tomenchuk 1990). Given the apparent strength of the basal depth measure, it appears reasonable to rely only on this measure as a means of placing additional sites in this seriation, in the absence of more complete metrics (e.g., the Gainey site, Michigan; see Table 1.1).

Based on the metrics from the Shoop site, the retrograde diminution of basal concavity depths appears to continue southward; at the same time there is greater overlap between the Bull Brook/Shoop site metric clusters than between Bull Brook and its more northern "neighbor" Vail. I hesitate to attempt to explain why the southward diminution of the basal concavity depth occurs; to carry this pattern much farther extinguishes the fluted point technology!

The strength of the observed clustering is sufficient to suggest that use of such metric data from smaller sites and find spots may provide a means by which additional sites may be grouped with their "larger site" counterparts, improving our understanding of the spatial distributions of related groups (and perhaps giving us a glimpse of Grimes et al.'s [1984] mating network) (see Table 1.1). Given the distributional "tails" in each metric cluster, assignment of find spot data is strongest only where the "new" specimen fits within a given cluster center. Geographical distance from the large site sample may serve as a guide in determining the accuracy of the assignment. Given how little we understand about the processes responsible for both the clustering and distributional "tails," we must remain open to the possibility that the range of variation is a reflection of not only individual skill in point production but also social-environmental interactions. Reverting to statistical averaging homogenizes variation to the population level. The more interesting insights are likely to be derived from intrasite analysis of a series of spatially discrete sites.

Latitudinal position (broadly approximated here) permits comparison of sites at similar latitudes (Table 1.1). Given the seasonal extremes typical of most northern environments (tempered in maritime locations today), it is reasonable to expect evidence of only seasonal use of many northward locations. Through time, however, under conditions of ameliorating climate, one would expect to see range expansion northward. Deviation from this trend may be an important indicator of the impact of the late Pleistocene climatic oscillations associated with the Younger Dryas cold interval, an interval that overlaps with the estimated maximum interval for Paleoindian occupation in the Northeast (11,000–10,000 B.P.) (Curran 1996). One might expect, for example, increased use of cooperative hunting units, with their occurrence varying according to season and habitat. A study of Netsilik seal hunting units nicely illustrates the effectiveness of a group size of about five hunters and their families. Such a size ensured adequate resource returns through a cooperative hunting effort where resources were unpredictably located (Balikci 1970). Similar group sizes appear frequently in the ethnographic record from around the world (Rogers 1963, among others). Northeastern Paleoindian sites of this age include Vail, Gainey, Wapanucket, Spiller, Neponset, and Holcombe. This model may also account for the structure of the larger sites, such as Shoop (16+ loci) and Nobles Pond (11+ loci), and, of course, Bull Brook (42+ loci). If extended family social units were relatively stable, a thorough interlocus analysis might reveal such relationships. Seeman et al. (1994:74) have successfully isolated and related spatially six of the eleven loci at Nobles Pond, employing raw material and refit analyses.

Interesting differences occur in the degree of metric overlap among the fluted point sites in this study, differences obscured when only metric means are used to characterize individual site collections. Some of these differences will be discussed below. Prior to this study, I had presumed that much of the variation within and between what appeared to be closely related assemblages was a product of sample size difference, occupation duration (measured by extent of attrition and recycling), and possible proximity, in time, to raw material source (Curran and Grimes 1989). There are now other factors to consider.

Bull Brook in itself forms a particularly strong metric cluster. Given that this grouping represents only "whole" fluted points, the metric variation can be expected to expand somewhat when the many basal fragments are added to the database. However, the Vail site, for which there is a larger sample size, including basal fragments, also forms a similarly strong and relatively distinct cluster. The greater overlap between the Bull Brook and Shoop site clusters, than between Bull Brook and the Vail site, may be explained as evidence of less "isolation" physically or closer social/temporal proximity between the former two sites. Shoop site metric and lithological "proximity" is clear at West Athens, Hill, and King's Road, in the Hudson River valley, and in the sample of some forty fluted points in Ritchie's 1957 survey (Funk 1977; Ritchie and Funk 1973).

There is greater overlap of the Vail metric cluster with Debert than with Bull Brook, suggesting closer temporal/spatial proximity northward, an observation that receives support from currently available radiocarbon evidence. The broad distribution of Debert point metrics (see Figure 1.1) was a complete surprise, since the metrics of other sites, both large and small, were relatively constrained. Given that measurements were based on only those artifacts illustrated in the Debert site report, I initially presumed the grouping had been preselected to illustrate the full range of variation in form. Instead, the sample represents the majority (twenty-two of twenty-eight) of the more complete specimens (MacDonald 1968:70). The metric clustering is unlikely to change dramatically with a complete sample, unless there are many more as yet unmeasured fragments from which one may extract basal concavity depths but not fluting information. Further analysis should be attempted. The unique distributional pattern is signaling a difference that deserves explanation.

Presuming that the metric variation is related to point function, rather than stylistic whim or widespread trade of projectile points, such a dispersed metric distribution for Debert leads to one of two interpretations: the site was used briefly over a long time span, during which period point forms changed, or, it is an indication of an extremely flexible approach to resource acquisition, that is, hunters were prepared for all eventualities (and were selective in matching target resource to point form). Based on his own field observations and analyses, MacDonald (1968:149) estimated that the accumulated site debris might represent an occupation span of a few decades, and a maximum group size of thirty to forty members, based on a boreal forest Naskapi-Montagnais ethnographic analog (Rogers 1963). The remarkably large size of some Debert points conjures images of hunters prepared to meet the giants of a dying race that have sought refuge in the last remaining open habitats of the far Northeast.

Beyond New England, metrics for the "Gainey-like" Nobles Pond and PaleoCrossing sites are critical for evaluating the degree to which this metric patterning may be extended north and westward of the Shoop site. A recent plot of metrics for thirteen Nobles Pond projectile points places this assemblage intermediate to the Shoop and Bull Brook/southern Ontario point forms, in accord with the latitudinally related variation noted above (Seeman et al. 1994). Close metrically to the type site of Gainey (Michigan), Nobles Pond may have served as the southern base camp counterpart to the probably seasonal site of Gainey, where six loci suggest the presence of an extended family band matching the size of the cooperative hunting units referred to above. Interestingly, six of a minimum of eleven loci at Nobles Pond are closely related lithologically (Seeman et al. 1994). Current lithic data indicate that the Gainey and Nobles Pond sites shared use of the same lithic chert source, Upper Mercer chert, ca. 75 km from Nobles Pond (Ellis 1989:143; Gramly and Summers 1986). Tankersley (1991) has demonstrated a complex distributional pattern of this Ohio chert.

On the basis of the spatial distribution of metric means for depths of basal concavities, for only the sites Dincauze (1993c) listed as "marshalling site" candidates, initially I would have suggested a site seriation similar to her proposal. However, the addition of metrics for smaller sites and find spots and closer inspection of the composition of the "large site" grouping produces a more complex picture (see Table 1.1).

A particularly revealing data set is derived from the survey of fluted points in collections of the Champlain Basin, Vermont (all likely of different proveniences) (Loring 1980). Averaging the metrics for the eight points (albeit a questionable procedure) produced a metric mean of 5.9 mm, clearly falling within the Bull Brook cluster, despite its location northward of 44 degrees latitude. This suggests a greater northward range extension in New England during the Bull Brook/Gainey phase than is suggested by mean metrics for the current Ontario sample. There is no indication as yet that these Vermont specimens are quarry-based finds nor that they may have been manufactured in any significant number on Hathaway formation cherts. This pattern suggests that the distribution of sites in southern Ontario and Vermont is more controlled by latitudinal position than a population expansion from west to east in these northern areas. This argument receives support lithologically (Table 1.2).

Additional small site and find spot evidence contributes support for an early entry into and exploration of the New England/Maritime region. Latitudinal

Table 1.2
Raw Material Use at New England-Maritime Fluted Point Sites

Phase / Site	Chert			Southern Jasper	Felsites		Other	Reference
	Gray, black	Red	NonNew England		Spherulitic	Other		
Shoop								
Hannemann, MA	possible (Munsungun)	no	possible	dominant	—	(blackish)	—	Hasenstab 1986a
Thornton's Ferry, NH	—	no	—	dominant	possible	(reddish)	possible	Stinson in Curran 1996
Kingsclear, NB	—	—	—	—	—	—	—	Keenlyside 1991
Bull Brook								
Dedic, MA	dominant	no	present	present	present	present	—	Gramly 1998; Ulrich 1979
Wapanucket, MA	dominant	no	present	present	present	present	—	Robbins 1968, 1980
Dam, ME	primary	present	present	present	present	—	Cheshire quartzite; quartz	Spiess et al. 1998
Bull Brook II, MA	dominant	no	present	present	present	present	—	Grimes et al. 1984
Bull Brook I, MA	dominant	present	present	present	present	present	—	Grimes 1979
VTCH197**	dominant	present	—	present	—	no	Cheshire quartzite	Peter Thomas, Pers. Comm.
Hedden, ME**	dominant	present	present	present	present	Saugus jasper tertiary	quartz secondary	Speiss and Mosher 1994; Speiss et al. 1998
Adkins, ME**	secondary	present	possible	no	no	no	quartz dominant	Gramly 1988
Intermediate Bull Brook-Vail								
Whipple, NH	dominant	present	possible	no	no	no	Cheshire quartzite; quartz	Curran 1984, 1987
Vail								
Vail, ME**	present	no	present	no	no	—	—	Gramly 1982 (cf. Spiess et al. 1998)
Morss, ME	no	dominant	no	no	no	—	—	Gramly 1998
Wheeler Dam, ME	—	present	possible	no	no	—	quartz	Gramly 1998
Spiller, ME	secondary	dominant	—	no	present	—	Nova Scotia chalcedony?	Hamilton and Pollock 1996; Spiess et al. 1998
Point Sebago, ME	dominant	secondary	—	no	present	—	Maritime chalcedony	Hamilton and Pollock 1996; Spiess et al. 1998
Debert								
Debert, NS	no	no	silicified siltstone	no	cobble tools only	—	Nova Scotia chalcedony	MacDonald 1968
Belmont Sites	no	no	—	—	—	—	Nova Scotia chalcedony	Davis 1991

*NonReading Prong jasper.
**Phase assignment based on lithic types; metrics not available.
***Forty-eight percent of the Vail collection is highly weathered.

gradient appears to be correlated with northern expansion in interior locations, but exploration along the maritime lowlands appears to have extended much farther northward at an early date. A Shoop/Bull Brook like fluted point find (ca. 4.5 mm), presumably on Munsungun chert (Keenleyside 1991), has been recorded as far north as Kingsclear, New Brunswick (>45 degrees latitude), well northward (latitudinally) of any similar find currently reported in the Great Lakes region. A Shoop size point on a reddish porphyry was recovered from the Thornton's Ferry site, New Hampshire (ca. 43 degrees latitude), adjacent to a small group of tools based on "southern-derived" yellow jasper (Curran 1994) and two points of similar size have been recovered from the Hannemann site, Massachusetts. One point from Hannemann is made of blackish felsite and the second, heavily reworked, is of yellow jasper. A small yellow-brown jasper assemblage has been collected from the site area (Hasenstab 1986a). The compositional similarities of the two assemblages together strongly argue for a southern-derived early entry into New England. In all cases the addition of a measure of basal thickness would improve the sorting accuracy, since "Neponset" points generally are both thinner and smaller than the earlier Bull Brook forms. Based on the metrics of a single point, one may cautiously place the small Dam site (Maine) within this early phase of New England colonization (cf. Spiess et al. 1998).

Of considerable interest is placement of the Whipple site within this metric system. The Whipple artifacts form a quite dispersed "intermediate" cluster, albeit on a very small sample size. Of the sites and find spots summarized here, only the Udora, Ontario, site collection (30 minutes latitude farther north and well west of Whipple) contains a cluster of points in the Whipple size range (transitional Bull Brook/Vail) (see Table 1.1). Divergence of the Whipple sample from the Bull Brook metric cluster requires explanation, since Grimes et al. (1989) have placed both sites within the Bull Brook phase, a process which carries with it a presumption of site contemporaneity. Grimes et al. suggested that the sites within the grouping be viewed as representatives of an open-ended mating network. If one were to extend that network "generationally" (considering "openness" in time), one could still view these two site components as related members, operationally a reasonable view, but not one usually considered by those using the "phase" construct. The strength of this divergence from the Bull Brook cluster will be reevaluated in the next section, since Grimes et al. had linked the two sites on the basis of use of a shared lithic source area.

The relationship of the remaining three Bull Brook phase members—Dedic, Bull Brook II, and Wapanucket—must also be considered here. Dedic is a potentially large site as currently defined by Gramly (1998). The metrics of the very limited Dedic site sample places this site within the Bull Brook cluster. The context of four of these points, however, must be viewed cautiously, since at least some of the artifacts originally ascribed to this site were very likely looted from the Whipple site (New Hampshire). Of the three measured points in the Bull Brook II sample, one each fall within the Shoop, Bull Brook, and Whipple metric clusters, a surprising metric range for a spatially limited site that appears to represent a short-term occupation (Grimes et al. 1984).

The positioning of the Wapanucket sample remains problematic. There is evidence of both Bull Brook and Neponset phase artifact clusters at the site (Robbins 1968, 1980). Grimes et al. suggested that two "aberrant" flared-ear points are a product of the reworking that is clearly evident in illustrations. Who, however, were the recyclers? Could the "Neponset" occupants have been responsible for these "aberrant" forms? Which component, then, is more clearly represented at Wapanucket? A search for more complete field records and find spot data from Lake Assawompsett is clearly in order, since the Wapanucket site has been listed as a Bull Brook phase member.

An independent data set derived from New England and the Maritimes is clearly needed to validate the clusters identified metrically and to test the colonization and mating network models set forth by Dincauze and Grimes et al. The variation in raw material use noted among nineteen sites from New England and the Maritimes (see Table 1.2) will serve as the basis for this evaluation. The explanatory burden falls heavily upon the following lithic observations, since one cannot account, simply, for the metric ranges observed within each site's assemblage.

VARIATION IN RAW MATERIAL USE IN EARLY NEW ENGLAND

Shared use of lithic and biotic resources is the measure by which Grimes et al. determined membership in the Bull Brook phase. The distribution of lithic raw materials at sites distant from the source is also the means by which numerous researchers have reconstructed Paleoindian band territories and annual exploitation ranges within the Northeast and beyond (Ellis and Lothrop 1989). Considerable work has focused on patterns of reciprocal lithic movement southwest-northeast along the former shoreline of glacial lake Algonquin during the Parkhill Phase (Ellis 1989; Storck and von Bitter 1989; Stothers 1996).

More recently lithic data sets have been used by researchers interested in identifying patterns of lithic movement that might yield clues to the process of colonization (Storck 1988; Stothers 1996; Tankersley 1994). Researchers are now equipped with a much more sophisticated and detailed body of evidence than that available to Witthoft (1952) and Ritchie (1957) when they proposed directions of movement within the Northeast based on the occurrence of nonlocal lithics at fluted point sites in the region. Dincauze (1993c) has incorporated lithic source interpretations into her seriation model.

Lithic Source Characterization

The descriptive work that forms the basis for raw material sourcing has barely begun in New England, beyond Pollock's (1987) work with the Munsungun Lake formation. There are seriously conflicting notions regarding the sources of the dominant lithics seen at numerous fluted point sites in New England (Byers 1954; Gramly 1998; Grimes 1979; Pollock et al. n.d.; Spiess and Wilson 1987; Spiess et al. 1998). Weathering processes, at least part of which may be culturally related in archaeological samples, have introduced additional difficulties for lithic identifications (Pollock et al. n.d.; Ritchie 1957; Witthoft 1952). As a result, one can rarely ascribe an archaeological specimen to its specific lithic source with any degree of precision. However, Pollock and colleagues (n.d.) have recently completed a distributional study of Munsungun Lake chert in some twenty fluted point sites, primarily from Maine. Pollock has provided lithic identifications for the Whipple and Bull Brook sites as well. He has also identified non-Munsungun raw materials observed in these site assemblages, including the use of spherulitc Mt. Jasper rhyolite (Pollock et al. 1996).

I have been able to expand the comparative sample through personnel observation and with the assistance of numerous researchers who have graciously shared their knowledge of lithic sources and assemblages. In this sorting process it has become evident that even broadly defined lithic categories are useful for identifying patterns of lithic source use. Such sorting will permit at least provisional evaluation of the models of Grimes et al. and Dincauze. Six lithic categories have been chosen for this preliminary analysis. These categories have been so broadly defined that error in category assignment is highly unlikely.[2] Still, even with such broadly characterized groups, occasionally it is not possible to be confident of the accuracy of assignment. For instance, work by Hatch (1994) and colleagues (King et al. 1997) has distinguished the jasper used at Bull Brook and several other New England sites from that from Reading Prong, Pennsylvania, the source area of the well-known Vera Cruz jasper. While the New England samples are more closely related to the Reading Prong group than other Middle Atlantic sources (Pennsylvania, Delaware, and Virginia) (King et al. 1997), Hatch (personal communication) suggests that there may be an as yet unidentified source positioned intermediately between the Reading Prong and the Bull Brook area, either now inundated offshore or perhaps found elsewhere in the New England extension of the Appalachians, possibly western Connecticut. These similar yellow-brown jaspers will all be referred to as "southern jasper" for the purposes of this study. If only "red jasper" is present, the designation is considered too broad and subject to error to be included. Abundance within a given site is indicated broadly for tool discards only, listed in terms of whether a given lithic was the dominant, secondary, or tertiary resource. A presence/absence statement is applied to the remaining identifications.

Interpretation of Lithic Connections

The metric study presented above serves as an important anchor upon which to develop an interpretation of the relationship between lithic raw material variation within New England sites and distant lithic source areas. These data suggest that early exploratory movements extended sufficiently northward along the Atlantic Coastal Plain that individuals or small scouting parties monitoring nonlithic resources could fairly easily have encountered the northernmost New England chert sources at an early date. The Munsungun Lakes region is accessible quite directly from the coastal plain via the Penobscot and Aroostook River drainages (Pollock et al. n.d.). Such a valley system would be a logical route for seasonal migration of animals such as caribou into the interior from the coastal plains. Documented portages between the Connecticut River and the Androscoggin River may also suggest a route by which the rhyolites of Mt. Jasper were dispersed throughout New England fluted point sites (Pollock et al. 1996).

The use of the northernmost lithic sources is thus possible. At issue is the extent to which they were employed, and at what point within the colonization and population expansion process within New England. In the lithic debris left behind by groups newly entering New England, one would expect evidence of the use of only one lithic source as the preferred lithic, from a source area in use before entry into New England. The Thornton and Hannemann sites match this expectation (Curran 1994; Hasenstab 1986a). The Hadley site in the Connecticut River valley (Massachusetts) may be a similar candidate (an assemblage of Hudson River valley green chert for which metrics are unavailable) (Curran and Dincauze 1977). Simplicity of explanation would also argue for a source that was readily available in time and/or space, for a dependable portion of an annual subsistence cycle.

As familiarity with New England's resources increased, new lithics would likely become incorporated into the raw material inventory. Where access to high quality lithics was limited, and yet the resources were sufficiently abundant or dependable to draw new colonists, regional alternatives may have been incorporated, as seen in the flexible use of felsite at the above mentioned sites of Hannemann and Thornton, as well as Dedic, Wapanucket, Bull Brook II, and Bull Brook I, among others.

As settlement and expansion of territorial range extended into the far Northeast and the Maritime provinces, one might expect that the addition to the lithic inventory of new source materials would increase incrementally. The addition of red cherts may be such a signal of increasing familiarity with northern chert sources. The Munsungun Lake Formation is the best candidate for the source of red cherts (although red cherts have also been reported in the Normanskill formation, New York), since its use is seen in greater abundance throughout Holocene Maine archaeological sites than elsewhere in New England, and it occurs in relative abundance at several Maine fluted point sites, the Spiller site in particular.

This interpretation places Bull Brook I secondary in time to both Dedic and Bull Brook II, contrary to the proposal by Dincauze (1993c). In fact, the lithic patterning nicely supports the idea of Bull Brook II as the early colonizing site for Bull Brook proper. Perhaps a small group of summertime hunters and gatherers took stock of resources before suggesting a larger group movement.

Only with subsistence sufficiency could regionalization of the population develop. The regional lithics then necessarily become the new dominants. The use of quartzite at Whipple may be an indicator of this regionalization process. The Dam site in Maine likely fits somewhere in the period of colonization, perhaps as an early northward exploration into Maine, given its lithic diversity (Spiess et al. 1998). The Adkins site, Maine (Gramly 1988), also within the Bull Brook metric cluster (but without jasper), may represent the first exploratory site into the Magalloway River valley, northwestern Maine.

In previous research, I presumed that the absence of "southern" jasper in such small sites as Whipple and Adkins was simply a product of an occupation too short for discard of all currently employed lithic types. The minimal yet persistent presence of jasper at Bull Brook II in multiple categories belies this assumption, as does its occurrence at several other small sites.[3] Evidence of the continued use of the "older" lithic source areas (i.e., the source of "southern" jaspers) would have important interpretative implications—that may be a reflection of the need to maintain familiarity with subsistence resources in formerly exploited areas, as would occur where resources were subject to significant spatial or temporal fluctuation or disparity. The importance attached to the maintenance of kin ties and mating networks could be similarly inferred. Its "disappearance" from northern assemblages is sending a similarly strong signal—group sizes were sufficiently large, and regional resources were sufficiently stable, that continued contact with a distant "ancestral homeland" was deemed no longer necessary.

While Curran and Grimes (1989) have suggested that the incorporation of poorer quality lithics into the raw material inventory may be a strong seasonality indicator, through time it may be a stronger reflection of the regionalization of Paleoindian groups within New England, where high quality lithics are unevenly distributed along the "northern tier."

Newly developing paleoenvironmental research has isolated evidence of a "brief" period of significant warming within the Younger Dryas, providing a window of opportunity for northward and interior exploration and colonization, ca. 10,600–10,500 B.P. (Cwynar and Levesque 1995; Spiess et al. 1995; Lucinda McWeeney, personal communication 1997). Based on the metric and lithic data in this study, and supported by radiocarbon evidence, it is during this period of warming that settlement of Maine likely began. The disappearance of southern-derived jasper in Maine assemblages and the possible introduction of Nova Scotia chalcedony (see Table 1.2) are perhaps the most dramatic indicators of such a regionalization process (Spiess et al. 1998:214, 217).

At the Debert site, where the dominant raw material is chalcedony presumably derived from a now-drowned source in Minas Basin (MacDonald 1968), ongoing research suggests the presence of minority lithics that may be southern in origin (Stephen Pollock, personal communication 1998). Expansion of the metric and lithic databases, including information from the Debert-related sites of Belmont I and II (Davis 1991), is important for a fuller understanding of Debert's position within the colonization process.

The sparse, yet wide, distribution of Vail-type points (at Plenge, New Jersey [Kraft 1973], throughout New York [Gramly and Funk 1990; Ritchie 1957], and into Ontario at Udora [Storck and Tomenchuk 1990]), all based on local lithics, demands further investigation, as well. By what process was this point form so widely distributed? Did the mid-Valders warm interval encourage low density population dispersal? Did the warm interval result in lower water tables and erosional episodes that may have obscured site evidence of this period? Slight readjustments in water levels in the vicinity of sites near the coast today could have resulted in the placement of similar habitation sites in positions now under water, including the now-drowned coastal plain.

The lithic pattern at Vail is somewhat of a puzzle itself. Under the present sorting system, the Vail site assemblage appears less diverse than its neighbors. Year-round isolation within the valley seems unlikely, however, given the currently harsh winter conditions and the inferred seasonal extremes during the Younger Dryas (Dincauze and Curran 1983). Despite a possible warming trend during the period of occupation, it is still likely that winters would have been brutal. The site size (eight loci) and content is suggestive of intensive processing efforts by a seasonal cooperative hunting group. Gramly (1982), however, has posited that the abundant discard was an additive process; that is, individual habitation areas were shelters that were occupied recurrently. Where then are the red cherts so dominant at other central and northern New England sites, in particular within the Vail metric cluster? Why are they absent at the Vail habitation site and yet present at the nearby kill sites? The answers may well be hidden within the numerous cherts identified as non-Munsungun or too highly weathered for determination; the weathered specimens comprise ca. 48 percent of the sample (Pollock et al. n.d.).

DISCUSSION

Despite the image of hearty Siberian hunters crossing over the Bering land bridge from the harsh climates of Siberia, the cultural ancestors of the earliest New Englanders seem unlikely to have faced such high-risk environments. Rather, I suspect they were faced with a "land of opportunity," as were their predecessors throughout the Eastern Woodlands. The low population density conditions suggest that resource opportunities must have drawn fluted-point-using peoples northward, not population pressures, even as groups expanded northward during the onset of the Valders cold interval.

I would suggest that the differences we see in northern assemblages are a reflection of the adaptive flexibility of early colonists (Dincauze and Curran

1983). They were able to adjust group sizes to take advantage of these resource opportunities. At the same time they were conservative in their choices, selecting only the most productive and/or stable large-patch environments as their resident group centers; all of the truly large sites are positioned either southward of New England (often palimpsets of occupation evidence) or within lowland large patch environments, particularly the Atlantic Coastal Plain of New England and the Maritimes.

Abundant lithic source data support the maintenance of contacts with southern locations, as small bands took advantage of seasonally productive (spring through fall) northern resource patches. It is from the residential base camps that the local population was able to expand or contract as environmental conditions permitted or dictated (Curran 1987). The extent of northward movement and population expansion within New England is thus a measure of those resource opportunities.

The occupation of Bull Brook undoubtedly occurred toward the beginning of the Valders cold interval. Its uniqueness might best be explained as a product of its use as a residential center, important for the maintenance of group ties, information and resource exchange, and organizing cooperative hunting units for short-term or longer-term forays from a reliable group center. A thorough study of within-site lithic variation may well provide fascinating insights into the nature of this cooperative process. This flexible structuring of a resident population requires an equally flexible archaeological definition. Grimes et al.'s (1984) mating network structure, with a generational component, most closely approximates the connections observed among the members of the Bull Brook phase. The databases within this study provide a reasonable means by which to judge group affiliation; the difficulty lies in deciding who should be excluded! In our attempts to bring order to a seemingly inexplicable diversity, we are creating boundaries where none exist.

On a continent-wide basis, we must carefully separate the components that have been inadvertently or wittingly combined under the fluted point tradition rubric (Anderson and Faught 1998; Ellis and Deller 1997). The metric and lithologic data presented here suggest there is value in attempting fine levels of discrimination in what appear to be relatively homogeneous assemblages. A closer look at Clovis assemblages beyond New England may reveal similarly identifiable distinctions. Meltzer (1989:484) has even suggested that "Clovis may represent a composite of migratory 'dribbles.'" It is reasonable to suspect that the earliest Clovis site assemblages will be found to be somewhat divergent in content from the later fluted point industries. The absence of a blade technology in the early fluted point components of the Northeast, in contrast to its presence at Clovis-period sites in the Southeast, parts of the Mid-West, and western Clovis sites, may prove to be such an important temporal distinction (Ellis et al. 1998). For the earliest sites, will the stronger links be to a generalized Upper Paleolithic tradition or to a Beringian blade core industry? Only time will tell.

ACKNOWLEDGMENTS

I am deeply indebted to an array of colleagues and friends for their infinite patience and support and, in particular, to my husband, John, and daughter, Clare, who developed a new time system referred to as "when the paper is done." I have benefited greatly from the generous sharing of unpublished data by Richard Boisvert, Steven Cox, Michael Gramly, Robert Hasenstab, Nathan Hamilton, Stephen Pollock, Duncan Ritchie, Arthur Spiess, Wesley Stinson, and Peter Thomas, as well as helpful conversations with David Anderson, Stephen Davis, Christopher Ellis, Albert Goodyear, James Hatch, C. Vance Haynes, Carole Mandryk, Lucinda McWeeney, Brian Robinson, N. W. Rutter, and Peter Storck. Special thanks for the support and assistance of Dr. Frederick H. West, William Eldridge, and John Grimes at the Peabody-Essex Museum, Salem. Figure 1.1 was drafted by Christine Raisig. The Sandersons kindly provided access to the Sugarloaf collection. Victoria Jacobson was extremely helpful in arranging the visit to the Dedic/Sugarloaf collections and assisting in their inspection. Stephen Pollock and Nathan Hamilton provided an assessment of lithic comparability for the Bull Brook and Whipple site collections and James Hatch analyzed the jasper from the Bull Brook site. The particular inspiration for this paper, very appropriately, is Dena Dincauze, longtime mentor and Paleoindian enthusiast, who was very supportive to this French teacher-turned-archaeologist, at a time when there were very few women doing field research and even fewer in Paleoindian studies. Her encouragement has been invaluable.

NOTES

1. The flared fluted points from the Templeton, Michaud, and Neponset sites may be considered "more fully Folsom" and technologically similar to the Barnes points of the Great Lakes Parkhill phase than to the larger, parallel-sided Bull Brook style points of New England. This author suggests the provisional use of the term Neponset phase for this grouping of sites (cf. "Michaud-Neponset" phase [Spiess et al. 1998:235]). This is based in part on the relatively large metric sample from Neponset and the predominant use of a distinctive spherulitic rhyolite for fluted point production there. The rhyolite previously referred to as Neponset rhyolite has been more recently described lithologically by Pollock and colleagues (1996) as Mt. Jasper rhyolite. Flared points similar in size and technology have recently been recovered from two fluted point sites in Jefferson, New Hampshire, where artifacts are also made of a spherulitic rhyolite that may represent a similar source (Bouras and Bock 1997). Four fluted points in a local collection in the Champlain Valley, Vermont, are identical in form to the smaller points at Neponset, and also are made of spherulitic rhyolite (Loring 1980). Neponset style points appear as ephemeral components at several presumably temporally discrete "early" sites (Bull Brook; Spiller); they also occur within more clearly mixed multicomponent sites (Wapanucket; Reagen).

There is the possibility that as our data sets expand we may be able to support a further division, that may be placed intermediate, technologically, between the points of the Bull Brook and Neponset phases (points that are flared, with deeper basal concavities and broader basal widths than the Barnes-Neponset cluster). Based on cherts (and possibly regional felsites), their best type site may be Michaud. Spiess and Wilson (1987) had previously noted similarities that led to their placement of the Michaud site within the Bull Brook phase grouping. The Searsmont point (Cox et al. 1994) may represent a further complication as a transitional form.

2. It should be noted, however, that these broad categories potentially obscure variation that may ultimately be very significant in determining the actual quarry sources employed. This is particularly true for the "gray, black" chert grouping. It very possibly represents a combination of Hudson River valley, Munsungun Lake, and possibly northern Vermont sources. Therefore, much more detailed work must be done to validate these observations.

3. The lack of diagnostic fluted points at the Heddon site is a critical absence. The presence of "southern" jasper suggests either a fit within the early Bull Brook cluster or placement in the later Neponset Phase, rather than an association with the Vail-Debert grouping, as the 10,500 B.P. date would suggest (Spiess and Mosher 1994; Spiess et al. 1995).

2

A Light but Lasting Footprint: Human Influences on the Northeastern Landscape

George P. Nicholas

> They are, of course, nomads—hunters and foragers who grow nothing, build nothing, and stay nowhere long. They make almost no physical mark on the environment. Even in areas which are still inhabited, it takes a knowledgeable eye to detect their recent presence. Within a matter of weeks, the roughly cleared camp-sites may be erased by sun, rain, and wind. After a year or two there may be nothing to suggest that this country was ever inhabited. Until one stumbles on a few old flint-tools, a stone-quarry, a shell-midden, a rock painting, or something of the kind, one may think that the land has never known the touch of man. (Stanner 1987:230)

Hunter-gatherers have often been credited with having no discernible "footprint" on the landscapes they have occupied. Their relatively small group size, low population density, and high mobility, along with an inherent conservation ethic, are seen as having allowed them to fulfill the role of "indigenous ecologists"— taking only what they need, without impact on the environment. This view has become so widely cited in recent years as to be taken as common knowledge (Callicott 1995). It has also become an important component in contemporary Native American self-identity (Deloria 1996).

Yet it is evident from detailed studies of historic hunter-gatherers at locations around the world that their presence on the landscape has often had a significant effect on animal populations and local vegetation patterns, although this is usually seen as being of only short duration. In fact, one reason that most hunter-gatherers move so frequently (Lee and Devore 1968:11) is to alleviate overharvesting of the local resource base (Kelly 1995:156)—whether translated as a conservation ethic or as an economic strategy to minimize effort. However, such activities as selective plant harvesting and animal hunting, forest clearance, and the use of fire as a resource management strategy would have had a longer-term influence on the landscape. This is perhaps most clearly seen in Australia where, despite Stanner's shortsighted observation, tens of thousands of years of "fire-stick farming" has transformed the vegetation history of the continent (Haynes et al. 1991).

This chapter examines the type and degree of potential or apparent influence that nonagricultural populations had on the shaping of the landscape of northeastern North America. The starting point is a brief discussion of indigenous peoples as "noble ecologists." This is followed by a review of such pertinent issues of human ecology as scale, points of contact, and the dynamic nature of landscapes. Human interactions with animal and plant communities are then examined at several different spatial and temporal scales. The chapter concludes with a discussion of the human role in regional landscape development.

NOBLE ECOLOGISTS

There is a kind of academic defense of the cultural integrity of indigenous peoples that, though well-intentioned, winds up delivering them intellectually to the imperialism that has been afflicting them economically and politically. I mean the paradox entailed in defending their mode of existence by endowing them with the highest cultural values of Western societies. So the Cree or the Maori or the Kayapó are supposed to be paragons of ecological knowledge. (Sahlins 1995:119)

Western understanding of nonagricultural lifeways has changed substantially during the last 500 years. In the mid-1600s Thomas Hobbes characterized life for aboriginal peoples as "solitary, poor, nasty, brutish, and short"—a phrase that has had astonishing longevity in public perception, policy, and law. This was countered by the equally unrealistic portrayal of the "Noble Savage" by Jean-Jacques Rousseau in the 1700s. A more balanced view of small-scale societies emerged in the late 1960s with the *Man the Hunter* conference (Lee and Devore 1968), which set the stage for much of the next twenty-five years. Recent studies (e.g., Bettinger 1991; Dahlberg 1981; Kelly 1995) have broadened our knowledge, while the growing participation of indigenous peoples themselves and the increased legitimacy of traditional knowledge open entirely new avenues of understanding for Western scholars (Inglis 1993; Nader 1996; Nicholas and Andrews 1997). Despite the wealth of information now available, there is still much misunderstanding about human-environment interaction.

There is a widely held view that aboriginal peoples, who generally see themselves as an integral part of the natural world, have achieved an enviable degree of equilibrium with their environment and may thus be viewed as successful ecologists (cf. Headland 1997). The "ecological success" of indigenous land use becomes most apparent when compared with historic and contemporary Western land-use practices and ethics, as Cronon (1983) revealed for colonial New England. Indeed, in the larger context of human affairs, the impact of preindustrial societies (and especially hunting-and-gathering peoples) has been minimal compared with industrialized ones (e.g., Goudie 1993; Turner et al. 1990). For hunting-and-gathering peoples in general, this has been achieved by several means. The first, and most important, relates to the characteristics of small-scale societies noted above. Small group size, low population density, high mobility, and similar factors mean that people tend not to be present at any one place in large enough numbers and for long enough time to leave a lasting impression. Not all hunter-gatherers exhibit these traits, of course; in northwestern North America, for example, what are viewed as "atypical" hunter-gatherers exhibited many of the features of horticultural societies, including sedentism and ranking (Hayden 1997; Matson and Coupland 1995). There, however, the impact of human activities upon the environment appears relatively slight due to the resiliency of the highly productive rainforest-maritime-riverine environment.

Second, there is also an implicit conservationist ethic embedded into the world view of many indigenous peoples. Creation stories and clan affiliations, for example, point to a time when humans and animals had not yet separated into their contemporary forms. For the Cree, to enter the spirit world is to go into, not out of, the real world, and it is there that animals live in lodges, smoke, gamble, and partake in other familiar activities. There is much here that supports broad and respectful considerations of the natural world by people. Such expressions of this world view as use of scapulamancy in determining hunting locations (Moore 1957; Speck 1977) further limit human impact through unconscious, random sampling in resource collection.

Despite these features, there may be apparent contradictions in this conservationist ethic. For example, however much they respect animals, Cree hunting techniques (at least historically) included the destruction of beaver lodges and the killing of all the occupants (Helm et al. 1981). More generally, recent studies by archaeologists (Dincauze 1993b) and geographers (Butzer 1992; Denevan 1992) identifying the impact of Native Americans on their landscape may not be popular because they counter the image of "Native Americans as noble ecologists" with ecological realism. Nonetheless, there is still a huge difference in the scale of environmental degradation—from very localized and generally short term for small, nonagricultural groups to regional and long term for modern industrialized societies. And it is by examining the type and degree of influence that these people had on the landscape, tempered by an understanding of both scale and ecological dynamics, that we can learn new things about the way things were and why.

LANDSCAPE DYNAMICS, SCALE, AND POINTS OF CONTACT

There has long been interest in environmental issues by archaeologists, and this is well documented in the Northeast (e.g., Johnson 1942; Sears 1932). There is, however, a distinction between what is often termed environmental archaeology, which is concerned foremost with reconstructing past landscapes and identifying resources available to, or utilized by people, and ecological archaeology, which goes beyond this to examine the relationships between the different components (including people) of those environments. In this context, such factors as scale, biological productivity, ecosytemic stability, and population dynamics become especially important.

Landscape Dynamics

Long ago archaeologists recognized the importance of the environment in interpreting past human affairs (see Butzer 1971:6–9). Clearly, one has to consider such factors as general climatic zone, landform type and distribution, plant and animal communities, precipitation, and soils types when interpreting particular sites or larger land-use patterns. A subsequent epiphany occurred with the advent of systems theory and the idea of ecosystems (see McIntosh 1991:193–241), the latter consisting not only of the sum of its parts, but also the various relationships that are present among these parts. These relationships can be recognized at several complementary levels. The most obvious is that of correlation; for example, plant communities are dependent on the types of soils present and upon local precipitation patterns. To this, we can add the concept of feedback, whereby the success of those plants may modify those soils, allow new species to propagate, and may eventually lead to a new microclimatic regime.

Another dimension is identified by those variables, such as primary and secondary biomass productivity, biotic diversity, succession, and stability, that define the nature of the relationship between the components of the landscape. As one example, ecosystem stability is defined as "resistance to and recovery from external perturbations" (Simmons 1989:16). This concept is pertinent to the developmental history of the northeastern landscape, and to understanding human adaptive strategies associated with periods of environmental stability and change. Further insights are possible when specific types and properties of stability are examined, such as inertia—the ability of a system to resist external change, or elasticity—the speed at which a system returns to a former state following a disturbance (see Simmons 1989:17). Attention to such factors encourages a shift from looking for correlations between climatic change and shifts in land-use patterns to identifying the points of contact between climate and land use (i.e., *how* does a climatic perturbation actually influence human behavior?). A pertinent example is the Little Ice Age, a period of cooler than present temperatures between about A.D. 1550 and 1800. People responded not to the drop in temperature per se (Baron 1988:42), but to the reduction in the length of the growing season, and to an increase in the availability and number of anadromous fish (e.g., Carlson 1995).

An ecological outlook may also prove important when examining anthropogenic influences on the environment. Although the type of impact that non-agriculturalists had was generally very local and short term, even this can have a cumulative effect. For example, selective harvesting of plants increased the availability of those plants with desired characteristics. Likewise, positive or negative pressures on animals or plants that acted as keystone species (i.e., species having a significant role in community organization [McNaughton and

Wolf 1979:690]) can contribute to the gradual transformation of the landscape. Finally, periods of disequilibrium in an ecological system can increase biotic productivity and diversity, and such episodes can have both anthropogenic causes and human behavioral responses.

A Matter of Scale

In addition to the type and degree of ecological variables to be considered, issues of scale are no less important. Not only must we consider differences in temporal and spatial domains (see Delcourt and Delcourt 1991; Dincauze 1988a), but note that events occurring at local and short-term parameters influence the larger and longer regimes of which they are a part. Dincauze (1987), for example, has discussed three scales of human interaction with the environment—micro, meso, and macro. Of these, archaeologists are most often concerned with what goes on at the microscale because this equates with individual behavior, activity areas, and sites. The majority of anthropogenic influences on the environment occurs at this level (Dincauze 1993b). There is also interest with the mesoscale in terms of landscape archaeology—the level at which people interact with the landscape, and landscape ecology—where biotic communities are defined. The effects of anthropogenic influence are more restricted here, and tend to be the result of large-area disturbances, such as fires, or the cumulative effect of many small-scale and short-term ones.

The remainder of this chapter examines possible and demonstrated anthropogenic influences on landscape development in the Northeast associated with three areas of human endeavor: hunting, fishing, and harvesting. This tripartite scheme encompasses a wide range of human activities, including subsidiary tasks, that represent points of contact between people and the landscape they occupy. These examples are selective rather than inclusive, and serve only to illustrate certain types and scales of behavior. For example, with hunting we can look at its positive and negative influences on animal communities that, in turn, may influence vegetation or wetland development. The type, intensity, and success of fishing also affect the target population, and have other influences as in the case of fish weir construction. Finally, the gathering of plant materials and other means of manipulating and harvesting resources can profoundly effect local and regional plant communities through selective harvesting, caring for "wild" plants, and fire management strategies.

HUNTING

Hunting activities may have a discernible influence not only on the species selected, but the landscape itself. In the two examples that follow, it is clear that hunting by small-scale groups could also have had positive or negative impact on the biological communities with which those species interacted.

Mammoth and Mastodon

The early postglacial environment in the Northeast was very different from that of today in terms of both vegetation and fauna. The most notable component of the late Pleistocene faunal communities was the megafauna (e.g., Laub et al. 1988). Both mammoth and mastodon were present on the Northeastern landscape soon after deglaciation and possibly until the beginning of the Holocene 10,000 years ago (McAndrews and Jackson 1988; Morse et al. 1996). Herd size and distribution appears significantly different from more western localities; the number and distribution of fossil sites, plus other paleoecological data, suggest that animals were solitary or part of small herds widely scattered on the landscape. To date, there is no direct evidence of the exploitation of such megafauna by Paleoindians in the Northeast (e.g., Steadman et al. 1997). However, mastodon were undoubtedly hunted and killed on occasion. Human interaction with megafauna, no matter how limited, likely influenced local environment conditions in several ways.

One "positive" effect would be a reduction of trampling, trail creation, and torn-out vegetation, all of which are associated with modern prosbosideans (see Haynes 1991). These large mammals are also prodigious consumers of vegetation. Haynes (1991:58) noted that an adult African elephant consumes 175 to 200 kg of plant material during a fourteen-hour day. Using the lower figure, we can estimate that their late Pleistocene cousins could have consumed 63,875 kg during a year, and 3,832,500 kg during a sixty-year lifespan.

Hunting is also associated with "negative" effects not only on the prey itself but also on the local and regional landscape. While no longer considered the primary factor in the extinction of Pleistocene megafauna, hunting by humans still contributed to their demise. Beyond this, humans may have had more indirect influences on local landscape. Mammoths and mastodons were probably a significant influence on localized vegetation in their role as keystone species. For one thing, probosideans are major producers of dung, transforming shrubs, twigs, grasses, sedges, and other materials into a soluble source of plant phosphorous, nitrogen, water, and other nutrients that would have been in relatively short supply on the early postglacial landscape. Hunting would thus reduce significantly fertilizer production and distribution on an emergent postglacial environment. For example, using an average of 125 kg of dung produced daily by an adult African elephant (Haynes 1991:90), the yearly production is 45,625 kg, with an lifetime estimate of 2,737,500 kg. Given these impressive figures, even a relatively small and scattered probosidean population was capable of making a substantial contribution to the early northeastern landscape; to paraphrase Dincauze (1993b), they were the "fertilizers of Eden."

Finally, if megafauna were keystone species, any increase or decrease in their population density and distribution pattern may have influenced other elements of early postglacial floral and faunal communities (see Owen-Smith [1988] for discussion on how North American probosideans may have acted as keystone species). Subsequent environmental changes, in turn, could have provided new opportunities for early human populations.

Beaver

More than any other animal, beavers have a profound influence on the landscapes they occupy. Beaver were and continue to be a major influence of landscape development in the Northeast. Beaver dams have a substantial role in pond and wetland formation and maintenance, and in the geochemistry of those waters (Johnston 1994). The degree to which beavers were hunted could have greatly influenced the local landscape. Little or no hunting would have had a positive effect on beaver populations, resulting in more numerous and extensive pondings that would create extensive wetland habitat, encourage certain trajectories of vegetation development, and reduce flooding (see Naiman et al. 1988). Intensive hunting, on the other hand, would lead to a reduction in local and/or regional beaver population, and to fewer and less extensive wetlands and the return of impoundments to preexisting conditions or new development sequences.

There is a long history of beaver hunting in the Northeast, and it appears to have been a widely sought resource throughout the Holocene. They occupied low, poorly drained areas in New England soon after deglaciation (Kaye 1962), and may have played a significant role in the development of the Great Dismal Swamp in Virginia (Oaks and Whitehead 1979:20). Not surprising, there is evidence of beaver hunting at such Paleoindian sites as Bull Brook in Massachusetts (Grimes et al. 1984). Based on ethnographic sources, a wide variety of hunting strategies was undoubtedly utilized. In the eastern Subarctic, for example, lodges were broken into in the winter and all escaping animals killed (e.g., Helm et al. 1981:152). While this may be a postcontact technique, it probably has considerable antiquity. Beaver were also killed individually by traps, as Goddard (1978:217) noted for the Delaware.

The intensity, frequency, and location of beaver hunting during the Holocene undoubtedly varied in response to the availability of the prey, as well as to local and regional economic needs, market pressures, and trade opportunities. Given the obvious correlation between beaver dams and wetland formation, however, it is likely that Aboriginal management strategies and/or conservationist practices developed quite early in the Holocene.

FISHING

The most obvious effect that fishing has is the pressure that it places on local fish populations. Such effects are probably quickly alleviated once the fishing stops, thus leaving no discernible impact on either the fish population or the local environment. However, other types of activities relating to fishing can have a more lasting impact.

In the Northeast, fishweirs generally consist of linear arrangements of vertical stakes and horizontal latticework consisting of saplings and branches; some incorporated rocks as an integral part of the structure. Ethnohistoric accounts indicate that they were widely utilized throughout the region by the Abenaki (Day 1978:153; Snow 1978:138), the Mahican (Brasser 1978:199), and by various groups throughout southern New England (Salwen 1978:162). Archaeological evidence of fishweirs is limited, however, most likely due to their relatively fragile character. Documented examples are found in Connecticut (Coffin 1947), Maine (Petersen et al. 1994), Massachusetts (Johnson 1942), and Ontario (Johnston and Cassavoy 1978). Construction requirements and the operation of weirs had potential influences on microhabitat formation and sedimentation, as the example of the Boylston Street Fish Weir illustrates.

The Boylston Street Fish Weir

The Boylston Street Fish Weir is a large set of weirs found in the vicinity of Boylston Street, in Boston, Massachusetts. Excavations earlier this century at several locations where the weir was exposed by construction were described by Johnson (1942). More recently, additional work was conducted in the late 1980s, as reported by Décima and Dincauze (1998), Dincauze (1988a) and by Newby and Webb (1994). The dates of weir construction, use, and abandonment have now been bracketed by radiocarbon assays of 5300 and 3700 B.P. (Décima and Dincauze 1998:165) and are thus associated with the Archaic period. There is little evidence of what fish the weir was created to catch, although they were most likely intertidal.

By archaeological standards, the Boylston Street weir site is immense, although Décima and Dincauze (1998) now contend that it actually represents numerous small weirs. At the Boylston Street section, the weir covers an estimated 20,000 m^2, with no indication of margins (Johnson 1942:24). With the addition of the area tested in 1988, it is evident that the weir(s) extended over a much larger portion of the Back Bay. From the standpoint of anthropogenic factors, the amount of wood collected to construct the weir was substantial. For the Mutual Life building section alone, Johnson (1942:27) estimated 65,000 stakes. To evaluate the potential local impact of this construction project, it is necessary to determine approximately how much wood may have been harvested.

Johnson reported the length of stakes ranging from "four to seven feet," and the width from "one to four inches"; the wattling consisted of a mass of branches and shrubs. Taking an average length of 5.5 feet (160 cm) and width of 2 inches (5 cm), one stake equals 132 inches^2 [nonmetric measurements correspond with modern lumber usage.] Accepting this, multiplying 65,000 stakes by 132 inches^2 and dividing by 144 (a board foot is 144 inches^2) equals 59,585 board feet. If divided by the 1,500-year period of weir construction indicated by radiocarbon dates, this provides an annual harvest of forty board feet/year, plus an unknown amount of wattles/brushwork, for the Mutual Life Insurance Building site alone. Alternatively, if we adopt a prelumberyard approach and assume that one stake equals one sapling, then 65,000 saplings total equal 43 saplings/year over 1,500 years. The latter estimate is more meaningful because what is most significant in assessing the local influence of weir construction and maintenance is not the board feet of lumber but rather the number of saplings that *did not grow* into trees. The annual harvest figures may also be considerably higher if the weirs were more extensive or numerous, if construction and maintenance were more episodic, and if the total number of saplings is not divided over 1,500 years.

One resource harvesting technique that may have limited or reduced the effect of wood collection for weir construction is coppicing, a practice by which trees are severely cut back and the resultant abundant sprouts later harvested, often on a five- to seven-year cycle (Buckley 1992). This practice, which is well documented in Europe where it has considerable antiquity (Coles and Coles 1986:86), has gained the attention of researchers working in North America (Anderson 1995). The majority of species represented in the sample of Boylston weir stakes analyzed by Kaplan et al. (1990)—beech, oak, alder, and sassafras—can all be coppiced.

The possibility of coppicing may help to explain why there is no discernible evidence in the pollen record of deforestation in the vicinity of the weir. Newby and Webb (1994:222) note that deforestation was not extensive enough to affect the abundance of any pollen type during the period of weir operation, and that, even if large numbers of "lower story" saplings were cut, pollen from the "upper story" would mask the event. They also state that there are no fluctuations in grass pollen percentage at a magnitude indicating human activity, but acknowledge the difficulty in identifying intense but episodic activities against the normal background. Coppicing would provide one means of obtaining a substantial amount of saplings without deforestation primarily by maintaining the levels of mature trees reflected in the pollen record. More generally, sapling cutting and the collection of fallen branches and drift wood may have affected local vegetation and animal communities by clearing the understory in forested areas or removing the source of nutrients available from decayed leaves and branches.

The weir undoubtedly had an influence on local fauna. Johnson (1942:18), for example, noted that it provided a habitat attractive to oysters, which "increased during the period when the weir was in use." Nelson (1942:56) took this further by suggesting that the weir functioned in part as an oyster farm. More recent studies tend to support both ideas. For example, the increase in shellfish species diversity and abundance after weir abandonment led Carlson (1988b:33–34) to note that oyster was minimally present in Back Bay prior to weir construction but increased in abundance after the weir was in place. This may indicate improved habitat, a cessation of oyster harvesting and clam digging, or some degree of both.

HARVESTING

Although both hunting and fishing are activities that garner much attention, the gathering of wild foods and other resources was unquestionably the economic foundation of most hunting-and-gathering systems. The word *gathering*, however, is inadequate in describing how hunter-gatherers make a living because it implies a very casual means of obtaining food. The increasing recognition of the detailed knowledge, conservation practices, and complex management strategies utilized by nonagriculturalists in North America temperate forest areas suggests that a more meaningful term, at least for some places, may be harvesting. This usage reflects not only a high degree of planning, but also the sustainable character of many small-scale, indigenous operations (also see Neusius 1986). As used here, the term encompasses the range of gardening and resource harvest strategies associated with hunter-gatherers (the latter including certain forms of hunting).

Gardening

The term *gardening* is now cropping up all over in reference to traditional resource management strategies (e.g., Anderson 1991; Dincauze 1993b). As with the term *harvesting*, its use represents a major transition in evaluating hunter-gatherer plant use. For example, in a review of traditional food-gathering techniques utilized in interior British Columbia, Peacock and Turner (1998) found that weeding, tilling, pruning, and transplanting were not only widely practiced but also considered by their informants to be vital to the health of the resource. These activities also have had a significant effect on the landscape by increasing, maintaining, or decreasing biodiversity levels. Weeding, for example, not only removes undesirable plants, but can, along with transplanting, significantly change the biotic composition of particular locations.

The actual harvesting or collection of plants has its own ecological dynamics. With some root crops, the more intensive the harvest, the greater the yield and the healthier the crop. This is due to the loosening of soils and to the creation of new propagules when portions of the harvested plant remain in the ground. We see in this case a counterintuitive correlation—that intensive harvesting can not only be sustained, but actually be beneficial to the plants. Cattail (*Typha* spp.) is one plant widely utilized in the Northeast (Nicholas 1991b) that may have similarly benefited from intensive harvesting. One potential danger, however, is that if this is indeed the case, then anthropogenic factors may have inadvertently contributed to the terrestrialization of wetlands as cattail responded favorably to human harvesting. This, in turn, could have reduced the size and extent of certain types of wetlands, and thus decreased resource diversity, productivity, and reliability in those areas.

Resource Harvesting

A number of activities fall under the category of resource harvesting, where resources other than food plants are managed for later collection. Coppicing and fire management strategies are two examples. Other types of resource collection, such as firewood collection, are qualitatively different as they require little, if any, planning.

Coppicing represents a form of timber management that is similar in some ways to farming. It would thus prove an ideal source of building material for weir construction because it involves a sustainable resource that is located near where it is needed. Coppicing has been identified as a resource procurement strategy utilized by Aboriginal groups in western North America to obtain basketry materials (Anderson 1995). The impact of coppicing will usually be limited to the local level and may have a minimal effect on vegetation succession.

Perhaps the most influential anthropogenic factor affecting the character of the northeastern landscape is the use of fire as a resource management strategy (Day 1953; Williams and Hunn 1982). To date, there have been only limited archaeological studies on fire history (e.g., Patterson and Sassaman 1988), although this practice is expected to have been utilized throughout the Northeast, and may have considerable antiquity. The parklike settings encountered by early observers were likely the result of burning, although this could include both lightning and human-set fires. Patterson and Sassaman's (1988) review of ethnohistorical accounts, of the criteria for distinguishing between different ignition sources, and of charcoal in pollen cores and other sources led them to conclude that fires were most common in areas of the greatest settlement during the late prehistoric period. It is thus likely that burning was utilized to enhance resource availability on either a regular or occasional basis.

Fire management strategies using controlled burning generally have one or more goals. Controlled burning can be utilized in land clearing; in this it also provides an influx of nutrients into the soil. In hunting, it can be used as part of an immediate return strategy to drive or concentrate game, or with longer-term goals of encouraging new browse that will attract deer that can later be exploited. Burning can also stimulate the growth of many different plants (e.g., berries) and improve the yield of the harvest. Finally, it creates and maintains ecologically heterogeneous mosaics (Turner 1991). The landscape changes resulting from human set fires occur at a much different scale than the other examples of anthropogenic influence noted above because fire modifies the structure and productivity of the biotic community, rather than individual members of that community.

As observed ethnographically, the location and timing of the burns were carefully controlled. In North America, these was usually being restricted to early spring or late fall (Patterson and Sassaman 1988:115; Turner 1991:68); elsewhere, such as in Australia (Lewis 1982), they were scheduled before the start of the rainy season. These were times when enough moisture was present to limit the extent and intensity of the burns, or rains were expected.

Undoubtedly, however, events sometimes did not go as planned and fires got out of control.

LONGER-TERM ANTHROPOGENIC INFLUENCES

Most of the examples described above involve relatively local and short-term influences. Even these, however, can have a lasting influence by setting the stage for other developments.

Fire management strategies may have long-term consequences for landscape development and vegetation history, particularly if frequently used. They can strongly influence the biotic composition of an area by removing fire-sensitive species and encouraging the spread of fire-tolerant ones, or by allowing the colonization of previously forested areas. Land clearing through burning may also increase erosion, removing soil and also increasing sediment loads in streams and rivers that, in turn, may influence fish and other organisms. Finally, fire not only encourages or constrains particular trajectories of forest development, something of obvious importance to people living in the Eastern Woodlands (e.g., Abrams 1992), but maintains levels of disturbance and heterogeneity, factors that generate biodiversity (e.g., Reice 1984).

Wetlands play an important role in human affairs, both in terms of providing many resources harvested by people and contributing to the character of the regional landscape (Nicholas 1998). They can be adversely affected by both anthropogenic and natural factors. Whether due to accelerated infilling resulting from harvesting, burning, increased beaver hunting, or natural environmental changes, a reduction in the number, size, extent, and distribution of wetlands, and changes in wetland type and composition, are correlated with an overall decline in ecological heterogeneity, a variable positively correlated with high human habitat values. This will also reduce the habitat utilized by the many birds and animals associated with these settings. In addition to affecting plant and animal habitat, a decline in beaver-controlled wetlands would increase stream velocity and erosion potential; decrease the amount of hydraulic residence time; decrease water depth; reduce acidity; and influence nutrient loads through nitrogen transformation and organic cycling (e.g., Cirmo and Driscoll 1993)—all factors that subsequently influence local biotic communities. Wetlands are also a major source of atmospheric methane (Naiman et al. 1991), which is linked to climate; anthropogenic changes in their number and composition may thus have large-area, long-term consequences.

Perhaps the most pervasive influence that hunter-gatherers had on the landscape stems from the selective pressures placed on plants and anthropogenic open habitat. In eastern North America, and possibly including the Northeast, these factors led to the local domestication of chenopod (*Chenopodium berlandieri*), marsh elder (*Iva annua*), sunflower (*Helianthus annuus*), squash (*Cucurbita pepo*) (Smith 1995), and a preadaptation to domesticates arriving from elsewhere. The increasing success of hunter-gatherers during the middle Holocene led to larger population sizes, higher population density, and more sedentary behavior. With such factors came greater anthropogenic pressures on the environment; for example, reduced mobility can translate into decreased recovery time for exploited areas. Larger, longer, and more intensive settlements would also influence local ecology by contributing to the formation of soil types, adding or removing appreciable nutrients, or increasing pH levels in occupied or utilized areas. When forest clearance for horticultural is added to this, shifts in local vegetation occur and erosion becomes even more pronounced (Burden et al. 1986), although comparable effects may also result from nonagricultural land clearance and/or use of fire as a resource management strategy.

Earlier in the Holocene, anthropogenic-induced landscape changes may also have occurred as people responded to the Hypsithermal episode, a period of significant warm, dry climatic conditions (see Dincauze 1989). In addition to influencing vegetation, this period of drier winters and summers and increased evaporation rates contributed to a subsequent decrease in lake levels (Webb and Newby 1987). Wetlands, as a reliable source of water, plant, and animal resources, may thus have been more intensively exploited than before or after. Such intensive land use during a period of environmental stress may have placed additional pressures on wetlands, which are susceptible to outside influences (Walker 1970), thus influencing developmental trajectories.

CONCLUSION

My purpose here has not been to criticize Aboriginal peoples for their role in modifying the landscape. Indeed, I have been working on a daily basis with them for the last eight years (Nicholas 1997). We *assume* that nonagricultural peoples left a light footprint, and this is more or less true—but it is prudent to examine such assumptions critically. In fact, if we consider that disturbance and heterogeneity generate biodiversity, we then acknowledge that human-induced disturbances have contributed positively to the character of the regional landscape. Likewise, if hunter-gatherers had not been active managers of the landscape they occupied, as seems likely, then the later Holocene history of the Northeast would undoubtedly have been much different. The spread of horticulture, the rise of ranked societies, and the cultural dynamics that accompanied them would then have required a different developmental route than they had.

ACKNOWLEDGMENTS

Dena Dincauze has been a profound influence upon my own research, as she has for most archaeologists working in the region. She created disturbances in my thinking and opened new patches in which she planted many of the ideas discussed here. I thank the editors of this volume for the invitation to participate, and patience for transcontinental delays. The initial aspects of this paper were prepared while on sabbatical at the Department of Anthropology, University of Auckland, New Zealand. I thank Doug Sutton and the members of the department, and especially Claire Reeler for typing and e-mailing the abstract of this paper while I was in transit to Australia. Finally, Catherine Carlson, Nancy Turner, Sandra Peacock, Rickard Toomey, and Kat Anderson were generous with information and ideas.

3

Paleoenvironmental Context for the Middle Archaic Occupation of Cape Cod, Massachusetts

Frederick J. Dunford

Cape Cod is a narrow, armlike peninsula situated on the Atlantic Coastal Plain in southeastern Massachusetts (Figure 3.1). Located in the southern Gulf of Maine and bordered on the north by Cape Cod Bay, on the east by the Atlantic Ocean, and on the south by Nantucket Sound, Cape Cod is a glacial landform created during the Laurentide glaciation of southern New England ca. 21,000–18,000 B.P. (Oldale 1989). Its landscape consists principally of end moraines and outwash plains which have been significantly modified by postglacial sea-level rise. In the last 12,000 years the southern shoreline of Cape Cod has retreated more than 150 km from the Great South Channel southeast of Cape Cod to its present position (Figure 3.2). Ocean currents over these millennia have eroded, transported, and redeposited glacial materials to form the Cape and Islands as they are today. Cape Cod is thus a landscape defined by the sea with a shoreline that is always in transition. Geologist Barbara Blau Chamberlain describes Cape Cod as existing in an "endless state of flux, alive with changes measured not in geologic eons, as in the more static inlands, but within life-times, decades, or even overnights" (Chamberlain 1964:xii). This observation has important implications for archaeologists studying Cape Cod or other similarly dynamic coastal environments, where there is an immediacy to environmental change.

The archaeological record of Cape Cod preserves, in part, a cumulative record of the responses made by specific human communities to environmental conditions at particular times and places in prehistory (Dincauze 1997:2). For example, the estuarine-based territoriality that characterized Late Woodland (1000–500 B.P.) settlement and subsistence systems on Cape Cod can be viewed as a response to sea-level stabilization and the development of the modern estuary systems after 2000 B.P. (Dunford 1993:5–6; Oldale 1992:98). However, the relationships between human communities and the environments they occu-

Figure 3.1
Cape Cod, Massachusetts

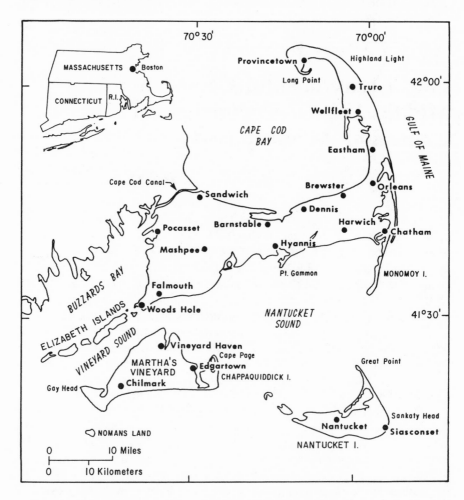

pied were never absolutely deterministic. I follow Dincauze (1997:3) in suggesting that "environmental variables do not define or determine the livelihoods of
human communities. The variables of a given space offer a finite range of conditions and material and biota; what humans make of those will always be con-
tingent upon the composition, size and especially technological complexity of the
human communities that occupy that space."

From this perspective, postglacial sea-level rise and the development of the
modern estuary systems may have provided environmental conditions that influenced the emergence of territoriality, for example, but historical events and
social processes would have tempered, to a great extent, the social partitioning

Figure 3.2
Landward Migration of the Southern Shoreline of Cape Cod, 12,000 B.P. to Present
(based on Uchupi et al. 1997)

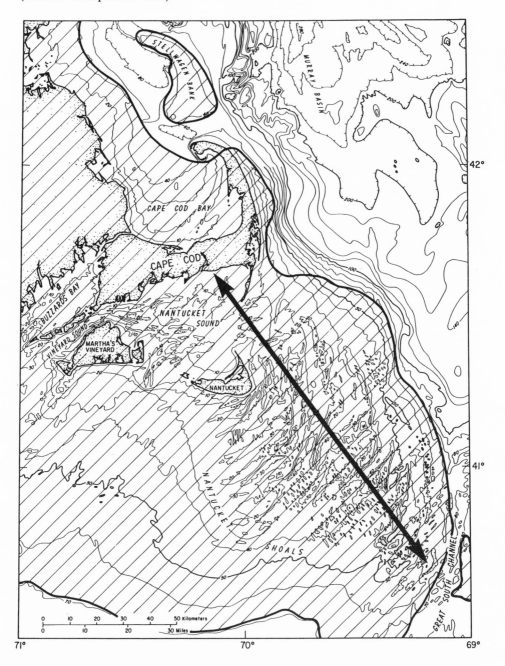

of the landscape. The development of estuarine-based territoriality during the Late Woodland on Cape Cod was an ecologically centered but socially charged phenomenon.

Postglacial sea-level rise also had significant implications for the human communities that occupied Cape Cod before 2000 years ago. This is not always immediately evident however, because the submergence of the coastal lowlands during the early Holocene destroyed a significant part of the archaeological record of the region. While an unknown number of archaeological sites from the Early and Middle Archaic (9500–6000 B.P.) have been eroded, the location of the remaining sites and find spots on Cape Cod provides a partial record of the settlement and subsistence systems and the communication and exchange networks that were truncated by the rising sea.

In this chapter I discuss Middle Archaic (8000–6000 B.P.) settlement and subsistence systems on Cape Cod in the context of postglacial sea-level rise and marine transgression of the coastal lowlands during the early Holocene. During that time the rapidly rising sea provided both opportunity and constraint for the human communities that occupied Cape Cod. While sea-level rise created especially productive, albeit transitory, marine ecosystems like estuaries and salt marshes, it also provided an increasingly circumscribed landscape as the southern shoreline of Cape Cod retreated more than 40 km between 10,000 and 6000 B.P.

I propose that the archaeological record of the Middle Archaic on Cape Cod provides insight into the manner in which local populations responded to these exceptionally dynamic environmental conditions. In this chapter, I provide a paleoenvironmental context for the Middle Archaic occupation of Cape Cod, along with a review of the current state of knowledge concerning the spatial distribution of Middle Archaic sites and find spots on Cape Cod. I also discuss the extent to which the geographic orientation of Middle Archaic sites on Cape Cod can be seen as a response to specific environmental conditions during that period.

PALEOENVIRONMENTAL CONTEXT

In developing a paleoenvironmental context for the Middle Archaic occupation of Cape Cod, I focus on three categories of environmental data specific to the period of 10,000 to 6000 B.P. First, I review evidence for modification of glacial Cape Cod by marine processes dating from 9500 to 6000 B.P. (Uchupi et al. 1997:32). This period represents the first of two phases in the modification of Cape Cod during the Holocene and is characterized as a time of massive erosion when sea level was rising rapidly (Uchupi et al. 1997:32). I present a series of paleogeographic maps to illustrate the landward migration of the shoreline during this period. Second, I examine the "sea level forcing of the freshwater aquifer" (Winkler and Sanford 1995:332) of Cape Cod as it relates to the development of freshwater habitat during the Middle Archaic. Finally, I summarize the palynological data from Cape Cod that indicate the establishment of a coastal, pine barrens environment during a period of warm, dry climate after 9000 B.P.

Marine Processes and the Development of Coastal Environments

Between 9500 and 6000 B.P. sea level was rising "at a rate of about 6 m/ 1000 yr from -30 m to -10 m below its present level." This resulted in "massive erosion" on the east and north sides of the Cape and the submergence of most of Nantucket Shoals, Nantucket Sound, and Cape Cod Bay (Uchupi et al. 1997: 32). As noted earlier, sea-level rise provided both opportunity and constraint for the inhabitants of the region. The rapidly rising sea created a series of relatively short-lived, but potentially productive marine ecosystems that could have provided important resources for the local population. At the same time, however, the marine transgression of the coastal lowlands drastically reduced the area of inhabitable land available to human communities (following Dincauze and Mulholland 1977:442–443), thereby constraining the spatial organization of settlement systems.

To illustrate the landward migration of the shoreline between 9500 and 6000 B.P., I developed a series of paleogeographic maps using sea-level curve data and modern bathymetry to approximate the position of the shoreline at 10,000, 8000 and 6000 B.P. (Figures 3.3, 3.4, and 3.5). The maps are not intended as precise reconstructions of the Cape Cod landscape at these times, but instead illustrate the manner in which the rising sea influenced environmental conditions during the period in question.

By 10,000 B.P. the rising sea had begun to submerge the lowland between the present day islands of Nantucket and Martha's Vineyard, creating a relatively protected embayment in the area that is now Nantucket Sound. Much of Cape Cod Bay had also been submerged by that time (see Figure 3.3).

Sea-level rise along the eastern shoreline of Cape Cod between 9500 and 6000 B.P. resulted in significant erosion of the eastward facing sea cliffs. Uchupi and colleagues (1997:63) have estimated that as much as 5 km^3 of sediment was eroded and carried southeastward during this period.

At the beginning of the Middle Archaic period, about 8000 B.P., most of Nantucket Sound had been submerged. The "hummocky topographic texture" (Uchupi et al. 1997:32), which characterizes the outwash plains along the southern margin of Cape Cod, provided for the creation of a number of protected embayments as the rising sea flooded low-lying areas. The submergence of Cape Cod Bay during the Middle Archaic also led to the creation of a large embayment when the lowland between the Billingsgate Shoal moraine and glacial Cape Cod was inundated (see Figure 3.4).

The creation of protected embayments along the northern and southern coasts of Cape Cod during the Middle Archaic provided favorable conditions for the development of especially productive ecosystems like estuaries and salt

Figure 3.3
Approximate Position of Cape Cod's Shoreline at 10,000 B.P.
(based on Uchupi et al. 1997)

Figure 3.4

Approximate Position of Cape Cod's Shoreline at 8000 B.P. The arrow indicates the distance between embayments on the southern and northern shoreline (based on Uchupi et al. 1997).

Figure 3.5
Approximate Position of Cape Cod's Shoreline at 6000 B.P.
(based on Uchupi et al. 1997)

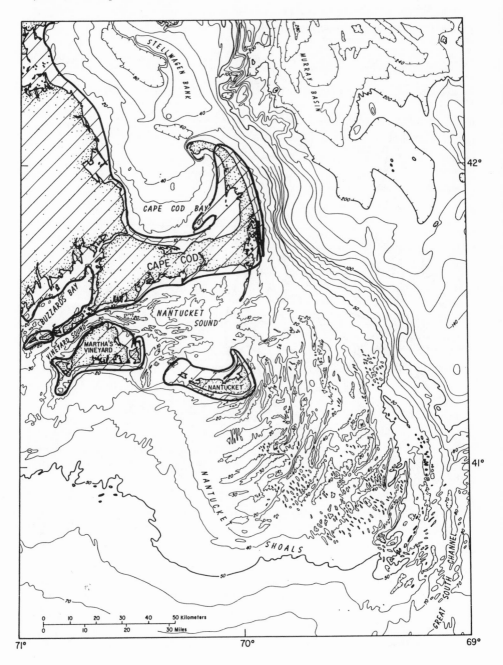

marshes. The distance between the embayment at the Billingsgate Shoal moraine and the embayments along the southern shoreline of the Cape at that time was only about 20 km (see Figure 3.4). As such, Middle Archaic sites were in relatively close proximity to coastal environments which provided concentrated, predictable, and highly productive resources.

Marine Processes and the Development of Freshwater Environments

The hydrology of Cape Cod is somewhat unique because the water table rests close to sea level and is recharged "only by the precipitation that falls locally" (Oldale 1992:138–139). As such, the development of freshwater ponds and wetlands on the Cape was influenced by postglacial sea-level rise and climate change. This observation has important implications concerning the amount of freshwater habitat that was available for human communities during the Middle Archaic period.

A recent study of freshwater ponds in the Cape Cod National Seashore, located on the eastern Cape, separated ponds into three groups characterized by "different development scenarios" (Winkler and Sanford 1995:311). Ponds in the first group have late-glacial histories and formed during the deglaciation of the region when ice blocks were lodged and buried in clay-rich outwash (Winkler and Sanford 1995:311). Because the basins of these ponds are relatively impermeable they have held varying amounts of freshwater, derived from surface runoff, from the time of meltout (about 11,500 B.P.) until about 6000 B.P. when the sea level forcing of the aquifer began to influence pond levels across the Cape (Winkler and Sanford 1995:312–323, 332). The second group of ponds were created in the same manner, but in outwash plains that were clay poor (Winkler and Sanford 1995:311). After meltout, these ponds became dry basins until approximately 6000 B.P. when "sea level rose and the freshwater lens intersected the dry basins" (Winkler and Sanford 1995:311). The final group of ponds in the study developed as interdunal bogs in the Provincelands after 1000 B.P. (Winkler and Sanford 1995:311) and are not relevant to this discussion concerning sea-level rise and the formation of freshwater environments during the Middle Archaic period.

Winkler and Sanford's observations concerning pond development have important implications for determining both the relative availability and spatial distribution of freshwater habitat on Cape Cod during the Middle Archaic period. The influence of sea level in elevating the water table was critical in creating freshwater ponds and wetlands on the now submerged coastal lowlands between 8000 and 6000 B.P. (see Figure 3.4). Indeed, the embayments along the northern and southern coast of the Cape were in all probability estuaries "where the seawater is diluted and partially mixed with water coming from the land" (Smith 1980:258). As noted earlier, estuaries are unusually productive places that provide resources that can be characterized as concentrated, predictable, and very productive. Therefore, Middle Archaic communities would have found coastal locations ecologically advantageous.

At the same time, however, inland locations would have provided fewer sources of freshwater. Ponds and wetlands on the interior of the Cape (the Group I ponds) were recharged only by precipitation. Therefore, the availability of freshwater habitat at elevations above the coastal lowlands was directly affected by seasonal fluctuations in precipitation and long-term climatic variation during the Middle Archaic period. After 6000 B.P., all the ponds and wetlands in the region were influenced by sea level (Winkler and Sanford 1995).

Vegetation and Climate History

The vegetation and climate history of Cape Cod during the Middle Archaic period can be derived from palynological analysis of radiocarbon-dated sediment cores taken from several ponds (Tzedakis 1987; Winkler 1985; Winkler and Sanford 1995). Between 9000 and 5000 B.P., a mixed, pitch pine-oak vegetation, referred to as pine barrens, became dominant "during a dry and hot climatic interval" marked by a measurable decrease in precipitation (Winkler and Sanford 1995:323). Pine barrens are plant communities that thrive on dry, open sandy soils, characteristic of the Cape's outwash plains (Winkler 1985:310). Pine barrens communities are also marked by a high fire frequency. Winkler and Sanford (1995:323) note that charcoal frequencies were higher on eastern Cape Cod between 9000 and 5000 B.P. than at any other time prior to European settlement. In addition to the dominant pine barrens community, more mesophytic trees like hemlock, white pine, and beech grew in protected basins and hollows that were seasonally moist (Winkler 1985:308; Winkler and Sanford 1995:323).

Summary of Paleoenvironmental Conditions

The Middle Archaic occupation of Cape Cod occurred during a time of significant environmental change. Massive erosion reshaped the sea cliffs of eastern Cape Cod. The marine transgression of the coastal lowlands south of Cape Cod and the inundation of Cape Cod Bay provided conditions favorable for the development of highly productive marine and estuarine ecosystems. In addition, the sea level forcing of the freshwater aquifer created ponds and wetlands on the coastal lowland, along the shore of Cape Cod Bay and in areas of low topographic relief on the present-day Cape. The availability of freshwater habitat decreased at higher elevations where water levels were perched and sensitive to seasonal fluctuations in precipitation. Pine barrens vegetation, common on the Atlantic Coastal Plain was dominant. Mesophytic species grew in moist, protected hollows, expanding across the Cape after 5000 B.P., when cooler, wetter conditions returned to the region.

THE MIDDLE ARCHAIC PERIOD ON CAPE COD

Evidence for the Middle Archaic occupation of Cape Cod has been summarized in a preservation planning document prepared by the Massachusetts Historical Commission (see Mahlstedt 1987). Thirty-four Middle Archaic sites have been identified on Cape Cod based on the presence of diagnostic bifaces which include Neville-like, Neville Variant, Stark, and Archaic Stemmed (Mahlstedt 1987:27–29). One site is located on western Cape Cod, thirteen are situated on eastern or outer Cape Cod, and twenty sites (61 percent of the total) are on the middle of Cape Cod in the area outlined in Figure 3.6. While collecting bias is certainly part of the reason that this distribution is skewed toward the mid-Cape area (Mahlstedt 1987:28), I believe that the paleoenvironmental conditions reviewed in the preceding section drew human communities to this area. In this section, I will briefly describe the spatial distribution of Middle Archaic sites in the mid-Cape area (Figures 3.6, 3.7), including the Run Hill Road site (Figure 3.7), which is the only systematically excavated Middle Archaic site in the area to date. I will then relate the distribution of Middle Archaic sites and find spots on this part of Cape Cod to the prevailing paleoenvironmental conditions between 8000 and 6000 B.P.

Site Distribution in the Mid-Cape Area

As noted earlier, a 1987 inventory lists 20 Middle Archaic sites for the mid-Cape area (see Figure 3.6). Middle Archaic assemblages have been collected from multicomponent Archaic sites on both sides of Bass River, Herring River, and the Stony Brook Valley (see Figure 3.7). More than half of the sites are found in two clusters at the Bass and Herring rivers. Each of these drainages developed within topographic lows on the outwash plain during the early postglacial. Both have been significantly influenced by the sea level forcing of the aquifer (Robert Oldale, personal communication 1997). Mahlstedt (1987:28) noted that several of the assemblages from these sites are particularly extensive, with one site alone yielding over 60 Middle Archaic points, primarily of the Neville-like variety. Mahlstedt (1987:28) also suggested that the cluster of sites at the Bass and Herring rivers is indicative of the significance of these locations to the local population during the Middle Archaic period. Since the publication of the inventory, several additional Middle Archaic find spots have been recorded for the mid-Cape area, but only one site has been systematically excavated.

The Run Hill Road site is an extensive, multicomponent Archaic site located 50 feet above sea level on the eastern shore of Upper Mill Pond, one of a series of contiguous glacial ponds that form the headwaters of Stony Brook (see Figure 3.7). Stony Brook developed during the early postglacial in a topographic low on the collapsed head of an outwash plain. Like Bass and Herring rivers, sea-level rise influenced the development of freshwater habitat in the valley after 6000 B.P. (Robert Oldale, personal communication 1997).

Figure 3.6
Portion of the Mid-Cape Area That Contains 61 Percent of the Middle Archaic Sites Documented on Cape Cod

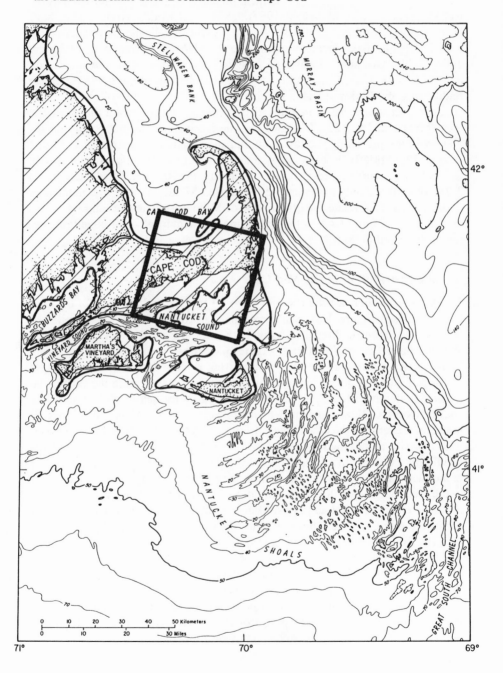

Figure 3.7
Middle Archaic Find Spots and the Run Hill Road Site
(based on Woodward 1944:11)

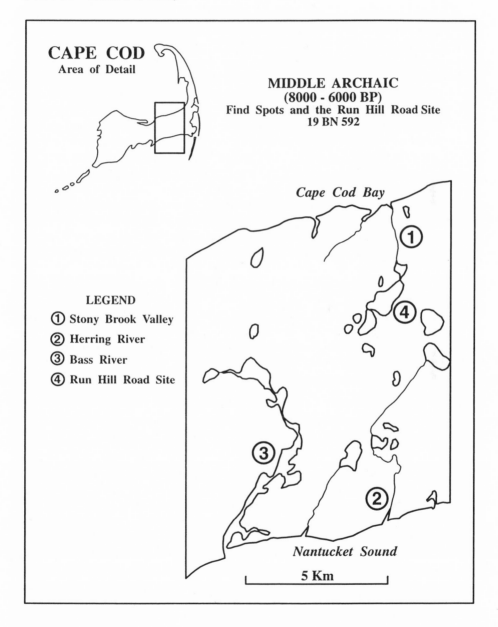

The Middle Archaic component of the site was derived from the excavation of a single, spatially discrete lithic reduction activity area. The assemblage contains 135 lithic artifacts and 6,842 pieces of debitage, providing an important record of tool production, use, modification, loss, and discard at a specific location.

While the artifacts and activities at the Run Hill Road site generally conform to patterns identified at other Middle Archaic sites in southern New England, two aspects of the assemblage are especially characteristic of Middle Archaic sites on Cape Cod. First, Run Hill Road Neville points were produced from flake blanks derived from cobble sources rather than bedrock outcrops. Small cobbles were also split by anvil-supported battering, to produce flakes that were subsequently used with little or no modification. On Cape Cod, bedrock is deeply buried and the selection of cobbles from the glacial drift represented a solution to the problem of lithic scarcity. Second, serrations are present on four of the bifaces in the Run Hill Road sample. Mahlstedt (1987:28) has indicated that a high percentage of the Neville-like bifaces in mid-Cape assemblages have "delicately serrated edges, a form common throughout the Cape." While serrations may be created at any point in an artifact's use-life, the cluster of serrated bifaces on Cape Cod may reflect functional or geographic variation within the Middle Archaic technological tradition of southern New England.

The site-specific interpretation of the Run Hill Road assemblage provides some insight into the manner in which human communities in the region responded to environmental conditions during the Middle Archaic (e.g., the adaptation of lithic technology to cobble rather than bedrock sources). Like lithic technology, settlement and subsistence systems were also influenced by environmental conditions. In fact, the distribution of Middle Archaic sites in the mid-Cape area is related to the development of new and productive environments between 8000 and 6000 B.P.

Paleoenvironmental Conditions and the Spatial Organization of Settlement and Subsistence Systems

Sixty-one percent of the Middle Archaic sites recorded for Cape Cod occur in the mid-Cape area. Two "closely related clusters of Middle Archaic sites" (Mahlstedt 1987:28) are located at Bass River (ten sites) and Herring River (four sites). Several find spots and the Run Hill Road site occur in the Stony Brook Valley. The significant density of Middle Archaic sites in this area is directly attributable to the ecological significance of the valleys during the Middle Archaic.

Bass River, Herring River and Stony Brook developed in topographic lows on the outwash plains of the mid-Cape area. The glacial ponds at the head of these rivers have developmental histories similar to the Group I ponds identified by Winkler and Sanford (1995). As such, water levels in these ponds were perched and sensitive to seasonal fluctuations in precipitation from the time of their formation (about 12,000 B.P.) until 6000 B.P. when the sea level forcing of the aquifer began to influence pond levels on Cape Cod. Therefore, during the Middle Archaic period these ponds would have represented a significant source of freshwater.

At the same time, however, conditions in the river valleys were somewhat different. During the time when the ponds at the head of the river valleys were perched and not influenced by sea level, "pond levels were not high enough to spill over into the river valleys" (Robert Oldale, personal communication 1997). Thus, water levels in the valleys were recharged only by precipitation until 6000 B.P. This is significant because the climate between 9000 and 5000 B.P. was warmer and drier than at present. Therefore, during the Middle Archaic period, valley basins may have been seasonally moist at higher elevations near the interior of the Cape. More extensive freshwater habitat existed at lower elevations near the coastal lowlands, where sea level influenced freshwater levels. On the coastal lowlands, highly productive estuary systems developed in extensive embayments which formed when the rising sea inundated low-lying areas.

CONCLUSION

Locations along Bass River, Herring River, and Stony Brook were significantly different places during the Middle Archaic period than they are today. During that time, the rivers were essentially elongated basins or valleys, which extended from glacial ponds at the interior of the Cape to estuaries at the shoreline. Varying amounts of seasonally available freshwater habitat existed at the higher elevations. Extensive freshwater wetlands were situated at lower elevations near the coast. By 6000 B.P. the sea level forcing of the aquifer began to influence freshwater levels throughout the valleys and tidal rivers began to develop.

These elongated basins or valleys were significant places on the landscape during the Middle Archaic. They provided a diverse and abundant mix of resources in a relatively concentrated area. For example, at 8000 B.P. the distance between Upper Mill Pond, the glacial pond at the head of Stony Brook valley and the embayment at the Billingsgate Shoal moraine was less than 10 km. The spatial distribution of sites indicates that Middle Archaic communities established essentially linear settlement and subsistence systems focused on these valleys. While the archaeological record has been truncated by sea-level rise, it is still possible to offer some observations concerning the spatial organization of Middle Archaic settlement and subsistence systems.

The proximity of the Middle Archaic sites at Bass River, Herring River, and Stony Brook Valley to both the north and south shore of Cape Cod at 8000 B.P. (see Figure 3.4) is indicative of the relatively low degree of mobility that would have been required to effectively exploit the diversity of resources that existed between the glacial ponds and the estuaries. In addition, the extensive nature of Middle Archaic site assemblages from the Bass and Herring rivers suggests that large settlements were established where resources were concentrated. As such, the organization of settlement systems on Cape Cod during the Middle Archaic period may not have been significantly different than the estuarine-based territoriality described for the Late Woodland (Dunford 1993). While residential relocation during the Middle Archaic would have occurred over longer distances (up to 10 km?) than during the Late Woodland, the pattern of resource utilization was essentially the same. It follows that there may be a significant degree of historical continuity in the spatial organization of settlement and subsistence systems in the region.

ACKNOWLEDGMENTS

I would like to thank the editors of this volume, Mary Ann Levine, Ken Sassaman and Michael Nassaney for providing me the opportunity to contribute a paper in Dena's honor. Dena has been an advisor, mentor, friend and a wonderful guide on my journey through the archaeological northeast. During the preparation of this paper, I had numerous conversations with John Cross and Robert Oldale which helped to clarify my thinking concerning matters archaeological and geological. Jeff Zwinakis, Robert Oldale, Peter Lajoie, and Carol Dumas, assisted with the graphics.

Part II

Rethinking Typology
and Technology

4

"By Any Other Name . . .": A Reconsideration of Middle Archaic Lithic Technology and Typology in the Northeast

John R. Cross

"What is it?" is one of the questions most frequently asked of archaeologists by the nonarchaeological public. On the face of it, the response to the question is a straightforward one—assigning a category or type name to an object. Yet artifact types are abstractions, created by archaeologists to sort objects into frameworks of time, geography, and culture. Artifact form is generated by a complex interplay of design, manufacture, and use history.

At an analytical level, artifact types define boundaries of inclusion and exclusion. Similarities in material culture may be interpreted in terms of broad cultural identity, historical continuity, or comparable levels of social complexity. Such similarities are the foundation for reconstructing culture histories at a "macro" scale, where time is measured in centuries and millennia and where traditions are the units of culture. Ultimately, however, artifacts and features were created by the actions of individuals as they balanced the opportunities, social constraints, and consequences of particular moments in time and space. Selective preservation, postdepositional disturbance, and techniques of excavation, recording, and interpretation are all filters that may distort or obscure the view of these actions by archaeologists.

The growing literature on the criteria for lithic tool design (e.g., Bleed 1986; Odell 1996) is a rich source of testable hypotheses that can move artifact analysis beyond an exercise in chronological ordering. In this chapter, I examine the technological and typological basis for Middle Archaic (ca. 8000–6000 B.P.) stemmed bifaces in the Northeast, drawing on insights from the Annasnappet Pond site in southeastern Massachusetts. Beginning at the general level of artifact types and cultural traditions, the discussion shifts to variables that address manufacture, use, and reworking—all variables that link artifact form and human action. I view this as a necessary first step in creating a prehistory that is relevant both to the region's peoples and to social scientists.

DEFINING THE MIDDLE ARCHAIC IN NORTHEAST PREHISTORY

Types establish a common frame of reference for archaeologists working within a region, but they also may impede communication with researchers working in adjacent areas. For the uninitiated, Northeast prehistory is a bewildering and somewhat insular world, with borrowed and "homegrown" terminology, a diffuse literature, and few clearly defined areas of agreement or disagreement among its practitioners. Historically, the Northeast is divided along intellectual fault lines and administrative boundaries that crosscut the area from Long Island to the St. Lawrence River, separating the prehistories of the United States and Canada, the Northeast and Mid-Atlantic regions, New York and New England, and even northern New England and southern New England from each other.

For much of the past twenty-five years, two themes have dominated the study of the Middle Archaic period in the Northeast: the apparent paucity of Early and Middle Archaic sites in the region and connections with cultures in the Southeast (Cross and Shaw 1996). Along with the development of a radiocarbon-dated framework for Northeast prehistory in the 1960s and 1970s came the realization that there were very few archaeological components dating to the period from 9000 to 5000 radiocarbon years B.P. William Ritchie (1969b:212–213) and James Fitting (1968) each suggested that the low productivity of the region's postglacial forests accounted for low human population densities. Although this explanation has been challenged on ecological grounds (e.g., Dincauze and Mulholland 1977; Nicholas 1990), the evidence remains sparse for the Early and Middle Archaic periods in much of the region (e.g., Funk 1991: 7). Researchers have sought answers in the shortcomings of existing artifact typologies (Robinson 1992), the deep burial of sites in alluvial settings, the erosion or inundation of sites by rising sea levels (Funk 1993:184–186; Nicholas 1991a; Sanger 1979), and the scarcity of datable materials in Middle Archaic contexts.

Dena Dincauze's (1971, 1976) reports on the Neville site in Manchester, New Hampshire, defined the Middle Archaic period for a generation of archaeologists working in the Northeast (see Starbuck and Bolian 1980). Through her definitions of Neville, Neville Variant, Stark, and Merrimack points as categories of Middle Archaic stemmed bifaces, Dincauze gave formal recognition and chronological standing to artifacts that previously had been described in generic outline terms (e.g., "hastate" [Ritchie 1969b] or "corner-removed" [Fowler 1963]). In the stemmed bifaces from the site, Dincauze saw technological and morphological parallels with two southeastern Middle Archaic biface types—Stanly and Morrow Mountain II—previously described by Joffre Coe (1964) for the deeply stratified Doerschuk site in the North Carolina Piedmont. According to Dincauze (1971, 1975b), the similarities among the Archaic Period projectile points of the Northeast, Mid-Atlantic, and Southeast regions provided evidence for an "Atlantic Slope Macrotradition" of cultural connection and continuity.

Coe's original description of Stanly points highlighted their distinctive technological and morphological features: straight stems; incurvate bases resulting from basal thinning; well-defined shoulders; symmetry—in plan view, cross-section, and longitudinal profile; noninvasive retouch of edges (i.e., flakes do not reach the midline); and a preference for rhyolite as a raw material. The morphological, temporal, and functional equivalent of the Stanly point at the Neville site was the Neville point (Dincauze 1976:26–29), and Coe's description of Stanly points applies on a trait-by-trait basis to Neville points. Dincauze (1976:26) has acknowledged "that Neville points may logically be considered variants of the Stanly Stemmed type," the only difference being size, with Neville points overlapping the smaller end of the size range for Stanly points.

On morphological and technological grounds, Coe's Morrow Mountain II points and Dincauze's Stark points are, for all practical purposes, indistinguishable (Cassedy 1983). Both types are characterized by comparatively thick cross sections, weakly defined shoulders, a tapered stem, and highly variable raw material quality. Morrow Mountain II and Stark points were assumed to be functionally and temporally equivalent artifacts. Both Coe and Dincauze envisioned a sequential relationship between Stanly/Neville points and the somewhat later Morrow Mountain II/Stark points.

Dincauze also identified "Neville Variant" points in the Neville site assemblage. These exhibit similar blade morphology to Neville points, but blade-stem angles are obtuse and the stem contracts to a rounded base, traits shared with Stark points. Initially, Dincauze suggested that Neville Variants were technologically (and perhaps chronologically) intermediate between Neville and Stark points, although the stratigraphic relationships between Neville Variants and these two point types were ambiguous at the Neville site (Dincauze 1976:29). For reasons discussed below, I consider the Neville Variant points to be part of the Stanly/Neville use-life trajectory.

As originally defined, "Neville" and "Stark" referred to site-specific populations of Middle Archaic points (i.e., "unbounded nodal clusters of attributes" [Dincauze 1976:26]). Dincauze used these terms primarily to define groups of technologically and morphologically similar artifacts from a single site. However, for purposes of intersite comparison, "Neville" and "Stark" could also be used as type names (Dincauze 1976:26). This duality in meaning has led to terminological confusion, as researchers resorted to "Neville-like" and "Stark-like" to identify similar artifacts from other sites (Eisenberg 1991; Johnson and Mahlstedt 1984). With few exceptions (notably Cassedy 1983), archaeologists working in adjacent regions have been unwilling or unable to scale this terminological barrier. I have chosen to use the terms *Stanly/Neville* and *Morrow Mountain II/ Stark* here as type names, emphasizing technological and morphological similarities for the Middle Archaic stemmed bifaces of the Northeast, Mid-Atlantic, and Southeast.

In geographical terms, sites with diagnostic Middle Archaic stemmed bifaces are limited to portions of the Northeast (Justice 1987). Funk (1993) stated that no Middle Archaic components are known from western, central, or northern New York. Wright (1978) illustrated a few examples of Stanly/Neville points from southern Ontario, but these were derived from a number of sites and collections. In Maine comparatively few Stanly/Neville or Morrow Mountain II/Stark points have been identified north of Flagstaff Lake in the northwestern part of the state or east of the Kennebec River. Several projectile points that are technologically consistent with Stanly/Neville and Morrow Mountain II/Stark points have been identified at the Hirundo site in the Penobscot drainage (Cross, personal observation 1996; Sanger et al. 1977).

The picture is complicated by the fact that evidence for the Middle Archaic period in the Northeast is not confined to components with Stanly/Neville or Morrow Mountain II/Stark points. Recently, researchers have identified assemblages of ground-stone rods, gouges, unifaces, and cores that date to the period from 8000 to 5000 B.P. in the region (Cole-Will and Will 1996; Robinson 1992; Sanger 1996). Chipped-stone projectile points are neither numerous nor standardized in these assemblages. For this reason, it appears likely that the Middle Archaic period has been underrepresented in the regional literature, because not all sites that date from 8000 to 5000 B.P. contain the familiar biface forms of the Southeast sequence, as outlined by Broyles (1966, 1971), Chapman (1976), and Coe (1964).

EXCAVATIONS AT ANNASNAPPET POND

The Annasnappet Pond site (19-PL-337) consists of nine loci of prehistoric activity on the margins of a spring-fed pond/cranberry bog complex in the upper reaches of the Taunton River drainage in Carver, Massachusetts (Figure 4.1). The site is located within a sandy outwash plain and is bounded on the north and west by the Monks Hill Moraine (Larson 1982). Data recovery excavations were undertaken at Annasnappet Pond by the Public Archaeology Laboratory, Inc., between 1992 and 1995 for the Massachusetts Highway Department as part of a planned highway relocation project (Doucette and Cross 1998). Three loci at the western end of the pond formed a nearly continuous distribution of Middle and Late Archaic cultural material over nearly 14,000 m^2 (Figure 4.2). The site area was tested at a 5-m interval with shovel test pits, and areas with features or high artifact densities were explored with contiguous 2 × 2-m units. In all, 720 square meters were excavated at these three loci.

There are substantial components at Annasnappet Pond that date to the Middle and Late Archaic Periods (8000–2500 B.P.), as well as limited evidence for fluted-point Paleoindian, late Paleoindian, Early Archaic, and Middle Woodland components (Doucette and Cross 1998). The excavations at the western end of Annasnappet Pond generated an impressive assemblage of Middle and Late Archaic material, including nearly 70,000 pieces of debitage, 166 Stanly/Neville points, 31 Neville Variants, 38 Morrow Mountain II/Stark points, 4 Merrimack points, cylindrical and winged atlatl weights, ground pieces of

Figure 4.1
Location of the Annasnappet Pond Site (19-PL-337) in the Taunton Drainage Basin, Massachusetts

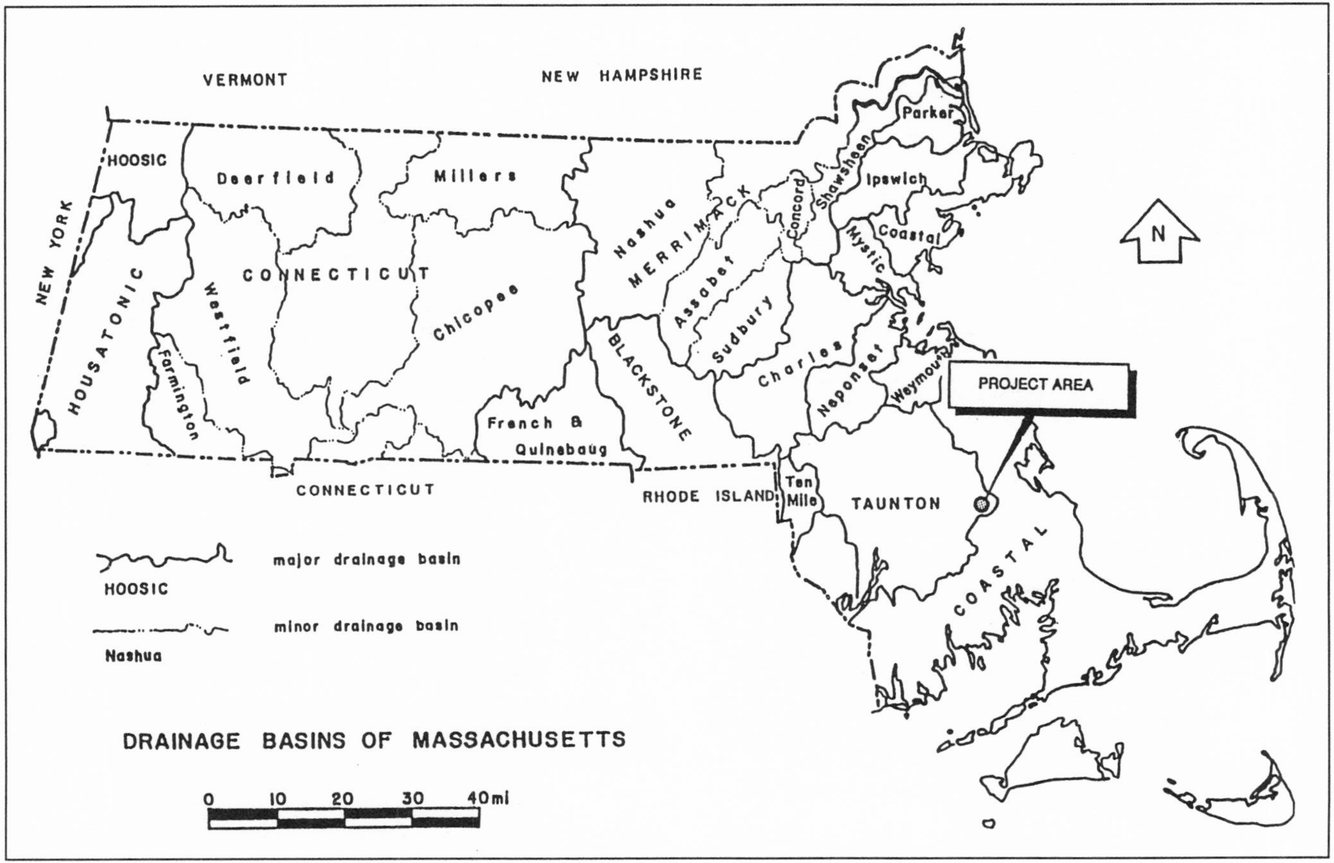

DRAINAGE BASINS OF MASSACHUSETTS

Figure 4.2
Archaeological Loci of the Annnasnappet Pond/Cranberry Bog Complex

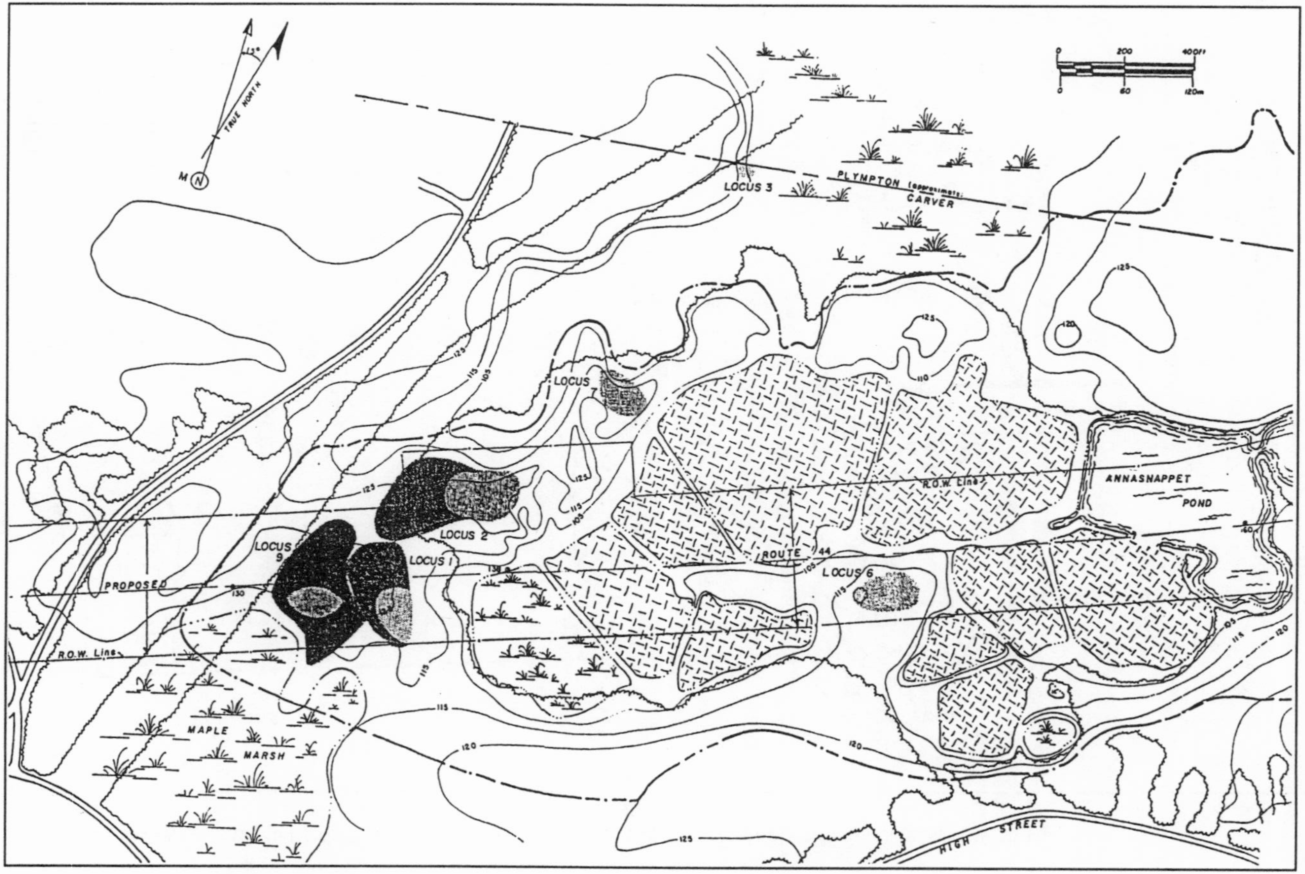

hematite, and a number of bifaces, drills, cores, and unifaces. A large full-grooved axe recovered from a pile of bulldozed earth at the south end of the Locus 1 sand pit is similar in form and technology to axes described for Middle Archaic contexts elsewhere in the Northeast (Dincauze 1976; Zeolli 1978).

The Middle Archaic assemblage from Annasnappet Pond is larger than assemblages of similar age from the Neville site (Dincauze 1976), NH 31-20-5 in Belmont, New Hampshire (Cassedy 1984; Starbuck 1982), Mohonk Rockshelter in New York (Eisenberg 1991), or the Lewis-Walpole site in Connecticut (Starbuck 1980). Nine radiocarbon dates from Middle Archaic feature contexts, including a date of 7570 ± 150 B.P. (Beta 58115) from the only known human burial in the Northeast associated with Stanly/Neville points, anchor the Middle Archaic chronology at Annasnappet Pond (Table 4.1).

Middle Archaic Mortuary Feature

The excavations at Annasnappet Pond identified 119 cultural features, including one mortuary feature. At the top of a sandy knoll at Locus 1, excavators identified the clear outlines of a large, oval pit feature (Feature 6) measuring 270 cm in length, 130 cm in width, and extending to a depth of 150 cm below surface (Figure 4.3). This feature contained red ochre, 188 calcined human cranial fragments, three Stanly/Neville stemmed bifaces, a Stanly/Neville drill,

Table 4.1
Radiocarbon Age Estimates for Middle Archaic Samples from Annasnappet Pond

Lab Number	Feature/ Locus	Conventional Radiocarbon Date	Calibrated Age (2-sigma range) Years B.C.	Calendar Years Ago
Beta-63078	21/1	7880 ± 240	7435–6195	9385–8145
Beta-58111	15/1	7840 ± 260	7435–6150	9385–8100
Beta-63079	6B/1	7660 ± 110	6640–6220	8390–8170
Beta-58115	6/1	7570 ± 150	6630–6055	8580–8005
Beta-63081	36/1	7430 ± 80	6415–6055	8365–8005
Beta-63080	22/1	7290 ± 120	6380–5935 5910–5880	8330–7885 7860–7830
Beta-58112	15B/2	7130 ± 110	6170–5725	8120–7675
Beta-57029	6/2	6470 ± 80	5520–5255	7470–7205
Beta-58114	21/2	6440 ± 120	5580–5205 5170–5135 5110–5095	7530–7155 7120–7085 7060–7045

Figure 4.3
Feature 6 at Locus 1, Showing Relationship of Cremated Cranial Fragments, Winged Atlatl Weights and Stanly/Neville points
(Doucette and Cross 1998)

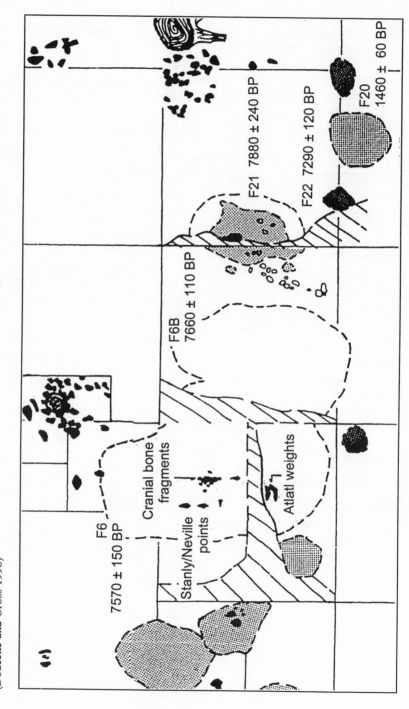

two winged atlatl weights (Figure 4.4), and a chipped slate preform (possibly for an ulu or semilunar knife). Charcoal from the feature yielded an uncalibrated date of 7570 ± 150 B.P. (Beta 58115). Calibrated (using the Pretoria Calibration [Vogel et al. 1993]), and expressed as "calendar years ago," there is a 95 percent probability that the actual date falls between 8580 and 8005 years ago. This date is among the earliest in the Northeast for a mortuary feature containing human bone. Robinson (1996) has described a number of features in New England that contain red ocher, calcined bone fragments, and/or artifacts that have yielded uncorrected dates of between 8500 and 6500 B.P. (e.g., the Morrill Point Mound in Salisbury, Massachusetts, and Wapanucket 8 in Middleboro, Massachusetts), although none of these is associated with Stanly/Neville components.

Within Feature 6, two Stanly/Neville points were aligned with the two winged atlatl weights in a manner that suggested the placement of atlatls and darts in a hafted (i.e., "engaged") position. The approximate lengths of the dart shafts are estimated at between 125 and 135 cm, given the relative positions of Stanly/Neville points and atlatl weights and the overall length of the pit. The association is reminiscent of William Webb's excavations of Late Archaic burials excavated along the Green River in Kentucky, which demonstrated that "bannerstones" were, in fact, weighted adjuncts to atlatl assemblies (Sassaman 1996; Webb 1946, 1957; Webb and Haag 1939).

Figure 4.4
Winged Atlatl Weights from Feature 6

A TECHNOLOGICAL PERSPECTIVE ON STANLY/NEVILLE AND NEVILLE VARIANT POINTS

The size of the Annasnappet Pond chipped stone assemblage allowed me to draw a number of inferences about Middle Archaic lithic technology. In general terms, the Stanly/Neville points in the Annasnappet sample were made from pre-form blanks, preferentially of rhyolites. On the basis of visual inspection, the majority of the preforms were identified as Blue Hills rhyolite, which outcrops 30 km north of the site (Duncan Ritchie, personal communication 1995). Similar preforms have been described in the regional literature as "U-base" bifaces because of the subrectangular shape of the base (e.g., Leveillee and Davin 1987). The presence of preforms broken during subsequent reduction and the low incidence of cortex in the debitage sample from Annasnappet Pond provides strong support for the inference that Stanly/Neville points were made from preforms that had been brought to the site.

With the exception of Stanly/Neville points from the burial, the archaeological sample at Annasnappet Pond consists largely of specimens that had been discarded as too small, too short, or too dull to be of further use. At 7.86 and 7.39 cm in length, respectively, the two Stanly/Neville points associated with the winged atlatl weights are longer than any from non-mortuary contexts at Annasnappet Pond, and their lengths exceed the maximum length values reported by Dincauze for the Neville site sample. The points from the burial feature had not experienced the same levels of attrition and reworking as points in the habitation assemblage.

Within the sample of Stanly/Neville points there is a second form of point that is well within the same technological tradition. Three of these are illustrated in Figure 4.5. Their larger size and broader haft element suggest a different function than the majority of Stanly/Neville points in the assemblage. The greater potential for incremental resharpening offered by the broad blade and the robust haft element are consistent with the functional morphology of bifacial knives.

Regardless of their size, all of the Annasnappet Pond Stanly/Neville points are characterized by several features, including an attention to symmetry in three dimensions (particularly of the edge), "micro-management" of the edge by the removal of small flakes that do not reach the midline of the biface, bifacial basal thinning that created a small indentation in the base in plan view, and a regular, lenticular cross section, often with a slight bevel created by resharpening (Figure 4.6). Dincauze (1976) reports that basal thinning of Neville points was usually unifacial. In the Annasnappet Pond Stanly/Neville sample, basal thinning was almost exclusively bifacial.

The regularity of the flaking on Stanly/Neville points from Annasnappet Pond often resulted in a finely serrated edge. Serration has often been viewed as an "early" trait within the Middle Archaic (Dincauze 1976), although serrated edges could be created during any resharpening episode. At the Neville site, there was a single serrated Neville point in the assemblage. By contrast, 25 of

Figure 4.5
Large Stanly/Neville Points with Serrated Edges on Two Points
and Reworking of Broken Point on the Right

0   5 cm

Figure 4.6
Representative Stanly/Neville Points from the Annasnappet Pond Site

0   5 cm

the 166 Stanly/Neville points in the Annasnappet Pond collection (15.1%) had serrated edges. Variation within the Stanly/Neville sample from Annasnappet Pond suggests that edge modification may have been either an individual preference or a way to compensate for a reduction in relative edge thinness during a Stanly/Neville point's use life.

Two kinds of resharpening/reworking patterns are represented on Stanly/Neville points from Annasnappet Pond: (1) incremental modification of the blade margins and (2) reworking following breakage. Incremental modification involves the removal of a series of small flakes along one or both edges to re-establish effectiveness for cutting or piercing. For Stanly/Neville points, resharpening focused on the portion of the blade above the shoulder. For this reason, width at the shoulder, absolute thickness, and stem attributes may be considered comparatively stable measures throughout the use life of a projectile point. On the other hand, overall length, the ratio of thickness to blade width above the shoulder, and the tip-to-shoulder silhouette are expected to vary over the course of a projectile point's use-life. Tip-to-shoulder profiles on incrementally-reworked bifaces are often incurvate or recurvate (see Cross 1990), and blade edges exhibit a slight beveling unifacially or bifacially when viewed in cross section.

During use as dart tips, Stanly/Neville points often broke, and exhibit the characteristic features of a transverse snap fracture which occur when the internal stresses created by an impact exceed the limited elastic properties of the stone (Johnson 1979). Breaks were most commonly observed at the stem/blade juncture among the Stanly/Neville points at Annasnappet. Mid-blade transverse fractures were also common. The comparatively large number of stem fragments in the assemblage is consistent with a pattern of re-use for the dart foreshaft. If the projectile point were to break upon impact, the foreshaft (with the stem fragment still secured in the haft) would be returned to a habitation or campsite, where it could then be fitted with a new projectile point. For this reason, stem fragments may be disproportionately represented at habitation sites, relative to tip and midsection fragments.

If a blade fragment were sufficiently large, it could be reworked into a smaller projectile point by creating a new stem (Figure 4.7). A snap fracture at the blade-stem junction creates a right-angle edge which is difficult to remove, particularly on a comparatively small biface fragment. As a result, the reworked stem often retains at the base a portion of the transverse fracture scar. All Neville Variants in the Annasnappet assemblage were made from bifacial preforms, and the lenticular cross section of the stem base (often retaining a flat surface) resulted from creating a new stem after the original point had been snapped during use. Dincauze (1976) attributed the flat surface on the base of the stem on Neville Variant points from the Neville site to a remnant striking platform on the flake blank from which the point had been made.

The second form of reworking occurs after a point had broken at the tip or in mid-blade. The proximal end (including the original stem portion) was

Figure 4.7
Two Scenarios for Reworking a Broken Stanly/Neville Point. Small Stanly/Neville and Neville Variant points from Locus 1 superimposed on one of the points from mortuary feature.

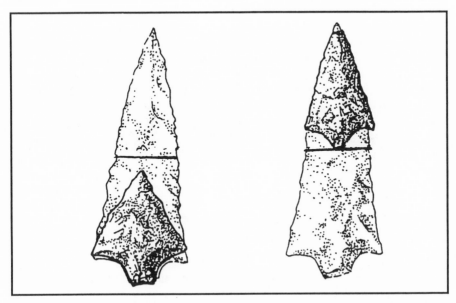

reshaped into a shorter point, resulting in a biface with a blade portion that is closer to an equilateral triangle in plan view than it is to the elongate isosceles triangle that is the characteristic shape of minimally-reworked points. The frequency of this kind of modification may be seen in a secondary mode for length and external shoulder angles within the Annasnappet Pond Stanly/Neville sample.

The production trajectory for Stanly/Neville points may be seen in the debitage and in the tools broken during manufacture. It is a trajectory that involves planned (rather than *ad hoc*) acquisition of raw materials. There is comparatively little cortex on the rhyolite debitage sample of over 30,000 pieces, reaffirming the position that the Stanly/Neville production trajectory progressed from preform to finished artifact at the site.

A TECHNOLOGICAL PERSPECTIVE ON
MORROW MOUNTAIN II/STARK POINTS

In their overall form, high degree of variation in techniques of manufacture, and selection of raw materials, Morrow Mountain II/Stark points from the Annasnappet Pond site contrast with Stanly/Neville points (Figure 4.8). The form of Morrow Mountain II/Stark points is consistent with tools that puncture, such as the stone tip of a thrusting spear. This suggestion has far-reaching implications, since it challenges the widely-held assumption that all objects classified as

Figure 4.8
Morrow Mountain II/Stark Points from the Annasnappet Pond Site

"projectile points" are functionally equivalent, analytically comparable, and temporally distinct groups of objects. The evidence from Annasnappet Pond indicates that the organization of production, mode of use, and expected use-life of Stanly/Neville and Morrow Mountain II/Stark points differed greatly.

The lithic raw materials used to make Morrow Mountain II/Stark points were drawn from a wider range of lithologies than those used to make Stanly/Neville points, and included quartz, quartzite, felsite, argillite, and indurated shale. Researchers working along the Atlantic seaboard have commented on this distinction (e.g., Blanton 1985; Blanton and Sassaman 1989; Cassedy 1983; Coe 1964; Dincauze 1976; Starbuck 1982). As a result of the highly variable raw materials used in their manufacture, Morrow Mountain II/Stark points exhibit considerable variation in morphological attributes. Points tend to be thick and have a limited potential for resharpening. As Dincauze (1976:34) has noted, Stark points appear to have been better suited for piercing than for slicing. Morrow Mountain II/Stark points, with their thick cross-sections and rounded shoulders, may have been used in hand-held thrusting spears, where repeated jabs may have been required. By contrast, the projecting shoulders of Stanly/Neville points would have enabled Middle Archaic hunters to anchor an atlatl dart in an animal target.

I infer a pattern of generalized manufacture for Morrow Mountain II/Stark points that proceeds from a cobble or flake blank to a finished point without the intermediate step of a preform that characterized the more highly formalized Stanly/Neville production trajectory. Along several scales—the number of steps in the production process, the spatial separation of production stages, and the temporal separation of production stages (Cross 1990)—the production of Morrow Mountain II/Stark points reflects *ad hoc* and de-centralized stone tool manufacture. The variation that has been described in the literature for both Morrow Mountain II and Stark points is consistent with (1) highly variable raw material quality; (2) replacement wherever and whenever necessary by the tool user; and (3) a functional emphasis on "pointedness" and strength, rather than on thinness or the potential for resharpening. In many ways, then, Morrow Mountain II/ Stark points contrast with Stanly/Neville points—in terms of production, function, discard, and in the social realm, where actions, opportunities, and status connect the static archaeological record to lives lived in the past.

DISCUSSION

The excavation of the human burial feature at Annasnappet Pond established the association of Stanly/Neville points with winged atlatl weights in a sealed, dated Middle Archaic context. Although Coe (1964) had identified winged atlatl weights with the Stanly component at the Doerschuk site in North Carolina, and Dincauze (1976) had described a fragment of an atlatl weight in Middle Archaic levels at the Neville site in New Hampshire, there had not been an unequivocal functional association of Stanly/Neville points with atlatl weights prior to the excavations at Annasnappet Pond. The suggestion that Stanly/Neville points were dart tips is supported by the data on breakage and resharpening within the Annasnappet Pond assemblage and reinforces functional interpretations derived from Stanly/Neville point morphology. The projectile points from Feature 6 provide a sense of the size of Stanly/Neville points in a non-discard context—they are longer than any reported from the Neville site and their respective lengths contrast strongly with other Annasnappet Stanly/Neville points.

The excavation of the mortuary feature provided a glimpse of imperishable material culture from a single event. Seldom have archaeologists had the opportunity to document Middle Archaic artifacts that are contemporaneous in an absolute sense. Gross stratigraphic measures (such as depth or soil horizons) and radiocarbon dating can establish contemporaneity only at a hypothetical level (i.e., within the realm of possibility).

From an examination of the form and technology of Middle Archaic stemmed bifaces at Annasnappet Pond, I conclude that Stanly/Neville and Morrow Mountain II/Stark points were not functionally-equivalent artifacts, nor were they created by comparable production strategies. Although there may be slight differences in the temporal ranges of the two artifact types, I consider it likely that there is substantial overlap as well. On the basis of technological and morphological evidence in the Annasnappet Pond assemblage, it appears that Stanly/Neville points were atlatl dart tips, produced from bifacial preforms and maintained as hunting gear. Three very large Stanly/Neville points in the Annasnappet Pond assemblage have broad blades and stems, and are interpreted as hafted knife blades. I suggest that Morrow Mountain II/Stark points were thrusting spear tips.

Data from Annasnappet Pond clarify a number of issues surrounding Middle Archaic chipped stone technology and typology, particularly the function of Stanly/Neville points as atlatl dart tips, the position of Neville Variant points within a use-life/rejuvenation trajectory for Stanly/Neville points, and the contrasting patterns for production and use of Stanly/Neville and Morrow Mountain II/Stark points. It is also fair to say that a host of fundamental questions and issues remain about the Middle Archaic Period, both at Annasnappet Pond and for eastern North America.

However, the data from Annasnappet Pond do not resolve the relative chronological positions of Stanly/Neville and Morrow Mountain II/Stark points. There was little or no net accumulation of sediment at the site over the past 10,000 years; artifacts entered subsurface contexts through a combination of freeze-thaw mechanisms and bioturbation (Doucette and Cross 1998). There was a general relationship between the recorded depth of an artifact and its relative age, but this measure was insufficient to resolve temporal relationships clearly. Coe (1964) had suggested a sequential relationship between the older Stanly points and the more recent Morrow Mountain types. On the basis of the coarse excavation levels at the Neville site, Dincauze (1976) argued for temporal overlap, with the relative percentage of Stark points increasing through time. The position taken here (that Stanly/Neville and Morrow Mountain II/Stark points were functionally and technologically distinct artifacts) raises the possibility that both kinds of bifaces were made and used at the same time.

It also became clear during the analysis of the Annasnappet Pond Middle Archaic assemblage that the vocabulary and conventional practices of archaeology are not well-suited to understanding macro-scale patterns or the historically-specific actions that created the archaeological record. On the one hand, why do types "work" over large units of space and time? At the scale of human experience and action, what processes or mechanisms sustain stylistic similarities and what processes or mechanisms transform them? It is difficult to move conceptually and semantically from the immediacy of face-to-face interaction to abstract, faceless artifact traditions that may span a thousand years and a thousand miles.

These issues are not new; they bear repeating as a reminder of what we need to know in order to understand the past, both in its generality and in its historic specificity. Archaeologists may, with some justification, be caricatured as shouting the answers to questions that no one is asking. Perhaps, as professional archaeologists, we have become so enamored of our hard-won knowledge and analytical expertise that typological classification has become an end in and of itself rather than the means to an end.

ACKNOWLEDGMENTS

The ideas expressed in this paper have grown through discussions with Leslie Shaw, Ken Sassaman, Fred Dunford, Stuart Eldridge, Dianna Doucette, Dan Cassedy, Richard Will, and Jim Bradley. I am grateful to John Rempelakis and the Massachusetts Highway Department for their support of the fieldwork at Annasnappet Pond, to the Native Americans who shared their insights and our concern for those who had lived at the site, and to the Massachusetts Historical Commission for their commitment to archaeological research within a cultural resource management framework. Field crews from the Public Archaeology Laboratory, Inc., under the direction of Dianna Doucette, set high standards for data collection and camaraderie. I am also grateful to Deborah Cox, and the laboratory staff at PAL, Inc. for their role in making the research at Annasnappet possible. Dana Richardi drafted the figures and Kirk Van Dyke took the photos that have been reproduced from the Annasnappet data recovery report.

5

A Southeastern Perspective on Soapstone Vessel Technology in the Northeast

Kenneth E. Sassaman

The geological formations of eastern North American offered a variety of raw materials of interest to prehistoric Indians. Among them were talc-rich rocks known today as soapstone or steatite. As early as 8000 years ago, Native inhabitants acquired soapstone for making components of weaponry, and later for ornaments, smoking pipes, and cooking stones and vessels. Aside from being soft and hence easy to carve, soapstone had thermal properties which made it particularly effective as a medium for cooking. Archaeologists have long regarded soapstone vessels as the prototype of the ceramic cooking pot, an innovation that at once enhanced the efficiency of food processing while setting the stage for further technological developments (e.g., Custer 1988; Gardner 1975; Smith 1986:30; Stephenson and Ferguson 1963:88; Witthoft 1953).

Soapstone vessels were made and used throughout most of the talc belt of eastern North America (Chidester et al. 1964), and they were exported to select locations as much as 500 km from geological sources (Figure 5.1). Differences in vessel size and shape attest to some subregional variation, although generally soapstone vessels were shallow, widemouthed containers with either flat or round bottoms and occasional lug handles. Their use as cooking vessels is evident in the carbon residue, or soot, that adheres to the exterior surfaces of some vessel sherds (Custer 1987, 1988; McLearen 1991; Mouer 1991; Ritchie 1959: 64–65, 74, 1965:170; Sassaman 1997).

In its capacity as a direct-heat cooking container, soapstone vessel technology presumably was an improvement over the indirect-heat, "stone-boiling" method used by generations of native hunter-gatherers to process nuts and other resources for consumption. Pottery vessels represented further improvements in thermal engineering, as vessel forms and ceramic composition became increasingly better suited for prolonged cooking (e.g., Braun 1983; cf. Smith 1986:43). Furthermore, because clays for making pottery were more widely available than

Figure 5.1
Map of the Eastern United States, Showing Generalized Distributions of
Archaeological Occurrences of Soapstone Vessels and Geological Formations which
Contain Talc-rich Deposits Quarried for Soapstone

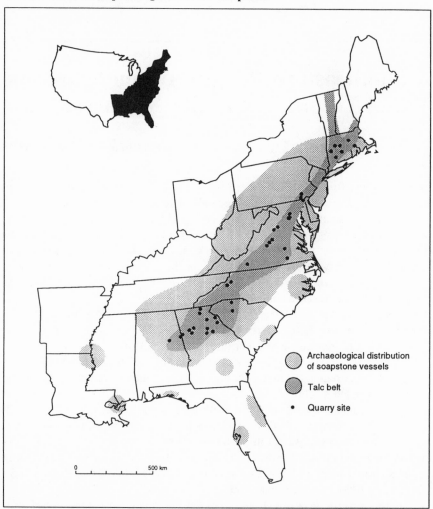

soapstone sources, the adoption of pottery greatly reduced acquisition costs, particularly for groups that resided far from outcrops of the talc belt.

The shift in cooking technology from stone boiling to direct-heat cooking—first with soapstone vessels, then with increasingly more effective ceramic forms—is a pervasive theme of eastern North American prehistory (Dent 1995: 182–184, 224–227; Smith 1986:28-30; 42–43). However, the timing and sequence of these changes are not paneastern. The Southeast was home to the oldest pottery in the East, dating to as much as 4500 radiocarbon years ago in the Savannah River area of Georgia and South Carolina, and in the St. Johns

River valley of northeast Florida. Soapstone vessels did not precede pottery in these areas; in fact, their local adoption postdates the oldest ceramic wares by as much as a full millennium. What is more, ongoing research on the chronology of soapstone vessels, which I summarize in this chapter, suggests that the innovation does not predate 3700 radiocarbon years B.P. anywhere in the Southeast, contrary to the widely held notion that its origins date to the beginnings of the Late Archaic period (ca. 5000–3000 B.P.) (Phelps 1983:26; Smith 1986:30).

Combined with the presumed antiquity of soapstone vessels, the demonstrated antiquity of southeastern pottery has long inspired northeastern archaeologists to look south for sources of innovations in the north (Gardner 1975; Ritchie 1959:62, 1965; Snow 1980:240–242). However, refinements in the chronology of southeastern vessel technologies provides ample cause for rethinking the causes and contexts for the origins of cooking technologies in the Northeast. Whereas pottery in the Southeast clearly predates ceramic traditions to the north, soapstone vessels in the Southeast are not a technological antecedent of pottery, nor do they predate their soapstone counterparts in the Northeast. It follows that simple diffusionist claims for soapstone vessel origins in the Northeast are no longer plausible. Furthermore, in neither region do soapstone vessels fit neatly into the technological sequence outlined above, a finding that undermines any lingering influences of nineteenth-century, unilineal evolutionary thinking. The eroded credibility of these dominant themes points to the need for increased attention to the particular historical and cultural contexts of alternative cooking technologies.

SOAPSTONE VESSELS IN HISTORICAL CONTEXT

Ever since soapstone vessels were first proposed as a diagnostic trait of the Northeast's Late Archaic period (Witthoft 1953), the Southeast has been regarded as the donor of innovations. Connections between the regions were inferred not simply from this technology alone, but from an entire cultural complex known as the Broadpoint Tradition. Its namesake is a series of broad-bladed, stemmed hafted bifaces that occur in Late Archaic assemblages along most of the Eastern Seaboard. In the Southeast, the tradition is best represented by the Savannah River Stemmed (Coe 1964), a biface type alleged to have deep historical roots in the region (Oliver 1985). In contrast, northeastern manifestations of the Broadpoint Tradition generally are considered intrusive to an indigenous narrow-point technological tradition. Diffusion, migration, and paneastern adaptive change are alternative explanations for the sudden appearance of broadpoint cultures in the Northeast (cf. Cook 1976; Custer 1984; Dincauze 1968, 1975b; Funk 1993:224–225; Ritchie 1965; Turnbaugh 1975; Witthoft 1953). More than simply the introduction of new traits, the broadpoint cultures of the Northeast apparently introduced an entirely new way of life centered on the intensive exploitation of riverine and estuarine environments (cf. Dincauze 1974). Given this context, soapstone vessels are viewed as a technological response to an increasingly demanding lifestyle (Dent 1995:203, 213; Gardner 1975).

Whereas the association between soapstone vessels and the Broadpoint Tradition in the Northeast is apparently certain, no such claim can be made for the Southeast. The landmark site for broadpoint technology in the Southeast, Stallings Island in the middle Savannah River valley (Claflin 1931), has never yielded a soapstone vessel sherd in the 1400 m² of excavation to date. This site is, however, home to some of the oldest ceramic vessels in the Southeast, Stallings fiber-tempered pottery. Importantly, the stratum containing Stallings pottery is stratigraphically superior to and distinct from the stratum containing broadpoints. Unfortunately, this unconformity was not sufficiently documented in the widely read report on Stallings Island (Claflin 1931). Fairbanks (1942) later contributed to this oversight by conflating the artifact types of both strata into a single trait list for Stallings Culture. More recent investigators have kept the two separate, noting differences in artifact types and subsistence patterns which appear to reflect wholesale replacement of one culture by another (Bullen and Greene 1970; Crusoe and DePratter 1976). Indeed, it now seems certain, as Waring (1968) suspected long ago, that the middle Savannah River valley was colonized by a population with roots on the coasts of Georgia and South Carolina. The indigenous people they displaced—local bearers of the Broadpoint Tradition known today as the Mill Branch phase (Elliott et al. 1994)—persisted for at least two centuries on the outskirts of Stallings territory (Sassaman 1998). They used neither pottery nor soapstone vessels, but they apparently interacted with their pottery-using neighbors on a regular basis. Why an innovation such as pottery would fail to cross seemingly permeable cultural boundaries is an issue of ongoing research.

Soapstone vessels never figured into the technological repertoires of Mill Branch and Stallings populations during the centuries of their coexistence (ca. 4200–3800 B.P.). Still, the middle Savannah valley was home to a soapstone *cooking stone* technology with origins extending back to at least 5700 B.P. (Sassaman 1993b). Throughout the Mill Branch and Stallings phases, soapstone was fashioned into perforated slabs for indirect-heat cooking, or stone boiling. Because of its superior resistance to thermal shock, soapstone was a vast improvement over cooking with clastic materials such as quartz and granite. Literally thousands of perforated slabs were uncovered at Stallings Island by Claflin (1931), who, like many of his contemporaries, mistook them for net sinkers. Made and used for centuries, soapstone cooking slabs eventually became obsolete when pottery was adapted for use over fire, but for many generations, until about 3500 B.P., they continued to be employed for cooking with ceramic vessels by Stallings people (Sassaman 1993a).

Soapstone cooking slabs were not used widely outside of the middle Savannah River valley. Perhaps because of their limited distribution, hence unfamiliarity to those working elsewhere, cooking slabs have sometimes been mistaken as perforated vessel sherds (e.g., Dent 1995:184). Such misidentification has conspired with other factors to perpetuate the falsehood that soapstone vessels predate pottery in the middle Savannah valley. To the contrary, the namesake site for early pottery, Stallings Island, provides absolutely no such stratigraphic evidence, nor do any of the other middle Savannah sites investigated to date (Sassaman 1998). What is more, the stratigraphy of one of the key sites for the Southeast's Broadpoint Tradition, the Gaston site in North Carolina (Coe 1964), is ambiguous in its alleged association between Savannah River Stemmed points and soapstone vessels (Sassaman 1997:10–11). In short, the proposal that soapstone vessel technology diffused northward with the Broadpoint Tradition is undermined at its very source.

Obviously, soapstone vessels were eventually made and used by many of the Southeast's prehistoric people, for they are found at sites throughout the region, including the middle Savannah area, where they occur most often at remote, interriverine sites. As I have argued, the stratigraphy of riverine sites in the middle Savannah suggests that soapstone vessels did not predate the local adoption of pottery. Sites of early pottery in Florida offer corroborative stratigraphic evidence (Bullen 1972), as do locations within the Poverty Point complex of northeast Louisiana (Gibson 1996). Precisely when soapstone vessel technology was used in the Southeast and how its timing compares with the Northeast is a matter of radiocarbon chronology.

Radiocarbon Chronology

Radiocarbon chronology for riverine sites in the middle Savannah valley is relatively thorough (Sassaman 1998). However, because these sites typically lack soapstone vessel sherds, none of their absolute dates apply directly to the innovation. What is more, interriverine sites that contain numerous soapstone vessel sherds offer few opportunities for radiometric or stratigraphic dating. Together these factors have impeded progress in dating soapstone vessels.

In lieu of features or other contexts for preserved organic matter in direct association with soapstone vessels, I began in 1995 a program to date soot adhering to the exterior surfaces of sherds using accelerator mass spectrometry (AMS) (Sassaman 1997). I have thus far obtained twelve age estimates on samples from eleven sites in five southeastern states (South Carolina, Georgia, Florida, Alabama, and Tennessee). The uncorrected assays range from 3620 ± 60 to 2590 ± 40 radiocarbon years B.P. Corrections for C13/C12 ratios alter estimates by no more than eighty radiocarbon years, and calibration does little to change the relative differences among them.

A graphic display of the AMS soot assays is provided in Figure 5.2, along with other, conventional age estimates from the Southeast (defined herein as all states south of Virginia, and east of the Mississippi River, but including northeast Louisiana) purported to date soapstone vessels. The entire inventory of seventy-five assays includes several run on charcoal from feature contexts with at least one sherd of a soapstone vessel; the bulk of the remaining assays involve

Figure 5.2
Radiocarbon Age Estimates for Soapstone Vessels in the Southeastern United States

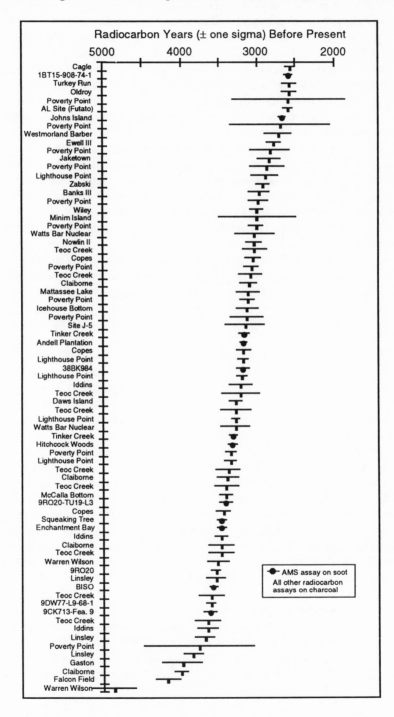

indirect associations with soapstone sherds. Only one of the assays predating the oldest soot date (i.e., >3620 ± 60 B.P.) is from a feature context. At the Falcon Field site in Georgia, charcoal beneath a rock cluster with a soapstone sherd yielded an uncorrected age of 4170 ± 150 B.P (Elliott 1989). At the time of its publication, this assay was regarded as the oldest date for soapstone vessels in the Southeast. The investigator has since reconsidered its validity, noting that the charcoal was perhaps not directly associated with the sherd (Daniel T. Elliott, personal communication 1997). The other assays predating the oldest soot date have either weak associations with soapstone sherds or standard deviations exceeding 5 percent of the mean value. Notably, the Gaston site estimate of 3900 ± 125 B.P. (published with two-sigma value of 250) was not only derived from charcoal collected from three different hearths (Coe 1964:97), none of which contained soapstone, but there is good reason to suspect that all of the soapstone sherds in the Late Archaic stratum were introduced by pit activities of subsequent Early Woodland occupants (Sassaman 1997:10–11).

In short, the Southeast radiocarbon record for soapstone vessels contains no unambiguous assays predating about 3700 B.P. The range of time bracketed by the oldest and youngest soot dates is endowed with many good associations between soapstone and dated organic matter. The radiocarbon centuries from 3500 to 3000 B.P. account for more than half of all assays, including eight of the twelve obtained from soot. A notable break in an otherwise continuous distribution is evident at about 2800 B.P., after which a series of younger assays, including two on soot, suggest the occurrence of a separate, late horizon for soapstone vessels. This is a pattern that may be paralleled in parts of the Northeast.

The program of soot dating has recently been expanded to include samples from the Northeast. Thus far only two such assays have been obtained, on soapstone vessel sherds provided by James Herbstritt from islands in the Susquehanna River of southeast Pennsylvania. Soot from a McCormick Island sherd yielded an estimate of 3190 ± 50 B.P. (Beta-116287), and one from Upper Bare Island gave an estimate of 2940 ± 50 B.P. (Beta-116286).

Three additional AMS dates have been acquired by James Truncer (1997) as part of his ongoing research on soapstone vessel technology in the Northeast. A sample of exterior residue (soot?) on a sherd from the Hunter Home site in western New York returned an estimate of 3420 ± 60 B.P. (AA-19136), well within the range of soot assays for the Southeast. The other two results, obtained from interior residues, deviate markedly from all soot ages. A sherd from the Hagerman site (36LY58) in north-central Pennsylvania is estimated at 4910 ± 75 B.P. (AA-19134), while one from the Christiana quarry (36LA189) in southeastern Pennsylvania is estimated at only 310 ± 65 B.P. (AA-19135).

These outlier assays are not corroborated by the full suite of radiocarbon ages purported to be associated with soapstone vessels in the Northeast (Figure 5.3; note that the recent age from the Christiana quarry sample is not included in this suite of fifty-two assays). Only two age estimates come close to the

Figure 5.3
Radiocarbon Age Estimates for Soapstone Vessels in the Northeastern United States

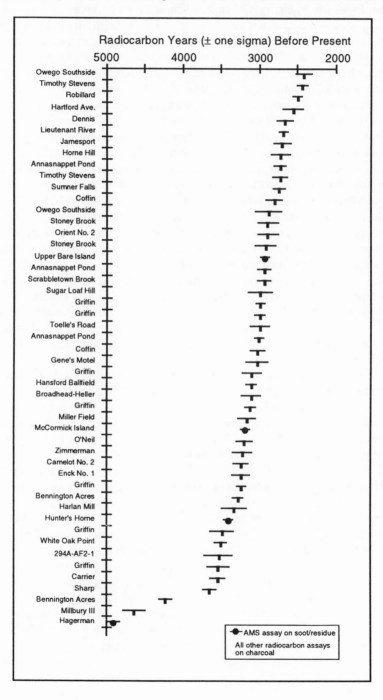

antiquity of the Hagerman AMS assay. Although Hoffman (1997) ascribed the Millbury III (Massachusetts) and Bennington Acres (Vermont) ages to soapstone vessels, neither of the investigators of these sites consider the associations credible (Doug Mackey, Alan Leveillee, personal communication 1997). Thus, the radiocarbon inventory for the Northeast, like that of the Southeast, includes no unambiguous assays predating 3700 B.P., Hagerman notwithstanding.

To compare further the two regional inventories, I converted the chrono-metric data into bar diagrams using only the mean values of the assays (Figure 5.4). Although they do not reveal tendencies in sample variance, these graphs enable some first-order analysis of interregional patterning. Basically, the distributions are very similar: both are attenuated toward the early end of the scale by a few ancient outliers (i.e., >3700 B.P.), both have a more or less unimodal shape centered on 3200 to 3100 B.P., and both have some stacking toward the recent end of the scale, particularly in the Southeast, where ages

Figure 5.4
Graphic Comparison of the Frequency Distributions of Radiocarbon Age Estimates for Soapstone Vessels in the Northeast and Southeast

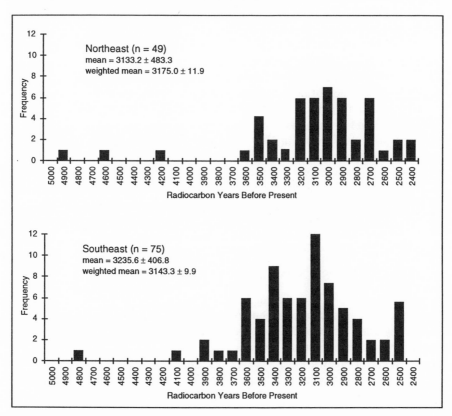

around 2500 B.P. are not uncommon. These general similarities are manifested in group averages, with the Northeast yielding a mean of 3133.2 ± 483.3 B.P. and the Southeast a mean of 3235.6 ± 406.8 B.P. Although the greater mean for the Southeast ages might be construed as evidence for a southerly origin for the innovation, the difference is not statistically significant due to the large standard deviations of either value (t = -1.215 [unpooled], -1.261 [pooled]; $d.f.$ = 122). Moreover, when individual sample variance is taken into account to produce weighted means (Long and Rippeteau 1974), the differences are reversed: the Northeast shows a mean of 3175.0 ± 11.9 B.P., while the Southeast has a mean of 3143.3 ± 9.9 B.P. Because weighting serves to reduce group variance, the difference in means is now statistically significant (t = 15.332 [unpooled], 15.946 [pooled]; $d.f.$ = 122).

Accounting for all potential errors of misascription and sample contamination is beyond the scope of this chapter. I have already pointed out problems with radiocarbon ages greater than 3700 B.P.; other problems no doubt exist among more recent ages. However, taken at face value—with potential errors distributed randomly across both sets of assays—the Northeast and Southeast radiocarbon records for soapstone vessels are very similar with respect to range and modal tendencies. There is little to recommend that soapstone vessel technology in the Southeast is older than its Northeast counterpart; if anything, Northeast origins may be slightly older.

The relatively recent ages for soapstone vessels across the East underscore the need to rethink the relationship of this technology to early ceramic vessels. Clearly the relationship between the two technologies varied from region to region. Across much of the Southeast, pottery preceded local uses of soapstone vessels by several centuries. In the Middle Atlantic region (Virginia, Maryland, Delaware, Pennsylvania, and New Jersey), the two technologies may have emerged in tandem, while in New York and New England soapstone may yet have preceded pottery by a century or two. Regardless of the timing of origins, soapstone vessels apparently enjoyed a resurgence in popularity after 2700 B.P., well after pottery was adopted across most of the East. It goes without saying that soapstone vessel technology cannot be viewed simply as the precursor of the ceramic cooking pot. More deliberate attention to the specific cultural contexts of alternative vessel technologies is in order.

SOAPSTONE VESSELS IN CULTURAL CONTEXT

In the balance of this chapter I explore more fully the cultural contexts of soapstone and ceramic vessel technologies, first in the Northeast, where they are widely regarded as progressive stages in a developmental sequence, and then in the Southeast, where pottery predates soapstone vessels by several centuries in certain areas. My own experience reconciling this reversed sequence in the Savannah River valley led to a better appreciation of the cultural circumstances surrounding technical choice. Specifically, I found it useful to consider how alternative technologies were actively manipulated to create and reproduce ethnic or cultural identity. In this regard, neither technology can be understood as merely technical solutions to mundane needs but, rather, as deeply entrenched, historically specific symbols whose significance can only be appreciated through detailed cultural reconstruction.

Northeast

Early pottery traditions and their relationships to soapstone technology in the Northeast are sufficiently varied to divide the region into two for the purpose of this discussion. The Middle Atlantic (Virginia, Maryland, Delaware, New Jersey, eastern Pennsylvania) boasts an early pottery tradition (Marcey Creek) whose design allegedly was inspired by a soapstone antecedent. In southern New England and New York, the first pottery (Vinette I) marks a dramatic technological break from soapstone vessels, although the two technologies apparently coexisted for several centuries.

Middle Atlantic. Soapstone vessels have long figured in the systematics of Middle Atlantic prehistory. They were the defining characteristic of Witthoft's (1953) Susquehanna Soapstone Culture, part of the so-called Transitional period. Although he lacked absolute chronology for this period, Witthoft (1953:14) was certain about the relative chronology of soapstone vessels and thus their "transitional" status: "[soapstone vessels] pertain to a very limited period in our archaeological history, and . . . they were not used by peoples before or after the Transitional Period; they represent the first form of cooking vessel, slightly earlier than pottery, and were soon supplanted by pottery vessels."

Although modern-day specialists in the Middle Atlantic long ago abandoned Witthoft's scheme (Kinsey 1972), soapstone vessels are still widely regarded as an early form of cooking vessel that was quickly rendered obsolete by ceramic technology (Custer 1984:84; 1989:167). Described as "experimental ware" (following Wise 1975), early pottery series in the region include Marcey Creek (Manson 1948), Selden Island (Slattery 1946), Bushnell (Waselkov 1982), and Croaker Landing (Egloff et al. 1988), among others (see Dent 1995:224–227). These early ceramic vessels are generally trough- or basin-shaped, with flat bottoms, wide orifices, and occasional lug handles. Their formal resemblance to soapstone vessels has led some to suggest that early pots were copies of stone precursors (Custer 1984, 1989; Stephenson and Ferguson 1963:180; Witthoft 1953:25). Notably, Marcey Creek and Seldon Island wares were tempered with soapstone.

The type site for Marcey Creek pottery provided stratigraphic evidence for the temporal priority of soapstone vessels over pottery (Manson 1948). A few other stratified sites in the Middle Atlantic region apparently corroborate the Marcey Creek sequence (e.g., Kent-Hally [Kinsey 1959]; Racoon Point [Kier and Calverley 1957]), while others show stratigraphic overlap between the two technologies (e.g., Seldon Island [Slattery 1946]; Koens-Crispin [Cross 1941];

Goose Island [Cross 1941]). Notably, all such stratified contexts were investigated long ago; comparable contexts have not been examined in the recent era. Whereas the quality of these excavations is not itself at issue, the lack of modern scrutiny is curious. Still, the cooccurrence of soapstone vessels and early pottery has not escaped attention, as some regional specialists allow that the former technology may have persisted well into the pottery era (Stephenson and Ferguson 1963:182; Stewart 1989; Thurman 1985).

As the chronology for soapstone vessels and early pottery in the Middle Atlantic continues to be refined, we may very well find that they were largely, if not fully, coeval, both dating as early as 3600 B.P., and then peaking in popularity from 3200 to 2900 B.P. If this indeed proves to be the case, the question then becomes: What were the conditions that allowed or encouraged the simultaneous use of soapstone and ceramic vessel technologies? In keeping with the dominant themes of Middle Atlantic prehistory, the answer would seem to be found in conditions, such as population growth and environmental change, which encouraged more intensive economic practices and increased settlement permanence (Custer 1984, 1989; Gardner 1975; Witthoft 1953). In this regard, either vessel technology may have helped to improve the efficiency with which foods could be processed through direct-heat moist cooking. However, given the formal and technological similarities between soapstone vessels and early pottery in the Middle Atlantic, the advantage of one over the other is unlikely to be manifested in mechanical performance but, rather, in relative manufacturing costs, particularly the costs of acquiring adequate raw material. Thus if early pottery represented the functional equivalent of soapstone vessels, its origins should be traced to locations removed from geological sources of soapstone, notably the Coastal Plain province.

Middle Atlantic radiocarbon chronology is too coarse-grained at present to posit the exact origins of the oldest pottery, although enough distributional data are available to suggest that limited access to soapstone was unlikely the determining factor in technical choice. Indeed, soapstone-tempered pottery is more common in the Piedmont province than in the Coastal Plain (Stewart 1989:57). And, whereas soapstone vessels are most common nearest quarries in the Piedmont and Fall Zone, they are distributed widely across the Coastal Plain (Stewart 1989:57). One of the more remote Coastal Plain locations in the Middle Atlantic, Dismal Swamp in southeast Virginia, received large numbers of imported soapstone vessels (Painter 1988). Soapstone-tempered pottery was also deposited regularly at Dismal Swamp sites (Painter 1988).

Obviously, factors other than ease of manufacture or access to raw material were at play. One possibility is that soapstone vessels and early pottery had significance beyond their role in everyday cooking. This is an idea recently examined by Klein (1997). In assessing the formal and technological qualities of early stone and ceramic vessels, Klein has suggested that they functioned primarily as containers for stone-boiling. He further suggested that soapstone vessel technology did not represent a vast improvement over traditional organic media (wood, basketry), primarily because of its high acquisition and manufacture costs. Instead, the value of soapstone, according to Klein, resided in its capacity as a symbolic medium of social interaction. He notes that the use of soapstone vessels in the Middle Atlantic coincided with a period of widespread soapstone exchange in the Southeast, particularly the Poverty Point exchange network. Spurred by opportunities for interregional alliance building, Middle Atlantic residents incorporated soapstone vessels in the highly social contexts of ritual and ceremony. Later, when the exchange networks of the Southeast ceased to involve long-distance importation of soapstone, Marcey Creek ceramics became a short-lived substitute for soapstone in the ritual lives of Middle Atlantic residents.

Klein introduced a variety of considerations that typically are overlooked in explanations for the origins of durable container technology in the Middle Atlantic. I agree that interregional exchange, alliance building, and ritual uses of vessels were integral factors in the adoption of innovations. On the specific details of Klein's model I find some points of disagreement, however. For one, Klein embraced the usual sequence of soapstone to pottery that underlies traditional explanations. Clearly, soapstone vessels and early pottery coexisted for a few centuries in the Middle Atlantic, even if the former preceded the latter by a century or two, which remains to be proved. Second, sufficient evidence exists to conclude that at least some soapstone vessels were used directly over fire. In addition to the sooting described earlier, thermogravimetric analyses conducted by Truncer (1997) on sherds from the Middle Atlantic verify that soapstone vessels were regularly subjected to direct heat. Assemblages of Marcey Creek pottery await similar use-wear analyses. Inferences based on form and technology must be tested with independent evidence to determine how vessels were actually used, as opposed to the intent of design engineering. Marcey Creek and soapstone vessels may not have been functional equivalents, despite their obvious similarities in form.

These provisos about Klein's model deliver us back to the issue of cooccurrence. In this regard, I suggest that much is being missed in the lack of attention to ethnic diversity among populations of the Middle Atlantic. One of the more striking aspects of early ceramic technology in the region is the incredible diversity of the so-called experimental wares. In addition to the soapstone-tempered pottery that coincides more or less with distributions of soapstone vessels, there are a variety of sand-tempered and grog-tempered wares that are as old, or nearly as old, as Marcey Creek and Seldon Island pottery (Dent 1995: 225–226). Many of the wares tempered with aplastics other than soapstone are concentrated on the outer Coastal Plain, geographically distant from Piedmont outcrops of soapstone. Still, the appearance of Piedmont lithic materials in Coastal Plain sites with early pottery suggests that Coastal Plain and Piedmont groups interacted on a regular basis. The ethnic affiliations of these respective groups and the nature of interaction are topics that are woefully underexamined. It stands to reason that choices of alternative vessels technologies had much to do with one's ethnicity, while the boundaries surrounding technical variants relate directly to rules of group formation and interaction. As I discuss at the close of this chapter, these very issues figured significantly in the differential use of alternative vessel forms in the Southeast. They may very well explain patterns of technological choice in southern New England and New York, as well.

New England and New York. Archaeologists in New England and New York have consistently, if not unanimously, confronted issues of ethnicity and cultural interactions in their explanations of technological innovation. Witthoft's Transitional Stage, while crafted for archaeological manifestations of the middle and lower Susquehanna River valley, was adapted by Ritchie (1965) to explain the introduction of broadpoint technology and soapstone vessels into New York. Similarly, broadpoint cultures are believed to be intrusive to a southern New England landscape inhabited by indigenous cultures of the narrow-point tradition. The first pottery in the greater region—Vinette I—crosscuts both areas, although its relationship to soapstone vessel technology is not uniform across this expanse.

The temporal priority of soapstone over pottery in New England and New York is not supported by stratigraphic data, for the region boasts few deep sites. Instead, the sequence is based on radiocarbon chronology and by the lingering influences of the same unilineal thinking that has affected all other regions. As in the Middle Atlantic, with soapstone vessel chronology being compressed toward the recent end, and ceramic vessel chronology extended farther back in time, the two technologies are converging on contemporaneity. Regional specialists might balk at the notion that pottery is as old as soapstone vessels (cf. Hoffman 1997), although most would agree that soapstone vessels continued to be made after pottery appeared on the scene (Ritchie 1965:163), at least in southern New England, where sites sometimes contain both technologies (Snow 1980: 258). This long history of soapstone vessels in the region actually encompasses two different traditions: a presumably early one associated exclusively with broadpoint cultures, and the later one centered on southern New England and Long Island, involving elements of both broadpoint and narrow-point cultural traditions known as the Orient Complex (Dincauze 1968, 1975b; Ritchie 1965).

Ceramic vessel technology in New York and New England marks a dramatic technological break from either variant of soapstone vessel technology. Dating as early as 3200 B.P., Vinette I pottery consists of coiled, grit-tempered, conoidal vessels marked by vertical or oblique exterior cord marking and horizontal interior cord marking. In form and technology, Vinette I pottery bears no resemblance to soapstone vessels. It occurs sporadically across sites of both narrow-point and late broadpoint affiliation in southeast New York and southern New England, and is occasionally found in association with early pottery of the Middle Atlantic as far south as southeast Pennsylvania (Kinsey 1959). Whereas New England/New York specialists generally agree that Vinette I pottery was an indigenous innovation, its precise context of origin is unknown. A few southern New England radiocarbon dates stretch origins back to as much as 3600 B.P.

(McBride 1984:124). Age estimates in the 3330–3100 B.P. range have been obtained from sites in southern New Hampshire (Bunker 1988; Howe 1988), on the northern fringe of its distribution, and on its western fringe in central New York (Ritchie 1965:158). Sparse occurrences in southeast Pennsylvania may be equally old (Custer et al. 1983). The use of Vinette I pottery peaks in the Meadowood Phase of central New York, which dates to about 3000 to 2500 B.P. and does not involve soapstone vessel technology. Southern New England sites of the Orient Complex often include early pottery, as well as soapstone vessels, although not typically in the same assemblages. Little of this Orient pottery is Vinette I; occurring with greater frequency are sherds of soapstone-tempered ware (Weeks 1971b) and other poorly known wares with possible affinities with Middle Atlantic pottery traditions (Dena Dincauze, personal communication 1998).

Central New York sites with soapstone vessels believed to predate Vinette I pottery are part of the Broadpoint Tradition that Ritchie (1965) attributed to Witthoft's Susquehanna Soapstone Culture. Both Witthoft and Ritchie regarded these occurrences as the northward expansion of broadpoint cultures whose ultimate origins laid to the Southeast. Soapstone vessels were considered a diagnostic feature of this intrusion, having been literally paddled by canoes up the Susquehanna River into central New York from quarries in southeast Pennsylvania (Witthoft 1953:25).

Ritchie's (1965:161) Frost Island phase embodies the proposed expansion of soapstone vessel technology into central New York, following on the antecedent Snook Kill phase of the Broadpoint Tradition. Dating from about 3600 to 3000 B.P., the Frost Island phase involved the use of soapstone vessels with formal similarity to those of the Middle Atlantic region; that is, they consist of oval to rectangular, shallow vessels with flat to nearly flat bottoms, straight or slightly outflaring walls and occasional lug handles. Exterior surfaces bear the traces of chiseling or gouging, while interior surfaces are smoothed. Ritchie (1965:161) suggested that such vessels were at first delivered directly by immigrant groups, but then acquired through trade with groups down the Susquehanna River who had access to the quarries of southeast Pennsylvania. New York offered absolutely no local sources of soapstone. According to Ritchie (1965:161), pottery making may have been stimulated by the lack of local soapstone sources: "The want of any suitable stone substitute for the steatite pot may have hastened the adoption of Vinette 1 ware which was being introduced into the New York area not later than 1000 B.C. (Ritchie, 1962)."

Modern research undermines Ritchie's model on two counts. First, it appears that soapstone vessels were not a major element in the early assemblages of the Frost Island phase. Few early assemblages (i.e., pre-3200 B.P.) contain soapstone, and there is absolutely no evidence for soapstone in the preceding Snook Kill phase (Funk 1993:198). It thus appears that soapstone vessels were added late in the Frost Island phase, along with Vinette I pottery (Funk 1993: 197–198). Second, recent sourcing analyses by Truncer and colleagues (1998)

eliminate southeast Pennsylvania or other Middle Atlantic quarries for most of
the soapstone artifacts sampled from New York sites, including five sherds from
the O'Neil site in Cayuga County, type site for the Frost Island phase (Ritchie
1965). These results suggest that southern New England quarries are the most
likely sources for many soapstone vessels in New York (Truncer et al. 1998:40).

The earliest expression of an intrusive broadpoint culture in southern New
England is the Atlantic phase, estimated by Dincauze (1972) to date from about
4000 to 3600 years B.P. This phase apparently did not include soapstone vessel
technology, exemplifying again the lack of unity between intrusive broadpoint
culture and this cooking innovation. The subsequent Broadpoint phase, Water-
town (3600–3300 B.P.; Dincauze 1968), is responsible for the earliest uses of
soapstone vessels in southern New England, although the defining contexts for
the innovation are mortuary rather than domestic. Burial ceremonialism involving soapstone vessels intensified in the ensuing Coburn (3300–3000 B.P.) and
Orient (3000–2500 B.P.) phases, the latter considered by Dincauze (1968, 1974)
to be the coalescence of 500 years of interaction between an indigenous population of the narrow-point tradition and descendants of the intrusive broadpoint
culture. Independent of Dincauze, Ritchie (1969a) drew a similar conclusion
about the coexistence of distinct cultural traditions from work on Martha's Vineyard.

In light of the Dincauze's and Ritchie's outlooks for a multicultural landscape in southern New England, it may be instructive to consider how soapstone
vessels and Vinette I pottery emerged in the arena of interethic relations. This
opens an array of complex issues that require detailed study. Did soapstone
vessel production and exchange in southern New England emerge in the context
of an expanding broadpoint cultural front as one of several means of alliance
building with central New York groups? Did successful ties with such groups
effectively preclude or thwart assimilation between indigenous and immigrant
populations in southern New England? Was the burial ceremonialism of southern
New England a context of mediating ethnic distinctions between indigenous and
immigrant populations, as suggested earlier by Dincauze (1975b:31)? Did the
ritual "killing" of soapstone vessels in mortuary contexts in southern New
England symbolize mediation? Did the growing technological contrasts in the
third millennium B.P.—notably the exclusive use of Vinette I pottery by Meadowood groups of New York and the coexistence of both soapstone and pottery in
Orient contexts of southern New England and Long Island—signify an end to
traditional alliances?

Answers to these questions elude us for now. Still, it is apparent that the
peak in popularity of soapstone vessels in southern New England occurred after
pottery was adopted, albeit lightly, throughout the region. This is the period of
about 2900–2700 B.P. that encompasses many of the radiometrically dated or
crossdated mortuary contexts of Orient affiliation. It likewise coincides with the
proliferation of pottery use in Meadowood contexts of central New York, contexts which exclude soapstone vessels. Given the ceremonialism surrounding

soapstone vessels in southern New England and the sharp interregional contrasts that emerged at this time, I would suggest that explanations for the choice of alternative vessel technologies reside in the interpersonal alliances, marriage opportunities, and descent rules which underwrote patterns of ethnic affiliation and interaction. Ultimately, these are issues of social organization about which many archaeologists consider impossible to know. On the other hand, much untapped potential awaits archaeologists in the study of technology from a social perspective, particularly as regards one of the chief dimensions of social identity in any society, gender. It is within gender that we find the fundamental dimension for social divisions through marriage, alliance, and descent. It follows that archaeological patterns of gender-specific technologies embody rules of social organization, much in the fashion that Hill (1970) and Longacre (1970) attempted to show with ceramic design in the Southwest. In the close of this chapter I provide a short summary of my own attempt at social reconstruction in the middle Savannah River valley during the time pottery and soapstone vessels appeared. This case study illustrates how technical choice embodies identities of gender and how such identities are extended, through unilineal social organization, to boundaries and emblems of ethnicity.

Middle Savannah River Valley

Before pottery appeared in the Savannah River valley around 4500 B.P., soapstone had a long history of use as a raw material for cooking stones and bannerstones among Piedmont residents with lineal ancestry going back at least 1200 years. The use of pottery was initiated by a distinct people who resided in the lower Coastal Plain and on the coast of Georgia. Their first vessels were flat-bottomed basins used for indirect-heat cooking with soapstone cooking stones and other rocks. Soapstone did not outcrop in the Coastal Plain, so it had to be acquired through direct, long-distance procurement, or, more likely, through alliances with Piedmont neighbors. Pottery was not adopted by individuals occupying the Piedmont, not even after innovations for direct-heat cooking rendered soapstone slab cooking unnecessary. I have argued elsewhere (Sassaman 1993a) that the resistance to technological change may have been grounded in efforts to perpetuate alliances predicated on soapstone exchange. I further suggested that the apparent ethnic distinctions between Coastal Plain and Piedmont groups paralleled gender relations as regards cooking technology, with females responsible for pottery innovations and men in control of soapstone acquisition and trade.

By 4000 B.P., Coastal Plain residents began to spend more time in the Fall Zone and lower Piedmont of the middle Savannah River valley. Their composition at this point may have resulted from the assimilation of Piedmont and Coastal Plain residents into one group, through marriage and other means. However, the emerging cultural expression archaeologists refer to today as Stallings appears to have been organized by rules of exclusion. Analysis of the technology and decoration of Stallings pottery suggests that Stallings Culture was matrilocal in its postmarital residence patterns (Sassaman and Rudolphi 1995). Men who were lineal descendants of Piedmont groups may have been able to marry Stallings women and then join their wives' groups, but there is nothing to suggest that such men were able to take Stallings brides away from their natal lands. The inequity of this arrangement may have been disadvantageous to Piedmont groups attempting to sustain themselves biologically and socially. Over the 200 years during which Stallings Culture rose to prominence in the middle Savannah (i.e., 4000–3800 B.P.), Piedmont groups became increasingly remote. Known today as the Mill Branch phase, small groups persisted in the uplands of the middle Savannah during this period, but completely abandoned the area after 3800 B.P. Certain enclaves of Mill Branch affiliation appear to have relocated into portions of north-central Georgia (Stanyard 1997), where they maintained a traditional lifestyle. Here they began to make and use soapstone vessels.

In one sense, soapstone vessels can be viewed as a technological solution to challenges facing descendants of Mill Branch Culture. However, they certainly had knowledge of pottery, and there is nothing yet from the archaeological record to suggest they experienced any new demands on cooking technology. Rather, the greatest challenges may have been in establishing new alliances and relations with regional neighbors and to build a new cultural identity from the remnants of their traditions. In this regard, soapstone vessels embodied the raw material of tradition (soapstone) and the form of innovation (pottery) that paralleled both the ethnic distinctions of their history (Mill Branch/Stallings) and the gender relations underwriting inequality (men:outsiders; women:insiders). For them, soapstone vessels may have symbolized the mediation of contradictions (ethnicity, gender) that had undermined more open, egalitarian social relations. Shortly after appearing, soapstone vessels were exported great distances into peninsular Florida, the Gulf Coast, and, eventually, to Poverty Point. They clearly had a conspicuous role in the intergroup relations of regional populations, many of which, by this time, had developed, or at least had access to, full-blown pottery technology (Finn and Goldman-Finn 1997). Alliances directed away from the middle Savannah River valley may have themselves contributed to the collapse of Stallings Culture. Classic Stallings Culture, with its elaborate pottery, large shell middens, and concentrated riverine settlement pattern, dissolved at about 3500 B.P. Appearing at the very same time, for the very first time in the middle Savannah, were soapstone vessels.

To summarize, variation in timing and uses of alternative cooking vessel technologies in the Savannah River region was embedded in the histories of culture building and ethnogenesis stemming from group interactions. The most conspicuous seams of variation resided at the level of ethnicity, or the boundaries of collectivities, but they emanated from domestic relations of gender and their community extensions of unilineal descent and unilocal postmarital residence. As such, the alternative technical choices can hardly be considered passive expressions of tradition. Rather, they were conscious and purposeful decisions, enacted to distance one from the constraints of tradition (structure) while simultaneously building new tradition of alliance and collectivism.

CONCLUSION

Improved chronology for soapstone vessels in the Southeast verifies that this innovation was not the technological precedent for pottery, as unilineal evolutionary thinking would have us conclude. Refined chronology also undermines simple diffusionist claims for the spread of soapstone vessel technology from south to north. The so-called Broadpoint Tradition may in fact have involved the northward migration of people from the Southeast to the Middle Atlantic, and then into central New York, southern New England, and beyond. However, soapstone vessels technology was not a part of this process. In each of the areas of their occurrence, soapstone vessels were adopted or developed at least 200 years after members of broadpoint cultural affiliation became established locally. The decoupling of emergent broadpoint cultural elements (e.g., flaked stone) and soapstone vessels underscores the inadequacy of normative models which view cultures as unified, integrated wholes, as in the now defunct Susquehanna Soapstone Culture of Witthoft (1953). Clearly, the origins of soapstone vessels and its relationship to pottery varied from region to region and need be interpreted in their specific historical and cultural contexts.

At the same time, soapstone vessel technology has all the hallmarks of a true archaeological horizon at about 3200 B.P. across much of the East, and a resurgence in use at about 2700–2500 B.P. in two widely separated areas, the Gulf Coastal Plain and southern New England, both of which involved mortuary ceremonialism. The factors accounting for such large-scale patterns are not likely to be independent of the local-scale processes which led to varying choices among alternative vessel technologies. The earlier horizon coincides with the beginnings of pottery making throughout the Middle Atlantic and areas of the Southeast apart from those with earlier, fiber-tempered pottery traditions. The later occurrences accompany widespread use of pottery across eastern North America. Rather than relegating soapstone vessels to the category of "ceramic prototype," we ought to consider more fully how soapstone vessels were among the consequences of cultural processes which circumscribed traditions of pottery. The Savannah River case study exemplifies one such process. Elsewhere the juxtaposition of soapstone and pottery may be structured by control over raw material sources, labor arrangements, or technical processes.

In examining social processes accounting for alternative vessel uses, it is important that analyses not be restricted to the simple presence-absence of particular technologies. For instance, soapstone vessel forms vary considerably across the Northeast. Orient vessels tend to have smooth exterior surfaces and rounded bottoms, while other Northeast forms tend to have chiseled exteriors and flat bottoms (Ritchie 1959:62; 1965:159, 161; Witthoft 1953). Within particular quarries of southern New England, vessels forms vary from oval and round to rectangular and triangular (Bullen 1940; Dixon 1987). Also, size within a single tradition of form varies; those in Orient and related mortuary contexts, for example, vary from 14 to 62 cm in length and 5 to 23 cm in height (Lord 1962; Ritchie 1965:170). The extent to which formal variation reflects diachronic trends is uncertain, but one cannot dismiss the possibility that contemporaneous producers manipulated form for diverse cultural purposes.

In a similar sense, vessel function is subject to cultural variations not directly related to utilitarian concerns. As noted earlier, the persistent of indirect-heat cooking with early ceramic vessels in the Savannah River valley arguably was the result of conscious efforts to perpetuate exchange alliances between groups. Similarly, the Chumash Indians of California resisted the adoption of Western cooking technology to perpetuate soapstone exchange alliances with channel island neighbors (Hudson and Blackburn 1983). What is more, function can be manipulated to break from alliance and tradition, as well as perpetuate it—that is, to build new culture and identity (e.g., Lemonnier 1992). Thus, detailed information of the actual functions of early vessel technology is highly relevant. Truncer's (1991, 1997) recent analyses of soapstone vessel function is a major step in documenting the full range of vessel uses in the Northeast. Advances in our understanding of the cultural contexts of alternative uses cannot proceed without such functional data.

Above all, renewed interests in the specific cultural and historical contexts of prehistory heightens the need to interpret vessel technology in the Northeast in its own, multifaceted terms. New insights await efforts to "center" the Northeast (Dincauze 1993a) as a legitimate arena of social process, to abandon theoretical programs that downplay historical process, and, perhaps most important, to deconstruct the typologies that preclude social variation (see also Chapters 4, 6, and 8, this volume). We have the potential to convert unilineal sequences into multicultural communities and, by extension, enhance greatly the interpretive relevance of archaeological data to the issues of power and ethnicity that are in the mainstream of contemporary anthropology.

ACKNOWLEDGMENTS

For providing information necessary to the successful completion of this chapter, I thank Mike Anslinger, John Cross, Dena Dincauze, Jim Herbstritt, Curtiss Hoffman, Alan Leveillee, Doug Mackey, Kevin McBride, Tracy Millis, Duncan Ritchie, Jim Truncer, and Greg Waselkov. Soot samples for AMS dating were provided by Mark Brooks, Tom Des Jean, Mike Finn, Jim Herbstritt, Al Goodyear, Eric Poplin, Frankie Snow, Bill Stanyard, Betty Stringfellow, and Steve Webb. For commentary that caused me to abandon the initial draft of this chapter and start again with renewed interest, I am grateful to Dena Dincauze, Mary Ann Levine, Tracy Millis, Michael Nassaney, and Jim Truncer. This research was supported by the Savannah River Archaeological Research Program (SRARP), South Carolina Institute of Archaeology and Anthropology, under cooperative agreement with the U.S. Department of Energy–Savannah River (Contract DE-FC09-98SR18931), and by a grant from the Archaeological Research Trust, South Carolina Institute of Archaeology and Anthropology. Program Manager of the SRARP, Mark Brooks, deserves my thanks for his unflagging support of this research.

6

Ceramic Research in New England: Breaking the Typological Mold

Elizabeth S. Chilton

Ceramic analysis and description as now practiced in the [Northeast] are more art than science. . . . Tests of firing temperature, mineral composition, friability and cohesiveness are not usually undertaken. Although admittedly expensive of time and money, the results of such tests would at least provide information which is directly relevant to cultural interpretation. (Dincauze 1975a:5)

Important technical and theoretical changes have taken place over the past thirty years in the way archaeological ceramics are analyzed in the United States (Nelson 1985:1). These changes have been slow in their diffusion to the Northeast. Ceramic classifications in this region have been based largely on decorative attributes, with time and space viewed as significant determinants of change. Because of an emphasis on cultural-historical questions, archaeologists have most often focused on attributes of ceramics that are thought to vary the most through time and are the easiest to identify, namely, decoration and rim characteristics. As a result, there has been relatively little research on variation in technical attributes of ceramics, such as paste, vessel size and shape, and evidence of firing conditions. Thus archaeologists have not adequately addressed the variety of choices made by potters along the production sequence. While there has been greater attention to technical attributes of ceramics in the last twenty years in the region, they are most often employed for description (e.g., Dincauze and Gramly 1973; McGahan 1989) or for answering cultural-historical questions within local areas (e.g., Luedtke 1986).

In this chapter I examine an alternative to the use of extant ceramic classifications in the New England interior for the Late Woodland Period (A.D. 1000–1600). In the greater Northeast, especially for the New York Iroquois, the Late Woodland period is perceived as culturally dynamic: agriculture becomes important for subsistence, communities become more sedentary, and population and the incidence of intercommunity conflict increase (Fenton 1978). However, for Algonquian peoples in the New England interior, particular in the middle Connecticut River valley, there is no evidence for large, fortified settlements and intensive horticulture (Thorbahn 1988; cf. Chapter 9, this volume). In fact, there is no evidence that maize was anything more than a dietary supplement in the interior prior to European settlement (Dincauze 1990:30, *contra* Snow 1980: 333). Instead, archaeologists encounter highly variable and short-term horticultural settlements that do not fit established cultural classifications (Chilton 1996b; Johnson 1992).

It is generally accepted that Native ceramics in the Northeast "evolved" over time from crude to fine: vessel walls became increasingly thinner, temper (crushed rock or other substance added to the clay) became smaller, and decoration or surface treatment became more elaborate and sophisticated (Fowler 1966; Snow 1980). Luedtke (1986) has shown these trends to generally hold true in eastern Massachusetts. As I will explore in this chapter, aside from evolutionary reasons, there are utilitarian reasons for choices of temper, wall thickness, and surface treatment (see Braun 1983; Luedtke 1986). In this chapter I examine some of these other explanations through an analysis of ceramics from three Late Woodland sites in the Northeast. First, I begin with an overview of Late Woodland ceramic research in New England.

NEW ENGLAND CERAMIC CLASSIFICATIONS

In southern New England, ceramic classifications are largely based on the work of Fowler (1945), Lavin (1986, 1988), Pope (1953), Rouse (1945, 1947), and Smith (1944, 1947, 1950). Ritchie's extensive work in central New York (e.g., Ritchie 1944) on the development of classification schemes was probably the impetus behind the development of similar schemes for coastal New York and Connecticut (McBride 1984:4). Ceramic classifications consist of types within larger ceramic traditions. These type-names serve as a kind of shorthand for a range of stylistic attributes and are used to refer to distinct archaeological cultures, which archaeologists in the region often conflate with ethnic groups (Lizee 1994a:4). Because most excavated ceramic sherds in New England tend to be small and fragmentary, little emphasis has been placed on using design motifs, as for the New York Iroquois; instead, decorative technique or surface treatment has been the primary focus of study (Childs 1984:186).

The principle Late Woodland ceramic traditions described by archeologists in southern New England include Windsor, East River, Guida, and Mohawk (Table 6.1). (I have not included Contact Period ceramics, such as Hackney Pond Phase [McBride 1984] or Shantok ceramics [Johnson 1993].) Smith (1947, 1950) and Rouse (1947) use paste characteristics to separate traditions, and then use surface treatment, decoration, and rim form to distinguish types. Following these researchers, Lavin has continued to build on the existing typologies for southern New England (Lavin 1986; Lavin and Miroff 1992).

Table 6.1
Common Ceramic Traditions and Types from Southern New England and New York, A.D. 1000–1700

Windsor Tradition

Sebonac (A.D. 1100–1400): simple conical vessels, shell temper, interior and exterior surface brushing, stamping, and dragging direction

Niantic (A.D. 1400–1700): thin walled, shell tempered, globular pots, with constricted necks, collars, and complex stamped scallop shell designs; sometimes with smooth interior surface

Niantic Incised: smooth, constricted neck, collared rims, incised decoration. Lavin (1988:15) suggests that these are "strongly reminiscent of Hudson and Mohawk Valley types"

Other types: Niantic Stamped, Niantic Linear Dentate, Niantic Punctate, etc.

East River Tradition

Bowmans Brook (A.D. 1100–1200): smooth interior, cord-marked exterior; rims decorated with horizontal rows of cord-wrapped stick impressions; incising not common

Clasons Point (A.D. 1200–1700): collared rims, globular bodies, stamping decreases as incising increases; plain surface treatment common; grit temper frequent, but shell tempering increases throughout; at the end of the period vessels "approximate forms of the eastern Iroquois" (Smith 1947)

Guida Tradition

Guida Incised (A.D. 1500–1700): gray to black; fine, micaceous temper; surface "flaky" or "silky." Designs of finely incised lines, very close together on narrow collars; Byers and Rouse (1960:17) have suggested that the motifs are "Iroquoian"

Other Guida types: Guida Cord Marked, Guida Fabric Marked, Guida Plain, Guida Stamped, and Guida "Miscellaneous"

Mohawk Tradition

Chance Phase (A.D. 1400–1500): incising replaces cord-impressing for collar and neck designs; fine grit temper, semiglobular shape; check-stamped and cord-marked replaced by smooth surfaces

Chase Phase types: Chance Incised, Deowongo Incised

Garoga Phase (A.D. 1500–1700): large, globular vessels, incised linear patterns on castellated collars, notches at base of collar

Garoga Phase types: Garoga Incised, Wagoner Incised, Otstungo Notched, Rice Diagonal

Sources: Byers and Rouse (1960); Kuhn and Frank (1991); Lavin and Kra (1994); McBride (1984); MacNeish (1952); Ritchie (1980); Rouse (1947); Smith (1947).

A striking amount of overlap exists among the traditions and types of New England's ceramic typologies (see Table 6.1). For example, attributes such as incised decoration, shell tempering, or cord-marked surface treatment crosscut many of the ceramic traditions. Lavin has often expanded the ceramic type descriptions of Smith (1950) and Rouse (1947) when she has encountered attribute combinations that do not fit the existing types (Lavin and Kra 1994). This adding of traits and noting of "exceptions" to the original type descriptions has contributed to a blurring of the distinctions between types. Lavin (1988:15) has admitted that it is often difficult to place sherds within known types, because they may exhibit traits belonging to more than one tradition.

One of the major repercussions of overlapping ceramic typologies in the Northeast is that incised, castellated ceramics found in the New England interior are often deemed "Iroquoian" (Dincauze 1974) and considered by archaeologists to be the effect of social interaction, diffusion, migration, trade, or female capture (e.g., Brooks 1946; Byers and Rouse 1960; Engelbrecht 1972; Lavin 1988; Snow 1992a). Unfortunately, the direction and source of presumed cultural influences are influenced by where the type names were first applied. For example, when Windsor Tradition pottery, first defined on the coast of New England, is found in the New England interior, it is often thought to be the result of coastal influences—without archaeologists having to demonstrate where and when the Windsor traits originated (e.g., Lavin and Miroff 1992; Lavin et al. 1993). Likewise, Byers and Rouse (1960), in their analysis of Guida ceramics, conclude that many of the incised design motifs are "Iroquoian." They suggest that this influence is indicative of direct trade in some cases, and the diffusion of "collars and incised designs" in others (Byers and Rouse 1960:28).

Ceramics of the New England Interior

There is relatively little published archaeological research on the interior of New England, particularly for the middle or Massachusetts portion of the Connecticut River valley (Snow 1980:330). No one has developed a ceramic classification specifically for the region; type names are often borrowed from New York and southern New England, with the assumption that New England peoples were greatly influenced by groups to the south and west (e.g., Byers and Rouse 1960; Johnson and Bradley 1987). Because the direction of change is not rigorously investigated, this assumption is self-validating.

The only ceramic type/tradition created specifically for the New England interior is the Guida Tradition. Byers and Rouse (1960) defined the Guida Tradition on the basis of collections from the Guida Farm site, Westfield, Massachusetts (Figure 6.1). Shortly thereafter, Fowler (1961:21) criticized Byers and Rouse for following a "questionable course of action in trying to superimpose an arbitrarily created Guida Tradition over all central New England ceramics." On the basis of my analysis of the Young collection from Guida Farm (Chilton 1996a), which includes the original type collection, it is clear that the Guida

Figure 6.1
Map of Southern New England and Eastern New York,
Showing Location of Study Sites

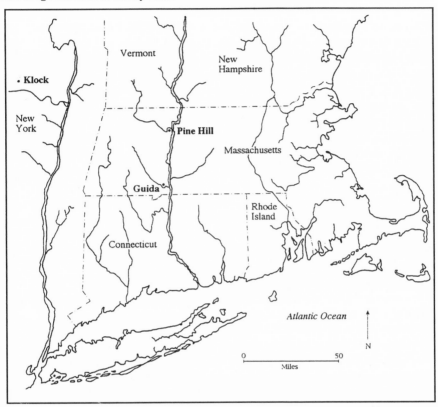

Tradition is nothing more than a residual category. That is, sherds that could not be attributed to other known ceramic traditions were relegated to the Guida Tradition. Importantly, because micaceous inclusions (muscovite) are the chief diagnostic trait of Guida ceramics, according to Byers and Rouse (1960), they may reflect simply the use of a specific set of clay or temper resources at the type site, not a "tradition" per se.

ATTRIBUTE ANALYSIS

What does it mean that we can't recognize pottery types . . . in Massachusetts? (Dincauze 1978a:6)

Archaeologists have come to realize in the past 20 years, that ceramic typologies have little utility in Massachusetts (Dincauze 1978a; Luedtke 1986). Archaeologists have sought an alternative in attribute analysis. The word *attribute* is probably the most misused and poorly defined term in analyses of material culture. In this analysis, I define an attribute as one variable of a ceramic vessel, such as surface treatment, color, inclusion type, or rim shape. An attribute state is thus one of any possible value or state for that variable, such as "cordmarked," "quartz," or "23 mm." Thus, each attribute has an infinite number of possible attribute states.

An attribute analysis can be the first step in the synthesis of a typology, since a type is considered to be a cluster or nonrandom association of attribute states. For example, Lavin (1986:3) viewed attribute analysis and typology as "complementary stages in the ordering of . . . data." However, attribute analysis does not necessarily lead to typology. In the previous section I described some of the problems associated with the typological approach as used in New England archaeology. While the creation of cultural-historical types continues to dominate ceramic studies in the region, in recent years there has been an increase in the use of attribute analyses that do not result in the formulation of cultural-historical types (e.g., Brumbach 1975; Chilton 1994; Dincauze 1975a; Dincauze and Gramly 1973; Finlayson 1977; Goodby 1992; Kenyon 1979; Kristmanson and Deal 1993; Lizee 1994a; Luedtke 1986; McGahan 1989; Pendergast 1973; Petersen 1980, 1985; Prezzano 1986; Ramsden 1977; Stothers 1977). In New England, Dincauze (1975a) and Kenyon (1979) paved the way for analyses of physical attributes of ceramics, such as characteristics of clay, aplastic inclusions, and the effects of firing.

Using an "attribute analysis of technical choice" (Chilton 1996b), the goal is to look for both variation and covariation within and between objects—not to formulate a typology. In such analysis, vessels are seen as a cumulative record of sequential attribute choices. The use of rim or sherd frequencies to describe ceramic assemblages has a long history in Northeast archaeology (Petersen 1985: 10). More recently, researchers in the Northeast have employed vessels as units of analysis (Dincauze 1975a, 1976; Dincauze and Gramly 1973; Luedtke 1980; Petersen 1980; and Wright 1980). Compared with sherds, vessels as units of analysis have greater relevance to interpretation of human behavior (Carr 1993) because vessels were the most likely units of meaning in prehistoric societies.

An attribute analysis of technical choice is designed to examine both technological *and* decorative aspects of material culture, both of which may exhibit "style" (Lechtman 1977). This kind of attribute analysis can and should be used in addition to existing typologies, as a means to acquire different kinds of information. For example, groupings of artifacts based on nonrandom associations of *decorative* attributes may crosscut groupings based on nonrandom associations of *technical* attributes (i.e., decorative style may or may not correlate with technical style).

The Data

As part of my dissertation research (Chilton 1996a), I analyzed ceramics from three Late Woodland sites in the Northeast: two in western Massachusetts (the Guida Farm site, Westfield, and the Pine Hill site, Deerfield) and one in the Mohawk Valley, New York (the Klock site, Ephratah; see Figure 6.1). These particular Massachusetts sites were chosen because they represent the best excavated and documented Late Woodland sites in the middle Connecticut River valley (see Chilton 1996a). The Klock site was chosen because it was one of the best documented Mohawk sites from the latter part of the Late Woodland period, and was, therefore, comparable in age to the Connecticut River valley sites. Because the study of Late Woodland ceramics in New England is strongly influenced by typologies created for the New York Iroquois, it was important to include an Iroquoian assemblage in this analysis.

Based on ethnohistoric accounts, the two Massachusetts sites are thought to have been inhabited by Algonquian-speaking peoples of the Connecticut River valley (most likely the Pocumtucks at Pine Hill and the Woronocos at Guida Farm). The Klock site has been interpreted by Kuhn and Funk (1994) as an early protohistoric Iroquois settlement, and was most likely occupied by a Mohawk community.

Several hundred ceramic sherds were recovered from the Pine Hill site, which was tested by the University of Massachusetts Archaeological Field School in the summers of 1989, 1991, and 1993 (Keene and Chilton 1995). Nearly 500 sherds were large enough to be used in the analysis. From these, fifty-six distinct vessel lots were identified. The Young collection from the Guida Farm site contains approximately 1,000 sherds which were large enough to be used in this analysis. From these, 108 vessel lots were identified. The collection from the Klock site has over 15,000 ceramic fragments. A random sample of 100 vessel lots was chosen in order to make it comparable in size to the Guida and Pine Hill collections.

To establish a vessel lot—that is, a group of potsherds determined to be minimally from the same vessel—at least nine attributes were recorded for each sherd: modal vessel wall thickness, inclusion material (i.e., temper or naturally occurring particles), size, and density, exterior and interior color, surface treatment (including decoration), and location of the sherd on the vessel. Inclusions were identified using $10\times$ magnification. Because it is extremely difficult to identify rock minerals in fired ceramic pastes, my inclusion designations are consistent, if not exact. Inclusion density was estimated using comparative charts (Terry and Chilingar 1955:229–234); because the amount of inclusion varies a great deal within ceramic pastes of hand-built pots, *estimates* of inclusion density are sufficient. The final vessel lot determination is based on overall similarity in the attributes analyzed.

Results

In this section I summarize a few of the more important technical attributes; other attributes analyzed, but not discussed here, include construction techniques, rim and lip form, and interior and exterior collar (see Chilton 1996a).

As might be expected, the ceramics from the Connecticut Valley Pine Hill and Guida Farm sites show many similarities. For example, the primary inclusion type at both sites was crushed quartz, followed by feldspar (Figure 6.2). In contrast, the most common inclusion types at the Mohawk Valley Klock site were feldspar (mostly plagioclase) and hornblende, which are both present in the metamorphic rocks of the nearby Adirondacks. It is important to note here that the optimal inclusion types for cooking vessels have thermal expansion coefficients similar or less than that of clay, such as grog, calcite, crushed burned shell, feldspar, and hornblende (Rice 1987:229). Quartz, on the other hand, is not an optimal inclusion type for cooking pots; it expands much more quickly than clay and can lead to crack initiation, especially if the particles are large. Therefore, on the basis of inclusion materials used, the Connecticut Valley ceramics would not have been ideal cooking pots, on the whole. Not only do the assemblages from the Connecticut Valley have different kinds of inclusions, but they also show a higher diversity of inclusion materials used, the implications of which I discuss later.

Inclusion density follows a similar, yet more striking pattern. Inclusion density was recorded as an ordinal variable (1 percent, 5 percent, 10 percent, etc.). The median inclusion densities for Pine Hill and Guida are 15 percent and 13 percent, respectively, while for Klock it is only 7 percent. The range of inclusion density is similar for Pine Hill and Guida: both have lower extremes of 3 percent, and upper extremes of 32 percent and 40 percent, respectively. Klock, on the other hand, has a range of 2 to 20 percent (note the much smaller maximum value). Usually, a densely tempered ceramic is stronger than one with lower density. However, the more temper in the paste, the more potential for shock from thermal expansion, especially if the temper is quartz (see Braun 1983, 1987). Therefore, the Connecticut Valley vessels would have been less resistant to thermal shock, but more resistant to mechanical stress, than the Klock site vessels.

Mean vessel wall thicknesses for assemblages from Pine Hill and Guida are 6.28 and 6.53 mm, respectively, with standard deviations of 2.4 and 1.9 mm. In contrast, the Klock site has a smaller mean thickness of 6.13 mm, and a lower standard deviation of 1.6, but the difference is not statistically significant. However, on the basis of body sherd curvature, the Klock vessels are, on average, 70 percent larger than those from Pine Hill and Guida (29 cm vs. 17 cm mean diameter). Because larger vessels are expected to have relatively thicker walls in order to support the additional weight, the wall thickness of the Klock assemblage is significantly thinner when vessel size is taken into account. Wall thickness directly affects vessel performance; vessels with thinner walls are more resistant to thermal stress but are less resistant to mechanical stress (Rice 1987).

Surface treatments (impressing, scraping, or smoothing of the surface of the clay before firing) on vessels from Guida and Pine Hill are also similar, while both differ significantly from the Klock site material (Figure 6.3). The Klock

Figure 6.2
Relative Frequencies of Vessels by Primary Inclusion Type and Site

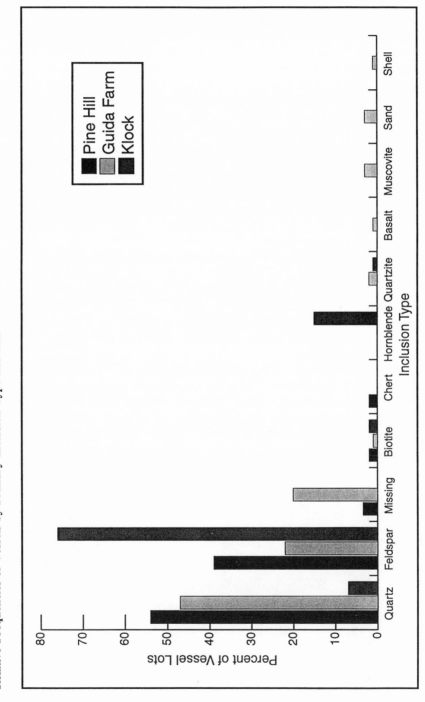

Figure 6.3
Relative Frequencies of Vessels by Surface Treatment and Site

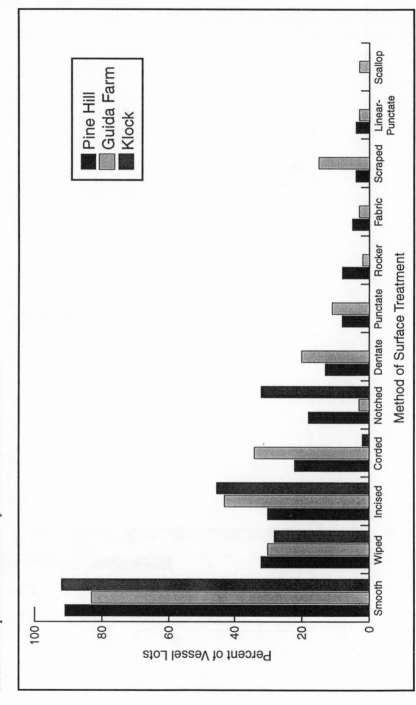

sample is exclusively smoothed, wiped, incised, and notched, while the samples from both Guida and Pine Hill show much more diversity: cord-marked, dentate-stamped, punctate, rocker-stamped, fabric-impressed, scraped, linear punctated, scallop shell-impressed, as well as smooth, wiped, incised, and notched. All of the rimsherds from the Klock site fit neatly into the established Iroquoian ceramic typologies (Kuhn and Funk 1994), while only two vessel lots from Guida and one from Pine Hill are typable (barring the Guida Tradition types, for reasons previously discussed). In all attributes analyzed, the Connecticut River valley ceramics consistently showed more diversity (Figures 6.4 and 6.5).

On the basis of the traditional assumption by archaeologists that dentate-stamping and fabric-impressing belong to the Middle Woodland period (A.D. 0–1000) and therefore predate incising, the assemblages from Pine Hill and Guida might appear to have Middle Woodland components. However, there is evidence that dentate stamping may also be a Late Woodland and even a Contact period trait, at least in New England. For example, at Pine Hill, on two occasions incised vessel lots were found in the same feature lens with dentate-stamped vessel lots. One vessel lot from Pine Hill exhibits both incising and dentate stamping, and two vessel lots from Guida have dentate-stamped collars (collars are thought to be an exclusively Late Woodland trait). It is clear from these examples that in the Connecticut River valley, unilinear evolutionary changes in surface treatment cannot be assumed.

DISCUSSION

What might these technical variations mean in the larger contexts of Late Woodland culture? In his analysis of Midwestern ceramics, David Braun (1983, 1987) suggested that the evolution from thicker-walled, more densely tempered vessels to thinner-walled, smaller tempered vessels represented a change in the intended uses of pots, and not an evolutionary technological improvement per se. More specifically, pots with larger inclusions and thicker walls are more resistant to mechanical stress. Conversely, pots with thinner walls and smaller inclusions may be less apt to crack when heated. But, these thinner-walled pots are more likely to break as a result of mechanical stresses (see Rice 1987). Surface treatment can also affect vessel performance. A rough surface, such as that produced by cord marking, fabric impressing or scraping, can increase thermal shock resistance and thermal spalling (Schiffer et al. 1994); a rough surface will also make a pot less slippery and easier to transport (Rice 1987).

As discussed previously, the Iroquois were dependent on maize for subsistence and were semisedentary. Also, they apparently produced pots that were better suited for cooking than for transport. The variety of maize (*Zea mays*) used by the Iroquois was Northern Flint or closely related varieties (Fenton 1978:325). Northern Flint has a thicker kernel wall than other varieties of *Zea mays* which makes it harder to process (Galinat and Gunnerson 1963:123–125). The New England variety of Northern Flint may have had especially thick

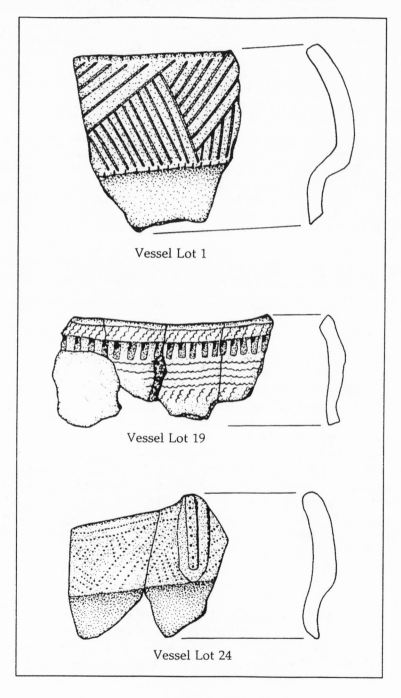

Vessel Lot 1

Vessel Lot 19

Vessel Lot 24

Figure 6.5
Sherds from Vessel Lots 5, 6, 15A, and 16A from the Klock Site

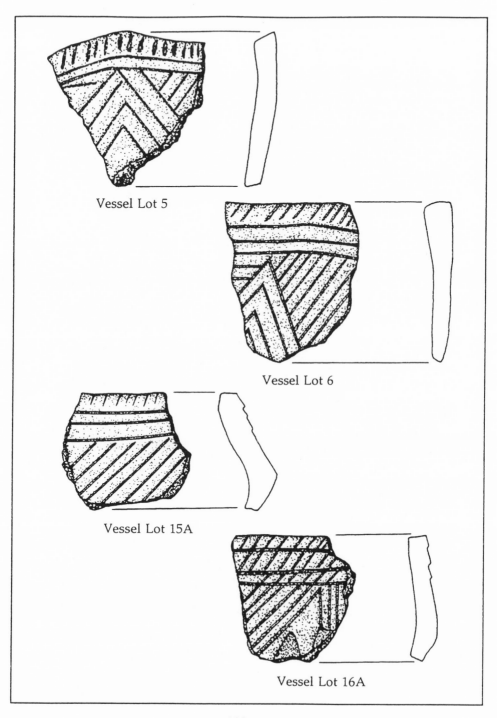

Vessel Lot 5

Vessel Lot 6

Vessel Lot 15A

Vessel Lot 16A

kernel walls, due to the relatively cold climate (Galinat and Gunnerson 1963: 123–125). The Iroquois most often cooked maize in stews that were simmered for a long period of time over a hot fire (Parker 1968). Thus, pots needed to be resistant to thermal stress.

In terms of settlement, the Iroquois resided in villages of 30 to 150 long-houses (Fenton 1978:306) for twenty-five to fifty years at a time (Tuck 1978: 326). Pots would have been made in similar social and ecological contexts each time, under predictable circumstances. In accordance with this expectation, the Iroquois ceramics in my sample show great internal homogeneity in terms of decorative and technological attributes.

In contrast to the Iroquois, the Algonquians of the Connecticut River valley were more mobile throughout the year and relied less heavily on maize and other seed crops (Chilton 1996a, 1996b). Accordingly, the Late Woodland ceramics of the Connecticut Valley were, on the whole, better suited for storing and transporting food than they were for cooking, as indicated by primarily dense quartz inclusions and slightly thicker walls.

Aside from issues of subsistence, there are social advantages to maintaining mobility. Johnson (1993) has suggested that mobility may have been a strategy of resistance to authority by the Algonquians of Southern New England—that is, the authority of certain native political leaders and (later) the English. By maintaining flexibility and mobility in their settlement practices, the Algonquians of the interior could literally "vote with their feet," which may explain the infrequent occurrence of warfare, at least prior to European contact. If the Connecticut River valley Algonquians were more mobile, and the boundaries were more fluid than those of the Iroquois, then the social contexts of ceramic manufacture would have been more variable—pots would not have been made in the same place and with the same people every time. For example, if groups of people were moving seasonally, and were fissioning and fusing with other groups at various times of the year, then the social and environmental contexts of ceramic manufacture and use would have been quite variable. Accordingly, we could expect the Late Woodland ceramics of the Connecticut River valley to show much more variability in surface treatments, inclusion type and inclusion density, as is the case.

CONCLUSION

To return to the quote by Dena Dincauze at the beginning of this chapter, I have tried to show that attention to nondecorative, technological aspects of ceramics is the key to understanding Late Woodland ceramic traditions and cultural dynamics in New England. It should be clear from this case study that ceramic classifications should not be imported across cultural borders. Also, because ceramics from the New England interior show tremendous variability in nearly all attributes analyzed, I suggest that a typological approach in this region is simply not warranted. While ceramic types may be defined for limited (particularly coastal) regions, they have little utility over the region as a whole (Luedtke 1986). Instead, the attribute analysis of both technical and decorative attributes has the potential to provide information about environmental and social contexts of production; intended vessel function; technological traditions; and social boundaries (Stark 1998). The analysis of technical attributes of ceramics are challenging in any region, but, as Dincauze (1975a) warned, it is the key to cultural interpretation. Rather than forever hiding in the shadow of the Iroquois, by breaking the mold of ceramic typologies in New England, archaeologists in the region will be free to seek models of cultural variation and change that posit New England Algonquians as the "center" (Dincauze 1993a) of unique processes of human experience.

ACKNOWLEDGMENTS

I thank Dena F. Dincauze who inspired my interest in ceramic analysis and who was the chair of my dissertation committee at the University of Massachusetts–Amherst. I also wish to thank the other members of my thesis committee, Arthur S. Keene, H. Martin Wobst, and Kevin Sweeney (Amherst College). Thanks also to Michael Sugerman (Harvard University) for computer assistance and David Schafer (Public Archaeology Laboratory) for brainstorming sessions and editorial comments. All potsherds were drawn by Maureen Manning-Bernatsky. A special thanks goes to Mary Ann Levine, Michael Nassaney, and Kenneth Sassaman for inviting me to contribute this paper and for organizing and editing this volume. Any flaws in this work are solely my responsibility.

Part III

Critical Perspectives on Entrenched Assumptions

become more permeable and vague, and are defined by an arbitrary decision about what density of materials constitutes a meaningful unit of analysis.

In the extreme, distributional "peaks" will be areas with large, dense, contiguous clusters of cultural material. Again in the extreme, the "valleys" will seem to be archaeological deserts, since the space between archaeological objects and features (or clusters) may be greater than the resolution of our standard methods of detection.

Under these conditions, our presence/absence tests have limited utility unless they are geared toward detecting a specific range of shapes, sizes, and densities of material clusters. We need to be more specific about what we are looking for (or, conversely, what we are willing to miss) with our testing strategies. Even if powerful statistics are not used to express ourselves, narrative assessments would be a good start. In other words, we will not find many sites in the thin part of the distribution (valleys) if we dig a narrow shovel test pit every 25 m.

In most places where the landscape has topographic relief, the odds are good that the peaks of the archaeological distributions are seen to have a direct and inverse correlation with elevation. This view was prevalent in New England for a long time. Thus, topographic valleys are seen as distributional peaks, and topographic peaks are projected as archaeological valleys.

This correlation may have some merit in terms of the sheer volume of cultural material per acre, but it does not reflect the probable number or significance of sites in a given zone. A trap we can all too easily fall into is to assume that the highly visible clusters we can identify in the lowlands and river valleys are substantially more numerous than the smaller, less visible clusters in the uplands. We simply do not know that to be true; moreover, it is highly unlikely in areas where most of the archaeological record was generated by people who spent the majority of the year in relatively small, mobile bands. While both the overall density of materials and numbers of large sites per acre in the traditional "high potential" zones is no doubt higher than elsewhere, the reality is that these zones represent just a small percentage (certainly less than 10 percent) of the state. If we thus prioritize the delineation and protection of zones with a "high potential" for yielding rich, dense, stratified sites at the expense of the rest of the state's land base, we virtually ignore the vast majority of sites (i.e., those located on the remaining 90 percent of the land).

Furthermore, it is an easy next step to assume that the rich lowland sites we protect are simply big versions of thin upland sites (Bender 1986). If that were the case, then lowland sites might indeed be inherently more interesting and significant because there is generally more to them, and the potentially time-consuming, labor-intensive search for the less obvious, higher elevation sites could be avoided.

However, we have yet to establish databases allowing us to compare the range of site functions, or seasons or eras of occupation, for example, between upland and lowland sites. If we plotted the location of different kinds of sites (e.g., contact villages, kill sites, lithic procurement workshops, vision quest spots), or functionally similar sites at different seasons, their distributions would have different shapes and slopes. If taken as a whole, however, the distributions would tend to level out (i.e., the site location patterns would not overlap). Collector activity and cultural resource management (CRM) surveys may well have reinforced the dominance of just one of several possible graphs/slopes by focusing on, for example, artifact-rich seasonal fishing villages. We may also find that the population of upland sites reflects a high proportion of single or limited component events—thereby offering more analytically robust opportunities than the more complex/disturbed deposits often associated with larger sites (Dewar 1986; Thomas 1986).

EXPANDING THE ARCHAEOLOGY OF THE ORIGINAL VERMONTERS

With this backdrop of topographic hyperbole, let me turn to a more personal and local level. My suburban Boston upbringing included a worldview assumption that most everyone who could do so lived on flat, well-drained, and reasonably low-lying places. My subsequent indoctrination into the prehistoric archaeology of New England did very little to alter this assumption: if the traditional syntheses of our archaeological heritage were any indication, the vast majority of Native Americans must have shared my suburban sensibilities.

Between the time of my first education in the archaeology of New England and the time I started working in Vermont, I worked with colleagues at the University of Massachusetts on a project titled "A Retrospective Assessment of Archaeological Survey Contracts in Massachusetts, 1970–1979" (Dincauze et al. 1980). This study taught us, among other things, that the distribution of known sites (loosely bounded, poorly defined, unstandardized clusters of archaeological materials) was a direct function of the number and intensity of surveys done in an area (Hasenstab and Lacy 1984)—a point which is still not always acknowledged.

I was therefore primed to ask questions about areas that were previously thought to be archaeologically "marginal" by the time I came to the Green Mountains. In fact, any reference to the marginality of the mountains only makes sense in relation to the abundant and fertile agricultural lands which lay to the East (the Connecticut River valley) and the West (the Champlain lowlands) of this generally moderate, rolling, and low northern end of the ancient Appalachians. The mountains themselves offered their own rich natural resource base, including deer, bear, and moose habitat; beaver ponds and meadows; fowl flyways; berries; mast; numerous medicinal plant species; and lithic raw materials. In addition, they were in proximity to areas of known archaeological sensitivity, had reasonably good preservation conditions, and were positioned strategically vis-à-vis major transportation corridors (see Jackson 1929) and river drainages.

Yet my literature review, background research, and interviews with archaeologists and local residents resulted in a striking absence of known sites, even previous archaeological inquiry. In fact, in 1984 the inventory of known prehistoric sites within the more than 350,000 acres of the Green Mountain National Forest consisted of three unverified "find spots" (Casjens 1978; Loring 1978). The only reference I can recall finding for a successful site survey near the Forest, but not on the Otter Creek, was Thomas et al.'s (1982) Ball Mountain Lake report which located a single component Late Woodland site along the West River (Jamaica, Vermont) at just under 900 feet elevation.

The apparent lack of sites in the Green Mountains ran counter to a growing number of precedents elsewhere in North America at the time which showed that there were significant populations of archaeological sites at high elevations. Sites had been identified in Wyoming (e.g., Bender 1986; Wright et al. 1980), the Colorado Rockies (Benedict 1981), areas surrounding the Great Basin (Bettinger and Thomas 1984), as well as in the geographically and/or geologically related Appalachian ranges of the Blue Ridge Mountains (Ayers 1976), Great Smoky Mountains (Bass 1977), other mountainous terrain in North (Mathis and Crow 1983) and South Carolina (Sassaman 1986), various locales in the Southeast (Barber 1984) and, potentially, right next door in New Hampshire's White Mountains (Cassedy 1986). It was also inconsistent with advice available closer to home (Dincauze 1980b) suggesting that we had not fully appreciated Native peoples' adaptations to the diversity of landscapes in New England. Such arguments provided the impetus to suggest that hunting, trapping, gathering, travel, refuge, lithic procurement, and sacred or ritual activities were all reasonable activities to have taken place in the mountains of Vermont.

The most obvious reason for the apparent dearth of recorded knowledge about archaeological resources in the Green Mountains was that we had not looked very hard or very often. Ironically, archaeologists—known to the public for our activities in remote and exotic locales—had not been attracted to Vermont's hills and mountains with the same intensity as tourists. Some archaeologists working in or near Vermont shared and encouraged my enthusiasm about the potential for sites in the mountains, but none had been in a position to investigate these expectations in the field. Since they had not, the mountains remained archaeological terra incognita.

To justify my request to U.S. Forest Service management to fund a prehistoric site survey program, I needed to identify why no one had gone before me—in effect, why I thought the inherited wisdom, or myths, about the lack of sites in the mountains was unfounded. I concluded that the primary reasons were to be found in the social and economic context in which we do archaeology (Lacy 1985, 1994). In brief: (1) prior to the advent of professional CRM, most sites were discovered through soil disturbance associated with farming (i.e., plowed fields) at lower elevations in alluvial deposits; (2) our twentieth-century, Euro-American view of the landscape did not encourage a search since the mountains were not "civilized" places to live or farm (but prehistoric economic systems would not have generated stratified land-use patterns parallel to our own anyway [see Sassaman 1986]); (3) archaeologists had rarely consulted with Native Americans about their understandings of past land use in the mountains, so our lack of knowledge was based in part on a culturally derived myopia (Lacy and Bluto-Delvental 1995); (4) the development of culture histories and typologies favored the identification of large, dense, stratified deposits characteristic of seasonal riverine gathering spots, which in turn influenced field survey methodology; and (5) CRM followed in the geographic footsteps of earlier site discoveries and therefore reinforced predictive models that were based on already existing data (see Dincauze and Lacy 1985), which takes us back to the beginning of this sequence.

In sum, the pattern of site discovery in Vermont, as elsewhere in northern New England and New York, was an artifact of the interplay between the money, ideology, science, population density, and systematic soil disturbances characteristic of modern Euro-American history, which, for the most part, excluded the mountains. This marginalization of higher elevation zones, and our willingness to leave it unchallenged, was analogous to the larger lack of a "centered" vision of New England prehistory (Dincauze 1993a), allowing us to accept that what we saw—or did not—was what we got.

PROSPECTING FOR EVIDENCE OF A
GREEN MOUNTAIN PREHISTORY

Given the baseline assumption of a continuous but unevenly (nonrandomly) clustered distribution of archaeological materials across the landscape; the rich resource base and strategic location of the Green Mountains; archaeological precedents for use of the mountains elsewhere in North America; and a socio-economic argument for why no one had yet focused on this large area of our state, the next challenge was to design and implement a survey strategy. While the long-term goal was to generate a predictive model for site locations, the short-term goal was a somewhat humbler task: to test the "null hypothesis" that prehistoric sites were rarely located in the mountains (Lacy 1988). Thus, the two basic questions were where and how to look.

I adopted practical, traditional site locational criteria (i.e., reasonably level, well-drained areas with access to fresh water, strategic travelways, unique landmarks, and/or rich or unusual natural resources), with the following caveats: (1) eliminate elevation as a predictive factor in selecting areas (this is, after all, the main feature of the myth: mountains are high places); (2) reduce the size/scale of the landscape units being considered (e.g., one acre spots are just as likely to contain interesting sites as more extensive areas); (3) downplay soils as predictive factors, except as gross indicators (e.g., do not assume that correlations between site locations and soil types, based as they are on distributions in alluvial contexts, have anything to say about site distributions in the mountains); (4) stratify ruthlessly within this sampling universe (i.e., eliminate "low" and "moderate" zones from consideration); and (5) freely use intuition, input from Native informants, and other underutilized sources of information or inspiration in the field to determine "hot spots" within larger environmental contexts (this includes consideration of view sheds, personal comfort, or evidence of modern-day preferences).

Having located areas based on these guidelines, I needed to establish how to test an area with appropriate intensity given the nature, size, and density of the sites likely to occur in the area. I chose to cluster three 40-cm^2 shovel test pits every 10 m within a 100 × 100-m "survey unit" grid. This level of intensity reduced both the diameter of, and the density of materials within, clusters confidently detectable through the use of test pits (this intuitively logical observation is quantifiable through modeling [see Hasenstab 1986b]). Small diameter clusters of materials would not fall between the grid intervals; low artifact densities at any test point had a good chance of being detected. The survey units grids subsumed both the phenomena we wished to observe (all or parts of a site) and the small-scale topographic variability characteristic of the mountainous terrain. An additional consideration was economics; that is, testing within this survey unit could usually be completed in a timely fashion.

Because survey units were placed selectively in areas considered to be "hot," and vast areas of the potential "sampling universe" (minimally, the 350,000-acre National Forest) were ignored, the strategy should be considered "prospecting" rather than sampling (Wobst 1983). The initial intent, after all, was to demonstrate that sites existed and were detectable, not that we could document their general distribution. The benefits derived from prospecting intensively in small areas, however, are the increased likelihood of site encounter and a more rigorous definition of archaeological "empty spaces" (i.e., at least we can know with certainty that clusters of material smaller and less dense than a certain arbitrary but calculable figure are not present).

As a result of subsequent field work, more than thirty sites have been identified. They are located across a range of elevations, from 700 feet (above mean sea level) along Otter Creek to over 3,000 feet, with no apparent clustering at or preference for lower elevations (Lacy 1994).

Of these sites, four merit mention here since they vary from the assorted "lithic scatter" sites I had anticipated finding (and which comprise the majority of the site inventory), and as such represent a subset of sites worthy of further attention. One is a large site (more than twenty acres) containing a substantial amount of small and medium quartzite debitage and at least one domestic hearth feature. The site is located along the edge of, and atop a knoll next to, an expansive beaver meadow at slightly more than 2,000 feet elevation. Significant associations beyond the beaver meadow include beds of ginseng (used moderately by Native peoples prior to the Contact period, but collected more intensively as a marketable trade item after contact) and a substantial upland pond less than half a mile away. Research on local lithic sources, analysis of float samples from the hearth, further testing, and exposure of working areas are planned.

A second site is a kilometer-long quartzite quarry (see Lacy 1987, 1997) consisting of a continuous series of activity areas at or near the ground surface, located on the side of a mountain. The site has a strong association with a spring-fed upland pond (at 1,900 feet elevation) and its former outlet stream. Given the quarry's large size and relative lack of disturbance, it offers a rare opportunity to press beyond lithic sourcing issues to questions about the organization of production at these kinds of sites (Lacy 1997).

Finally, two scatter sites (not found through our testing strategy), which lie at the northern and southern summits of a linear mountain ridge providing a strategic vista over a significant drainage in southwestern Vermont, have significance as well. Beyond the archaeological and locational interest, these two sites are actively monitored and perhaps used (at least recognized) today by Native people. This was initially determined by the presence of tobacco pouches tied in branches above the scatters, and subsequently confirmed through contacts in the Abenaki community. One reason given today for the sites' location is the presence of numerous medicinal plants on the lower slopes leading up to the summit. We plan to pursue more oral historical information specific to this site and to add this microenvironment/landform to our predictive model.

CONCLUSION

On the basis of the evidence presented here, it is clear that Native Americans did use the mountains of Vermont during prehistory. The myth that they did not do so persisted until recently because of the social and economic forces that shape why, how, and where we do archaeology. We should therefore be cautioned against relying too heavily on known site inventories as indexes of how prehistoric people used the landscape. Given our biased sample of the region it is possible that this distribution reflects as much about how twentieth-century folks have been using and thinking about the landscape as it does about people in prehistory. This should have serious implications for archaeologists doing environmental review, although recognizing the implications and being able to do anything constructive about them in the short term may be two entirely different propositions.

Furthermore, we have evidence that sites in the uplands are not exclusively small, low-density scatters (e.g., Lacy 1987). But even if most of them are, there is no good reason to suppose that they are simply subsets of large lowland sites, nor that they would be insignificant based solely on their size or material richness. We need site-specific analyses of a number of sites from a range of environments and elevations before we can address this issue completely. Funding and conducting analysis on sites discovered within the National Forest remains a challenge in the present economic environment, but we are obligated and committed to following through on the sites we have identified to date.

Standardization of methods for site detection in the forested landscape of New England is one of the by-products of the CRM boom of the 1970s and 1980s (Dincauze et al. 1980; Dincauze and Lacy 1985; Lacy and Hasenstab 1983). This took place, for the most part, away from the uplands and mountains in areas which were more likely to contain large, high-density sites. Given the demonstrably broad range of variability in the density and distribution of archaeological materials, we should not expect that one strategy can yield equally sensitive results in all environments. This, too, has obvious implications for archaeologists in the regulatory and environmental review aspects of the business.

Parenthetically, there is yet another myth that must be addressed here: the notion that relations between archaeologists and Native Americans are inherently contentious (see Lacy 1989; Lacy and Bluto-Delvental 1995). This is relevant, because if we choose to pursue knowledge about the use of the mountains we may be opening a door to a set of sites with a disproportionately high percentage of sacred and traditional use components (as per Lacy et al. 1992). It has been my experience that archaeologists trained in traditional departments have not been provided with a perspective which allows them to readily appreciate the values and concerns of the Native peoples whose lives they may well be affecting. As we expand our search for the actual shape of site distributions, and the range of variability expressed by these distributions, we may also be opening new wounds. Establishing communication about cross-cultural ways of understanding sites and treating them respectfully will yield social, cultural, preservationist, and scientific benefits.

Finally, I think it would be ironic to presume that our present inventory gave us an accurate reading on hunter-gatherer behavioral systems if the small, dispersed sites likely to have been characteristic of these peoples' living patterns for the majority of the year are not an integral part of our data sets. Our present inventory is likely top heavy with aggregation points reflecting some seasonal and functional subset of those systems. We must recognize that there is potentially a whole population of uninvestigated sites which could introduce significant new variability into our interpretations. Since most of Vermont and northern New England's prehistory is the story of various hunter-gatherer economic adaptations to a "diversity of landscapes" (Dincauze 1980b), it may well be these marginalized "valleys" of the distributional continuum that we need to study in order to achieve a more complete and "centered" understanding of regional systems and broad-scale land-use patterns.

ACKNOWLEDGMENTS

Thanks to Dena Dincauze for her grand ideas, attention to detail and logic, and the insight to ask whether my take on "critical thinking" derived from cynicism or skepticism. (I'm still thinking about that one.) My appreciation to the Green Mountain National Forest for its ongoing support. And as always, thanks to Barbara, Jameson, and Mackenzie, who help me maintain a healthy perspective on how and where archaeology fits in the larger scheme of things.

8

Critical Theory in the Backwater of New England: Retelling the Third Millennium

Elena Filios

Critical theory, one of the stars in the constellation of postprocessual archaeology, has much potential to illuminate social relations in the distant past. Whether it is a distant black hole or an approaching comet has depended on where one stood, both paradigmatically, geographically, and temporally. Over the past decade, the central debates in archaeology have focused on the relationship between theory and method. Critical archaeology is one of a number of strains of postprocessual archaeology that developed in the 1980s (see Preucel [1991b] for an excellent review of postprocessual archaeologies).

All archaeologists must confront the dilemmas and solutions of gathering and interpreting data. Where paradigms differ are in what are considered relevant variables, appropriate methods, and adequate measures of evaluation. For critical theorists, interesting variables may range from the social to the ideological, modeling the social environment, or the meanings embodied in material culture. For many critical theorists, there are many ways to do science. The goal is not to provide the *truth*, but instead to provide a retelling of the past. One of the goals of science, critical or mainstream, is to identify variables, state the conditions under which they will vary, and the relationship among them in order to understand the range of variation in the data. Critical theory provides retellings that explore dynamic sets of variables and which demonstrate interesting variation in the data in new ways.

In this chapter, I provide a retelling of the third millennium (3000–2000 B.P.) in southern New England emphasizing social variables. Social variables are ones that focus on other people, that is, that focus on the social environment and social interactions as the sources of cultural change. I examine social variables in relation to hunter-gatherer use of space. These kinds of variables are often overlooked in favor of natural variables which characterize the climate and/or natural resources, or technology. A social model provides an opportunity to examine some strengths and weaknesses of a critical approach to the distant past and to offer a retelling of the cultural sequence which allows us to see variation in the data in new ways and to explain the variation differently. In fact, the retelling may not be a convincing argument, in the conventional sense of science. Instead, evaluation of this story is based on its ability to help us understand that even "science" is a story when applied to the deep past, and that a new social story is plausible. Several different, even contradictory, arguments can explain the same set of fragmentary data.

CRITICAL ARCHAEOLOGY

The focus of critical archaeology has been on making inequalities, power, and domination explicit. It is "critical" in that the questions asked reflect back on the process of doing archaeology and include (1) how we define research questions, (2) how we know what we know, and (3) what function our results have within the contemporary culture. The goal is to critique our understandings of the past and to relate them to the contemporary cultural context in which the archaeologist works (Leone et al. 1987). There is no single way to do critical archaeology. A variety of approaches which have been labeled symbolic, feminist, or Marxist have emerged over the last decade and a half. Respect for this variety is part of the critical perspective. However, most critical archaeology shares two general assumptions about the world and about culture.

First, following from the work of sociologist Anthony Giddens (1979), and based on the philosophical perspective of the Frankfurt School (Held 1980), culture is conceived of as a self-reflexive system of meaning. That is, culture is a set of meanings and understandings of the world that people use to actively participate in daily life. People constantly create, use, and manipulate culture. Material culture is the physical embodiment of this symbol system, conveying meaning and communicating information. Material culture actively creates the context for behavior: "The daily use of material items within different contexts recreates from moment to moment the framework of meaning within which people act" (Hodder 1982:10).

Second, critical archaeology seeks to explain the past, but at the same time to situate the work of the social scientists within the cultural context that produced it—to critique the theories, methods, and conclusions. The goal is to examine contexts of inequality, and to make explicit how those in power mask domination and inequality. Self-reflection is expected to lead to action aimed at changing current conditions of inequality. Analyses of the social context and biases of archaeologists are central to critical archaeology.

Critical archaeology has had its greatest success in offering alternative views of the past in historic and ethnohistoric contexts. The reasons for this concentration are several. Most historic contexts involve complex, state-level societies characterized by social stratification and inequality. Furthermore, in historic contexts, documents may provide the multiple lines of evidence necessary to make strong arguments for interpretations which would be tenuous based on arti-factual evidence alone. Documents provide an independent source of confirma-tion.

For archaeologists who work with the distant past, documents do not exist to aid in our understanding. Many problems beset the archaeology of the deep past, whether processual or postprocessual. The archaeological record is often very difficult to read because it is a combination of numerous events subject to disturbance, and biased by recovery techniques which can never collect all necessary data. Processual archaeologists developed middle-range theory to fill in the methodological gaps, to try to tease apart the individual behaviors that create the archaeological record. Dating to the 1800s (Trigger 1989), ethno-graphic analogy and ethnoarchaeology was resurrected by processual archaeolo-gists (Binford 1978; Schiffer 1976; Yellen 1977) and was used in part to address these gaps (Preucel 1991a:20). However, as Wylie (1989) and Wobst (1978) have both noted, ethnographic data are not unbiased but are themselves theory laden and subject to similar types of sociological influences that affect archaeo-logical data.

If doing critical archaeology of the deep past begins with these serious handicaps, what does it have to offer? The answer lies with equifinality (Filios 1990:3). Several different, often contradictory arguments may explain the same fragmentary set of facts. As Gero (1991:126) has noted, the facts themselves may be above dispute, but the explanations we choose will vary depending on the social context of the scientist.

NATURE VERSUS CULTURE

With its roots in the political-economics of capitalism, critical theory would seem to have little to offer to the student of the deep past or of egalitarian societies. Critical archaeologists interested in the prehistory of egalitarian societies have few precedents for spinning a yarn, a story, of a political econ-omy of egalitarianism. The originator of modern political economy, Marx, was little interested in precapitalist societies, except as stereotypical antecedents to capitalism (Bloch 1983). He did not focus his gaze on the dynamics, variation, or history of these societies. These dynamics and variation are often overlooked in the search for what people in the past were eating, wearing, and using as tools.

Many, though not all, of these prehistoric cultures were egalitarian societies. Egalitarian societies are those in which people have equal access to resources and equal access to prestige. There are no institutionalized inequalities, though there are, of course, differences among individuals (Fried 1967). Egalitarianism is one means of organizing people in social groups; it is not synonymous with hunting and gathering. Not all hunter-gatherers live in egalitarian societies, and not all egalitarian societies make their living by hunting and gathering. As Kelly (1995) has documented, there is a foraging spectrum. In the third millennium in New England, people made their living by hunting and gathering and lived in egalitarian societies.

But egalitarian societies are as varied, as changing, as cultural, as any other. The power of a political-economic analysis is the ability to see the competing interests, to visualize the conflict, to acknowledge the differences among people in what is often assumed to be a socially homogeneous and static way of life.

Furthermore, the appreciation in critical archaeology that there are multiple perspectives on reality applies to both archaeologists and prehistoric actors. Humans are conscious agents of their own culture. People are social actors, not automatons. Focusing on agency prompts us to conceive of egalitarian cultures as *cultural* rather than *natural*; to recognize that the social environment is as important as the natural environment in the operation of culture. People endow their environment with meaning. The resources available in the environment are culturally defined, as are the means appropriate to exploit them. Further, within any culture, various individuals or groups have competing and often contradictory agendas which change through time (Bender 1985). Critical archaeology of egalitarian societies strives to break open the technoenvironmental models of processual archaeology, and to include social variables in our explanations (Filios 1990).

SOCIAL VARIABLES AND SPACE

Prehistoric peoples of New England lived in a built environment. These hunter-gatherers, as did all peoples, constructed space as they adapted to their natural and social environments. Space is an active variable in the creation of the social environment. Space is not simply a passive variable, the stage set within which social action takes place but directly creates the context for social behavior, promoting or inhibiting it.

Prehistoric peoples constructed space through the creation of infrastructure, both technical facilities and social facilities, which represent resources that are beyond the capacity of individuals to provide for themselves. Technical facilities structure how production is organized and space is constructed. In particular, how facilities are constructed, where they are located, and how they were used has implications for the way production is organized. Not all technical facilities create infrastructure. For example, hunting snares are likely to be constructed, used, and maintained by individual hunters. In contrast, to be effective, drivelines require a group of people, thus, they create infrastructure. Furthermore, different facilities require different divisions of labor. The types of facilities and divisions of labor among prehistoric peoples affect patterns of mobility. Thus, research into the construction of technical facilities provides one methodological avenue for investigating divisions of labor and mobility, one means for retelling the past.

Three aspects of facilities may affect mobility. Mobility should be affected by production that is organized to increase cooperative labor, interdependence, and equity. In particular, I want to evaluate how long facilities may have taken to construct, how many people may have been involved in their construction and use, and how they are constructed. This will allow me to evaluate productive interdependence, and social mobility. One indication of cooperation relies on estimates of labor requirements for construction or use. Increased numbers of people required for construction or use indicates cooperation. Likewise, increased time required for construction indicates increased equity. Technical facilities thus have social as well as energetic consequences.

Social facilities include social institutions and systems of meaning such as (1) information (Moore 1981); (2) access to mates via social alliances bolstered by social knowledge such as genealogies (Wobst 1974); (3) social institutions, such as mediators or socially significant items of nonlocal material and the social networks that provide them (Root 1984; Wiessner 1982); and (4) investments that have a delayed return such as land terracing, or social investments which require long periods of learning (Gilman 1981).

THE THIRD MILLENNIUM IN NEW ENGLAND

The third millennium in New England was a time of considerable cultural change and social diversity (Dincauze 1990). At least three cultural units were probably interacting in the region. People who used objects of the Orient, Meadowood, and Small-Stemmed stone tool traditions occupied the region simultaneously (Dincauze 1968:88). The first ceramics appear in the region at the beginning of the period, at approximately 3000 B.P. (Dincauze 1990; Lavin 1986). The significance of this technological change is unknown, but pottery changed the way production of containers was organized. Further, interaction with the people and ideas coming out of the Adena area of the Midwest probably contributed to the social dynamism of the period. Dincauze (1990:28) sees a settlement pattern shift during the time, with more numerous, small sites in the uplands, and larger sites in the lowlands, a pattern which McBride and Dewar (1981) also identify for the Connecticut River valley. We can expect that issues of mobility and autonomy may have been contested in this social environment, as my analysis of the Flynn site aims to illustrate.

The Flynn Site

The Flynn site, located on the Housatonic River in western Connecticut (Figure 8.1), was excavated by the American Indian Archaeological Institute in 1980 and 1981. Flynn is located on the first terrace above the river, between the present floodplain and a kame. There is a stream to the south forming the southern boundary of the site (Figure 8.2). The total area excavated was approximately 250 square meters.

Several radiocarbon ages suggest that Flynn was occupied during the beginning of the third millennium. Following the abandonment, slack water covered

Figure 8.1
Location of Flynn Site in Northwest Connecticut

the site, and a sterile sand deposit sealed the third millennium occupation levels. A C-13 corrected age on charcoal from the slack water deposit of 2585 ± 185 B.P. (GX-09361) provides a *terminus ante quem*. A second age of 3160 ± 620 B.P. (TX-4166), based on a charcoal sample taken from a fire-cracked rock hearth, gives an estimate of the occupation itself. The assemblage from the site consists of 24 fire-cracked rock features, mixed midden deposits and other features, and lithic debris of chert, "jasper," quartz, quartzite, and argillite. Thirty-six bifaces and more than 1,500 pieces of debitage were recovered. Projectile points are Orient and a variety of small-stemmed quartz points (Ritchie 1971). A small amount of grit-tempered pottery was recovered.

One of the most interesting aspects of the third millennium occupation at Flynn are the numerous fire-cracked rock features. Rock features at Flynn represent technical facilities that would be permanent features on the landscape during its period of use. Based on estimates I elaborate on below, the features required 160 person hours to construct. This much labor may indicate cooperation, and

Figure 8.2
Plan Map of Excavation Block at the Flynn Site

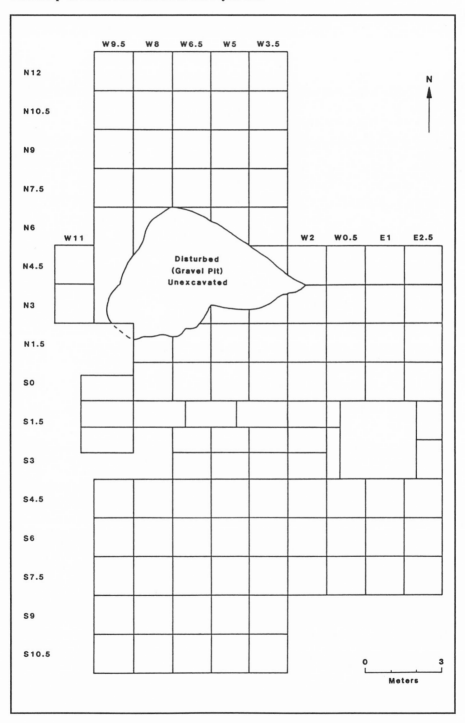

such investment would tend to attract people repeatedly to the same space for prolonged use. Some of the rock features are very thick and may indicate repeated use. In prehistoric geography, Flynn may have become "the place with the rocks," a significant cultural feature on the landscape.

The rock features at Flynn range from small hearths, about 30 cm in diameter, to large concentrations, also known as rock platforms (Figure 8.3). In all there were twenty-four fire-cracked rock features located in the approximately 250 m² excavated. Seven of these rock features measured more than 1 m in diameter. Only about half of the features discovered were removed and the rocks weighed. The total weight of fire-cracked rock removed from Flynn is nearly one ton. We can conservatively estimate that the total feature assemblage was comprised of about 4,000 pounds of rock.

Assuming that the rocks for the features came from the kame to the west of the site, a maximum distance of 100 m, an estimate of a range of time required to collect and transport the rock which was removed and weighed can be reached. Based on an estimate of 160 pounds per hour for a strong man, the rock features at Flynn represent a *minimum* of twenty-five person-hours. For a smaller woman already burdened with a load or with children, an estimate of

Figure 8.3
Plan Drawing of Feature 11 at the Flynn Site

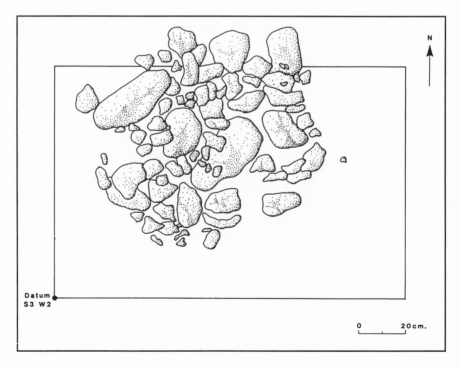

Datum
S3 W2

0   20cm.

twenty-five pounds per hour is reasonable. At a rate of twenty-five pounds per hour, 160 person-hours were required to collect and transport the rock.

Using Lee's (1979) estimate of a forty-two-hour work week for the Ju/'hoansi, this represents a minimum of 0.6 person-weeks and a maximum of 3.8 person-weeks. Therefore, the rock features at Flynn suggest a significant investment in time.

Many of the features at Flynn are "platforms," or large concentrations of rock. Platforms appear at more than half a dozen sites in southern New England, such as the Lighthouse site in northwestern Connecticut (Feder 1994), and Shattuck Farm on the Merrimack River in Massachusetts (Luedtke 1985). They are often assumed to be communal fish-drying facilities or meat-smoking facilities (see for example Feder 1994:117).

To evaluate the hypothesis that the platforms at Flynn are communal facilities we need to analyze how they were constructed and used. The composition of the individual features may reflect cooperative labor to make or to use. Most of the rocks in these features would require only one person to transport. Cooperative labor for construction was not required for moving most of the rock.

Determining how the features were used is more problematic. Few organic remains were recovered from flotation of the feature fill. Some mammal bone, numerous charred nut shells and several oyster shells, all of which may relate to the function of the feature, were recovered. While it would be tempting to suggest that these were fish-drying platforms because of the proximity to the river, no fish remains were recovered. Deer meat smoking or drying is more plausible. Soil acidity and preservation problems result in a lack of data, and the function of the features cannot be firmly determined.

Size and structure of the features may be more indicative of their use. Rocks in many of the smaller features fit together suggesting that they were fractured in use and are in situ. These are likely hearths for cooking or for heating of small groups of people. However, size alone is not a good indication of use. Large features do not necessarily suggest cooperative use. Apart from size, we need to demonstrate in situ deposition. Several of the larger features are scattered. None of the rocks in these features fit together suggesting that they were redeposited. These features are probably discard piles.

A third kind of feature at Flynn is a large, cohesive rock hearth. Within these features there are usually several rocks which fit together suggesting in situ fracture. Also, these features may include several larger rocks which would have been easier to transport by more than one person, suggesting some cooperative labor, either in construction or use.

Collectively, the rock features at Flynn indicate a large investment in time, an investment which people would tend not to walk away from. Analysis of construction aspects of features at Flynn suggest that some of them generated conditions for productive interdependence and cooperation. They thus may indicate that mobility was constrained, that people returned to the site repeatedly to use these technical facilities.

Social Facilities at Flynn

In addition to technical facilities, social facilities act to shape the built environment of the hunter-gatherers who occupied the Flynn site. Access to social networks is one of several variables I identified as indicating social facilities. I presume that the presence of nonlocal lithic materials indicates access to social networks. This assumes that lithic materials were not procured personally by the users. Raw materials from Flynn were identified macroscopically.

The distribution of raw material types at Flynn is shown in Figure 8.4. In New England, red chert is often termed Pennsylvania jasper indicating its source, although local sources have been recently identified in southeastern Massachusetts (Luedtke 1987) and northwest Connecticut (Nicholas 1990). It is separated here from other varieties of chert. Jasper comprises about eight percent of the total. Note that these other cherts comprise almost 60 percent of the total. There are few bedrock sources for cherts in southern New England, and I have estimated that they would have to have been transported at least 75 km. Using an estimate of a day's walk at 25 km, this represents a three-day distance. The remaining materials, including quartz and quartzite, are available locally. Twenty-two percent of the collection is quartz; seven percent is quartzite. Nonlocal materials and the social networks that supplied them were important to the people who occupied Flynn during the third millennium.

Figure 8.4
Relative Frequencies of Raw Material Types Present in Flaked-stone Assemblage from the Flynn Site

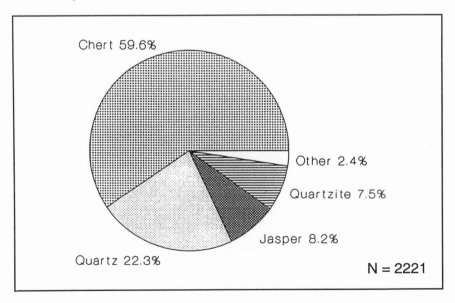

PROBLEMS AND A THEORETICAL SOLUTION

Several problems arise from the methods employed to evaluate the investment in facilities, both technical and social. One problem stems from the way rock features were excavated. Running out of time, the excavators exposed features, mapped them, and then back filled. The rocks were not removed or weighed, biasing the results, and reducing the estimate of time invested in these facilities. Perhaps more serious, is my assumption that *time* is the critical variable in evaluating the significance of these features, reflecting my own ethnocentrism.

Finally, reconstructing social networks through the identification of nonlocal materials is problematic. Chert sources vary considerably, and macroscopic identifications are notably unreliable (Luedtke 1992). Further, lithic sources are not so distant as to be necessarily accessed through social networks alone.

The origin of native copper, long thought to be the true sign of extraregional trade during the third millennium, poses a similar problem. Local sources for native copper, most especially in glacial drift, have recently been identified. Levine (1996, Chapter 12, this volume) explores implications for our models of hunter-gatherers and their exchange systems in New England. Similar critiques may be applied to the exchange of stone.

Do such methodological problems leave the critical archaeologist in the dirt? Many of these same problems confront archaeologists who seek to explain past behavior by recourse to ecological models and distributions of natural resources. We can evaluate some of the ideas about hunter-gatherer construction of space by returning to a more theoretical consideration of the problem.

Studies of hunter-gatherer settlement are confronted by an interesting paradox. It is widely recognized that mobility is related to production. It is also widely recognized that mobility is a means of creating and maintaining egalitarian society. Often, models of hunter-gatherer settlement pattern stress one perspective or the other, relating mobility to resource procurement or to social relations.

Probably the most well-known example of models of hunter-gatherer mobility that relates mobility to production is research by Lewis Binford. Binford (1980) has suggested two patterns of hunter-gatherer mobility strategies, which are the ends of a continuum: foraging and logistical. He relates these two patterns to resource structure and resource distribution. He suggests that hunter-gatherers living in environments characterized by dispersed resources tend to follow a foraging strategy. In contrast, hunter-gatherers who live in environments where resources are clustered and seasonal tend to follow logistical strategies.

Even though Binford recognizes the continuum of mobility strategies, his two named categories lead many of us to expect dual patterns of settlement. (Archaeologists, like everyone, tend to think in categories, not continua.) Sites of people following a logistical strategy should tend to all look different, whereas sites of people following a foraging strategy would all tend to look the same.

However, mobility is also a means for maintaining egalitarian society. For example, Richard Lee (1979) has suggested that the Ju\'hoansi "vote with their feet." The Ju\'hoansi move to avoid conflict and to maintain their autonomy. Patterns of mobility are affected by both energy capture and by social dynamics.

One way of resolving the paradox between these two approaches is to recognize that production systems are affected by social dynamics as well as energetic requirements. Work is always carried out within a social context. Issues of egalitarianism are contested in the productive sphere.

Analyzing how work is organized is one method of making variations in the social context of work visible. At one end of the scale, work that is organized so that individuals are independent and returns are immediate are those in which we would expect to see the greatest degree of autonomy and the most mobility. At the other end of the scale, work is organized so that it is necessarily cooperative, interdependent, and returns are delayed. At this end of the scale, we would expect the least autonomy and the least mobility. These are the extremes. We should expect considerable variation in the ways hunter-gatherers organize work and in mobility and autonomy. Furthermore, we should expect different aspects of production systems to be contradictory as issues of autonomy are contested, some aspects reflecting more interdependence and some more autonomy. We should also expect considerable variation in settlement size, and structure. My research (Filios 1990) has demonstrated that third millennium sites vary considerably in features, and in scale of procurement of raw material.

Taken together the discussion of the two variables at the Flynn site may point the direction for a retelling of the third millennium. The goal here has not been to provide a totally convincing argument, but a plausible one. An alternative explanation is that the features and debris at the Flynn site are the result of consciously created and culturally defined work practices and social relations. The site is one which was repeatedly visited, with permanent facilities providing opportunities for cooperative labor and social aggregation. In the complex social environment of the time, it may have been a place where egalitarian social relations were reinforced or challenged.

The result of modeling mobility in this way is that variation is more expectable and explainable. Rather than two types of mobility, we should expect a range of variation in settlement types. Rather than explaining this variation as random error or sample bias, we take it as the result of both productive and the social processes. We thus arrive at a model that links the political with the economic, a model of the political economy of hunter-gatherer mobility.

The lesson here is that we can spin many theories about society or subsistence. By using some low-tech methods, we can evaluate these theories and expose some surprising variation, thereby developing a critical archaeology of the deep past, and a retelling of part of the third millennium in southern New

England. As a result, we do not constantly recreate the same cultural-historical categories, for example, Late Archaic or Early Woodland.

In New England archaeology, typology is rampant and it limits our vision. Typology is useful when it usefully manages variation, ordering the data so that variation can be seen and explained. However, in New England, typology tends to overwhelm the variation in data. When the focus is on determining the time and cultural affiliation of the site's occupants, diagnostic projectile point types (Ritchie 1971) are useful in ordering the data. However, projectile point types may be unrelated to social variables and can get in the way of understanding variation related to these variables.

Critical archaeology provides a means to productively use the sometimes confusing array of variation in the data to conceptualize dynamic social relations. As a result, New England no longer looks like an archaeological backwater, but the center of the pool.

ACKNOWLEDGMENTS

My career in archaeology has been shaped by my relationship with Dena Dincauze. She has always provided rigorous critique, which has benefited my ideas, challenged my spirit, strengthened my argument, and sharpened my prose. My appreciation of the third millennium, its complexities and dynamics, were developed through listening to her lectures and discussing my work with her. Her legacy to archaeology is as much in what she has given to her students as in her own writings. For that I am grateful.

I would also like to thank Russell Handsman and the staff of the American Indian Archaeological Institute of Washington, Connecticut, for providing access to the Flynn site materials. I am also grateful to Michael Brault, Robert Paynter, and Martin Wobst for their assistance. Maureen Manning-Bernatzky, who drafted Figures 8.1, 8.2, and 8.3, also has earned my thanks. Finally, the editors of this volume, Mary Ann Levine, Michael Nassaney, and Ken Sassaman, provided helpful critiques and useful advice, which have greatly improved the chapter.

9

Fishing, Farming, and Finding the Village Sites: Centering Late Woodland New England Algonquians

Robert J. Hasenstab

In a recent article Dincauze (1993a) argued that we should not evaluate New England Algonquians in terms of how they measure up against their neighbors to the west—the Iroquois—who have their own unique identity. Rather, we should study Algonquian culture in its own right and, if anything, contrast it with that of the Iroquois. We should seek to identify what makes New England Algonquian culture unique from all other cultures in Native North America.

What makes New England Algonquians unique is perhaps best explained by their environment and their adaptation to it. New England marks the northern-most extent of viable maize horticulture along the Atlantic coast of North America (Mulholland 1988). At the same time, it marks the southernmost extent of migration of Atlantic Salmon and certain other anadromous fish species (Carlson 1988c). Thus New England Algonquians were in a position to exploit both the rich anadromous fish resources of the North Atlantic and the bountiful tropical cultigens of the southern latitudes. Osborn (1977) has pointed out that some of the densest human populations around the globe have arisen where high-protein, reliable marine resources have been juxtaposed against high-calorie cultivated grain crops. Indeed, in certain parts of North America, unusually high population densities were attained in locations of abundant fish resources and optimal maize habitat, for example in the meander belt zone of the Mississippi River valley and along the shores of Lake Simcoe in the Huron area of Ontario.

There are suggestions that New England Algonquians exploited both re-sources. Thomas (1976) cited two ethnohistorically documented Native calen-dars—one from the Connecticut River valley and another from the Kennebec River valley in Maine. Both calenders are defined in terms of the seasonal cycles revolving around maize horticulture and fishing. Thomas pointed out that neither calendar mentions hunting, suggesting that terrestrial game resources were a secondary concern.

One would expect that if Algonquians were reaping the benefits of fishing and farming, they could have developed populations at least as visible archaeologically as those of their Iroquoian neighbors. Certainly the Atlantic Coastal Plain has a milder climate—more favorable for maize—than that of the Iroquois homeland of upstate New York and Ontario. And the Algonquians' fish resources, which come from the sea, were far more reliable and less exhaustible than were the deer herds on which the Iroquois depended for their protein. Yet the archaeological record for New England shows a meager and scattered Algonquian population. Nowhere in New England are recorded the kinds of villages that are documented in the Iroquois area, namely, large, multiacre aggregates of longhouses surrounded by palisades. Is this lack of village sites an accurate reflection of Algonquian settlement, or are large villages simply not recognized because of ethnohistoric biases, poor preservation, or inadequate archaeological methods? This question will serve as the subject of inquiry for this chapter. I argue that New England Algonquians possessed a unique potential to develop large population aggregates and village settlements, and that in fact they did but that evidence for it has yet to be recognized by archaeologists.

WHERE ARE THE VILLAGES IN NEW ENGLAND?

The question of whether New England Algonquians ever developed villages was addressed in a symposium organized by the late Peter Thorbahn entitled "Where are the Woodland Villages" (see Kerber 1988b). Before the symposium participants could address the question, they had to first define what a village is and how one would appear in the archaeological record. Thorbahn (1988:48) stated that a village is a settlement containing multifamily dwellings, features, and a variety of artifact categories. This implies a place where large social groups would have lived for an extended period (long enough to construct features) and would have carried out a range of activities—to be distinguished from special purpose sites such as resource procurement stations or sacred sites.

Luedtke (1988:58) adds that a village ought to have a regular plan. This would distinguish it from a recurrently occupied base camp where dwellings might be erected haphazardly from one occupation to the next. A village should have a deliberate structure, reflecting planning and organization among a set of social units, such as bands or clans. Luedtke argued further that a village ought to be occupied most of the year, echoing Thorbahn's criteria for artifact diversity. This would distinguish it from a seasonal aggregation site, such as a fishing encampment. It should be noted, however, that even in the Iroquois area, villages were not always occupied year round. White (1963) pointed out that earlier villages were vacated during winter months for hunting forays and in some areas, such as the Huron area, villages were vacated during summer months so that women could tend remote corn fields.

Thus, an example of a village in New England might appear as a ring of wigwams spaced around a central area with a variety of features and artifacts represented. To date, such an archaeological plan has not been identified.

UMASS RESEARCH: WHERE ARE THE VILLAGES
IN THE CONNECTICUT RIVER VALLEY?

When I began graduate school at University of Massachusetts–Amherst (UMass) in the fall of 1978, it was an exciting time for Late Woodland research. Dena Dincauze's seminar on New England Indian Ethnohistory was enrolled beyond capacity. Paynter and Thorbahn (1975) had recently completed a survey of the I-391 corridor in the Connecticut River valley and had developed a predictive model for Late Woodland villages, resulting in identification of the presumed village site of Indian Crossing in Chicopee, Massachusetts. Ulrich (1979b) was preparing to lead data recovery at the Indian Crossing site and was writing a dissertation on the Connecticut River valley Late Woodland, studying soil maps in an attempt to predict village locations. Peter Thomas (1979a) was just completing his dissertation on Contact period villages in the valley. Moore and Root (1979) were completing a Survey and Planning Grant on aboriginal anadromous fish exploitation in the valley. Paynter (1979) published results of a symposium held on the middle Connecticut River valley. Later that year, a conference was held at UMass and that served as the birth of the Conference on New England Archaeology, which remains active to date. At that conference, Dena Dincauze (1980b) delivered her landmark paper on research priorities. She stressed the need for research on the development of horticulture among New England Algonquians. She also stressed the need to examine Algonquians in their own right—a theme she was forced to repeat thirteen years later (Dincauze 1993a). In 1980 Dincauze led a graduate seminar titled "Sociocultural Boundaries in Archaeology" in which we examined Algonquian ethnic identity vis-à-vis their Iroquois neighbors to the west.

Despite this flurry of interest in Late Woodland archaeology and the research it inspired in the Connecticut River valley, not a single village, save the Contact period fort excavated by Thomas (1979a), was identified. Dincauze (1980a) led a field school in Northfield and another in Hadley, both examining alleged aboriginal fortifications, only to determine that the earthworks examined were historic field markers. The Indian Crossing site did not materialize as the horticultural village it was thought to be. Neither evidence of structures (i.e., postmold patterns) nor maize remains were found during the dig (although a single corn kernal turned up in the lab years later). Subsequent multiyear UMass field schools led by Art Keene likewise failed to identify villages—one seeking the village of Norwottuck on the Northampton Meadows and another seeking Pocumtuck in Deerfield.

This string of disappointments, combined with similar negative evidence in southeastern Massachusetts and Rhode Island, along with the publication of

Ceci's (1982) hypothesis that villages were a Contact phenomenon, led researchers to seriously doubt whether Late Woodland villages ever existed in New England. The consensus of the "Woodland Village" symposium participants was that despite the scarcity and even lack of evidence for pre-Contact Late Woodland villages throughout New England, sufficient survey has not been conducted to rule out the possibility that such sites actually exist. Just because no villages have been found does not mean they do not exist (Thorbahn 1988: 55).

The issues presented in that symposium will be reviewed here and will be further examined. I argue that maize horticulture was adopted in a substantial way and that villages did develop, but that archaeologists to date have not identified them. I compare the situation in New England with that in New York and attempt to explain why Late Woodland villages have been recognized in the Iroquois area but not in New England.

WHY DO WE NOT SEE THE VILLAGES?

In Thorbahn's (1988:55) lead article for his symposium, he posed three possible explanations for why we have not identified any Late Woodland villages in southern New England. These are (1) "There were no Native American villages prior to the historic period," (2) they have been "destroyed by Euro-American development," and (3) they are "very hard to find and recognize." I will evaluate each of these explanations.

The Ceci Hypothesis: There Were No Pre-Contact Villages

I have named this explanation after its author, the late Lynn Ceci (1982). I believe that this hypothesis is probably true in certain parts of New England where nucleated settlements were limited by the environment. For example, in eastern Massachusetts, Luedtke (1988:63) argued that the soils are so poor and patchy that only small plots could be cultivated here and there, thus accounting for the ethnohistorically observed scattered settlement pattern. Her claim that the environment in this subregion could not support consolidated settlements may very well be correct. Likewise, in the Worcester uplands of central Massachusetts, Hoffman (1989) rightfully argued that the climate is too cold to have provided an adequate frost-free growing season and thus could not have supported reliable horticulture.

In other subregions of New England, however, I believe both the climate and the soils would have permitted productive horticulture and that villages could have developed. Probably the most obvious such region is the lowland valley of the Connecticut River—the largest river in New England. There is, in fact, ethnohistoric evidence that villages existed in this region prior to contact with the English. In 1634, prior to the English arrival in the valley and the year of a severe smallpox epidemic among the Natives, William Bradford (1912) described a village in the middle Connecticut River valley north of the Dutch fort at Hartford:

Ther was a company of people lived in the country, up above in the river of Conigtecut, a great way from their trading house ther, and were enimise to those Indeans which lived aboute them, and of whom they stood in some fear (b[e]ing a stout people). About a thousand of them had inclosed them selves in a forte, which they had strongly palissadoed about. 3 or 4 Dutch men went up in the begining of winter to live with them, to gett their trade. . . . But their enterprise failed, for it pleased God to visite these Indeans with a great sicknes, and shuch a mortalitie that of a 1000, above 900 and a halfe of them dyed, and many of them did rott above ground for want of buriall. (p. 193)

Unfortunately, this is only the beginning of English settlement in the valley and marks the beginning of most modern historical research (e.g., Thomas 1979a). By the time the English arrived, smallpox had decimated an estimated 90 percent of the Native population in the valley and probably had a profound impact on Native culture. Mulholland (1988:145) reports a lack of ethnohistoric documentation for inland portions of southern New England, noting that most early accounts are given by explorers sailing along the coast. Thus, we have very little information on the lifeways of Native groups at the time of contact in inland riverine valleys.

In contrast, the Iroquois were less affected by the smallpox epidemics and retained much of their native culture throughout the seventeenth century. Snow (1992b:Table 2) reports a reduction in population of northern Iroquoians during the seventeenth century from 22,000 to 8,920, indicating a survival rate of 40 percent overall. During that time they were thoroughly documented by Jesuit missionaries and others who produced a comparatively vivid picture of native life.

In summary, it appears from the limited ethnohistoric record that villages did exist in parts of southern New England at the time of contact, but we have very limited descriptive information for them.

Villages Sites Destroyed by Euro-American Development

The second of Thorbahn's explanations probably has merit. Iroquois villages in New York state generally escaped the impacts of Euro-American development. There villages tend to be in upland locations away from navigable waterways where most Euro-American settlement occurred. This is because the Iroquois sought remote, defensible locations and because they cultivated upland limestone till soils which supported nitrogen fixation by beans (Hasenstab 1996, n.d.). Thus, most Iroquois village archaeological sites survived historic urbanization which typically occurred along rivers.

In New England, by contrast, the uplands are not productive agricultural areas. The soils, derived from igneous and metamorphic bedrock, are acidic, rocky, and shallow (Hunt 1967:181–183). Upland intervales, which contain patches of rich alluvial soil, were probably unfavorable for climatic reasons. In the higher elevations temperatures decrease with altitude and the rugged terrain promotes cold-air drainage into the narrow valley bottoms, creating frost pockets. Instead, only the broad, lowland riverine floodplains provided both the soils and climate favorable for horticulture. It was precisely these valleys that were the focus of Euro-American settlement and hence destruction of archaeological sites (Snow 1980:320).

It has been suggested that the major falls along the rivers, representing prime fishing locations, were foci of aboriginal settlement and at the same time were the locations of massive nineteenth-century industrial development which would have wiped out archaeological sites. Such sites would have included fishing stations but probably not horticultural settlements. The falls sites tended to be a focus of Middle Archaic settlement, such as, for example, the Neville site in Manchester, New Hampshire (Dincauze 1976), or the WMECO site at Turners Falls, Massachusetts (Chapter 14, this volume; Thomas 1980). These fall-line locations are characterized by hard, rugged bedrock and sandy outwash soils and would not have been favorable areas for horticulture. It is unlikely that Late Woodland horticultural sites—if they existed—would have been located in these mill-town areas.

Rather, it was the early seventeenth-century English settlements that probably impacted Contact-period village sites. Thomas (1976:4) has pointed out that the initial English settlements in the Connecticut River valley—at Agawam, Hadley, and Deerfield, for example—were sited at the locations of former aboriginal maize fields. Given that high ground on the floodplain was at a premium, it is likely that both English and Natives alike chose the same ground on which to place their settlements. It is possible that these historic towns have been superimposed over earlier, Contact period villages.

Finally, another type of site that may have been destroyed by Euro-American development is the coastal village. Because of the requirement of native horticulture for limey soils, maize fields were likely located on extensive shell middens. For example, in Trumbull's (1818:43) review of Connecticut tribes he noted: "At Milford, the Indian name of which was Wopowage, there were great numbers; not only in the centre of the town, but south of it, at Milford point. In the fields there, the shells brought on by the original inhabitants are said to be so deep, that they never have been ploughed, or dug, even to this day." Unfortunately, it was these same shell middens that were mined by early farmers as a source of lime for their fields (Ceci 1984; Ruffin 1844). It is likely that any village sites situated atop shell middens would have been hauled away.

In summary, both early Euro-American riverine settlement and the systematic destruction of coastal shell middens could account for the apparent lack of Late Woodland village sites in New England. However, because native horticulture was shifting and fields would have been moved from place to place, at least some locations of horticultural settlements should have survived historic land alterations.

Village Sites are "Hard to Find"

Of Thorbahn's three explanations for lack of villages, I favor this one the most. Perhaps the main reason why there are so many more recognized Iroquoian villages than Algonquian is simply their geomorphic context. As I stated above, Iroquois villages tend to be in upland locations, in fertile agricultural areas that are under the plow today. Artifacts are visible in the plowed fields, signaling the presence of sites below, and when the plow zone is stripped away, the subsoil surface reveals an essentially two-dimensional site in plan view (see Ritchie and Funk 1973).

By contrast, New England Algonquian villages would be situated in stratified alluvial floodplains. Mulholland (1988:152) noted the major tribal groups in the Connecticut River valley at the time of contact were located within the range of fertile floodplain soils. In fact, the tribal clusters that Thomas (1976:4) outlined were situated at the major zones of floodplain alluvium throughout the valley: the Sequins at Hartford, the Tunxis in the Farmington valley, the Agawams at Springfield, the Woronocos along the Westfield River, the Norwottucks at the Hadley/Northampton Meadows, the Pocumtucks in the Deerfield lowland, and the Squakeags at the Northfield Meadows.

Unfortunately, any village sites on the floodplain will be "hard to find." Jahns (1947) reported that the 1936 flood alone deposited an average of eleven inches of flood silt throughout the Connecticut River valley. That is essentially the thickness of an entire plow zone which likely has obscured many sites. Moreover, Lindner (1988) has demonstrated the difficulties of identifying archaeological sites on floodplains given the dynamics of fluvial processes including erosion, deposition, and redeposition.

Any sites that are fortunate enough to have survived flood action will be buried by alluvium, stratified, and essentially three-dimensional in structure. Unlike two-dimensional Iroquois sites, three-dimensional stratified alluvial sites will be extremely difficult to peel away to reveal living floors and expose settlement patterns. For example, at the Indian Crossing site, our sampling strategy consisted of a grid of meter squares excavated to depths of 2 m. It is extremely difficult to expose broad-area settlement patterns with this sort of sample of "telephone-booth" excavation units. Meter squares revealing features were expanded to expose the limits of the features, but not beyond where the activity areas of their users would have been.

Similar problems with floodplain testing were experienced several kilometers down river in West Springfield at a sixty-eight-acre parcel of prehistoric horticultural potential (Mulholland et al. 1983a). There, backhoe test pits measuring roughly a meter wide by 2.5 m long by 2.5 to 3 m deep were excavated to examine the subsoil. Three possible fire hearths and five stained soil horizons were encountered, most being one to two meters below surface (Mulholland et al. 1983a:39–45, figures 19–27). Although the investigators considered "the possibility that the features observed are small portions of the larger sites," those sites were not sought because "the cost of locating them would be high"

(Mulholland et al. 1983a:44). I contend that the opening of a sample area could have been affordable, but apparently the investigators felt such testing would not be justified given the perceived low artifact density (see below). The effect of their decision to dismiss the site was to satisfy the client and avoid the risk of exposing potentially significant results and added mitigation costs.

In recognizing the difficulty of testing floodplains, Peter Thorbahn (1984) himself devised a methodology for analyzing such samples from stratified deposits. Termed "depositional mosaics," his method compares artifact distributions across space at various levels. It assumes a "telephone-booth" type of sample unit and implicitly admits the impossibility of observing broad-area contiguous exposures—exposures that Luedtke (1988:58) argued are necessary for recognizing village sites.

Another difficulty of identifying Late Woodland horticultural villages, even in the Iroquois area, would be their comparatively low artifact and feature density owing to their brief period of occupation resulting from shifting horticulture. Many archaeologists do not realize just how low the density of such sites can be and what to expect in their test units. Thorbahn (1988:51), for example, in his definitive paper, expressed his disappointment at the artifact densities at the Swift site and his reason for dismissing it as a possible village—the densities being 152 artifacts per square meter at Locus I and 22 at Locus II. He stated: "Frequencies of artifacts per unit area are among the lowest that have been reported for sites in the region" (Thorbahn 1988:51). However, the regional sites to which he refers are typically multicomponent base camps reoccupied for thousands of years. Perhaps a bit more credible in this regard is the West Springfield study cited above, which recovered only seventeen artifacts from eight of eighty-one test pits. The authors concluded that "the project has an unusually low prehistoric artifact and feature density" (Mulholland et al. 1983a:iv).

When examining actual horticultural village sites, artifact densities are not as high as one might expect. For example, at the Gannagaro village near Rochester, New York—a National Historic Landmark—a survey of 179 shovel tests produced two or more artifacts in only 18 percent of the tests (Hasenstab 1984: Figure 7; Hayes et al. 1978). Even lower densities were observed from the Squakeag village of Fort Hill in Hinsdale, New Hampshire, the subject of Thomas's dissertation. There, excavation of some 300 contiguous square meters revealed an artifact density of 1.4 items per square meter (Hasenstab 1984: Figure 5; Thomas 1979a:Figure 19). In short, encounters of village sites by standard test pitting strategies are likely to be dismissed as mere "lithic scatters" or low-density use areas.

Finally, one other difficulty in finding Late Woodland villages is in identifying their overt signs, namely, palisade fortifications. In New York there is a one-to-one correspondence between palisade earthworks and villages. Most Iroquois villages have been identified by their palisade embankments. Conversely, most earth embankments encountered on the landscape and mapped by early archaeologists were of aboriginal origin. Euro-American settlement did not begin in upstate New York until after the American Revolution. Shortly thereafter, land surveys for the Erie Canal—construction of which began in 1817—began recording earthworks, all of which were built by preceding native inhabitants. By 1851 the Smithsonian Institution had compiled a comprehensive inventory of these sites (Squier 1851), which today serves as a baseline for Iroquois archaeology.

Such is not the case in New England, where Euro-American settlement began in the mid-1600s. By the time antiquarians began writing about archaeological sites in the late nineteenth century, 200 years of Euro-American farming had modified the landscape. Ancient fence embankments constructed of earth had been built, abandoned, and were grown over by large trees. These so-called "ha-has" (see Bullen 1942) confound any attempts by modern archaeologists to identify aboriginal fortifications. Dincauze (1980a) experienced this difficulty in her Northfield field school. I also led an investigation of an embankment in Greenfield which turned out to be the Deerfield Common Fence surveyed in 1793 (Hoit 1793). Most recently, in 1995, the UMass field school under the supervision of Elizabeth Chilton (personal communication, 1995) excavated an alleged embankment of the Pocumtuck fort which turned out to be an historic fence line.

An additional factor confounding the "ha-ha" problem is that New England Indian forts were not necessarily synonymous with villages, as were the Iroquois forts. Iroquois forts are invariably associated with cemeteries and refuse middens and contain remains of longhouses. In New England, on the other hand, forts were often used solely at times of siege and did not serve as habitation sites (Luedtke 1988:62; Mulholland 1988:154). Perhaps this is because habitation areas were on the vulnerable floodplain while forts were placed in the rugged uplands. In the Iroquois area this separation was unnecessary because both fields and forts were in uplands. In sum, Algonquian villages may not have the advantage of being marked by palisade enclosures, and any enclosures found are liable to be devoid of any artifactual or feature remains, thus exacerbating the difficulty of finding either site, let alone a pair of them.

Many scholars have thus argued that Late Woodland Algonquian villages either never existed or have all been destroyed. I, however, believe that they did exist and that they remain on the landscape but simply have not been identified.

EVIDENCE THAT HORTICULTURAL VILLAGES EXISTED

It appears at the time of contact that horticulture was a deeply rooted part of Native life in New England. It was an important part of ideology, as revealed by Thomas's (1976) calender study cited above. For example, in the Connecticut River valley, seasons were reckoned in horticultural terms: "when they set Indian Corne"; "when ye women weed their corne"; "when they hill Ind Corne"; "when Ind Corne is eatable"; and "ye middle between harvest & eating Ind Corne" (Pynchon 1645–1650; Thomas 1976). Maize was a major component of the native food economy (Bennet 1955; Butler 1948). Huge quantities of maize were grown and stored, as evidenced by the Pocumtucks who had enough corn in storage that they could easily sell 500 bushels to the English settlers of Connecticut in March of 1632 (Trumbull 1850:1:11–13). Substantial quantities of maize were being grown in the Connecticut River valley centuries before European contact, as revealed at the Morgan site (Lavin 1988) and the Burnham-Shepard site (Bendremer et al. 1991).

Other archaeological evidence of precontact horticulture includes the ubiquity of stone hoes (Fowler 1946, 1948, 1954, 1973), which were likely used for hilling corn. Corn hills, thought to be native in origin, have been documented in Northampton, Massachusetts (Wilder and Delabarre 1920) and elsewhere (Hallowell 1921) and have been excavated on Cape Cod in association with a Native habitation (Mrozowski 1994).

Remains of large "granary pit" complexes, thought to have been used for storing surplus maize, are documented throughout the middle Connecticut River valley in local town histories (see Mulholland et al. 1982:49-51; Sheldon 1972:77, 78; Temple 1887:27–28, 34; Temple and Sheldon 1875:34-38; Trumbull 1898:173). These have been investigated by archaeologists, with two major complexes mapped in the Deerfield valley (Mulholland et al. 1983b:49-51, Figures 7A and 11A), and actual features excavated at Fort Hill in Hinsdale, New Hampshire (Thomas 1979a), at Fort Hill in Springfield, Massachusetts (Johnson 1990; Wright 1897), and at the Burnham-Shepard site in Connecticut (Bendremer et al. 1991). These granary pits typically occur atop well-drained gravelly terraces bordering the floodplains, that is, on the glacial delta deposits formed around the perimeter of glacial Lake Hitchcock. The terraces provided a dry storage environment and easy access from the floodplain maize fields.

Actual evidence of villages has been revealed but typically only when large exposures of soil matrix have been opened. Perhaps the most prominent exposure was the 1936 flood, when removal of silt at the Bark Wigwams site in Northampton, Massachusetts, is said to have revealed a large Native cemetery (Ed DeRose, personal communication 1982) and a series of "council fires" (Earl Parsons, personal communication 1989). In Montague, Massachusetts, a complex of granary pits was exposed along the Connecticut River (Lionel Girard, personal communication 1989; Hasenstab and Holmes 1990). During the mid-1980s, stripping for a shopping plaza parking lot in Westfield, Massachusetts, exposed a large Late Woodland habitation site strewn with triangular projectile points, pottery, and features (Randall Moir, personal communication ca. 1983). In Rhode Island, machine stripping of the RI-102 site revealed a large area of Late Woodland features including large storage pits—this despite meager artifactual evidence having turned up on the shovel test survey (Morenon 1986).

Other wide-area excavations by archaeologists have exposed house patterns and evidence of intensive horticulture. Along the Connecticut River in Vermont at the Skitchewaug site, Heckenberger et al. (1992) uncovered two house pits of oval wigwams and features containing charred maize. Similar finds including an oblong wigwam were made along Wappinger Creek in New York at Site 230-3-1 of the Iroquois Pipeline survey, just west of the Connecticut border in Algonquian territory (Cassedy et al. 1993). Along the Kennebec River in Maine at the Norridgewock site, Cowie et al. (1992) exposed a Contact period Abenaki settlement containing a 25-m-long longhouse and evidence of maize horticulture.

In summary, bits and pieces of Late Woodland settlements have been uncovered here and there throughout New England, including granary pits, corn hills, cemeteries, and house patterns. Most of these finds have been made either by happenstance or else within the pre-defined rights-of-way of cultural resource management (CRM) projects. Nowhere has an entire contiguous settlement been excavated, furthering the contention that villages do not exist. I question whether it was the aboriginal settlement pattern that was scattered, or simply the archaeologists' sampling of it.

DISCUSSION: WHAT WAS THE NATURE OF LATE WOODLAND SETTLEMENT?

At present we have insufficient data to define Late Woodland settlement in New England. Until we begin to expose large areas surrounding Late Woodland find spots, either through massive stripping during CRM projects or else through long-term, continued research programs focused on selected sites, we will be left with the question of whether or not Late Woodland villages existed.

In the end, it will not be a simple dichotomy of either nomadic camps or sedentary central villages that characterize New England Algonquian settlement, but rather something in between. Even White (1963:5–6) noted that Iroquoian settlement was made up of constellations of sites utilized by communities—communities such as those that Thomas (1979a) studied ethnohistorically in the Connecticut River valley. White (1963:3) noted that Iroquoian settlements were governed by seasonality—from year to year—and by periodic movement—over a period of years—because of long-term resource depletion (e.g., horticultural soil or fire wood). White notes that villages were accompanied by a variety of special-purpose resource procurement sites.

Luedtke (1988:58) argued that New England Algonquian settlements would have been determined by both location and seasonality, that is, by the availability of subsistence resources over time and space. As an example, Thomas (1979a) argued that Connecticut River valley communities dispersed into the Berkshire hills each winter to hunt. I argue that this pattern may be a product of the fur trade and the need to trap beaver, as White (1963:6–7) has argued for the Iroquois. White (1963:6-7) also argued that villages were likewise abandoned during the summer months for trading expeditions. One might question whether Connecticut River valley villages, such as that reported by Bradford (1912:193), were not the product of European trading posts such as Dutch Fort Hope at Hartford. Ceci (1982) argued this for Long Island Contact period villages. In short, a variety of factors—including natural and cultural—must be considered in modeling subsistence and settlement among Late Woodland New England Algonquians.

The main subsistence and settlement concerns addressed here are fishing and farming. Were these carried out at the same place, at the same time, and were they centralized? In addition to considerations of time and space, I would add a third dimension, gender, because fishing is believed to have been the domain of men and farming that of women. Dincauze (personal communication, 1979) has suggested that perhaps the apparent lack of horticultural villages was the result of scheduling conflicts, namely, between harvesting anadromous fish and sowing maize during the spring season. Pynchon (1645–1650) noted in the Connecticut River valley that the Native peoples "began of catching fish" during "Namossakkesos—part of March and part of April" and that "they set Indian Corne" during "Squannikesos—part of April and part of May." Were the two activities performed in the same location in succession? Did fishing continue through the season? Carlson (1988c) noted that various anadromous fish species ran up the rivers at different times of year, which could have extended the fishing season.

Several basic questions regarding scheduling and location of fishing and farming need to be addressed if one is to model Late Woodland settlement. Were the two activities split between the genders or were they shared (e.g., did women smoke the fish that the men caught)? Was fishing carried out at the traditional, natural locations, namely, the falls, or were cultural locations created in the form of weirs, at locations desirable to the users such as at floodplain farm sites? For example, at the Crego site, an Iroquois village on the Seneca River in New York, a stone fish weir was found in the river just upstream of the site (Pratt and Pratt 1987). Were horticultural sites aggregated or scattered, shifting or semipermanent? Were fish caught by men used to fertilize the corn hills planted by women? Ceci (1975) argued that fish were not so used, due to the difficulty of hauling them into the fields. If fields were located adjacent to weirs, perhaps this would not have been so difficult. Currie (1994:68) has identified cod fish bones and organic deposits in the soil of corn hills at the Smith site, suggesting that fish were in fact used as fertilizer, at least on Cape Cod. Finally, in terms of treatment of the resources, we must ascertain whether fish were being cured and where. Were they hauled in canoes to habitation sites, or processed elsewhere? Likewise for maize: where was it being husked, dried, and shelled? Were both resources stored and if so, were they stored in underground pits to allow abandonment of the site and later return, or were they tended inside year-round dwellings (see DeBoer 1988)?

In sum, to reconstruct Late Woodland subsistence and settlement systems in the various subregions of New England, we must define where fishing and farming sites were located and what their seasons and durations of occupation were. Only then can we begin to understand the relationship between these subsistence pursuits and the possibility of village settlement.

SUGGESTIONS FOR FUTURE RESEARCH

In terms of background research, we need to enhance the ethnohistoric data base for the early Contact period, especially in the inland riverine valleys where it is most lacking but where horticultural villages are most likely to have existed. It is unfortunate that historical research only begins (e.g., Thomas 1979a) when Native lifeways were devastated by epidemics. The major epidemics of 1616 to 1619 (along the coast) and 1634 (inland) had severe impacts on Native populations (Carlson et al. 1992). Current ethnohistoric knowledge coincides with the availability of English documents to the researchers. Prior to 1634, however, western New England was a Dutch colony and records for that area are in the Dutch language and are archived outside New England. Dutch explorer Adrian Block sailed up the Connecticut River in 1614, and in 1623 the Dutch settlement of Fort Hope was established in Hartford where it thrived for a decade until the epidemic of 1634 and the subsequent English takeover. Thus, there ought to be a decade of preepidemic records pertaining to the Dutch settlement and its interaction with local natives. These records should be sought as Shirley Dunn (1994) has done for the Mahican of Eastern New York. Some information may be available in the recently translated New Netherland papers at the New York State Archives (Gehring 1988).

Next, we cannot rely solely on CRM surveys as the source of settlement data, for their rights-of-way are arbitrary and restricted. More systematic, research-oriented survey work needs to be done. At the same time, attention should be paid to land alterations taking place in the locations Thomas (1976:4) proposed were Contact period villages, for example, the historic English settlements of Deerfield and Hadley. Other areas to examine, according to my own hypothesis regarding aboriginal horticulture (Hasenstab n.d.), include limestone areas, such as the upper Housatonic and Hoosic drainages and parts of the Narragansett basin, and coastal shell middens and areas surrounding them.

Regional surveys should be driven by predictive models generated by settlement models with locational implications (see Luedtke 1988). Such models can be informed by and implemented with geographic information systems (GIS). Most of the New England states now have statewide GIS databases including soil and terrain maps. An example of a locational model for Late Woodland villages might include proximity to river channels (including abandoned ones) for fishing, alluvial soils for horticulture, high ground for habitation, gravel terraces for storage, and rugged uplands for fortification.

In addition to GIS, remote sensing could be used to enhance survey. Satellites with multispectral scanners are currently scanning the earth's surface at resolutions of 3.5 m and may scan at even finer resolutions in the future. These data will allow identification of such features as middens, palisade ditches, and fish weirs.

Subsurface testing within sites must transcend the traditional method of shovel testing, which is inadequate for exposing village settlement patterns

(Kerber 1988a:66, 70; Luedtke 1988:58). Following Kerber's and Luedtke's advice, machine stripping can be used to expose living floors, geophysical probing to identify features. On elevated terraces with minimal stratification, the plowzone can be removed to expose the subsoil surface. Where this method is too costly or unfeasible, a "dead furrow" method can be used, plowing the site and shovel-clearing the end furrows of each plow swath (see Hasenstab et al. 1990). This method produces a venetian-blind-like view of the subsoil surface.

On stratified sites where stripping is not feasible, slit trenches or other methods can be used to identify buried living floors. Soil cores can reveal middens and buried soil horizons. Probing rods or ground penetrating radar can reveal stone pavements used for fish smoking. Magnetometers can identify fire hearths and resistivity meters can detect pits and house floors.

Lab analyses can aid in understanding site function in terms of subsistence and settlement. Luedtke (1988:61) advocated floral and faunal analysis to ascertain seasonality. Currie (1994) has used soil analysis to identify fish remains; this can be applied to midden soils and feature fill. Luedtke (1988:59–60) suggested isotopic analysis of existing human skeletal remains to evaluate the dietary contribution of maize. Little and Schoeninger (1995) have already performed such a study on Nantucket, although their results suggest maize was not a dietary staple there.

In summary, a variety of methods can be employed to study Late Woodland settlement and subsistence at a variety of scales, from regional settlement down to soil microfossils. By going beyond simple shovel tests and artifact counts, we will be able to test hypotheses about the nature of Late Woodland settlement and whether or not villages ever existed.

CONCLUSION

This chapter has argued that Late Woodland Algonquian villages may have existed in the riverine valleys of New England and may have been positioned to take advantage of the rich fish and farming resources these habitats offered. This view runs counter to that of most researchers, who see New England Algonquian settlement as characterized by scattered temporary camps. I contend that such a model is the product of scattered sampling: shovel test pits and "telephone booth" style units revealing scatters of artifacts and occasional features. Deeply stratified alluvial deposits prohibit the exposure of broad contiguous prehistoric surfaces. Most field tests are terminated at the initial phase and the results are dismissed as insignificant scatters. Such interpretations are rewarded by client satisfaction and ensure continued contracting.

This model, I argue, needs to be contested, and soon, before it's too late. As the pace of development in New England continues to accelerate, more and more of the landscape is "gobbled up"—particularly the riverine valleys along the interstate highway corridors on the flat terrain so favored for development. If we do not take action soon, the archaeological resources needed to test this model will be no longer be available. At best, they will have become so fragmented that it will be impossible to falsify a hypothesis of scattered settlement. The prehistoric cultural identity of New England Algonquians will then be lost forever.

ACKNOWLEDGMENTS

I thank Dena Dincauze for the many stimulating discussions we had during my graduate training regarding Late Woodland archaeology in the Connecticut River valley, for cultivating my interest in the subject, and for supporting me in my involvement in both CRM work in the valley and in the work of the Norwottuck Chapter of the Massachusetts Archaeological Society.

10

Community and Confederation: A Political Geography of Contact Period Southern New England

Eric S. Johnson

Open almost any book about seventeenth-century New England, and you may be presented with a map of indigenous groups. In many cases, these maps depict a limited number of "tribes," separated by solid boundary lines (Figure 10.1). In this chapter I point out some of the problems inherent in such maps and the model of political geography that they reflect and perpetuate. I propose an alternative model, one that is more dynamic, more varied, more cognizant of the community basis of indigenous political organization and thus provides a better framework for understanding the Contact period. Finally, I turn to patterns in material culture, specifically ceramics. Do these somehow coincide with one or the other models? The answer is that generally ceramics show no distinct styles that can be linked with one specific community or confederation, with one exception, "Shantok" pottery, which was made by members of the Mohegan community and their close allies.

What does a map of bounded tribes imply about political organization? It implies stasis and homogeneity, both within and among political units. Also it implies that the only political unit is the tribe. Such a picture of political organization is, in some respects, a legacy of eurocentrism and colonialism. Seventeenth-century Europeans from highly stratified, monarchical states, struggled to describe what were essentially egalitarian, communal societies, whose leaders were truly public servants. European writers tended to view native societies in familiar terms, or to use familiar terms to describe unfamiliar forms of political organization for which their language lacked appropriate words. Early English chroniclers like Roger Williams (1973:201) and Daniel Gookin (1970: 20) characterized native governments as monarchies with the principal sachem equivalent to a king (e.g., King Philip).

Representations like these also suppress variation in the political landscape. For example, the political organization represented by the two units labeled

Figure 10.1
Typical Map Showing Native American Tribes of Seventeenth-century
Southern New England Separated with Solid Boundary Lines
(Note location of Shantok)

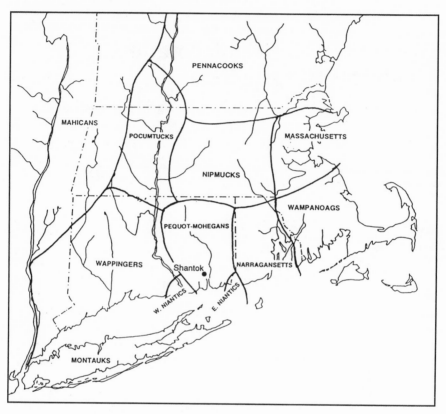

Narragansett and Pocumtuck differed in significant ways. Both territorial units actually contained a number of distinct communities: groups of people sharing a common territory containing one or more settlements. The Narragansett communities were much more closely linked through ties of kinship, alliance, trade, and ideology, and thus formed a more coherent political entity than did the more autonomous communities subsumed under the label Pocumtuck (Figure 10.2). In a recent study of documentary, archaeological, and linguistic data, Kathleen Bragdon (1996) has argued that depending on whether they occupied coastal areas, inland river valleys, or uplands, native people of southern New England pursued different subsistence practices, and maintained different settlement systems and sociopolitical organizations. However, by representing native communities as identical sorts of bounded territories, the map in Figure 10.1 implies

Figure 10.2
Seventeenth-century Native Communities of the Middle Connecticut River Valley

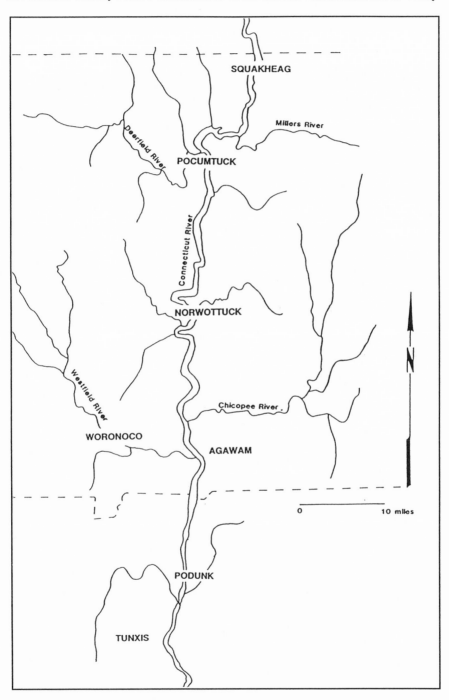

that they are identical sorts of polities. Even within the boundaries of one of these units, political organization, allegiance, and identity could be quite varied and were often extremely dynamic. Maps like this cannot convey those qualities; instead, they mask them.

Maps of any kind are, perhaps inevitably, static. The political landscape was, however, dynamic, especially at the supralocal levels that are depicted in the map. Patterns of alliance sometimes shifted rapidly during the seventeenth century. Ties between communities were forged, strengthened, weakened and/or ruptured under the pressures, constraints and opportunities that arose from the fur and wampum trade, epidemics, European settlement, and wars.

COMMUNITY AND CONFEDERATION: A CONTEXT FOR CONTACT

It has long been recognized that a different model of political organization is needed to express the dynamic and heterogeneous polities of this region. The model offered here explicitly recognizes the often shifting or inexact nature of supralocal political boundaries and territorial expansion, contraction, and/or instability of supralocal polities, which are viewed as confederations of local communities. Recognizing this, we can see that changes such as expansion, contraction, or internal upheaval may have been normal consequences of political strategies within or among confederations of relatively autonomous communities.

The basic unit of the model is the community: a group of people sharing a territory, in which their occasionally shifting settlements are located and having as their political leaders one or several sachems, with important contributions from other individuals. Before proceeding with the model, I examine more closely the powers, responsibilities, and limitations of sachems.

The term *sachem* refers to individuals whose power and authority could vary under different circumstances. The power of an individual sachem should not be assumed, but should be a topic of inquiry. Generally, sachems played important roles in decision making; they allocated land-use rights, distributed the products of large-scale communal activities, made decisions regarding alliance, warfare, and trade, and resolved conflicts (Rosier 1843:156; Williams 1973:203; Winslow 1841:304–305, 361, 364). However, the ability to make and implement decisions always depended on community consent, which placed significant limitations on the decision-making powers of sachems. "Their sagamore," Gookin wrote in about 1674 (1970:20), "[does] not [decide] any weighty matter without the consent of his great men or petty sagamores." Williams (1973:202) wrote, "The Sachim, although they have an absolute Monarchie over the people; yet they will not conclude of ought that concerns all, either Lawes, or Subsidies, or warres, unto which the people are averse, and by gentle perswasion cannot be brought" (see also Winslow 1841:360–361).

In addition to the responsibilities of decision making, sachems had material privileges. For example, they occupied larger houses and received substantial gifts from community members (Bradford and Winslow 1841:226; Williams

1973:62, 63, 123, 124, 201, 206, 227, 235; Winslow 1841:361–362; Wood 1977:97–98). However, these "privileges" were employed in meeting the responsibilities of the position. The larger sachems' houses served as meeting places and as lodgings for visitors. Most, if not all, of the goods and services to which sachems laid claim enabled them to meet material responsibilities. The sachem fed and lodged important guests, gave gifts to allies, and took care of any persons in the community who were unable to take care of themselves (Williams 1963:26, 58). According to Winslow (1841:361), "Every Sachem taketh care for the widow and fatherless, also for such as are aged and in any way maimed, if their friends be dead, or not able to provide." The responsibilities of the sachems clearly indicate some of the qualities they were expected to possess: wisdom and diplomacy in decision making, skill in oratory and debate (Williams 1973:235), and generosity with material goods.

These qualities were not necessarily enough to make one a sachem. It was imperative that a would-be sachem belong to the correct lineage. English accounts of succession vary considerably and are somewhat contradictory but suggest that although succession was generally from father to eldest son, rules of succession were flexible enough to allow for the best qualified candidate from among a sachem's close kin to succeed to the position. Both women and men could aspire to the position of sachem (Josselyn 1833:308–309; Winslow 1841:361; Wood 1977:97).

Most community members were outside of this limited group and could not become sachems. However, positions of power, authority, and responsibility were accessible to all adults. Status could be achieved by demonstrating generosity, by learning rituals or the arts of healing, by displaying wisdom in political counsel or bravery in battle (Williams 1973:124, 192–193, 215; Winslow 1841:356, 359), or by leading in the creation or continuation of community traditions, becoming what Mohegan tribal historian Melissa Fawcett has termed a sociocultural authority (Fawcett-Sayett 1988). These positions or social roles recognized and rewarded achievement, independent of genealogy. Although the office of sachem was not open to all, there were alternative positions of status and authority that were open to any who had the necessary ability. The seventeenth century also brought new opportunities for achieving status as deaths from epidemics opened leadership positions to new individuals and Europeans brought opportunities for trade, alliance, and wage labor that allowed individuals to acquire wealth and prestige outside of traditional means (see Nassaney 1989:86; Sainsbury 1975).

The community affiliation and political identity of individuals appears to have been relatively fluid. Perhaps the best of many documented examples of this fluidity is the absorption of many Pequots into the Mohegan and Narragansett communities after the Pequot War in 1637. The key to fluidity of identity was the kinship ties among different communities, which were created by intercommunity marriage or local exogamy. Every individual had extensive networks of kin or other allies along which he or she could move relatively freely. This freedom of movement limited the coercive power of the sachem and obliged the sachem to govern by consent. However, the degree of fluidity itself might be constrained by factors such as warfare, the consolidation of communities following epidemics, or changing patterns of alliance.

Archaeological evidence in the form of patterns of variation in material culture, particularly ceramics, is consistent with this model of fluidity of individual identity, the political primacy of the community, and the ephemeral and highly variable nature of confederation. Although the ceramics of precontact southern New England show a wide variety of form and decoration, there is no indication that these variations reflect social boundaries between communities or even between confederations (see Chapter 6, this volume). Robert Goodby's (1994) analysis of Late Woodland and Contact period ceramics from the Narragansett Bay area uncovered significant diversity in stylistic attributes both within and among sites, along with evidence of an intensification of decorative treatment in the Late Woodland and Contact periods. However, within the Narragansett Bay region, Goodby was unable to differentiate local decorative styles among communities or even to distinguish between Narragansett and Pokanoket ceramic styles. In his words, "While ceramic style was socially and culturally significant, it was not used by potters to mark their affiliation with particular local communities or larger 'tribal' entities" (Goodby 1994:4–5).

In summary, indigenous political organization rested on a strong communal, egalitarian ethic, with considerable personal autonomy and fluidity of identity. A balance of privileges, obligations, and rights constrained the behavior of community leaders. During the seventeenth century, these balances were occasionally disrupted, and community leaders were sometimes able to abrogate traditional constraints.

Communities were never isolated; individuals and families typically sought to create alliances and kinship ties with members of other communities. As a result, ties of kinship and political, economic, and social cooperation crosscut and linked communities. A group of communities, bound together by such ties among their members, could form the nucleus of a larger political entity, which I call the confederation. It is these confederations and their member communities that are the precursors of the present tribes of southern New England.

The most important political figures in the confederation were the principal sachem or sachems. The privileges, responsibilities, limitations, and aptitudes of the principal sachems were similar to those of the community-level sachems, but larger in scale and scope. Thus, the principal sachem often had little coercive power over the local communities in his or her confederation and relied on the building of consensus in decision making. Under this system, local community leaders enjoyed considerable autonomy.

Principal sachems generally had close kinship ties, both real and fictive, to the sachems of individual communities. William Simmons and George Aubin's (1975) study of kinship among the Narragansetts, who were not the only seventeenth-century confederation but were certainly one of the largest, revealed close family ties among the principal and local-level sachems of the Narragansett confederation and its close allies in the mid-seventeenth century. During this time the principal Narragansett sachems were Canonicus and his nephew Miantonomi. Ninigret, son of a sister of Canonicus, was the sachem of the eastern Niantics, and Wepiteamock, a brother of Ninigret, was the sachem of Manisee (Block Island) (Simmons and Aubin 1975; Stiles 1916:28; Williams 1963:37). Despite potential confusion over the exact meaning of kinship terms, these intermarriages between the leading families of the nuclear communities of the Narragansett confederation and its close allies must have strengthened the ties of kinship among the most important sachems and helped to keep the nucleus of the confederation stable. However, this strategy also had potential dangers; sachems from allied communities who married into the core families may have gained additional authority and even claims to the principal sachemship. Perhaps Uncas, the Mohegan sachem, is an example of the dangers of such close kinship ties. His marriage to the daughter of Tatobem, principal sachem of the Pequot confederation until 1633, probably gave him additional status, which he needed to legitimize his claims to Pequot allegiance after the Pequot War (Johnson 1996: 39).

Within the confederation, the autonomy of local communities appears to have varied considerably depending on a number of factors, including the personal qualities of the principal and local sachems, the size of the respective polities, distances separating the two, and closeness of genealogical ties. Outside of this nucleus of closely linked communities were others, called "tributaries," which were subordinate to the nuclear communities and were less strongly tied into the confederation through kinship. It is among the tributaries that political influences were most volatile.

Tributaries acknowledged their subordinate status by presenting wampum (the usual medium of tribute) to the nuclear communities. This relationship, however, was not necessarily exploitative. In return for their payment, tributaries expected to receive goods and/or services from the recipients. Such expectations are reflected in a speech Miantonomi, the principal Narragansett Sachem, made in 1642 to the Montauks, a tributary community. In this speech (Gardener 1897:141), Miantonomi exhorted his listeners to pay no tribute to the English. He said, "For they are no Sachems, nor none of their children shall be . . . there is but one king in England, who is over them all, and if you would send him 100,000 fathom of wampum, he would not give you a knife for it, nor thank you." Thus tributaries expected to at least be thanked for their payments and to receive some goods as tokens of appreciation. They also expected a degree of security by virtue of their ties to a more powerful group.

Miantonomi's speech also emphasizes the importance of the status and behavior of the recipient in the eyes of the tribute payer. Tribute was paid only to those who were worthy to receive it and the English were not worthy because they were neither true sachems, nor was their behavior appropriate for a sachem. Thus tributary relationships between groups appear to have been modeled (at least ideally) on the relationship between a sachem and his or her people. The people might give goods and services to the sachem but only if the sachem proved worthy of respect by fulfilling his or her duties, as redistributor of surplus, protector of the weak, and model of deportment. Similarly, tributaries expected the leaders of the groups to which they paid wampum to function as redistributors on a regional scale, to be generous, protective, and worthy of respect.

Tributaries, again mirroring the relationship of people to their sachems, were often able to realign themselves with new allies in a more advantageous relationship, thus limiting the exploitive power of the recipients. When patterns of alliance became unstable, the balance of power between tributary and receiver shifted, or tributaries were called upon to give above and beyond normal expectations, the flow of goods might even reverse. For example, Miantonomi, having already spoken against payment of tribute to the English, later that year called upon the Montauks to join with him in attacking the English and instead of receiving gifts, as was usual, he gave them gifts (Gardener 1897:141).

However, like the relationship between sachems and their subjects, the relationships between groups and their tributaries could, and did, change as circumstances changed. It was possible, under some conditions, for groups to exploit their tributaries, draining them of surplus while returning little in the way of protection.

Rather than viewing tribes as the static, internally homogeneous clones implied by bounded maps, they should be viewed as confederations of autonomous communities. Around a relatively stable nucleus of between one and a handful of communities whose leaders and membership were linked by numerous ties of kinship was a less stable margin. Here, with weaker ties to the nuclear communities, greater autonomy permitted allies and tributaries to follow their own interests, sometimes to the point of leaving one confederation for another. This view shifts the focus to individual communities and their circumstances in an environment of confederates, allies, subordinates, superiors, and adversaries. It creates a picture of a very dynamic political environment, wherein the actions of confederations, communities, interest groups, and individuals may be better contextualized and understood.

SACHEM UNCAS AND THE MOHEGAN COMMUNITY

As an example of understanding political action in this context, I consider a brief sketch of the actions of the Mohegan community, and of Uncas, the man who served as the community sachem. Before 1636 the Mohegans were close but subordinate allies of the communities that formed the nucleus of the Pequot confederation. The Mohegans and Pequots were linked by many kinship ties; Uncas himself was married to the sister of the Pequots' principal sachem, Sassacus. Although the Pequot confederation at one time had many allies and tributaries in southern Connecticut and Long Island, and was perhaps the region's most powerful polity after the Narragansetts, the confederation began to fall apart as a result of epidemics, conflicts with the Dutch, the Narragansetts, and other Native groups, and the death of the principal sachem Tatobem (Sassacus's father) at the hands of the Dutch in 1634. By 1636 the Pequots had lost almost all of their tributaries, most of whom realigned with the Narragansetts. Even Uncas, despite his kinship with Sassacus, had made several unsuccessful attempts to overturn his community's subordinate status (see Salisbury 1982:206–215). When the English attacked the weakened Pequots, Uncas and the Mohegans joined in eliminating their former allies as a regional power.

By regarding the Mohegans as one community within a complex and dynamic Pequot confederation whose internal ties were snapping under the pressures of war, disease, economic change, and a volatile balance of power, we can better understand the actions of its members and of their representative. This is only one example of how the model of community and confederation holds great explanatory potential.

After the Pequot War, Uncas and the Mohegans made effective use of their new English allies and both existing and new ties of kinship with Pequot survivors, to create a Mohegan confederation centered around the Mohegan community of Shantok. Shantok was (and is) located along the Thames River around present-day Montville, Connecticut (see Figure 10.1). By the mid-seventeenth century, the community center was a palisaded settlement which was sometimes called Fort Shantok. Portions of this site were excavated in the 1960s by archaeologists from New York University (Salwen 1966; Williams 1972).

The residents of Shantok were of very diverse origins: Mohegans, Pequots, refugees from eastern Massachusetts, individuals from Long Island, and people from other southern New England Native communities. Out of this diversity of people, the Mohegans forged a group that was cohesive enough to grow rapidly and compete successfully with the Narragansetts for the allegiance of former Pequot tributaries.

Competition between the Mohegans and Narragansetts eventually flared into open war. In 1643, between 300 and 400 Mohegans unexpectedly defeated an attacking force of some 1,000 Narragansetts and captured their sachem Miantonomi, whom Uncas executed after first securing the collaboration of the United Colonies. The Narragansetts attacked again in 1645, and again in 1657. Each time the Mohegans were rescued by the intervention of their English allies (De Forest 1964:211–218, 253; Forbes 1947:19–20; Johnson 1996; Winthrop 1908: 2:157).

In the course of this competition, Uncas was able to abrogate some of the traditional constraints on the powers of a principal sachem, and several Mohegan tributaries complained of his behavior. The Pequots of Naumeag (present-day New London, Connecticut), for example, protested Uncas's "oppressions and outrage" and "injustice and tyranny" in extorting tribute and imposing decisions without seeking consensus (De Forest 1964:231; Forbes 1947:131, 281–282; Pulsifer 1859:97–103). Uncas was able to do this by using the military and political support of his English allies, to whom he lent his people's support in return. He also benefited from the increasing constraints on individual and group mobility, realignment, and autonomy that resulted from expanding European settlement and the hot and cold wars of the mid-seventeenth century (Johnson 1996:37–44).

Because of the pattern of alliances and enmities, a social boundary grew up around the Mohegans. Many of their Native neighbors were either committed enemies in a state of perpetual cold war (the Narragansetts and most of the Connecticut River communities), or reluctant allies (the Naumeag Pequots). Although the Mohegans were allied with their English neighbors, there was certainly a clear social boundary separating them. Finally, the Mohegans were engaged in intense competition with other Native communities for a dwindling land base, an unreliable fur trade, and increasingly belligerent and slippery English and other European allies. Under these social, political, and military conditions, group cohesion must have been under some strain. Indeed a Narragansett-inspired attempt to rally Pequots from the Mohegans around the Niantic sachem Ninigret in 1649 suggests that the Narragansetts attempted to exploit the diverse origins of the Mohegans in order to split the Mohegan community. On the other hand, many of the Mohegans, including Uncas and those who had an interest in maintaining his position, may have tried to encourage and affirm a unified community identity and to practice or encourage any behavior that stressed unity within their community.

In struggling to create a unified group from disparate parts and to maintain cohesion under a variety of pressures, the Mohegans expressed and promoted their community identity through material culture. Despite a diversity of women potters coming from different communities, the ceramics from Shantok show distinctive consistencies that express Mohegan identity.

THE POTTERY OF SHANTOK

Shantok pottery is typified by large, thin-walled, globular or elongate-globular bodied pots, with round bottoms, pronounced shoulders, constricted necks, and thickened or applied high collars with up to four, often conspicuous, castellations which occasionally terminate in modeled nodes. Collars (including lips, lobes, nodes, and castellations) are exuberantly decorated with impressed, punctate, modeled, or extruded designs. Bands or plats of horizontal, vertical, or diagonal impressed lines are common on collars (Figure 10.3). Bodies are plain, with smooth interior and exterior surfaces.

Although Shantok pottery shares many decorative attributes with contemporary wares, such as the range of decorative motifs, it can be distinguished by certain decorative characteristics. Specifically, the highly visible applied or extruded lobes or notched rings along the base of the collars (Rouse 1947; Williams 1972:346–355) are considered to be almost entirely unique to Shantok ware. The prominent castellations and their occasional modeling is also most

Figure 10.3
Ceramic Sherds from the Fort Shantok Site

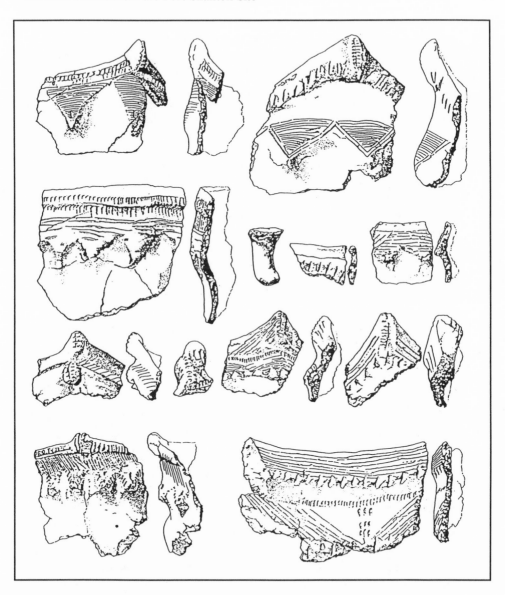

Source: "Ceramic Traditions and Sequences in Connecticut" by Irving Rouse, *Bulletin of the Archaeological Society of Connecticut*, vol. 21 (1947). Courtesy of the Archaeological Society of Connecticut.

often associated with Shantok ware, although Niantic ware and other north-eastern pottery styles occasionally exhibit these attributes. It has also been suggested that Shantok potters may have used a more restricted range of clays for their characteristic pots than did their contemporaries in other Native communities (Lizee et al. 1995).

So distinct are the ceramics from Shantok that they have defined one of the standard pottery types of southern New England: Shantok ware. Shantok pottery is believed to have originated as a postcontact ceramic type produced exclusively by the Mohegans (Lizee 1994b; Lizee et al. 1995; McBride 1990). Its distribution is largely restricted to southern Connecticut, west of the Thames River, within the historic Mohegan homeland, including Fort Shantok. A sizable sample has also been recovered from Fort Corchaug, Long Island. The Corchaug community had close ties to the Mohegans and may have been a Mohegan tributary after the Pequot War (Smith 1947; Solecki 1950; Williams 1972). Although a few individual pieces of Shantok-like pottery have been reported outside of these areas, other kinds of ceramics predominate at seventeenth-century sites (McBride 1990:99; Mrozowski 1980:86–87; Salwen 1969:86 Saville 1920:87–88; Simmons 1970:89–91).

The women who created ceramics at Shantok (and elsewhere) and gave the vessels form and decoration were concerned with creating both functional cookware and containers that carried social information. Among the social issues or messages that may have been addressed or expressed through pottery were those most closely associated with women's status in the family or in the community. The importance of agriculture and agricultural land, one of the sources of women's economic power, was doubtless one significant aspect of gender politics, as were the maintenance and transformation of traditional gender roles (hunting, gathering, farming, trading, politics, and ritual), obligations, and privileges (see Handsman 1990). Women were also active participants in political struggles that crosscut gender lines, competition or cooperation among families, residential or descent groups, lineages, communities, or confederations. One of these political processes was the development and elaboration of community or supracommunity political identity. The nature of this identity appears to have been transformed at different times and places and in response to different pressures, constraints, and opportunities. I have argued that among the Mohegans, and perhaps among some of their allies on Long Island, the issue of group identity was of particular importance. The distinctive pottery of Fort Shantok is one expression of this identity.

Although the elaborately decorated vessels of Shantok, like most of the Native ceramics of seventeenth-century southern New England, certainly contain an abundance of messages, many of which are lost to us, one of the most important of these was Mohegan identity. Moreover, this message is perhaps unique among southern New England ceramics, which, as noted above, generally do not appear to mark community or "tribal" affiliation.

Cooking pots should provide a suitable medium for such a message. Food, cooked and served in ceramic vessels, was an important part of ritual and political negotiation. The pots made and used by Mohegan women would be seen by members of the community, relatives living outside the settlement, other allies, and other individuals in politically charged settings (see Johnson 1993:263–304; also Wiessner 1983, 1990; Wobst 1977 for more general discussions of style and information exchange).

Shantok pottery's singular, easily recognized qualities, its distribution, and the social and political environment in which the women of Shantok made their pots, suggest that Shantok pots were an expression and assertion of Mohegan identity. In signaling their affiliation with the Mohegan confederation through their ceramic arts, Mohegan women created a unique style, expressing a unique social situation in southern New England.

CONCLUSION

Let us return to the subject of maps. How should we map the political geography of seventeenth-century southern New England? First, let us certainly retain the names of the tribes, or confederations, as I have termed them. But we must eliminate the boundary lines between them, as most recent scholars have done in the maps they choose to accompany their texts (e.g., Bragdon 1996; Jennings 1975; Salisbury 1982). What most of these maps lack is communities; few show more than a dozen or so.

As important as eliminating boundaries is including as many individual local communities as we can, as in the map in Figure 10.2. Including as many local communities as we can identify immediately gives a picture of a complex and dynamic political landscape; it fills in otherwise blank areas that contribute to what Russell Handsman (1989) has called "silenced" Native histories. It implicitly recognizes the significance of the community in Native politics, recognition that can help us to understand the variety of ways in which the indigenous people of southern New England experienced and responded to the European invasion. Such a map challenges us to explore the various ways in which communities confederated, divided, contested, and struggled to survive in a hostile new world order.

ACKNOWLEDGMENTS

The ideas expressed here have gone through a long journey, and at each step they have been enriched by the encouragement and constructive criticism of many people. Dena Dincauze first sparked my interest in this subject and thereafter has continually encouraged and inspired me. I have, in addition, benefited tremendously from discussions with and comments from, among others, Claire Carlson, Elizabeth Chilton, Fred Dunford, Robert Goodby, Russell Handsman, Arthur Keene, Mary Ann Levine, Patricia Mangan, Kevin

McBride, Michael Nassaney, Barry O'Connell, Rita Reinke, Paul Robinson, Neal Salisbury, Kenneth Sassaman, Janet Spector, and Michael Volmar. Thank you all.

Part IV

Interdisciplinary Perspectives on Northeastern Prehistory

11

History of Zooarchaeology in New England

Catherine C. Carlson

. . . they ain't no such animile. (Smith 1929)

Just over 100 years ago, G. F. Eaton (1898) undertook the first extensive study designed explicitly to investigate archaeological fauna in New England. Based on fieldwork conducted in 1897, Eaton reported on the shell middens of Block Island, off the southern New England coast. It is thus fitting to look back over the last century and review the history, goals, and contributions to science that the study of archaeofaunas has provided to our understanding of New England's past. Since the earliest days of recovering bone samples from New England's sites, the identification and analysis of the animal bones and shells that represent part of the harvested resource base of past peoples have illuminated the relationship between indigenous people and their environments. Emerging in the process has been a clearer understanding of paleoenvironmental stability and change, human subsistence and dietary patterns, social organization, and settlement patterns. Analysis and interpretation of archaeofaunas have become more sophisticated over the last three decades in North America. Issues of taphonomy, sampling, quantification, bone morphology, faunal extinctions, zoogeography, seasonality indicators, butchering and bone breakage, and carbon isotope analysis, to name a few, are all indicative of the degree of complexity and broad scope of research going on today with archaeofaunas.

This chapter examines the history of the development of zooarchaeology in New England with a focus on precontact studies. It is not the goal to review all faunal reports ever produced in New England but to provide enough examples of work on a broad range of topics to outline the scope of the contributions made. A major problem in doing this type of review is that much recent faunal work is contained in often inaccessible parts of the "gray literature" of contract archaeology, a situation not unique to New England. Even where analyses are published, unless the faunal research is presented as a separate entity or an appendix, it often gets only broadly summarized with reference to the unpublished report that contains the actual details of the sampling, identification, and quantification. This has had the effect of relegating much faunal research to the status of technical work, which has undoubtedly suppressed the number of academic-oriented students going into the field. Another problem noted by Dincauze (1981:70–71), is that in the early 1980s it was "not clear yet whether the promise of zooarchaeology, as a technical specialty for archaeologists, can be realized in the context of reduced financing for archaeological research staffs." Significantly, zooarchaeology faculty positions at universities in New England are today as rare as hen's teeth.

Until the 1970s there was a general attitude in archaeology that faunal remains were considered not as worthy of collection as artifactual material, or that only the large bones should be saved for analysis. We are undoubtedly still living with the legacy of this attitude in the design and publication of zooarchaeological research and in academic and museum appointments. This is not to minimize, however, the number of examples of significant research that can be found in the literature of New England archaeology. In evaluating the importance of environmental data and paleoenvironmental reconstruction in archaeology, Dincauze (1981:52) pointed out that "it is an expensive undertaking, requiring much staff time and extensive laboratory facilities. It can never recreate for us real environmental amenities. Why, then, do it?" She responded that "the answer must be that the evaluative description of ancient environments provides the archaeologist with data crucial to the full achievement of the archaeological (ultimately the scientific and humanistic) value of the human behavioral relics studied" (Dincauze 1981:52).

PIONEERING RESEARCH

An early pioneer of the field, G. F. Eaton is remarkable for recognizing the scientific value of archaeofaunas, for which he received a Ph.D. at Yale University in 1898 (Eaton 1898). Interestingly, he identified many of the same issues that zooarchaeologists continue to grapple with today. Eaton (1898:7) asked questions pertaining to the "former Indian inhabitants" of Block Island. He noted that "few records are extant which give any information about the manner of life of these aborigines. What food could they procure upon a bleak storm-swept island?" Citing earlier geological work that recognized that the numerous "shell-heaps" found on the Island were human features and contained the bones of animals, he set out in 1897 to undertake fieldwork explicitly to collect samples to answer these questions.

Eleven shell middens were identified on his map of the island, and he noted with concern that many of the sites were being destroyed by road construction. He collected bone and shell samples from six middens, from which he identified to species eleven mammals (including *Homo sapiens*), nineteen birds, three turtles, eight fish, nine molluscs, and one crustacean. No quantification of the relative amount of bone for each species was given, nor were his field sampling methods described; however, the fact that he had collected small fish, bird, and reptile bones suggests that he was concerned with identifying the total range of fauna present.

The issues about the faunal collection that Eaton considered relevant are still of importance in research today, including age, condition of bone, presence of extinct and rare species, distribution patterns of the common fauna, climate changes, seasonality of the fauna, geological environment, and bone technology. For example, he observed that the middens were pre-European contact in age because of the absence of European artifacts but also postglacial because of the presence of only modern faunal species. The rare presence of gray seal (*Halichoerus grypus*) suggested to him possible past fluctuations in range of the seal due to such factors as changing water temperature. He also discussed the extinction of the great auk, which had occurred by 1844 (Greenway 1958), and the seasonality of the bird. He identified taphonomic and butchering processes, including evidence for marrow extraction, missing articular ends, tooth marks probably from dog gnawing, and degrees of burned bone. In many respects it is difficult to think of any issues that we think of as important in faunal analysis today that he did not address. He did not, however, attempt to quantify the relative amounts of the different species, or contributions to the diet. Yet given the serious methodological difficulties inherent in this, as witnessed by the debates in modern studies about how to quantify bone samples (e.g., Crabtree 1985), his silence on this matter may indicate his insight on the problems of such analysis.

While Eaton's work was remarkable for its time, the archaeology of the first half of the twentieth century can generally be characterized as focusing on the artifacts and features with less regard for faunal materials. For example, Warren K. Moorehead's (1922, 1931) extensive early surveys and excavations, sponsored by Phillips Academy at Andover, were not concerned with recovering faunal materials.

Shell middens, however, were recognized early on as a special type of site where animal bones were frequently found. The earliest published excavations of shell middens were those of Jeffries Wyman (1868) and F. W. Putnam (1882–1883, 1887) on the "kjoekkenmoeddings," "kitchen middens," or "shell heaps" on the coasts of Maine and Massachusetts, where the presence of bone remains were noted, including specific reference to several species. Eventually one of Moorehead's associates, Walter B. Smith (1929), undertook an excavation on the Jones Cove Shell-Heap in Frenchman Bay, Maine. His charming prose describes how these "first shore dinners" provide "unpremeditated monuments" to the early inhabitants of the Maine coast, which "took much time and industry—also many clams" but are also made up of animal, bird and fish bones. He wondered about the age differences in seemingly similar middens, and whether they represented the activities of tribes who were "exclusive occupants year after year" (Smith 1929:3–4). Under another heading called

"Miscellaneous Bones," Smith remarks on bone butchering and breakage, and on the use of bone for the manufacture of implements. He is also quite honest about the limited treatment given to the excavated bones and the difficulties of species identification that continue to the present day.

A list of the various animals represented would be given if the writer could, but his knowledge of osteology is practically only that gained by a few days of shell-heap work. It gives him a little satisfaction to add that a few of his fellow workers were nearly as ignorant.

We learned much, but some of this knowledge was not absolutely accurate. We could positively identify bear teeth (canines only) though similar teeth of smaller animals kept us guessing. Incisors of beaver and of porcupines were also readily recognized, but we were not always sure of which from t'other. In some cases we could tell moose antlers from those of deer.

A man who really knows much of bird anatomy pronounced a certain light, hollow bone to be "*almost* that of the great auk," though he qualified this statement by adding "or turkey, or something."

One of the searchers thought he had discovered something when in accidentally breaking a hollow bone he was amazed to find another bone fitting snugly inside. . . . What kind of an animal had double bones? An extinct species, or something new? This question was decided by some of the diggers, without the aid of an expert. They found: That "they ain't no such animile."

Such trifling incidents are mentioned merely to emphasize the desirability of a competent "bone sharp" in the crew of shell-heap diggers, that data of scientific value be not over-looked, particularly that concerning those types of life which will never again occur on earth (Smith 1929:2-24).

Ten years later, W. S. Hadlock (1939) took heed and employed a "competent bone sharp" in his analysis of another shell midden at West Gouldsboro, Maine, the Taft's Point shell midden. He provided a list of eighteen species identified from the site by Glover M. Allen of the Museum of Comparative Zoology at Harvard College, indicative of a growing trend towards the use of zoological experts for osteological identifications.

Subsequent to these and other early shell midden excavations, Charles C. Willoughby's book, *Antiquities of the New England Indians*, summarized the various excavations of "shellheaps," although he focused little on the faunal remains recovered (Willoughby 1935:200–213). This may be due to the fact that he considered that the bones formed "a very small fraction of the deposits," and that "little attention has been given to their stratification" (Willoughby 1935: 202). He provides an interesting review, however, of the Damariscotta shell heaps in Maine, which he calls "the most remarkable shell-heaps in New England" because they are New England's largest middens and consist primarily of a single species of shellfish, the American oyster (Willoughby 1935:206).

Richard P. Goldthwait (1935) also recognized the uniqueness of the Damariscotta oyster heaps, a species for which only small relic populations still exist. Goldthwait attempted to quantify the numbers of shells represented, with loss due to erosion and mining for chicken feed factored into his equations. In addition, he examined the relationship between sea-level change and previously warmer water temperatures to explain the absence of oyster populations today.

Another unique site investigated in the early days of New England archaeology was the Boylston Street Fish Weir. The site was first described by Willoughby (1927) but extensively investigated under the direction of Frederick Johnson of Phillips Academy in the 1940s. Johnson's (1942) study was remarkable in having utilized detailed analysis of the molluscs to understand environmental and climate change in Boston Harbor. Johnson (1942:ix) noted that "archaeologists are slowly recognizing that their field is no longer susceptible to strict definition . . . studies of all the organisms from specific deposits must be interpreted" in order to understand the environmental context of sites. With the exception of a small sample of shore-bird bones identified by Glover Allen of the Museum of Comparative Zoology at Harvard University, the faunal analysis focused on the shellfish remains. The molluscs were identified and interpreted from both cultural and paleoenvironmental perspectives. The three distinct layers of shell that had accumulated in Boston's Back Bay indicated a change from warm- to cold-water fauna, and a rise in sea level. However, it was also noted that the number of oysters increased in the weir zone, prompting speculation by Thurlow Nelson, who undertook the oyster analysis, that the feature may have functioned as an oyster culture farm and not as a fish weir. Johnson used zoological specialists to identify the twenty-two species of molluscs, the oysters and the barnacles, and presented their analyses as separate chapters in the final publication. The Boylston Street Fish Weir project set a new standard for archaeofaunal and paleoenvironmental analysis in New England. More recent research in the 1980s, involving new collections and identifications on shell as well as fish remains, in concert with radiometric studies and other paleoenvironmental analyses, await final publication (Carlson 1988c, Dincauze 1985).

MODERN ZOOARCHAEOLOGY

Following the development of radiocarbon dating in 1950, and with it the ability to more accurately control the chronology of sites, archaeologists began to focus on the refinement of other scientific techniques and their applications to archaeology. One of the first projects in New England directed toward the development of problem-oriented zooarchaeological methodology was that of William Ritchie who undertook excavations at six shell middens on Martha's Vineyard between 1964 and 1967. The primary goal of his study "in coastal ecology and adaptation" was to see if there was "myth or reality" to the idea of a uniquely "coastal culture" in contrast to the inland sequences of New York. He also wanted to provide a radiocarbon-dated cultural sequence for southern New England, incorporating "critically conducted, problem-oriented excavations" (Ritchie 1969a:v). He chose Martha's Vineyard because it contained numerous undisturbed stratified shell middens, unlike the more densely settled areas of the mainland coast.

Although an earlier study had identified faunal remains from two middens on Martha's Vineyard (Byers and Johnson 1940), Ritchie's (1969a:vi) methodology was intended to "provide full descriptions of the stratigraphy, features and associated food remains and artifacts." The sampling for the faunal remains was revolutionary because for the first time in New England column samples were collected and screened with fine mesh (⅛ inch and 1/16 inch) to recover small elements, although the main excavation units were not screened. Dr. Joseph H. Waters of the Department of Biology, Villanova University, provided "his invaluable volunteered service in the identification and study of the osseous and shell remains" (Ritchie 1969a:vii). Waters (1965, 1967) had earlier published analyses on other shell midden fauna from Maine, Connecticut, and Massachusetts (Nantucket), and later identified the fauna from the Turner Farm site in Maine (Bourque 1973). He identified thousands of bone and shell fragments, and quantified them according to total pieces (bone count) and total individuals (minimum number of individuals), and also the column samples by weight. The thoroughness of the study is evident in the issues he addressed: the relative importance of species, cultural selection for larger/older individuals, seasonal versus annual indicator species, seasonality on antler, inshore versus offshore indicator fish and birds, comparison of terrestrial and coastal hunting patterns, temporal changes in species abundances, range changes in species (i.e., gray seal), overharvesting of clam beds, environmental changes in pond salinity, and dogs as food. On the basis of Waters's extensive faunal analysis, Ritchie (1969a) argued that the trend in subsistence from the Late Archaic through the Woodland periods was one of initially forest-adapted peoples who gathered easily procured shellfish, to one of increasing harvesting of more elusive shellfish combined with shallow-water fishing, to finally one of a people undertaking pelagic (open ocean) fishing and hunting of sea mammals, but always heavily supplemented by terrestrial game. He also suggested a shift away from a mobile settlement pattern to one of semisedentism or "perennial residency" at favored locations until shellfish became exhausted. He was not, however, willing to concede to a distinct coastal Archaic culture that was fundamentally different from the Laurentian tradition of inland New York.

Following the work of Ritchie and Waters, a growing number of research projects incorporated the analysis of archaeofaunas. In 1977 Robson Bonnichsen and David Sanger (1977:124) argued that faunal research, "which is not simply a technical service for an archaeologist," must involve a close working relationship between faunal analyst and the field archaeologist because "the faunal analyst's job is certainly more than one of merely providing the archaeologist with a list of identified bone elements and species" (p. 109). They advocated documenting site distributions patterns through the use of computer data banking to integrate the faunal remains with the other site data. The need for integration increasingly required that archaeologists be trained as faunal analysts.

Themes in Modern Zooarchaeological Research

A number of research themes in the analysis of archaeofaunas have become evident over the last three decades. An outline of the major themes, and examples of studies, are briefly presented to indicate the scope of research topics.

Paleoindian Subsistence and Paleontology. There are few faunal collections in New England that are of Paleoindian age given the acid soils of the forests, and because of coastal submergence for the pre-5000 B.P. period. Certain paleontological collections hint at the types of Late Pleistocene elephants, cervids, and fishes that were potentially available to Paleoindian hunters (Guilday 1968; McAllister et al. 1981; Moeller 1984; Oldale et al. 1987). Archaeological evidence consists of calcined bone fragments of caribou and beaver from the Bull Brook and Whipple sites; unfortunately however, the limited nature of the samples do not provide strong evidence for a Paleoindian subsistence focus, such as on the hunting of big game like the caribou (Spiess et al. 1984–1985).

Archaic Subsistence. Research on Archaic subsistence has centered on understanding both the shift from Late Pleistocene to Early Holocene resource utilization, as well as resource change throughout the Archaic period (Spiess 1992). Like those from Paleoindian sites, Archaic faunal collections are rare due to poor preservation conditions and coastal submergence of sites. There are a few inland sites such as at Turners Falls on the Connecticut River where fish and other fauna were recovered that may be Early Archaic in age (Curran and Thomas 1979; Chapter 14, this volume); the Eddy site at Amoskeag Falls on the Merrimack River where shad, alewife, turtle, snake, and deer were identified (Carlson 1990b); and the Wadleigh Falls site fauna identified by Spiess that contains a high percentage of turtle and snake bones in addition to deer, osprey, and shad (Maymon and Bolian 1992). New evidence has recently been published on the Early Archaic components at the Sparrow and Brigham sites in Maine (Spiess 1992), in addition to a summary of Middle Archaic inland sites. The Smyth site at Amoskeag Falls also contains Middle Archaic fauna that indicate utilization of forest species (beaver and deer) and freshwater wetlands (turtle, snake, and fish) (Carlson 1982).

Late or Terminal Archaic assemblages are found in both coastal and inland settings, and include the analyses of Seabrook Marsh (Robinson 1985), Turner Farm midden (Spiess and Lewis 1995), Goddard midden (Bourque and Cox 1981), Hunter Farm (Spiess 1992), Hirundo site (Knight 1985), Young site (Borstel 1982), several rockshelter sites (Carlson 1990a; Dincauze and Gramly 1973; Huntington 1982; Swigart 1987), and a freshwater midden in Concord, Massachusetts (Largy 1995b).

Ceramic/Woodland Coastal Subsistence. By far the vast majority of faunal collections in New England have been recovered from Ceramic/Woodland period coastal shell middens because they are above the level of coastal submergence, and their alkaline matrix provides excellent faunal preservation. A wide range of terrestrial mammals, marine mammals, birds, fish, and shellfish was utilized during this time period. The geographical scope of collections that have been analyzed for northern New England include sites in Passamaquoddy Bay (McCormick 1980; Sanger 1986), Acadia (Carlson 1980, 1981; Sanger 1980), Penobscot Bay (Belcher 1989; Bourque 1973, 1995; Bourque and Cox 1981; Morse 1975; Spiess and Hedden 1983; Spiess and Lewis 1995), Boothbay (Carlson 1986a; Chase 1988; Hancock 1982), Casco Bay (Yesner 1984), and the New Hampshire coast (Robinson 1985). Projects in coastal southern New England include those in the Merrimack estuary (Barber 1980, 1982, 1983), Boston Harbour (Carlson 1986c; Luedtke 1980; Nelson 1975), Duxbury (Largy 1995a), Cape Cod (Fitzgerald 1984; Hancock 1984; Shaw 1990), Narragansett Bay (Bernstein 1990, 1993; George 1993; Kerber 1994, 1997; Thelfall and Bowan 1981), Martha's Vineyard (Ritchie 1969a), Nantucket (Carlson 1990c), and Block Island (Bellantoni 1987). These studies indicate that by the late prehistoric period people were opportunistically utilizing the local resources of the land and sea in a generalized subsistence pattern.

Faunal Extinctions and Range Changes. Archaeological fauna have made contributions to understanding zoogeographic changes in species. In particular, possible range shifts are indicated for Atlantic salmon (Carlson 1988b, 1992, 1995), swordfish (Bourque 1995; Robinson 1985; Strauss 1979), mastodon (Moeller 1984), caribou (Spiess et al. 1984–1985), gray seal (Eaton 1898; Waters in Ritchie 1969a), great auk (Eaton 1898; Waters in Ritchie 1969), and oyster (Goldthwaite 1935; Johnson 1942). Given the flexible and nonspecialized nature of prehistoric subsistence practices, these limited extinctions probably had little impact on the ability of people to hunt and gather food.

Sampling, Identification, and Taphonomy. Although all faunal remains are derived from samples of some type, the issue of representation of small species and bone elements was first addressed by Ritchie (1969a) when he used column sampling on Martha's Vineyard. Carlson (1986a) compared column screening with fine window mesh against excavation samples screened with ¼-inch mesh for the recovery of fish remains in Boothbay, Maine, and determined that small species such as Tomcod and Alewives were lost in the larger screens. Problems in species identification have been discussed in distinguishing caribou from deer (Spiess et al. 1984/85), in distinguishing Atlantic salmon from trout (Carlson 1992), and coyote from dog (Kerber 1997). The taphonomic process of bone shrinkage and sample bias due to calcination was experimented with by Knight (1985), and by Spiess et al. (1984–1985) and Spiess (1992).

Seasonality and Growth Ring Analysis. Seasonality using faunal remains has been estimated through the presence or absence of seasonally restricted or migratory species (Barber 1982; Bernstein 1993; Carlson 1986a, 1990c; Ritchie 1969a; Robinson 1985; Spiess and Lewis 1995), sectioning of mammal teeth for growth rings (Bernstein 1993; Bourque et al. 1978; Spiess 1990; Spiess and Lewis 1995), sectioning of shellfish growth rings (Bernstein 1993; Chase 1988; Greenspan 1990; Hancock 1982, 1984), fish otoliths and vertebral growth rings (Carlson 1986a, 1988; Spiess and Lewis 1995), eruption of deer and seal teeth

(Spiess and Lewis 1995), and bird medullary bone (Spiess and Lewis 1995). All of these methods have their particular problems in accuracy and are addressed by the various studies.

Coast vs. Interior Settlement Patterns Comparisons. Faunal materials have been used to address the question of whether the prehistoric settlement pattern was one of separate coastal and inland adaptations, with potential sedentism on the coast, versus one of a transhumant cycle between the coast and inland of river-drainage oriented groups. Snow (1968) employed ethnohistorical accounts to suggest that river drainages were geographic containers of prehistoric communities, whereas Ritchie (1969a) first proposed potential coastal sedentism but eventually ruled out distinct coastal-adapted groups. Other scholars have contributed faunal analysis to the debate, generally conceding that there is little to rule out the possibility of year-round coastal habitation (Bernstein 1993; Carlson 1986a; Chase 1988; Sanger 1982; Spiess 1990).

Subsistence Diversification. On the basis of the increase in the numbers of different shellfish and vertebrate species on Martha's Vineyard from Terminal Archaic to Late Woodland, Ritchie (1969a) first suggested that there was a trend of increasing utilization of larger numbers of species, in particular shellfish, fish, and marine mammals. Recently, Bernstein (1993) and Bourque (1995) have argued similarly for subsistence diversification through time on the southern and northern coasts, respectively. Whether or not these trends are actually real—as opposed to artifacts of different sample sizes, preservation conditions, or cultural changes in mobility patterns from early to late periods—has not been thoroughly addressed. Ecologists have shown that as one collects more samples of animals in an ecosystem, one will identify more species, and the same must apply to archaeological assemblages of fauna.

Special Topics in Faunal Analysis. A number of projects have focused on specific problems with fish remains, such as the role of anadromous fish (Barber 1980; Brumbach 1986; Carlson 1988b, 1992; Dincauze 1976; Yesner et al. 1983), fishing strategies (Belcher 1989; Carlson 1986a; Handley 1996; Yesner 1984), specific use of particular species such as salmon (Carlson 1992, 1995) and swordfish (Bourque 1995; Robinson 1985; Strauss 1979), or general fish usage (Carlson 1980, 1981, 1990c; Huntington 1982; Rojo 1987; Spiess and Lewis 1995). Several scholars have also recently undertaken specialized analyses on shellfish (Barber 1982; Chase 1988; Hancock 1982, 1984; Kerber 1985a, 1985b; Nelson 1975; Ritchie 1969a), and on dogs (Butler and Hadlock 1949; Greenspan 1993; Kerber 1997; Kerber et al. 1989). Other projects have looked at the use of faunal bone in technology (Tyzzer 1943), or for understanding the technology of capture of various species (Dincauze 1985; Johnson 1942; Peterson et al. 1984). In some instances, archaeofaunas are published for their zoogeographical value in biological sciences (e.g., Rhodin and Largy 1984; Waters 1967).

Wild versus Domesticated Foodstuffs. While there were no domesticated animals in New England in precontact times, other than dogs, comparisons have been made about the relative contributions to the diet of wild foodstuffs and the introduction of maize in the Late Woodland period of southern New England (Bendremer et al. 1991; Ceci 1979; McBride and Dewar 1987). Isotope analysis of human, dog, and deer bone from Staten Island suggests that maize was not a component of the marine resource coastal diet (Bridges 1994).

Social Organization. Faunal remains have been used in limited studies as indicators of prehistoric social complexity (Carlson 1992) and social status (Strauss 1979), and in nineteenth-century socioeconomics (Harrington 1989; Singer 1985). This is an area of research that needs further development.

Historical Zooarchaeology. Historical archaeology has also used faunal analysis in several contexts, including studies of the early cod fishery in Maine (Carlson 1983b; Faulkner 1984), as well as subsistence at Fort Pentagoet, Maine (Carlson 1983a; Faulkner and Faulkner 1987), the Sherburne House (Carlson 1986b; Harrington 1989), the Simons House (Savulis and Carlson 1989), and the Ryder-Wood House (Carlson 1989b).

Theses and Dissertations. Several masters theses and Ph.D. dissertations have been written using faunal remains as the principal database. These include the analysis of the Turner Farm fauna (Morse 1975), the Passamaquoddy Bay fauna (McCormick 1980), the Hirundo fauna (Knight 1985), Boothbay shellfish (Hancock 1982), Boothbay fish (Carlson 1986a), Boothbay nonfish (Chase 1988), Block Island fauna (Bellantoni 1987), and a regional analysis of New England's fish fauna (Carlson 1992). Unfortunately, these studies are frequently unpublished, even though they contain some of the most detailed faunal analyses available for the New England region.

CONCLUSION

One of the most striking features about the history of zooarchaeology in New England is its time depth. Since the late nineteenth century, antiquarians, archaeologists, zoologists, and museum curators have been collecting, discussing, identifying to species, and publishing on faunal remains recovered in archaeological contexts. In the early period, osteological identifications were done by zoologists. Beginning in the late 1970s, archaeologists began to train themselves in the science of zoological bone identification, and, coupled with refined site sampling techniques, formed a new, albeit small, subspecialty called zooarchaeology. They have become the new "competent bone sharps" desired by Walter B. Smith (1929).

With the development of zooarchaeology came the need to prepare comparative skeletal collections in archaeology laboratories. Today some of the most comprehensive vertebrate collections in New England were developed by archaeologists and are located at the Maine State Museum in Augusta, the Archaeology Lab at the University of Maine at Orono, the Zooarchaeology Lab at the Peabody Museum, the Archaeology Labs at the University of Massachusetts at Amherst and at Boston, the University of Connecticut Anthropology Lab, and the

American Indian Museum in Washington, Connecticut (formerly the American Indian Archaeological Institute). In addition, there are large zoological collections that are accessible to archaeologists, such as the Harvard University Museums of Natural History (formerly the Museum of Comparative Zoology), and the zoology collections at Northeastern University, Yale University, and the University of Massachusetts at Amherst.

Much of the zoological research in New England has been descriptive, but basic classification is the essence of good science, and even in the antiquarianism of the pre-radiocarbon period, osteological identifications were performed by highly trained vertebrate zoologists, representing the first application of science to archaeology. Research has generally focused on the utilization of faunal resources in hunting, fishing, and gathering traditions, and their role in cultural adaptation and change. In some instances human impacts on the environment, such as faunal extinctions, or in increasing natural resource productivity, is also studied (see Chapter 2, this volume). Dena Dincauze (1993b:44) has written "Particularly here in North America, we accept that the European invaders of the 16th and 17th centuries found what they called a 'virgin land' . . . [but] What they called 'wilderness' had been home to people for over twelve thousand years, and had been indelibly changed by their presence." These remarkable data for understanding the nature of human and environmental relations in precontact New England are today being carefully and painstakingly coaxed out of the record of archaeofaunas.

ACKNOWLEDGMENTS

I am indebted to Tonya Largy for providing me with information on her faunal work and various comparative collections. Arthur Spiess kindly sent me some of his recent publications. To George Nicholas I am thankful for expert editorial advice and cooking. I thank Mary Ann Levine for her considerable patience and encouragement in getting the job done. Mostly I would like to acknowledge Dena Dincauze who, since our first acquaintance in 1981, has inspired me in immeasurable ways. Any errors in fact or interpretation are my own.

12

Native Copper in the Northeast:
An Overview of Potential Sources
Available to Indigenous Peoples

Mary Ann Levine

Since the discovery of ancient copper mines along the shores of Lake Superior in the 1840s, archaeologists have been intrigued with the prehistoric utilization of native copper. This 150-year fascination has resulted in the development of diverse research traditions. Although the focus of research on native copper has continually changed over the last century and a half, one assumption has not. From the mid-nineteenth century onward, scholars have generally assumed that indigenous people in the Midwest, Southeast, and Northeast all obtained native copper exclusively from the Lake Superior area. An early advocate for this perspective was Sir Daniel Wilson, one of the most respected and influential archaeologists of his day (Trigger 1966, 1981). Wilson (1855, 1856) traveled to the westernmost portion of Lake Superior to investigate ancient copper mines and issued the following statement regarding the procurement of native copper: "To this northern copper region American archaeologists are universally agreed in referring the source of most, if not all, the copper tools found in the ancient burial mounds of the Mississippi Valley, and other parts of the continent equally remote from the northern lakes" (Wilson 1855:204).

By the early 1900s the Lake Superior hypothesis was the dominant model for explaining native copper procurement despite the fact that some researchers called attention to its shortcomings (Beauchamp 1902; Duns 1880; Otis 1949). More importantly, the widespread acceptance of the dominant model among northeastern archaeologists was achieved in the absence of systematic large-scale testing to evaluate its validity. The Lake Superior-centric model has thus become an extant truism in northeastern archaeology (for a more detailed discussion of the historical development of the dominant model see Levine [1996]). The intransigence of this model may be seen as one further example of the marginalization of northeastern prehistory by reference to unexamined old folklore and assumptions (Dena Dincauze, personal communication 1993).

The traditional one-source model dismisses the existence and possible utilization of native copper deposits outside of the Lake Superior region and as such undermines our evaluation of the resourcefulness of indigenous peoples in the Northeast. Current perspectives on procurement prohibit serious consideration of how intensively prehistoric populations were aware of their environment and how actively they sought to define it. This model also gives short shrift to the technological capabilities of indigenous peoples in the Northeast. Many proponents of the dominant model claim that since Lake Superior copper sources were utilized to the exclusion of others, copper-working techniques were limited to the Lake Superior area and copper was traded into the Northeast in the form of finished artifacts.

The Lake Superior model also assumes that copper resource utilization practices among northeastern hunter-gatherers were static and stable for 6000 years. Inherent in the dominant model is the notion that the presumed strategy for procuring copper is timeless. Current discourse makes no allowances for the possibility that only local sources were utilized, or that both Lake Superior and other copper sources were procured with one or the other predominating at different points in time. Another deeply rooted assumption in the traditional one-source model is that copper resource procurement was not characterized by regional variation. In other words, the possibility that there was synchronic and diachronic variation in the utilization of native copper has been ignored. The prevailing model therefore assumes a timeless uniformity within the history of northeastern native groups.

Although several different data sets including those derived from geochemical analyses and ethnohistory can be used to assess this deeply entrenched model, I present only one line of evidence to evaluate the dominant model in this chapter. I provide a comprehensive survey of geological sources of native copper in the Northeast to suggest that indigenous peoples had a number of resource procurement options and may have thus availed themselves of these options. Although the multitude of lithic and clay sources available in the Northeast has long been acknowledged, the wide array of copper sources has been hitherto undocumented in the archaeological literature. Providing such an inventory of sources is a necessary precursor for any provenance study designed to chemically characterize copper from geological and archaeological contexts. As the geological origin of native copper cannot be distinguished macroscopically, sensitive analytical techniques that identify the chemical composition of this metal must be utilized to determine whether ancient copper workers procured this valued raw material from distinctly different deposits. Although I have already undertaken such a study (Levine 1996), this chapter solely reports on the range of geological sources present throughout the Northeast.

NATIVE COPPER

Native copper is an exceptionally pure, soft, and malleable red metal. Prior to approximately 7,000 years ago, artifacts of native copper were not a part of the material culture repertoire of indigenous peoples in North America (Beukens et al. 1992). It is in the Lake Superior region, a copper-rich area, that native copper first appeared in the form of utilitarian tools. Native copper artifacts first appeared in the Northeast during the Late Archaic period (ca. 5000–3000 B.P.). During this time native copper was transformed into a number of different tools including adzes, knives, conical points, and tanged points. Although large assemblages of native copper artifacts have been unearthed in some Late Archaic contexts, sites dating to this period usually yield only one or two native copper implements.

In the Early Woodland period (ca. 3000–2000 B.P.), native copper continued to be worked into tool forms, but artifacts for personal adornment, particularly beads, prevailed. Several distinct varieties of native copper beads were manufactured including elongated tubular beads, cylindrical beads crimped onto leather thongs, and rolled beads strung onto cordage. In contrast with Late Archaic assemblages, those of Early Woodland age are characterized by hundreds, and sometimes thousands, of small copper artifacts. Within both time periods, copper artifacts have been recovered from several cultural contexts; however, burials predominate. Native copper continued to be crafted by indigenous peoples into the historic period.

Native copper occurs in a number of different geologic environments in the United States and Canada. Most scholars agree that there are two different kinds of native copper formations, primary and secondary (Rapp et al. 1990). Primary native copper generally occurs in mafic igneous rock including the lava flows of Lake Superior. Rapp and colleagues (1990:480) indicate that the geochemical condition that allows the primary formation of native copper "is the interaction of copper-bearing fluids with iron-bearing minerals in the host rock." Secondary formations of native copper occur within oxidized zones of copper sulfide deposits (Rapp et al. 1990). Different and unrelated geological events are thus responsible for the occurrences of native copper. In the Lake Superior area, native copper generally occurs in basaltic lavas and related sedimentary rocks formed during the Precambrian Era. Some native copper deposits in New England, the Middle Atlantic States, and eastern Canada are associated with red sandstone beds formed during the Mesozoic.

Although the native copper deposits along the shores of Lake Superior were exceptionally large and have received much scholarly attention, several other sources of native copper that formed through unrelated geological events were accessible to indigenous people in the past. Because these deposits in eastern Canada, New England, and the Middle Atlantic States were smaller than those in the Lake Superior area, they were of little interest to nineteenth-century capitalists and economic geologists. However, there is no reason to believe that these sources were not valued by indigenous people who might have significantly depleted small concentrations of ores near the surface. It is important to note that native copper sources known today represent only those not exhausted prehistorically; sources heavily used in the past may not remain for identification or may be represented by only scant traces. Although copper found outside of the Great Lakes can occur as float in glacial deposits displaced from bedrock sources (Glock 1935a, 1935b; Salisbury 1885), it can also occur as lode deposits, significantly along the flanks of the Appalachians. The following sections provide a summary of native copper sources in eastern Canada, New England, and the Middle Atlantic States, as well as in the Lake Superior area.

LAKE SUPERIOR SOURCES

There are a number of native copper deposits widely distributed along the north and south shores of Lake Superior. This area is home to the world's largest deposits of native copper. Native copper occurrences range from tiny specks to massive pieces weighing up to several tons (Lankton 1991:5). South shore deposits are concentrated primarily in upper Michigan along the Keweenaw Peninsula, a seventy-mile-long narrow finger of land (Lankton 1991:3). Native copper deposits occur from Keweenaw Point southwestward through northern Wisconsin and Minnesota (Butler and Burbank 1929:16; Thomas 1993).

Native copper-bearing rocks of Keweenaw age (1.1 billion years old) also occur along the north shore from Duluth to Grand Portage, Minnesota. In this area lies Isle Royale, a forty-five-mile-long copper-rich island situated on the northwestern part of Lake Superior (Figure 12.1). Eastward, there is a gap in the distribution of native copper from Grand Portage at the Minnesota-Ontario border to the Thunder Bay/Black Bay district of Ontario (Butler and Burbank 1929:16; Clark 1991:149–150). Native copper then occurs continuously in scattered outcrops along the north shore as well as on islands in the area from Nipigon to Sault Saint Marie (Clark 1991:151). Copper-bearing locales include Saint Ignace Island, Simpson Island, Point Gargantua, Point Mamainse, and Michipicoten Island (Carter 1904:147).

Although European explorers were familiar with native copper deposits, early French and British attempts to mine copper were unsuccessful. Initial expeditions were understaffed and lacked appropriate transportation and mining technologies (Lankton 1991:7). Profitable exploitation of copper occurred in the 1840s when the U.S. government extinguished indigenous title to land in the Keweenaw and Isle Royale districts (Wilson and Dyl 1992:8). When the Chippewa/Ojibwa ceded this land in the 1842 Treaty of La Point, the government seized control of it for serious mineral exploitation. According to Rickard (1932:230), 30,000 square miles were ceded and the Ojibwa were relocated without ever having received full payment for their land.

Following the implementation of the treaty, vast quantities of native copper were encountered in a number of mining locales in the Lake Superior region. According to Krause (1989), the Keweenaw area alone produced well over 10 billion pounds of native copper from the 1840s to the 1940s. In the Keweenaw area, native copper was mined from over sixty localities associated with nineteen separate copper-bearing lodes (Wilson and Dyl 1992:30–31). Many of these

Figure 12.1
Distribution of Native Copper Sources in the Lake Superior Region
(based on Clark 1991:150)

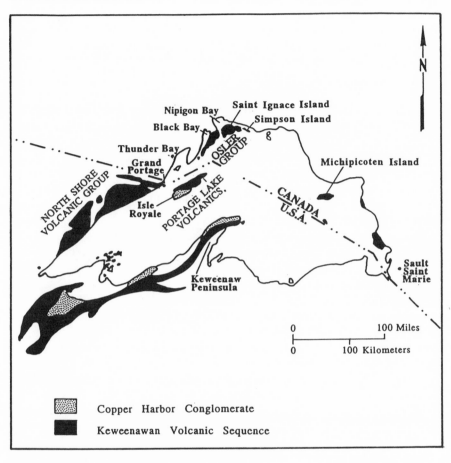

early American and Canadian mines congregated around indigenous mines and thus obliterated them.

EASTERN CANADIAN SOURCES

There are a number of native copper deposits distributed throughout eastern Canada in Québec, Nova Scotia, New Brunswick, Newfoundland, and Labrador (Figure 12.2). In Québec, minor occurrences of native copper have been reported. Some native copper was found in drift in the Chaudière Valley whereas thin plates of native copper were retrieved from red slate, near St. Henri, in the bed of the Etchemin River (Logan 1863:515; Traill 1970:166). The Etchemin

Figure 12.2
Distribution of Native Copper Sources in Eastern Canada

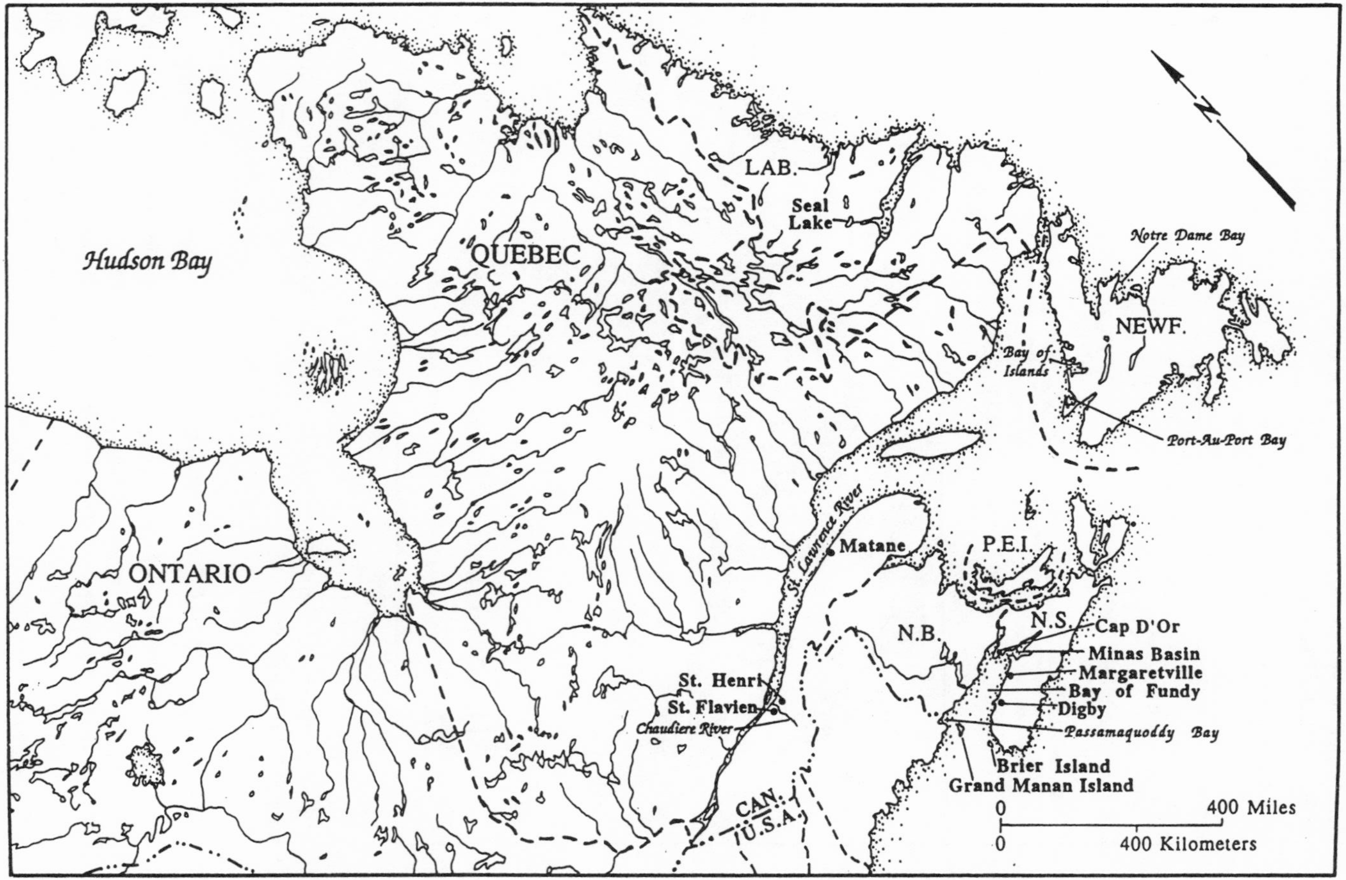

and Chaudière are tributaries of the St. Lawrence River near Québec City. Smaller specimens of native copper were also reported in a bed of amygdaloidal diorite at St. Flavien (Logan 1863:515). Near Matane, farther up on the south shore of the St. Lawrence estuary, several small pieces of native copper were found in an eruptive mass of diorite (Ells 1904:56). In contrast to Québec, the Maritime provinces have yielded impressive native copper deposits.

Nineteenth-century geological accounts report on the Bay of Fundy deposits, in addition to a number of other copper-bearing locales in the Maritimes. The Bay of Fundy is an arm of the Atlantic Ocean that separates Nova Scotia and New Brunswick. Gilpin (1880:75) noted that the "trap of the Bay of Fundy has . . . yielded grains and lumps of metallic copper sometimes weighing fifty pounds." More specifically, native copper occurs at various points throughout a 50-mile stretch of the north side of the Bay of Fundy. Native copper occurrences have been encountered from Five Points westward to Cap D'Or. Ells (1904:14) reported that at Cap D'Or, native copper can be readily seen. Dawson (1878:107) stated that Cap D'Or yields evidence for native copper ranging from large masses weighing several pounds to minute grains. There are also reports of native copper discoveries on the south side of the Bay of Fundy in Margaretsville, Nova Scotia. At this locale, small but abundant masses of native copper have discovered (Woodward 1944:117). Farther south at Annapolis and Digby, pieces of native copper weighing several pounds were found on the beach (Ells 1904:15). Even farther south at Brier Island and at Peter's Point, Dawson (1878:113) located what he described as irregular masses of native copper. All of the Bay of Fundy nuggets that I handled in museum contexts were lustrous and smooth from having been rolled along the beach. They were also free from any inclusions. Because such nuggets would have been easily and readily accessible to indigenous peoples, the native copper from the Bay of Fundy seems ideal for the fabrication of artifacts.

Native copper also occurs in nearby New Brunswick where this province's southern coast meets the Bay of Fundy. Native copper, in unspecified quantities, has been reported at Little Salmon River. Native copper has also been encountered at Clark Point in the Passamaquoddy Bay area (Traill 1970:164). A number of copper nuggets have also been found on Grand Manan Island (Ells 1904: 19). Bailey (1899:19–20) noted that "scattered nodules or irregular strings or bunches of pure copper have been frequently met with" on Grand Manan.

Native copper is also found in Newfoundland. Native copper in the form of arborescent thin films is found in small concentrations at Tilt Cove Mine and a number of other localities along Notre Dame Bay. It also occurs in small strings and nodules embedded in trap rock near Port-a-Port Bay and the Bay of Islands along the west coast of Newfoundland (Howley 1882:38).

Labrador possesses sizable native copper deposits as well. Geological exploration in the 1950s confirmed the existence of fifteen separate native copper occurrences along a 24-mile stretch of land near Seal Lake. The copper ranged in size from stringers and small blebs to large nuggets. At two localities where trenches were placed, geologists retrieved a number of copper nuggets each weighing several pounds and one measuring eight inches across (Evans 1952:111). Although native copper is distributed throughout eastern Canada, the literature reviewed here suggests that it was more abundant in Labrador and Nova Scotia than in Québec.

NEW ENGLAND SOURCES

Some of the most dramatic occurrences of native copper outside of the Lake Superior region have been discovered in New England, particularly Connecticut (Figure 12.3). A mass of native copper weighing nearly 200 pounds was found in glacial drift one-half mile north of East Rock, outside of New Haven (Dana 1887:146). This specimen is now on display at Yale's Peabody Museum. Like any other that could have been happened upon in pre-contact times, this mass could have been easily worked into hundreds of points or thousands of beads. In addition, a six-pound piece was turned up through plowing twelve miles from New Haven near Wallingford (Silliman 1818:55). Silliman (1818:56) described this specimen as "beautiful virgin copper, with rudiments of large octahedral crystals of native copper upon its surface."

A number of smaller pieces of native copper have been found throughout Connecticut as well. A button-sized lump of native copper was located in a trap ridge near Plainville (Hulbert 1897:24). Shepard (1837:41) noted that a number of smaller lumps had also been found in trap rock in Farmington. Near Mt. Carmel, nineteenth-century road construction exposed a thin seam or vein of native copper in the trap rock (Blake 1888:70). Blasting threw out small pieces of native copper from one-eighth to one-quarter of an inch thick and two or three inches long. Even such small, flat pieces could have provided the raw material for a number of beads with only minimal handling. And finally, unspecified amounts of native copper were retrieved from Bristol (Cochrane 1896: 512; Hitchcock 1823:116), Lambert's Mine in Orange (Shepard 1837:41), and Cheshire (Bateman 1923:154). In the 1800s native copper was thus frequently encountered throughout Connecticut in both drift and trap rock.

However, the actual extent of native copper in Connecticut prior to the 1800s is difficult to ascertain. Some reported examples of native copper deposits were not well documented when they were discovered and cannot be examined further since they ceased to exist. For example, in the early 1700s the Higley copper mine in East Granby purportedly produced copper of great purity (Gray 1982:204). Much of the copper was shipped to England for smelting. Harte (1945:154) stated that "[w]hile the mine in its time produced a very considerable amount of rich ore, its chief claim to fame is on the score of Higley's bootleg currency, struck from native copper." Without proper authorization, Higley utilized native copper to manufacture the first copper coinage in America. Our understanding of the native copper deposits in East Granby are thus limited because few examples of the Higley Coppers survive. In addition, in 1790 a

Figure 12.3
Distribution of Native Copper Sources in New England

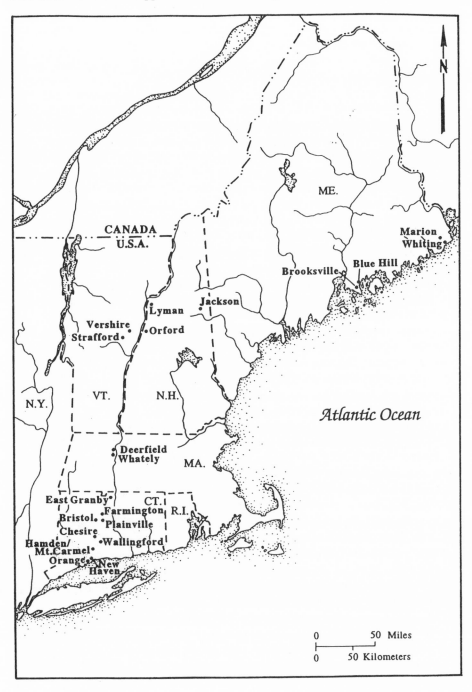

ninety-pound mass of native copper was discovered by a man gathering fruit in Hamden near Mount Carmel (Barber 1836:221; Hulbert 1897:24; Pease and Niles 1819:124). The copper was lying on the surface and was still attached to a rock by threads of metal (Silliman 1810:149). By 1810 nothing remained of the specimen, which had fallen into the hands of a coppersmith, the son-in-law of the discover, who "considered it as very free of alloy, and used it in the course of his business" (Silliman 1810:149). Evidently, the ninety-pound mass was melted down for commercial purposes. Although our understanding of Connecticut's native copper sources is necessarily incomplete, available evidence unequivocally demonstrates that native copper was present in quantities significant enough to allow for the manufacture of artifacts in prehistoric times.

Native copper occurs in Massachusetts as well. Hitchcock (1823:116, 1841: 422) reported that a specimen of native copper weighing seventeen ounces was found in a plowed field in Whately. Additional specimens, one weighing sixteen ounces (Hitchcock 1844), and the other two and one-half pounds (Anonymous 1862) were also found as float in Whately. One of the specimens is now part of the Pratt Museum collection at Amherst College. Like those recovered near New Haven, the Whately float copper was free of inclusions and could have been fashioned into a variety of tools without complication. Weed (1911:33) reported that the Triassic sandstones of Massachusetts included native copper at "many localities." Deerfield is one such locality. The Berkshire Museum in Pittsfield, Massachusetts, houses a piece of native copper attached to a fragment of red sandstone from Deerfield. Native copper thus existed in Massachusetts as float on the surface and adhered to host rock in modest amounts. Even such modest quantities could have been transformed into dozens of artifacts.

In contrast to southern New England, northern New England possesses only minor traces of native copper. Native copper occurrences in Maine are extremely rare and have usually been discovered in mine contexts. At the Twin Lead Mine in Blue Hill, miners discovered a massive quartz vein permeated by a number of minerals including native copper (Anonymous 1880b:232). A superintendent's report from the Mammoth Mine, also located in Blue Hill included the following passage: "Yesterday we broke into considerable native copper" (Anonymous 1881b:57). A report on the Manhattan Mine in Brooksville included this statement: "Considerable black oxide of copper has been encountered and also some native copper" (Anonymous 1881a:185). At the Hercules Mine also near Brooksville native copper along with copper silicate was reported (Bartlett 1880:246). One report on the mineral occurrences in the towns of Marion and Whiting announced the discovery of a surficial deposit of native copper. It stated the following: "Native copper has been discovered, very rich, one of the best surface showings of copper ever found in Maine" (Anonymous 1880a:357). Regrettably, no data on the actual magnitude of these surface finds were offered. Given the lack of relevant detail in this description, it is difficult to assess the likelihood of indigenous use of native copper from Maine.

In their volume on the geology of New Hampshire, Meyers and Stewart (1977:20) noted that "metallic copper is a rare mineral in this state." They reported that small amounts were found in a tin mine in Jackson, a town located in the White Mountains near the Maine border. They also stated that dendritic native copper occurred along the Connecticut River in Orford and Lyman (Meyers and Stewart 1977:20; Morrill 1960:29–30). Eugene Boudette, State Geologist for New Hampshire in 1991, stated that native copper may be found in what he termed the Gardner Mountain–Woburn, Québec mineral belt (Eugene Boudette, personal communication 1991).

The actual extent of native copper deposits in Vermont is a matter of debate. C. B. Adams (1845:30), an early state geologist for Vermont, reported that a mining agent found a single loose fragment of native copper weighing four ounces on Copperas Hill. In a footnote he suggested that the native copper may have been put on the ground for purposes of deception. George H. Perkins (1900:6), his successor, stated that "[t]here is no native copper, like that found in the Lake Superior region, in Vermont." A decade later Perkins (1910:34) reported that small pieces of native copper had indeed been discovered in 1861 in Strafford and Vershire. Yet in a subsequent publication, Perkins (1921:301) argued that anyone prospecting for native copper in Vermont was searching in vain.

Curiously, an even later report by Perkins (1930) included information that may be potentially contradictory. Although he first noted that native copper had never been found in Vermont he later stated: "Copper has several times been reported as found in Vermont, and small pieces have been picked up here and there, but it appears to be quite certain that these were all 'finds' that is they did not originally occur here" (Perkins 1930:157). When asked about the Adams-Perkins debate, Charles A. Ratté, state geologist for Vermont in 1991, reported that he was not personally familiar with any native copper in Vermont and if it did exist it would be thinly distributed (Charles A. Ratté, personal communication 1991).

MIDDLE ATLANTIC SOURCES

Several sizable native copper deposits have been reported in the Middle Atlantic states, especially New Jersey (Figure 12.4). Native copper has been found in many localities throughout the state and has taken the form of minute grains, thin sheets, nodules, nuggets, and large masses occurring in both surficial and mine contexts (Woodward 1944:13). Early mining reports shed significant light on the extent of native copper deposits in New Jersey.

In the early 1700s Schuyler Mine, one of the oldest mines in New Jersey and the United States, was being worked for copper (Figure 12.5). According to some sources, in 1719 an enslaved African who labored on Arent Schuyler's estate happened upon a piece of copper (Rickard 1932:7; Woodward 1944: 43). This specimen was analyzed in England and determined to be 80 percent

Figure 12.4
Distribution of Native Copper Sources in the Middle Atlantic States

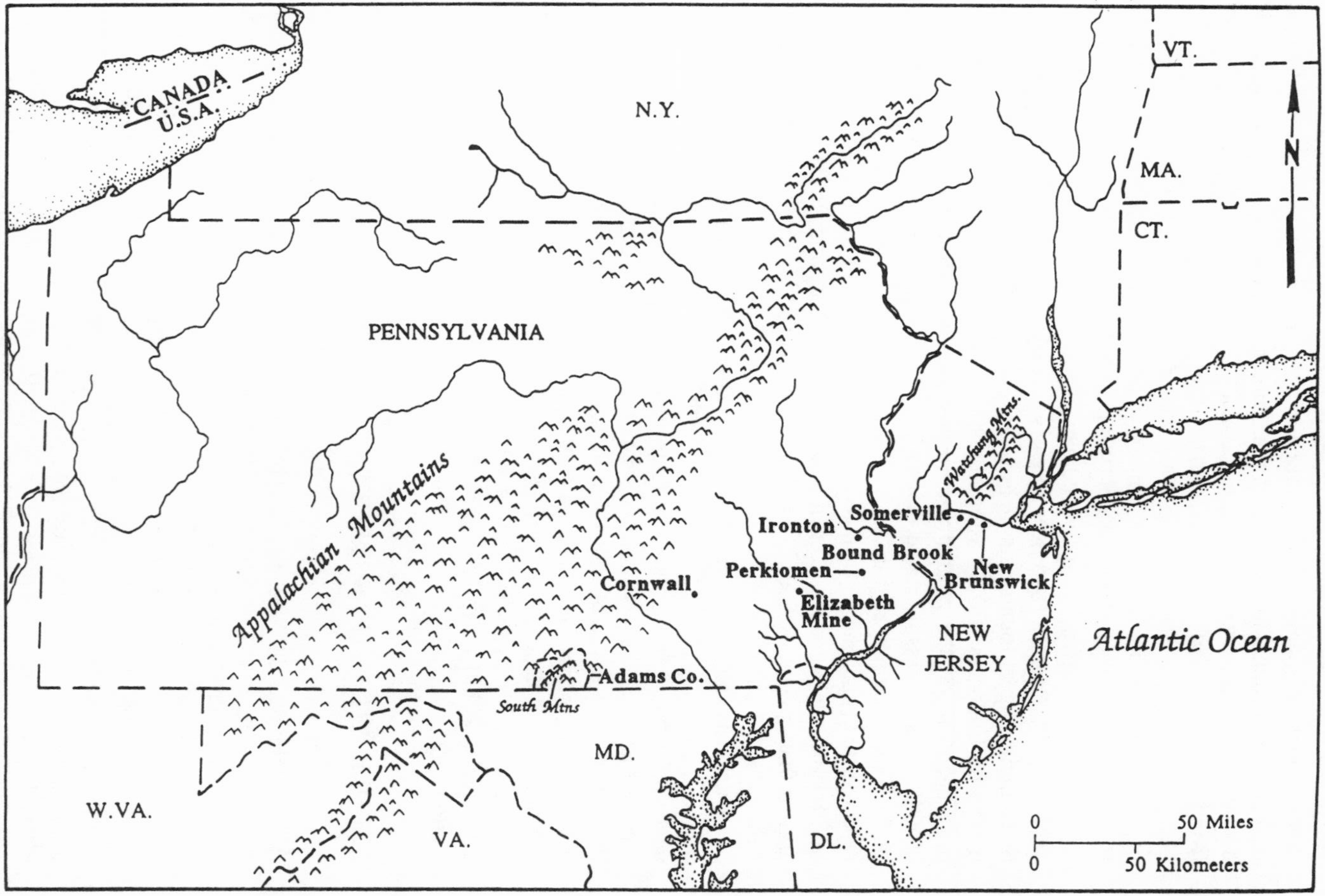

Figure 12.5
Distribution of Native Copper Sources in the
Watchung Mountain Region, New Jersey

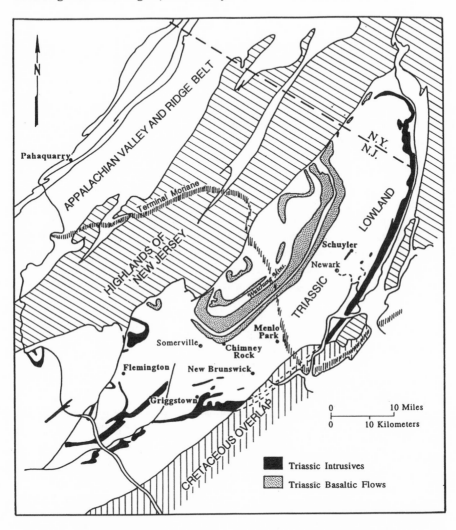

metallic copper (Woodward 1944:44). On the basis of that result, the specimen was variously interpreted as being native copper (Bishop 1868:548; Rickard 1932:7), chalcocite, or chrysocolla (Woodward 1944:43). According to George Rapp (personal communication 1995) if this specimen was indeed metallic copper and not alloyed, the high percentage of copper indicates that the specimen was native copper. For the first few years this mineral, which must have been native copper, was gathered only from the surface. It is reasonable to suggest then that the surficial occurrences of native copper must have been substantial. After a few years, the mining operations proved enormously profitable as underground shafts were sunk (Woodward 1944:58). By 1731 enslaved Africans had retrieved 1,386 tons of copper from Schuyler Mine (Woodward 1944:46). The mine was even worked into this century and continued to yield occasional specimens of native copper (Lewis 1907a:247, 1907b:42).

The discovery of copper on the Schuyler estate stimulated interest in searching for native copper in neighboring areas around the Watchung Mountains. The ridge slopes near Somerville and Bound Brook were carefully combed and resulted in the discovery of an impressive quantity of native copper fragments. Woodward (1944:77) stated that "[a]s much as 1,900 pounds of the native metal in various masses is said to have been discovered before 1754." More specific information on where and how this copper was retrieved is provided by Beck (1839) and Lewis (1907b). Beck (1839:107) stated that in Somerville, native copper nuggets weighing 5 to 10 pounds were discovered on the surface. He also noted that a 128-pound mass was plowed up on the mountain slope in Somerville (Beck 1839:108). A seventy-four-pound portion of this specimen was preserved and is still housed at Rutgers University Geological Museum. Given its high quality and size, this mass could have undoubtedly provided the raw material necessary for the fabrication of hundreds if not thousands of tools. Commercial mining operations soon followed these discoveries. The American Copper Mine was formed to retrieve additional copper. Woodward (1944:80) stated that "[a]s in the case of all New Jersey copper prospects, the first Somerville operations were wholly conducted from shallow trenches and surface excavations, no deeper pits being sunk until the surficial deposits had become exhausted." After describing subterranean shafts that had been sunk from 1,110 to 1,240 feet, Hamilton (1904:109) stated that the deeper part of the mine was the most encouraging and "[t]he values are now practically all in native copper."

Spectacular occurrences of native copper have also come from the area near New Brunswick. Between 1748 and 1750, 200 pounds of native copper in the form of numerous five- to thirty-pound nuggets were plowed up in a field in New Brunswick where Rutgers University now stands (Lewis 1907b:151). The New Brunswick Mines were opened in 1751 and miners immediately encountered a sandstone bed plated with thin sheets of native copper. Similar sheets of native copper about an eighth of an inch thick and one or two feet long were found in a neighboring area (Lewis 1907b:152).

Native copper has been reported from a number of other mines in the Watchung Mountain area of New Jersey. At the Menlo Park Mine seven miles northeast of New Brunswick, native copper occurs on the rock surface and as thick sheets and films in joint cracks of the shale (Woodward 1944:99). At the Chimney Rock Mines, specimens of native copper from one-half to one-and-a-half pounds were encountered (Hamilton 1904:110). The mines at Griggstown (Lewis 1907b:138); Hoffman (Woodward 1944:95); and Flemington as well as towns such as Stanhope, Woodbridge, East Belleville, and Bergen Hill (Canfield

1889:8–9) have also all yielded native copper. Given these descriptions of the historic landscape, it is reasonable to suggest that New Jersey's prehistoric landscape necessarily included large and readily accessible native copper resources.

Native copper in the form of small flecks, wires, lumps, and masses occurs throughout the South Mountains of Pennsylvania (see Figure 12.4), most especially in Adams County (Bascom 1896; Bevier 1914; Fauth 1978; Stose 1910, 1932; Stose and Bascom 1929). Native copper has been reported from mine contexts (Frazer 1877, 1880; Henderson 1884; Rose 1970) as well as surficially (Bailey 1883; Stose 1932).

Bailey (1883:88) noted that at the Wagamon farm in Adams County "excellent surface indications are present, of native copper, and oxide of copper, plentifully disseminated in a fine quartzite epidote." What is described by Stose (1932:136) as "float copper" was found on the surface at many places between newly established nineteenth-century mining prospects in Adams County. For example, native copper float was found at the Bingham farm near Mt. Hope (Stose 1932:138). Bailey (1883:89) provided the following description of the surficial deposits of native copper at Mussulman Hill, also known as Snively Mine.

In approaching the apex of the hill along the strike of the deposit, the surface of the ground is literally covered with wonderfully rich native float pieces weighing a ton or more sticking full of native copper and oxide of copper being visible. One piece of native metal weighing 27 pounds was picked up by Dr. Snively, the former lessee of the property, within a few feet of the shaft.

Stose (1932:138) doubted, however, whether so sizable a mass of native copper was ever recovered from this locale. Given the presence of a 300-pound mass of native copper recovered from a mine in the same region, I suspect that it is entirely possible that a 27-pound mass could have been recovered. Sometime in the 1970s a 300-pound mass was retrieved by Earl Shindledecker, an employee at the Virgin Mine (Melba Shindledecker, personal communication 1993). This specimen is now part of the Jay Lininger Mineral Collection in Dillsburg, Pennsylvania.

Native copper was frequently encountered at the Virgin Mine, now on land quarried by the GAF Corporation. According to Lininger (1991:2) the Virgin Mine yielded the richest mass of native copper in all of the South Mountain area. Earl Shindledecker preserved and dispensed thousands of specimens of native copper and accessory minerals which would have been destroyed since they were of no significance to the greenstone mining operation (Lininger 1991:2). Other sources provide additional information on the Virgin Mine, reporting that bright native copper in fine wires was found at the contact of the epidote and sheeted greenstone at a depth of 125 feet (Stose 1932:136) whereas strings of bright native copper were encountered at a depth of 150 feet (Stose

1910:126). Bevier (1914:60) noted that an even deeper zone was thickly impregnated with native copper.

There are at least seven mines within five miles of the Virgin Mine that also include native copper. At the Gingham Mine located one mile from the Virgin Mine, native copper in the form of specks and blebs was reported (Stose 1910: 126). At the Reed Hill Mine, a half mile north of the Bingham Mine, native copper specimens weighing over a pound were found in the soil and wash (Stose 1910:127). Flecks of native copper were encountered at the Russell Mine, located a mile and a half north of Reed Hill (Stose 1910:127). At the Snively Mine, or the Mussulman Hill prospect, native copper was obtained from the dump (Stose 1910:127) and in the form of three- to four-pound masses (Henderson 1884:88). The greenstone at the Eagle Metallic Mine was impregnated with "fine specks, stringers, and sheets of native copper" (Bevier 1914:59). The Hayes Creek and Headlight mines also contained native copper occurrences (Stose 1910:128–129).

Minor occurrences of native copper have been found outside the South Mountain area in eastern Pennsylvania. Native copper occurs at the Ironton Railroad Company's mine in Lehigh County (Prime 1878:70), Kober's and Perkiomen mines in Montgomery County (Earl 1950:6; Wherry 1909:734), Elizabeth and Wheatley mines in Chester County (Benge and Wherry 1908:6–7), and at the Cornwall Mine in Lebanon County (Lapham and Gray 1973:123; Lesley and D'Invilliers 1886:512, 548). The Middle Atlantic landscape traversed by indigenous people in the past was characterized by the widespread distribution of native copper nuggets and masses in procurable contexts.

CONCLUSION

Lake Superior sources of native copper are much celebrated for a variety of reasons. The abundance of these deposits coupled with their economic profitability drew attention to the region from an early date. Because so much wealth was generated from the exploitation of these deposits, the Lake Superior area has enjoyed a unique position in both the popular and scholarly discourse concerning copper, so much so that it is commonly held to be the only source of high grade, pure native copper. However, the metal is not as rare and as localized as previously believed.

Native copper does exist in a variety of other localities throughout eastern North America. Specimens, often of remarkable size and purity, have been identified throughout the region. Furthermore, the majority of native copper specimens that I have handled from outside of the Lake Superior area were of very high quality and thus appropriate for tool making. Such occurrences were free of inclusions and could have been transformed into a variety of tools without difficulty. In contrast with Lake Superior deposits, native copper sources from eastern Canada, New England, the Middle Atlantic states were not economically significant in the nineteenth century and thus were understudied by modern economic geologists. As a result, these sources of native copper have been neglected in the geological and archaeological literature. Although the decision to utilize a resource is determined by a number of factors, it is clear that if indigenous peoples during the Late Archaic and Woodland periods wanted to procure copper from local sources, those resources would have been available and suitable for working.

ACKNOWLEDGMENTS

First and foremost I would like to thank my mentor, Dena Dincauze. She has never failed to provide prompt and insightful comments and advice on my work. I will always be grateful for the opportunity to have studied with her. I am also indebted to Martin Wobst who was invaluable in the design and implementation of this research project. A special thanks goes to Rip Rapp, Director of the Archaeometry Laboratory at the University of Minnesota at Duluth for sharing his wealth of knowledge on native copper. My gratitude is further extended to James Delle, Michael Nassaney, and Ken Sassaman for commenting upon earlier drafts of this article. Maureen Manning-Bernatzky, graphics artist for UMass Archaeological Services, carefully drew the maps that illustrate this chapter. The research for this article was undertaken while I was a recipient of a Doctoral Fellowship from the Social Sciences and Humanities Research Council of Canada.

13

Radiocarbon Dating of Shell on the Southern Coast of New England

Elizabeth A. Little

In "Song for all Seas, all Ships," Walt Whitman (1927:222) spoke poetically of "Old Ocean." Radiocarbon dating, too, sees the ocean as old. That is, plants and animals in marine food webs appear to be older in radiocarbon years than contemporary plants and animals that lived in atmospheric webs. Furthermore, the variation in $^{14}C/^{12}C$ through time in the ocean differs from that in the atmosphere. This means that the radiocarbon ages of marine materials need special adjustments and calibration in order to represent ordinary calendar years.

In this chapter, I introduce radiocarbon dating, explain briefly why fractionation and reservoir corrections followed by age calibrations are necessary, and show how to do them. Lastly, I add five pairs of shell and charcoal ages to the existing southern New England database of four pairs used to determine the marine reservoir age.

RADIOCARBON

Taylor (1987) and Taylor et al. (1992) give overviews of radiocarbon studies since their beginning in the late 1940s, which are the basis for this brief introduction to radiocarbon. The isotope carbon-12 (^{12}C), with six protons and six neutrons in its nucleus, makes up most of ordinary carbon. The isotope ^{13}C has seven neutrons, while ^{14}C has eight neutrons and is unstable. Cosmic rays in the upper atmosphere bombard nitrogen-14 with neutrons and produce ^{14}C, which then disperses throughout the atmosphere, oceans, and biosphere. Each ^{14}C atom has a small and constant probability of decaying in any instant. By decay is meant giving off a beta particle (a high energy electron) and becoming ^{14}N again.

Radiocarbon provides a clock that starts when an organism dies. Alive, an animal or plant exchanges carbon with its reservoir. Alive, an animal or plant exchanges carbon with its environment. After death, existing ^{14}C in the organism decays, but no new ^{14}C is taken in. As the number of ^{14}C atoms of carbon decreases, the rate of emission of beta particles decreases. Thus the sample's ^{14}C activity at any time, compared to its initial value, reflects its age of death. Radiocarbon ages can be measured by counting either the emission rate of beta particles or the number of ^{14}C atoms, per gram of carbon. The former is done with an ionization detector, and the latter with an accelerator mass spectrometer. The ratio of the measurements on a sample as compared to a 1950 terrestrial ^{14}C standard determine the radiocarbon age of the sample (see Stuiver and Polach 1977:355).

FRACTIONATION CORRECTION

Isotopic fractionation is the discrimination against heavier carbon isotopes during chemical or biological processes. It is proportional to differences in atomic mass. This makes it possible to find the correction for fractionation in ^{14}C by measuring the fractionation in ^{13}C. $\delta^{13}C$ (delta 13C) is the difference in parts per thousand between the ratio $^{13}C/^{12}C$ in a sample and in a standard. $\delta^{13}C$ can be measured on a mass spectrometer, or, for many materials, can be estimated from a table (e.g., Stuiver and Polach 1977:358).

To obtain a fractionation corrected or *conventional* radiocarbon age (Stuiver and Polach 1977), one adds about 16 ^{14}C years for each 1 o/oo of $\delta^{13}C$ more positive than -25 o/oo (Taylor 1987:121–122). The fractionation correction for shells, for which $\delta^{13}C$ is close to 0 o/oo, makes their age older by about four hundred years. For charcoal, with $\delta^{13}C$ usually about -25 o/oo, the correction is zero and archaeologists often ignore it. Both assumptions are often worth checking (see Table 13.1; Little 1995).

RESERVOIR CORRECTION, R(t)

Newly formed ^{14}C created by cosmic rays disperses throughout the atmosphere and terrestrial biosphere in a matter of years. Thus most land plants and animals contain proportions of $^{14}C/^{12}C$ in equilibrium with the atmosphere. But in the ocean, which has much more carbon than the atmosphere, as well as many deep, poorly mixed basins, ^{14}C can require thousands of years to mix. As ^{14}C decays to ^{14}N, the result is a marine environment low in $^{14}C/^{12}C$. Animals and plants living in such waters have fewer ^{14}C atoms per gram of carbon than their contemporary terrestrial counterparts. To obtain a correct age for a marine plant or animal, therefore, its radiocarbon age measurement must be adjusted for the ^{14}C age of its marine habitat, or, to use the terminology of the field, for its Marine Reservoir Age. This phenomenon has interested geologists since at least 1952 (Kulp et al. 1952; Taylor 1987:sections 3.3.3, 5.5.1; McNichol 1996).

To test this theory experimentally, in 1991 I collected some fresh bluefish from Nantucket and several live twigs from Lincoln woods and took them to

Geochron Labs for a comparison of their radiocarbon activity. The mean conventional age of the bluefish was 555 ^{14}C years older than that of the twigs (Table 13.1).

To enable archaeologists to adjust and calibrate marine radiocarbon (^{14}C) ages to estimated calendar years, Stuiver and Braziunas (1993) have modeled a worldwide difference, over the past 10,200 ^{14}C years, between the ^{14}C ages of a sample from the top seventy-five meters of the ocean and a contemporary sample incorporating atmospheric carbon. They call this difference, which varies with time, the Marine Reservoir Age, and denote it as R(t), measured in ^{14}C years. Stuiver and Braziunas (1993:Figure 5a) assume that R(t) averages over time to about 400 ^{14}C years, with a variation generally less than 100 years. The ^{14}C concentration in ocean water also varies with depth, but the surface layer provides most marine biological resources used by humans.

The model, R(t), requires a regional correction, ΔR in ^{14}C years, to account for local oceanic effects. ΔR is a constant over time unless there are major changes in climate, currents, upwelling, or bomb testing (see McNichol 1996). Figure 13.1 gives ΔR values in the North Atlantic Ocean available in 1993.

A determination of the local ΔR needed for Stuiver and Braziunas's (1993) marine calibration procedure requires a pair of δ^{13}C-corrected radiocarbon ages for contemporaneous marine and atmospheric samples. Alternatively, a radiocarbon age on a marine sample of known calendar age can be used to provide a pair of ages. Figure 15 of Stuiver and Braziunas (1993) provides a handy aid to calculation of ΔR.

CALIBRATION

Calendar years are what we use every day. Even after adjustments for fractionation and reservoir ages, radiocarbon years are still not equal to calendar years. The chief reason for this is the change through time in ^{14}C production (Stuiver and Braziunas 1993).

A radiocarbon age corrected for fractionation and reservoir age may be converted to calendar years by reference to tree ring calibration curves or tables. Radiocarbon years are usually reported as ^{14}C years $\pm$ σ B.P., where σ (sigma) is standard deviation and B.P. means before 1950. After the age is calibrated, it is reported as Cal B.C., A.D., or B.P., expressed as xxxx(mmmm)yyyy, where mmmm is the mean, xxxx is the mean less σ, yyyy is the mean plus σ.

To calibrate an atmospheric sample, one converts the δ^{13}C-corrected ^{14}C age to Cal years using atmospheric calibration curves or tables (e.g., Stuiver and Pearson 1993). To calibrate a marine sample, one first subtracts ΔR from the δ^{13}C-corrected ^{14}C age and then converts the result to Cal years with the marine calibration curves or tables (Stuiver and Braziunas 1993). *Radiocarbon* (1993: 35[1]) included a computer disk with CALIB 3.0 (DOS; Stuiver and Reimer 1993) to perform these calibrations, and a recent MAC or DOS CALIB 3.0.3 can be downloaded from < http://weber.u.washington.edu/ ~ qil > .

Table 13.1
Terrestrial and Marine Pair Ages from Massachusetts and Rhode Island Sites

Location		Lab. No.	Material, $\delta^{13}C$ o/oo	^{14}C years B.P. $\delta^{13}C$-cor.	ΔR[a] ^{14}C years	Cal A.D. years[b] $-\sigma$ (mean) $+\sigma$
MASSACHUSETTS						
Boston Harbor:	Calf Island[c]	GX-3652	charcoal, -24.9	410 ± 110		1420 (1462) 1641
	Calf Island[c]	GX-7456	M. arenaria, +1.8	860 ± 115	-10 ± 150	1311 (1418) 1485
		GX-3652	charcoal, -24.9	410 ± 110		1420 (1462) 1641
	World's End[c]	GX-7457	M. edulis, +0.4	685 ± 135	-185 ± 168	1435 (1522) 1675
		GX-15664	charcoal, -25.6	765 ± 70		1223 (1279) 1294
		GX-15661	M. arenaria, +2.6	1065 ± 70	-85 ± 99	1185 (1268) 1312
Cape Cod and Nantucket:	Brewster[d]	GX-19564	charcoal, -26.1	865 ± 95		1036 (1212) 1278
		GX-19318	M. mercenaria, +1.6	1150 ± 90	-100 ± 131	1052 (1184) 1279
	Nauset[e]	GX-9550	charcoal, (-25)	1265 ± 130		655 (774) 952
		GX-9551	M. arenaria, +2.0	1570 ± 120	-80 ± 177	638 (725) 881
	Nauset[e]	GX-9553	charcoal, (-25)	180 ± 115		1643 (1678-1941) 1955
		GX-9554	M. mercenaria, +1.2	590 ± 110	-60 ± 159	1504 (1651) 1715
	Nauset[e]	GX-9558	charcoal, (-25)	890 ± 150		1011 (1168) 1284
		GX-9559	M. mercenaria, -0.1	1090 ± 155	-170 ± 216	1050 (1244) 1349
Quidnet[f]:		GX-4528	deerbone apatite, (-13)	1770 ± 160		79 (253,304,314) 432
		I-9734	C. virginica, (+1.2)	2060 ± 80	-70 ± 179	113 (230) 340
RHODE ISLAND						
Pt. Judith[g]:		β-67425	charcoal, (-25)	480 ± 110		1398 (1436) 1611
		β-67424	shell, (0)	820 ± 60	-90 ± 125	1397 (1439) 1489
Average ΔR (9 pairs):					-94 ± 53	
MASSACHUSETTS						
Lincoln		GX-17860	1991 Twigs, -31.2	113.9 ± .6 %Mod.		
Nantucket		GX-17859	1991 Bluefish, -17.9	106.3 ± .6 %Mod.	R = 555 ± 90 ^{14}C years	

[a] ΔRs estimated from Stuiver and Brazuinas (1993:Figures 15a,17a).
[b] Dates calibrated using CALIB 3.0.3 (Stuiver and Reimer 1993; $\Delta R = -95 \pm 45$ ^{14}C years).
[c] B. Luedtke, personal communication 1990.
[d] Strauss (1994), Little (1994).
[e] Borstel (1984).
[f] Little (1984).
[g] Leveillee et al. (1996); ($\delta^{13}C$): estimated.
For subtraction, $\sigma = (\Sigma\sigma_i^2)^{1/2}$; for averaging, $\sigma = (\Sigma\sigma_i^2)^{1/2}/N$, for N pairs.

Figure 13.1
North Atlantic Geographic Distribution of Coastal ΔR values in ^{14}C years
(based on Stuiver and Braziunas 1993:Figure 16)

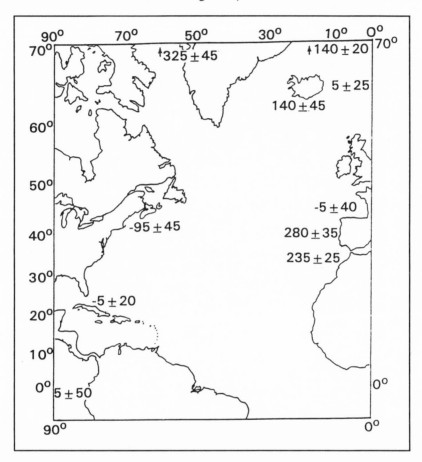

MEASUREMENT OF ΔR FOR MASSACHUSETTS AND RHODE ISLAND

Stuiver et al. (1986:955) gave ΔR values for many coasts of the world. However, they provided only one data point on the entire eastern coast of North America between southern Florida and Baffin Bay. To estimate ΔR for the New England coast, I compiled radiocarbon ages for pairs of marine remains with a known age of death or with associated charcoal or deer bone radiocarbon ages from archaeological deposits of coastal New England (Little 1993). Four of the Massachusetts pairs from Cape Cod and Nantucket, dating between 200 and 2000 calendar years ago, established a ΔR = -95 ± 45 ^{14}C years for Massachusetts (Figure 13.1; Little 1993; Stuiver and Braziunas 1993). Data earlier than 2000 years ago and outside of Massachusetts are scarce and I continue to collect pair data (Little 1994, 1995).

In the present chapter I add five pairs of shell and charcoal, three from Boston Harbor (Little 1993), and new pairs from Brewster, Massachusetts, and Point Judith, Rhode Island. Each of the now nine pairs consists of a radiocarbon-dated marine shell and an associated terrestrial date from an archaeological site in coastal Massachusetts or Rhode Island (Figure 13.2; Table 13.1).

The two new pairs of radiocarbon-dated shell and charcoal samples have provided a striking test of the Massachusetts ΔR. Alan Leveillee and Burr Harrison (1996) encountered an apparent 340 ^{14}C year difference between shell and charcoal ^{14}C ages from a Late Woodland cemetery, RI-110, at Point Judith, Rhode Island. The two samples came from two nearby pit features in a Late Woodland cemetery. Because of the apparent difference in dates, Leveillee initially concluded, with some reluctance, that the use of the cemetery covered a

Figure 13.2
Map of the Southern Coast of New England, Showing the Sites Discussed in the Text
Key: (1) Calf Island; (2) Worlds End; (3) Brewster; (4) Nauset; (5) Quidnet; (6) Point Judith. 41°N to 42°N is 70 miles (112 km), and 70°W to 72°W is 104 miles (166 km).

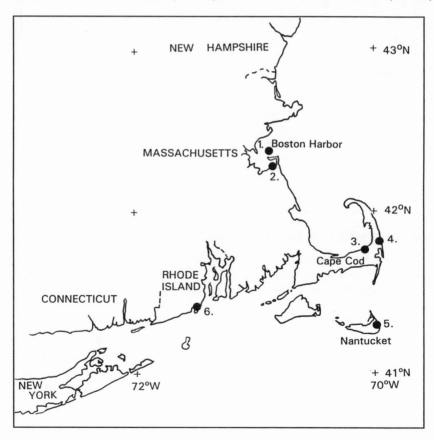

span of 340 years (Alan Leveillee, personal communication 1995). In fact, after reservoir correction with ΔR = -95 $\pm$ 45 ^{14}C years and an appropriate terrestrial or marine calibration (Stuiver and Reimer 1993), the dates of charcoal and shell become Cal A.D. 1398(1436)1611 and Cal A.D. 1397(1439)1489, which are remarkably close (Figure 13.3)!

Another pair of shell and charcoal samples came from a site at Myrick's Pond, Brewster, Massachusetts, excavated by Alan Strauss (1994). This provided an opportunity to radiocarbon date a *Mercenaria mercenaria* (quahog) shell and wood charcoal found in the same level in the same small pit (1.6 m $\times$ 1.2 m, with a maximum depth of 0.50 to 0.55 m; Little 1994; Strauss 1994). The pit is thought to contain a single component; that is, that its shell and charcoal were deposited at the same time (Alan Strauss, personal communication 1993; Strauss 1994). A comparison of the δ^{13}C-corrected ages of the shell and charcoal gives a mean age difference of 285 ^{14}C years. But marine calibration with ΔR = -95 $\pm$ 45 ^{14}C years gives a shell age of Cal A.D. 1052(1184)1279, which is essentially the same as the charcoal's Cal A.D. 1036(1212)1278 (see Figure 13.3), because the mean of each date falls well within the error range of the other.

In summary, for the charcoal and shell pairs at the Point Judith and Brewster sites, the 1993 Massachusetts ΔR gives calibrated shell dates almost indistinguishable from charcoal dates plus or minus one sigma.

Furthermore, using Stuiver and Braziunas (1993:Figure 15) to calculate ΔR, the nine pairs from Nantucket Island, Cape Cod, Boston Harbor Islands, and Rhode Island give an average ΔR = -94 $\pm$ 53 ^{14}C years for the Massachusetts coast. The small difference between this value and the Stuiver and Braziunas (1993) value for ΔR based on four pairs is well within the accuracy of the methods of determining ΔR.

DISCUSSION

According to Stuiver and Polach (1977:356–357), radiocarbon labs have generally assumed a marine reservoir age of 400 years for shell from nonpolar regions. With this assumption, the estimated fractionation correction (+400 years) and reservoir correction (-400 years) cancel each other. However, with atmospheric calibration curves for both marine and terrestrial samples, the method gives only an approximation within 100 years of the ages calibrated with Stuiver and Braziunas's marine model (Little 1993). Another reason for calibrating shell ages by the marine curves is that these curves have smaller variations (wiggles) than atmospheric curves, due to the dampening effect of the large oceanic carbon reservoir. The results, with measured fractionation and reservoir ages, should be more precise than past approximations.

The variations in ΔR for our nine pairs can be due to poor pair association, as well as to the statistical fluctuations of radiocarbon dating. Finding more pairs can reduce the σ value of the average ΔR.

Figure 13.3
The Charcoal and Shell Ages from Point Judith, Rhode Island, and Brewster, Massachusetts. Shown as (a) δ^{13}**C-corrected (conventional)** ^{14}**C years B.P., and (b) cal A.D. years.** Note how marine reservoir correction and calibration bring the conventional shell ages in (a) to dates in (b) that are nearly identical with the calibrated charcoal dates.

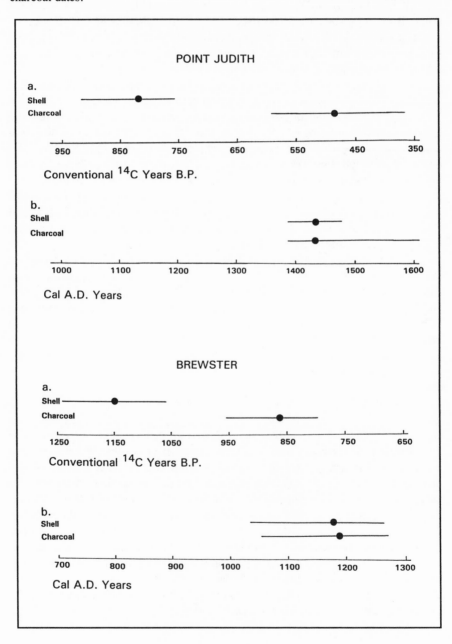

The five additional charcoal and shell pairs support the 1993 Massachusetts ΔR and extend it to Rhode Island. The now nine ΔR values in Table 13.1 from pairs of Middle and Late Woodland Period shell and charcoal or deer bone from Point Judith, Nantucket Island, Cape Cod, and Boston Harbor, can be averaged to give ΔR = -94 ± 53 ^{14}C years. Because this value does not significantly differ from the Massachusetts ΔR = -95 ± 45 ^{14}C years published by Stuiver and Braziunas (1993), I recommend the continued use of the 1993 ΔR for Massachusetts and using it for Rhode Island as well.

On the coast of California, radiocarbon ages of shell and charcoal pairs dating between 6000 and 9000 ^{14}C years B.P. from a stratified site show an increase in ΔR of up to 350 ^{14}C years over earlier and later ΔRs, and appear to reflect an increase in upwelling (Erlandson et al. 1996). Southon et al. (1990) tentatively reported similar findings on shell and wood for the Northwest Coast around 6400 ^{14}C years B.P.

If early sites on the East Coast can provide good associations between charcoal and shell, we, too, might find changes in ΔR with time. Investigations into reservoir values at large shell middens with Archaic components on the coast of Maine (Sanger 1981) and the lower Hudson River (Little 1995) suggest that multicomponent shell middens are likely to be highly disturbed and give shell dates without consistent relationships to associated artifact styles or charcoal dates.

The use of charcoal and wood in these analyses also raises questions about the age of the wood when it was deposited at the site (Long and Rippeteau 1974: 206). Southon et al. (1990:202) emphasized the care needed in selecting appropriate pairs of samples. Short-lived terrestrial materials that might have been eaten with the shellfish, such as nuts, seeds, or bone of small animals, should make the best samples for pair dating. Another alternative is to date museum shells that have a recorded date of collection. Research on shell collections housed at museums has failed so far to locate Massachusetts shells collected at known historic dates.

RADIOCARBON REPORTING AND ITS PROBLEMS

Pitfalls lurk in loosely described radiocarbon dates, especially those reported in the past. The late William Ritchie (1969a) reported maize at Martha's Vineyard at A.D. 1160 ± 80 years (on charcoal). By the conventions of his time, he assumed that ^{14}C years equaled calendar years and obtained his date by subtracting the reported radiocarbon age from 1950. Working backward, the radiocarbon age must have been 790 ± 80 ^{14}C years B.P., which calibrates (Stuiver and Pearson 1993) to Cal A.D. 1192 (1263) 1290. This is a sizable 100 years later than Ritchie's published A.D. date and highlights the problems of dates inadequately described in the literature.

Today, in contrast to Ritchie, who stayed with charcoal, we date all kinds of materials with a wide variety of δ^{13}C values. On the lab form may be the words "δ^{13}C-corrected," or "not corrected for fractionation in nature" (presumably meaning not δ^{13}C-corrected), or no qualification (meaning no corrections or equal and opposite estimated δ^{13}C and R corrections [Watters et al. 1992:40]). In the resulting confusion, many archaeologists were also unaware that, if maize kernel ages are not δ^{13}C-corrected, the ^{14}C age can be 200 years too young (Hall 1967), and, if a δ^{13}C-correction is made on shell, a marine reservoir age correction must be applied in order to avoid errors of 300 to 400 years.

Recently, Beta Analytic corrected Nantucket shell ages by an estimated +400 years for fractionation. The lab then calibrated these ages using Stuiver and Braziunas (1993) with ΔR = 0 (Rainey and Ritchie 1994). In other words, they used a marine calibration program with a 400 year (rather than our measured 305 year) average reservoir age. These procedures must be made clear to the archaeologist. Similarly, warnings in the CALIB 3.0.3 User's guide (Stuiver and Reimer 1993) about not correcting twice for δ^{13}C suggest we should all clearly state corrections that we make.

Recommended practice in this changing field is to report:

1. the lab number
2. the material tested, including species, if known
3. the radiocarbon age in ^{14}C years B.P. $\pm$ one sigma
4. whether the age is δ^{13}C-corrected or not
5. the δ^{13}C value, if known or estimated
6. the calibrating data set and ΔR, if ages are calibrated

SUMMARY

Radiocarbon dating is a valuable tool for the archaeologist. This chapter has introduced the topic in general terms, and described some of the adjustments necessary to calibrate a radiocarbon age to an approximate calendar year. For marine samples such as shell, not only a fractionation correction, but also a reservoir age correction is required before calibration to Cal years.

Five additional pairs of archaeological marine shell and charcoal samples, from Boston Harbor, Brewster, and Cape Cod, Massachusetts, and Point Judith, Rhode Island, have been added to the four pairs that formed the data base for the 1993 reservoir age correction, The results support the published ΔR value of -95 $\pm$ 45 ^{14}C years for Massachusetts (Stuiver and Braziunas 1993; Little 1993), and they extend its geographic range to Rhode Island.

The marine reservoir age is well recorded in shell. Now that we can handle radiocarbon dates on Massachusetts shell with confidence, we welcome measures of ΔR north and south and through time on the North Atlantic Coast.

And, in conclusion, consider this: the bones of all of us who are coastal dwellers and eat bluefish, shellfish, or other seafood will show an old ^{14}C age from Whitman's "Old Ocean."

ACKNOWLEDGMENTS

For contributions to the Brewster dates, I thank the Nantucket Maria Mitchell Association and Alan Strauss. Alan Leveillee provided background on the Point Judith dates. Dena Dincauze first put me on the track of the marine reservoir and fractionation corrections for radiocarbon ages on the northeast coast. I am grateful for her continuing encouragement.

Part V

Contributions from Cultural Resource Management

14

The Significance of the
Turners Falls Locality in
Connecticut River Valley Archaeology

Michael S. Nassaney

Up through the classificatory-descriptive period of American archaeology (see Willey and Sabloff 1993), Northeastern archaeologists marched in step with their colleagues elsewhere in the continent in the use of a cultural-historical paradigm to organize archaeological remains. Distinguishing artifact types and their spatial and temporal associations were important initial tasks needed to impose order and facilitate communication and comparison within and between regions. As the New Archaeology came into vogue, many researchers sought to address questions about the past that had potentially broader anthropological significance. There began a shift from an interest in culture history to a more generalizing scientism whereby the archaeological record was viewed as a laboratory to test models and establish laws of human behavior (Trigger 1989:294–303). Processualism was practiced most vehemently in the Midwest and Southwest where well preserved ecofacts and architectural remains could be used to reconstruct settlement-subsistence systems within a regional, ecological context. As the broad outlines of culture history were established and the goals, methods, and research orientation of American archaeology began to change, some archaeological sites and regions attracted greater attention than others, even though "the anthropologically interesting matters are what people did and how they did it" (Dincauze 1993a:36) regardless of time or space.

This paradigmatic reorientation coincided with the growth and development of cultural resource management (CRM). In some circles this meant that finding and mining archaeological sites were paramount even though rigorous research designs aimed at hypothesis testing were the ideal. As a result, much of the work remained object oriented. As a colleague once casually remarked, "Archaeology is artifacts, or it is nothing" (cf. Willey and Phillips 1958:2). In the past, National Register eligibility criteria often led researchers to sites that exhibited what I have elsewhere called "cultural superlatives"—the largest, oldest, or deepest archaeological manifestations in a region (Cobb and Nassaney 1991:3).

These attributes were also sought in the Northeast, despite more than three centuries of European colonization and land modification that had adversely affected the aboriginal archaeological record. Moreover, the record consisted predominantly of the remains of band-level societies, which were thought to represent most of New England's indigenous peoples (Thomas 1980:76). These relatively small-scale societies lacked year-round sedentism and the labor investments entailed by dependence on cultivated crops and residence in fortified towns (Dincauze 1993a:36). As theoretical interest shifted toward understanding cultural processes and the emergence of cultural complexity, regions and societies that lacked the hallmarks of complexity were ignored or seen as peripheral.

As Dincauze (1993a) has recently pointed out, band-level societies and their material remains are the antithesis of Euroamerican values of dominance, competition, and wealth. The dynamics of relatively egalitarian societies have been underappreciated by North American archaeologists, thus creating an image of Northeast prehistory as "a marginal, culturally retarded outlier of the eastern United States" (Dincauze 1993a:33). Insofar as Northeastern archaeologists have not celebrated the potential contribution of their data base to questions of broad anthropological significance, they are themselves partly to blame for the image of their subject of study.

In this chapter I argue that as long as Northeastern archaeologists fail to promote the anthropological relevance of their work and maintain parochial interests, the archaeology of the region will be seen as marginal by practitioners elsewhere in North America. I see their concerns as parochial when they fail to demonstrate how archaeological information can have theoretical and practical application beyond the immediate problem at hand; research questions cast in a narrow, cultural-historical frame will be of limited interest beyond a handful of scholars. The only way to salvage Northeastern archaeology (and Northeastern archaeologists!) from marginality is to emphasize the comparative approach while maintaining a historical orientation.

To demonstrate that Northeastern archaeology can have a broader audience and contribute to significant anthropological issues, I examine the history of archaeological investigations in the Turners Falls locality of the Connecticut River valley in western Massachusetts (Figures 14.1, 14.2, and 14.3). The locality, which is defined spatially as those portions of the towns of Gill, Greenfield, and Montague that lie in proximity to the Turners Falls, has a rich archaeological heritage that has been known since the early nineteenth century and has attracted increased avocational and professional interest over the past three decades. In the late 1980s, I had the opportunity to synthesize the archaeological and historical background of this locale for two CRM projects (Nassaney 1988; Nassaney et al. 1989). Since then it has occurred to me that despite a number of potentially interesting sites in the area and steady efforts to investigate them by amateur and professional archaeologists alike, three archaeological

Figure 14.1
Turners Falls and the Connecticut River Valley in Southern New England

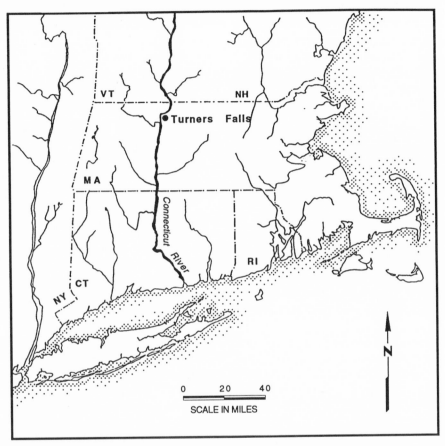

projects conducted over the past quarter century stand out as having transcended local concerns. The Turners Falls Airport, Western Massachusetts Electric Company (WMECO), and Russell Cutlery projects have attracted interest beyond western Massachusetts because they have contributed or have the potential to contribute to questions of regional, continental, and even global importance.

In the remainder of this chapter I discuss how the archaeological findings from each of these projects can be used to address issues of broad anthropological significance. All of the projects were associated with properties that were either on or eligible for inclusion in the National Register of Historic Places and all were conducted with minimum funding. The goals of each principal archaeologist varied, as did the circumstances that led to site investigations in each project. Yet each site has produced data that are compelling enough to warrant

Figure 14.2
The Greater Turners Falls Locality Showing the Locations of
Major River Confluences in Franklin County, Massachusetts

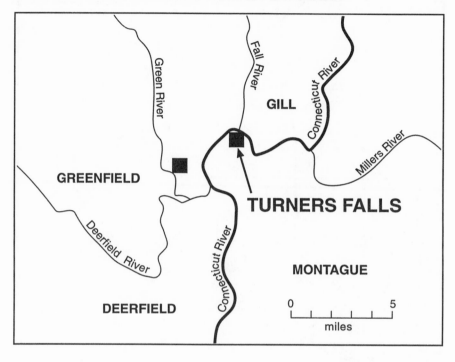

interest beyond the local scale. The hope is that the following discussion will be part of a growing trend to highlight the importance of sites that lack precious artifacts and spectacular monuments as a means to transform the false image of marginality that tarnishes the Northeast's past. I provide some background information on the environmental and historical contexts of the locality before discussing each project's contributions to our understanding of culture history and culture process in the region.

ENVIRONMENTAL AND HISTORICAL CONTEXTS

The Turners Falls locality is environmentally unique in the Northeast. It includes one of the largest falls on New England's largest river and marks the northern extent of the Connecticut River valley lowland. Thus it coincides with a major biotic ecotone that also exhibits ecological diversity at the local scale. The locality also lies near the confluence of three tributaries: the Deerfield, Fall, Green, and Millers rivers (see Figure 14.2). The most prominent feature in the locality is, of course, the Great Falls, once called Peske-ompsk-ut by the local Native American peoples ("the place where the river is divided by the cleft

Figure 14.3
The Riverside Archaeological District and the Turners Falls Historic District
Shown in Relation to the Physical and Cultural Landmarks of the
Turners Falls Locality

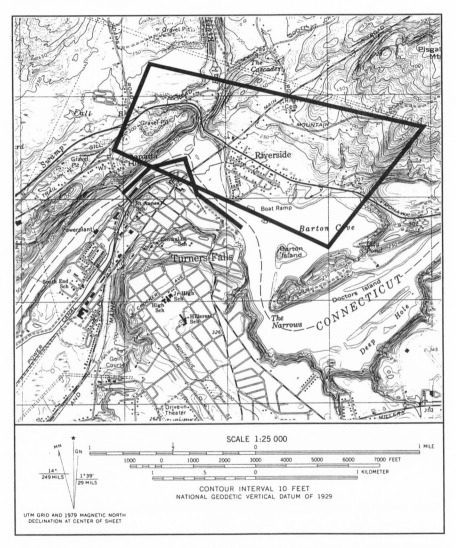

rock"). The name *Turners Falls* became associated with these cataracts in the nineteenth century. Today Turners Falls refers both to the falls created by an artificial dam and the planned industrial village situated to take advantage of the available water power in the nineteenth century. To a large extent, the history of Native and Euro-American occupation in the locality is the history of human accommodation to and exploitation of the falls. Thus, the geological and glacial conditions that led to the formation of the falls have been an important backdrop for the cultural, political, and economic geography of the region since the end of the Pleistocene (for more information on the geological history, surficial geology, and paleoenvironmental reconstructions of the region, see Brigham-Grette and Wise 1988; Curran and Dincauze 1977; Dincauze 1978b, 1988b; Dincauze and Mulholland 1977; Hartshorn 1969; Jahns 1966; Koteff et al. 1988; Larsen 1984; and Stoughton 1978).

By the end of the Pleistocene, the area began to support vegetation that included various plant food products as well as suitable habitats for numerous edible and fur-bearing animals. Of particular note were the plentiful and predictable anadromous fish that could have been easily taken in the immediate vicinity of the falls. Exploitation of fish resources is well documented historically and the archaeological record testifies to the importance of fish in the human diet prior to contact (see Carlson 1988c; Curran and Thomas 1979; Thomas 1980).

Sustained Euro-American settlement did not occur in the Turners Falls locality until the early eighteenth century (see Lockwood 1926:755), although the territory was already well known in colonial history since it figured prominently in King Phillip's War (1676) as the site of a military encounter between colonial forces and Native Americans (see Bagnall 1875; Sheldon 1895). The first permanent European settlers arrived in the 1720s and soon established important commercial activities dominated by agriculture, sawmills, cornmills, taverns, and lumbering (Holland 1855:393–394; Lockwood 1926:755). The numerous rapids and falls along the river, however, were a serious obstacle to the expansion of trade and transportation. To overcome the difficulty of navigating the falls and rapids, an act of the legislature of Massachusetts was passed in 1792, which incorporated the Proprietors of the Locks and Canals on the Connecticut River for the purpose of rendering the Connecticut River passable for boats and rafts in the Commonwealth (Holland 1855:305). This led to the construction of a timber dam and a canal on the east side of the river at Turners Falls (Holland 1855:308–309; see also Nassaney 1988:45–45, Figure 7; Pressey 1910). The canal served to facilitate water transportation until the 1850s when it became outmoded by the faster and cheaper rail freight rates.

In 1864 the provisions of the Proprietors charter were changed to allow the waters of the Connecticut to be leased for power purposes (Abercrombie 1925:9) and in 1866 work began on the reconstruction of the former dam, enlargement of the canal for water power, and building a planned industrial village designed to rival the manufacturing cities of Lowell, Lawrence, and Holyoke (Abercrombie 1925; Carls 1934; Cloues 1974; Stone 1930). The Russell Cutlery soon became the largest employer providing jobs for over half of those working in manufacturing (Nassaney and Abel 1993). Although never reaching the size and prominence of Lowell, the industrial development had profound effects on the physical landscape and demographic composition of the region that are still evident to this day. Even a casual observer will note numerous late nineteenth-century buildings in Turners Falls along the canal, Avenue A, or elsewhere in the downtown area. In the early 1980s the Turners Falls Historic District was listed on the National Register to recognize the integrity and unique architectural characteristics of this planned industrial village.

BRIEF HISTORY OF ARCHAEOLOGICAL INVESTIGATIONS

Interest in the natural and cultural history of the region began in the 1830s when quarrying activities exposed dinosaur fossil footprints (Little 1984). These ancient traces were followed by discoveries of human antiquities often as a result of agricultural and early industrial activities. The Turners Falls locality soon became known for its abundant aboriginal remains. As one mid-nineteenth century historian noted: "Montague abounds with the common Indian relics, as that was once the grand resort of the Indians in their fisheries for shad and salmon" (Holland 1855:398). Nineteenth-century authors frequently commented on the ubiquity of native artifacts which they interpreted as evidence for a long and intense period of indigenous occupation (e.g., Bagnall 1875:1).

Local landowners and antiquarians alike amassed large collections of artifacts from the region, although many were poorly documented and others have since disappeared. For example,

some few arrowheads, tomahawks and cooking utensils have been found near the Farren House (Grand Trunk Hotel), and a year or two ago the skeletons of several Indians were exhumed on L street; but on the lands of T. M. Stoughton, Lemuel Barton, and Dr. Roswell Field of Riverside, relics of every variety have been found. Mr. T. M. Stoughton has, perhaps, secured the greatest number, but having parted with many to different colleges and museums, Dr. Field, possibly, has the best collection in his cabinet. Mr. Barton has a fine collection, and so also has Mr. Albert Smith. . . . In Dr. Field's collection are mortars, pestles, pipes, tomahawks, knives, drills, gouges, chisels, pots, and dozens of other things used by the Indians in camp and on the battle field, all of which are made of stone, and no iron tool of any kind was used in their manufacture. (Bagnall 1875:1–2)

As might be expected, many amateur archaeologists have contributed time and effort to investigating the region's archaeological record. The usefulness of their work for understanding the past is, in large part, dependent upon the quality of their investigations. Several artifact collections are known for the study region, though most older collections have limited provenience information.

Shelley Hight (1978, 1979, 1980) summarized information on local collections in conjunction with the preparation of a National Register nomination for the Riverside Archaeological District. Riverside was listed in the National Register of Historic Places in 1980 in recognition of significant archaeological remains in the Turners Falls locality north of the river (see Figure 14.3). The boundaries of the district extend from Adams Road on the west to the Lily Pond area of Barton Cove on the east. Its northern boundary lies just north of the Riverside cemetery and it extends to the Turners Falls village on the south.

The following discussion of sites and collections is meant to be illustrative and not exhaustive. It serves to demonstrate the high archaeological sensitivity of the locality and its potential for examining a range of research questions regarding 10,000 years of human occupation. Many of the materials in the collections described below may have come from Riverside, though other archaeological sites are surely represented. An early collection was made in the late nineteenth to early twentieth century by Jacob Bowne, a Springfield librarian. Although Bowne collected primarily from Springfield north to Hadley, he also purchased from George Sheldon the collection of Dr. Anson Cobb, a former Deerfield resident who later moved to Montague (Hight 1980:25). This collection, which was donated to the Springfield Science Museum in 1926, also contains individually purchased items from Turners Falls (or Riverside), including a slate semilunar knife from Captain Andrew Smith of Turners Falls.

The Montague historian Edward Pressey (1910) reported that a "Mr. Smith" uncovered seven flexed burials at Riverside. Albert Smith (perhaps the Smith who found the burials), a local landowner, had donated a 418-piece collection to the Carnegie Library of Turners Falls in 1913. It included 338 projectile points, eleven gouges, four axes, thirty-six potsherds, two pestles, and a swordfish sword according to the Carnegie Library Accession and Loan Records (1909–1925).

Henry Barton also donated many artifacts to the Carnegie Library. It is likely that many of these objects came from the area around Barton Field (later Barton Cove), which took his name. In 1909 the collection was listed as having 313 pieces, although Hight (1979) listed 427 pieces seven decades later. Whether or not all these items were donated by Barton is unclear. Dr. Hitchcock of Amherst College also supposedly contributed a collection of arrowheads and fossils (his main interest) acquired while work was being done on the canal and dam in Turners Falls. None of these materials could be readily identified in the Library during my search in 1988 (Nassaney 1988:33). Unfortunately, theft and poor curation practices have limited the research value of materials held by the Carnegie Library. In July, 1988, the collection consisted of approximately 200 unprovenienced objects in a locked case including projectile points (side-notched, contracting stem, triangular shapes); stone knives; a few celts, gouges, and grooved axes; plummets; hammerstones; potsherds; a swordfish sword; a human femur; and a perforated stone (Nassaney 1988:33).

Another well known collector and local authority on the early history and prehistory of the Pioneer Valley was Walter S. Rodimon (Johnson and Bradley 1987). Rodimon began collecting along the alluvial terraces of the Connecticut River and its tributaries between South Hadley and Gill, Massachusetts, in 1897. Rodimon identified seven small collecting sites in the Riverside District, as well as one site elsewhere in Gill (19-FR-66 to 73). Diagnostic artifacts from the Middle Archaic to Late Woodland period are represented, including a very finely carved stone pipe of a hooded figure retrieved from "an ancient Indian burial ground in Riverside, Gill overlooking Turners Falls" (Rodimon 1963 quoted in Hight 1979:1). Rodimon's interpretation of the pipe as evidence for the presence of Irish Culdee monks in New England around A.D. 900 remains unsubstantiated. His notes and collection of more than 5,000 objects were purchased by the Springfield Science Museum in the late 1980s and have been studied by Johnson and Bradley (1987).

Walter Rodimon interested Ed DeRose in artifact collecting when Ed was still a boy (Ed DeRose, personal communication 1988). According to Janice Weeks (personal communication to S. Hight, 1980), Rodimon and DeRose collected at Fort Hill in the Riverside District in the 1920s. DeRose and his wife Wilma also excavated at Fort Hill with the Norwottuck Chapter of the Massachusetts Archaeological Society (MAS) in 1969 and 1970. His artifacts probably derive from these excavations, as well as from other favorite collecting spots.

Another repository of Fort Hill artifacts is the American Indian Archaeological Institute, Washington, Connecticut. Here lies the collection of Edward H. Rogers who excavated in Gill in 1915 and 1916. Much of this collection is derived from mortuary contexts though little skeletal material was preserved or retained. Rogers's notes do not always clearly indicate specific provenience, and it is likely that some artifacts come from other locales outside of the Riverside District (Hight 1980).

The discoveries of aboriginal inhumations in the course of agricultural activities and industrial development in nineteenth-century Turners Falls were usually noted with interest. As early as 1895, Sheldon wrote authoritatively that "distinct modes of burial prevailed" (1895:78). He had apparently seen enough aboriginal inhumations to identify extended and flexed burial patterns. A single instance of a third mode was noted in 1881 by Mr. Stoughton and his son William on a hill north of Route 2 across from Main Road Cemetery. There they found twelve graves two feet below the surface that "had been extended and radiated from a center, head outwards, the feet resting on a circle five or six feet in diameter" (Sheldon 1895:78). They were interred with many stone weapons and a number of smooth (rattle?) stones. Interestingly, Rogers also noted that "water washed pebbles" were often found in graves (Hight 1980:18).

Three burials reported to be "from the banks of the Connecticut in Gill, Massachusetts," curated at the Deerfield Museum, are thought to be from Riverside (Sheldon 1920). The more recent (1978) excavation of a house foundation east of Fort Hill exposed two burials, one of which was reburied in the bank of Heal-All Brook (Hight 1980:5). Two burials (an inhumation and a cremation) were also excavated at Fort Hill by the Massachusetts Archaeological Society. A flexed adult male was found in association with a small stemmed quartz point, several projectile point preforms, a possible net sinker, and a paint cup (Hight 1980:41). The cremation consisted of calcined bones placed inside a cranium with no clear artifactual associations. Skeletal remains are curated at the University of Massachusetts, Amherst and are being treated according to the guidelines stipulated by the Native American Grave Protection and Repatriation Act of 1990.

Most of the aboriginal remains discussed thus far have come from Riverside north of the river. It appears that this side of the river was the preferred location for human occupation and resource exploitation (Nassaney 1988). The south side of the river apparently experienced significantly less intensive human activity if the sporadic archaeological discoveries made there since the late nineteenth century are any indication. Several inhumations were found during the construction of L Street, and prehistoric artifacts were also present at the site of the Grand Trunk Hotel at the corner of Avenue A and Second Street (Pressey 1910:61; see also Bagnall 1875; Nassaney 1988:Figure 3). An archaeological locational survey conducted in 1988 identified aboriginal artifacts in five shovel test pits placed approximately 100 m west of the former site of the Grand Truck Hotel, also known as the Farren House (Nassaney 1988:91–93). These materials included quartzite chipping debris ($n = 60$); several flakes of chert, argillite, and quartz; eight pieces of fire-cracked rock; and more than 10 g of charcoal associated with an occupational surface buried beneath 50 to 60 cm of artificial fill.

Several other CRM projects have been undertaken in the greater Turners Falls locality (other than those mentioned above) since the 1970s, though most of this work has been confined to site identification with limited intensive survey (e.g., Barber 1977; Bawden 1980; Dincauze et al. 1976; Hasenstab 1982; Mulholland et al. 1983; Weeks 1971a:3). Testing in the area of Cabot Woods southwest of the falls disclosed several concentrations of prehistoric cultural material dating to the Archaic and Woodland periods (Bernstein 1989a, 1989b; Johnson and McArdle 1986, 1987). Charcoal recovered from two prehistoric hearths have produced radiocarbon dates of 730 ± 190 B.P. and 3870 ± 100 B.P. (David Bernstein, personal communication 1989). Finally, recent work has been conducted by Timelines, Inc., at the Mackin Sand Bank site about 0.5 km northwest of the Falls on the western edge of the Riverside District (Elena Decima, personal communication 1997). This work was initially stimulated by CRM concerns as the site was threatened by a construction project. During the site examination and subsequent follow-up work, numerous features, diagnostic projectile points, and aboriginal ceramics were identified that testify to a long sequence of site use perhaps beginning in the Early Archaic. The dominant raw material for chipped stone tools during the Archaic period is quartzite, whereas chert was preferred in the succeeding Woodland period. Woodland ceramics have also been recovered, although their precise age has yet to be determined. Two copper beads and charcoal suitable for carbon-14 dating were collected from several features that appear to be hearths. Ongoing analysis is oriented toward understanding vertical and horizontal stratigraphy and the formal-temporal attributes of various artifact types including a nearly complete ceramic vessel.

Occasionally, archaeological sites have been investigated with an explicit research design aimed at collecting data to evaluate questions of broad anthropological and historical significance. Work was conducted at the WMECO site between September 1971 and November 1972 under the direction of Peter Thomas, then a graduate student at the University of Massachusetts, with assistance from Janice Weeks and the Norwottuck Chapter of the MAS. The site proved to be "a multi-stratified Middle Archaic to Middle Woodland site . . . [with] a remarkable similarity to the Neville site on the Merrimack River in Manchester, New Hampshire" (Thomas 1980:73). Thomas (1980:75) sought to explore two basic questions: (1) Why has Riverside consistently attracted prehistoric groups? and (2) What types of social dynamics were operative among these populations?

In the late 1980s two CRM-related projects were conducted by personnel affiliated with the University of Massachusetts Archaeological Services (UMAS). A UMAS survey to develop a master plan for the Turners Falls Airport led Robert Hasenstab (1986a, 1987) to document a collection of Paleoindian artifacts made by Paul Hannemann from the vicinity of the project area. Although subsequent field work provided limited information on site structure and the distribution of materials, the formal attributes of the artifacts in the Hannemann collection demonstrated the great antiquity of this collection.

At the other end of the temporal spectrum, Nassaney and coworkers spent several days in 1986 and 1987 conducting backhoe testing and limited data recovery at the site of the former Russell Cutlery Company along the canal (Nassaney et al. 1989). The project area was initially investigated to locate and identify Native American remains. Although deep testing revealed that the natural stratigraphy had been disturbed by the construction of the Cutlery to a depth of at least 2 to 3 m, architectural and artifactual remains of cutlery production were found that helped to document some of the poorly understood aspects of early industrialization (Nassaney et al. 1989). A careful study of the remains was warranted because the site was one of the contributing properties to the Turners Falls Historic District, listed on the National Register for its significance in industrial history. Intensive documentary work and interpretations of the material record have provided information that contributes to ongoing debates about technological innovation, deskilling, and the efficacy of the American system of interchangeable parts (Nassaney and Abel 1993, 1998).

In sum, the Turners Falls locality is marked by a high density of aboriginal and historic archaeological sites encompassing the entire span of human occupation. In the remaining section of this chapter I summarize our current understanding of the culture history of the region with an emphasis on the contributions provided by anthropologically oriented research.

CULTURE HISTORY

The Turners Falls locality has yielded archaeological evidence for human occupation from the end of the Pleistocene to the present. The Paleoindian period (12,000 to 10,000 B.P.) is represented by a Clovis-like fluted point recovered from a former terrace of glacial Lake Hitchcock in Riverside (Lionel Girard, personal communication 1988). Archaeological testing in this area above the 250-foot contour failed to substantiate this site (Dincauze et al. 1976:45–48), although a possible hearth was uncovered with heavy equipment 4.5 to 5 feet below the surface (Hight 1979).

South of the Connecticut River the Paleoindian period is better represented near the Turners Falls Airport at the Hannemann site situated at the north end of the Montague Plain. According to Robert Hasenstab (1986a, 1987), Hanne-mann, an avocational archaeologist who found the site, thinks that this location was used by Paleoindians to ambush migratory caribou herds traveling across the plain. Numerous fluted points and other diagnostic materials (e.g., channel flakes, end scrapers, gravers), as well as lithic debitage of red and yellow Penn-sylvania jasper, attest to the antiquity of this occupation (Hasenstab 1987). The wide range of tools has led investigators to suggest that the site served a habita-tion function. Unfortunately, the eroded edges of the site have yielded most of the finds thus far (Hasenstab 1987:17). Nevertheless, Hasenstab (personal com-munication 1997) insists that the site appears to exhibit structure and the main part of it is undisturbed, thereby making it eligible for inclusion in the National Register of Historic Places.

Although the Hannemann site has yielded limited contextual information, the site assemblage has contributed (albeit indirectly) to a sophisticated model for understanding the pioneering efforts of the earliest occupants of eastern North America. The model is not based on what the assemblage is, but what it is not. It is significant to note that when the site was first threatened with destruction, Dincauze specifically requested Hasenstab (1986a:3) to collect "explicit informa-tion on site structure and the distribution of materials." These data would allow the assemblage to be compared with other Paleoindian assemblages throughout the Northeast.

In a recent collection of papers on eastern North American archaeology, Dincauze (1993c) compiled information on aspects of artifact style, lithic raw material, lithic technology, intrasite spatial configuration, and tool-kit diversity from a range of large fluted-point sites in the Northeast. The similarity among these sites (and contrasts with smaller sites such as Hannemann, Whipple, and others) supports an argument that the large sites may have been formed as rela-tively long-term marshaling sites to organize small groups exploring and coloniz-ing unfamiliar territories. These large sites were likely used only once as tempo-rary aggregation sites at the time of initial settlement. After the territory was explored, new activities occurred that left a different archaeological signature. If this interpretation is correct, then by implication, Clovis populations in the region had no immediate predecessors. Such a conclusion should be of enormous interest beyond the Northeast, given the continuing efforts to determine the timing of the peopling of the New World. In principle, the logic of the compara-tive method used to assess the significance of assemblage variation in the region can be used to evaluate the presence of pioneering human groups elsewhere in

North America and beyond. Thus the Hannemann site and the model to which it has indirectly contributed have significant implications for problems of continental, if not global, scale—when did the first peoples occupy the Northeast, was Clovis first, and how do colonizing populations organize themselves in unknown environments (see Chapter 1, this volume)?

The Early Archaic period (10,000 to 8000 B.P.) is even more sparsely represented in the region. Morgan Wood of Northampton collected a single bifurcate projectile point from the Mackin Sand Bank site (19-FR-12) in Riverside (Hight 1979), and the recent work there by Timelines, Inc., has also recovered possible Early Archaic projectile points. Cultural materials affiliated with the Middle Archaic period (8000 to 6000 years B.P.) have also been recovered from the Mackin location. Robert Hasenstab (personal communication 1988) has examined an assemblage of over 100 Middle Archaic points made of local quartzite reportedly collected or dug from the site.

Other Middle Archaic components have also been documented from Riverside. Excavations at Fort Hill yielded Otter Creek projectile points and a quartz crystal plano-convex scraper (Hight 1980). The latter artifact has been associated with Early and Middle Archaic occupations (Curran and Thomas 1979). The WMECO site (19FR15), first investigated systematically in the early 1970s, contains a component dated to this period. Projectile points morphologically related to Neville and Stark types (see Dincauze 1976) were recovered from the stratigraphically lowest levels (Thomas 1980:75). Furthermore, the site contains a cultural stratigraphic sequence from the Middle Archaic through Middle Woodland periods. In addition to chipped stone tools, debitage, and ceramics, the site has yielded faunal remains and charcoal suitable for dating in undisturbed context.

The identification of stone tools at WMECO formally similar to those from the earliest occupational levels of the Neville site marks an important watershed in the history of archaeological investigations in the region. WMECO is among the few sites in New England that exhibit well delineated cultural stratigraphy, dating back to 7800 years B.P. Thus, it has been useful for establishing a local and regional chronological sequence. In addition, the earliest components contain artifacts that are similar to Neville and other Middle Archaic forms along the Atlantic seaboard (e.g., Broyles 1971; Coe 1964). This suggests that indigenous peoples in New England were participating in broad regional processes which would have linked them to technological and cultural developments elsewhere in eastern North America. Site investigations also represent a relatively early demonstration of pre–Late Archaic occupation in the Connecticut River valley (see Starbuck and Bolian 1980).

The goals of the investigations, albeit implicit, were similar to those developed for the Neville site, suggesting the influence of Dincauze's (1976:5) work. Thomas (1980) was able to: (1) demonstrate the validity of the stratigraphy, (2) describe and date the cultural sequence, and (3) define patterns of site utilization. The last point is perhaps most germane to this discussion, because it constitutes an early attempt to implement an ecological approach in New England archaeology. Arguing that there is a relationship between environment, subsistence, and society, Thomas (1980:80–84) reconstructed the environment of an "exploitation territory," or catchment, to examine the criteria for site location. He then derived testable implications for resource usage from these reconstructions to be compared against the archaeological record. The site was shown to be a prime location "within an annual subsistence region covering at least several hundred square miles along the Connecticut River, including the Deerfield, Millers, and Fall River watersheds" (Thomas 1980:84). Faunal remains from the site were used to evaluate changing animal exploitation strategies through time.

Thomas (1980:90–92) also tried to make the work anthropological by exploring the social dynamics of the site's occupants. Using expectations of band-level social organization developed by ethnologists and archaeological theorists (e.g., Damas 1969; Steward 1969; Wobst 1974), Thomas (1980:91) proposed that Riverside may have been an important location for the maintenance of communication networks among "minimal bands." Changes in the frequencies of local and exotic raw material used for chipped stone tools also suggests that social networks expanded during the Late Archaic (Thomas 1980:92).

An increase in the frequency and size of Late Archaic sites in the region, along with evidence for expanded interaction, suggests higher population densities during this period. This pattern is mirrored in other parts of the Northeast. The three major Late Archaic traditions of southern New England—Laurentian, Small Stemmed, and Susquehanna—are all represented in the region. Projectile points of the Laurentian tradition (Brewerton, Otter Creek) seem to predate the Susquehanna tradition points of Atlantic, Susquehanna, and Orient types (Curran and Thomas 1979). However, their relationship to the Small Stemmed tradition is not well understood. Small stemmed points are most common and were found in association with a burial at Fort Hill (Hight 1979). Hight (1979) has suggested that the social ramifications of the possible coexistence of two different traditions (Small Stemmed and Susquehanna) would constitute a significant research problem in the region.

Paleoenvironmental reconstructions once led archaeologists to propose that the Late Archaic expansion coincided with the climatic Hypsithermal, a period of drier conditions reflected in the faunal record at WMECO where aquatic reptile remains diminished in frequency (Thomas 1980:85). Our current understanding of the timing of the Hypsithermal (ca. 8000–5000 years B.P.) challenges the idea that climatic change can account for the expansion. Furthermore, an increase in population also corresponds with changing patterns of nonsubsistence resource acquisition. Thomas (1980) noted that nonlocal lithic raw materials (chert, rhyolite) supplant local sources of quartz and quartzite during the Late Archaic period, a trend that suggests more extensive exchange networks. Social relationships must ultimately be considered in reconstructing explanations of Late Archaic cultural dynamics.

The Woodland cultural sequence is well represented in the Turners Falls area, both within and outside of the Riverside Archaeological District. Early Woodland (3000–2000 B.P.) materials have been recovered from the WMECO site and Fort Hill, as well as other areas within Riverside. Diagnostic artifacts include Meadowood points, Adena-type blocked end tube pipes, and Vinette I pottery. The latter material has been found at the Q-Narrows site, on Barton Cove north of the Connecticut River. Investigations conducted here by the MAS have yielded numerous Late Archaic and Early Woodland artifacts eroding from potentially datable cultural features at the edge of the cove (Jane McGahan, personal communication 1988). Fluctuations in the elevation of the river have made these deposits especially vulnerable to erosion and redeposition.

Fragments of a somewhat unusual ceramic vessel (represented by six sherds) were recovered from Fort Hill at the Casley site (19FR14). Tempered with steatite and quartz, the sherds are similar to apparently contemporaneous pottery from the Wilson site in Pennsylvania that dates to the transition between the Archaic and Woodland periods (Weeks 1971b). Artifacts associated with the steatite-tempered pottery include steatite vessels, Susquehanna points, and the use of rhyolite as the predominant raw material for chipped stone tools (McCann 1962 cited in Weeks 1971b). Careful examination of sites associated with steatite-tempered pottery may help to resolve the uncertain chronological relationship of stone bowls and ceramic containers along the Atlantic Coast in Eastern North America (see Chapter 5, this volume).

Middle Woodland (2000–1000 B.P.) components are also represented at Riverside and two sites have been excavated outside of the district. The Wills Hill site (19-FR-37) consists of a single component interpreted as a camp occupied by one or two families during the late summer (Thomas 1979b). Tool manufacture and maintenance using dolomitic mudstone, a local resource, appear to dominate activities at this site. Excavations have also been conducted at the Greenfield Landfill site (19FR159) by the MAS. The site was originally reported by Ed DeRose, a local amateur archaeologist (personal communication, 1988), who recovered Middle Woodland pottery, projectile points, and a rolled native copper bead (Robert Hasenstab, personal communication 1997).

The last prehistoric period recognized in the region is called Late Woodland (A.D. 1000–1600). Its most diagnostic artifact is the triangular-shaped Levanna point. Late Woodland components have been identified beneath Barton's Cove when this former agricultural field was exposed in 1971. Site survey and excavation recovered 153 artifacts, including Levanna and Brewerton points and a bead (Hight 1979). Late Woodland pottery has been recovered from Fort Hill at the Casley site and Late Woodland materials are scattered throughout Riverside, though the WMECO site lacks Late Woodland pottery (Thomas 1980:75).

Evidence of aboriginal occupation of the area during the Contact period (A.D. 1620–1676) is poorly documented archaeologically. Although European sources suggest that the region was fairly heavily populated during this period (e.g., Sheldon 1895), no large habitation sites have been located. Hasenstab (1987:22, Chapter 9, this volume) has proposed that when maize was introduced into the region sometime during the Late Woodland period, preferred settlement locations would have shifted away from the Turners Falls area toward the more fertile agricultural lands of Deerfield and Northfield. Thus, late prehistoric and early historic settlements near the falls may have been confined to specialized activities related to the seasonal exploitation of fish.

Despite the designation of the Turners Falls Historic District to the National Register, the practice of historic archaeology in the Turners Falls locality remains in its infancy. By the 1870s, the town was a bustling industrial community with numerous factories and ancillary services to sustain the mills and their workers. Many of these buildings are still standing. Thus far, there have been few efforts to systematically study these historic resources. During an archaeological locational survey conducted in the late 1980s for the proposed Turners Falls Heritage State Park, two areas were subjected to site evaluation (e.g., see Nassaney 1988:96–98). One area was the former site of the Farren House or Grand Trunk Hotel. This 1872 hotel built in the French Empire style was torn down in the 1960s. The remains of associated buildings (e.g., a carriage shed and blacksmith shop) were found to lack integrity. Architectural remains associated with the Montague Paper Company complex located immediately below the dam are potentially eligible for the National Register.

Perhaps the most famous industrial enterprise ever established in Turners Falls was the John Russell Cutlery Company. The company, which was founded in 1833 by John Russell along the banks of the Green River in Deerfield, made high quality edge tools such as chisels, knives, and other types of cutlery. Russell revolutionized the cutlery industry by introducing mechanization to produce interchangeable parts (Taber 1955:36). Russell's business grew steadily. By 1865 it along with the Lamson & Goodnow Company in Shelburne Falls, accounted for 49 percent of all the cutlery produced in the United States (Taber 1955:122). After a series of fires in the shop and a growing recognition of the inadequacy and obsolescence of the facilities at the Deerfield location, Russell decided to relocate and modernize his operation by moving it to the planned industrial village of Turners Falls.

Construction of the new plant in Turners Falls began in 1868 and it allegedly became the largest cutlery factory in the world when it was completed in 1870 (Merriam et al. 1976:23). The factory buildings varied from two to four stories high with each floor having fourteen-foot ceilings (Figure 14.4). The buildings were laid out in a large rectangle with a central courtyard comprising a total of 160,000 square feet of work space and capable of accommodating 1,200 employees. All shop processes were organized so that goods moved the shortest distance possible from one operation to the next—a veritable blueprint for scientific management in the work place (Nassaney et al. 1989). Technological innovations transformed the labor process and subdivided cutlery making

Figure 14.4
The John Russell Cutlery Company in the 1880s (from *Picturesque Franklin*, 1891)

into standardized and routinized tasks further severing the conception and execution of labor (see also Nassaney and Abel 1993, 1998).

The cutlery survived in Turners Falls until the 1930s when it was merged with the Harrington Cutlery and moved to Southbridge, Massachusetts (Taber 1955). The factory complex was abandoned in the 1940s and remained standing until 1958 when WEMCO had it demolished. The foundations and the remains of the partially collapsed raceways were still visible in the 1980s, despite the use of the site as a landfill.

In 1987 UMAS was contracted to conduct an intensive survey at the cutlery site (Nassaney et al. 1989). After examining extant documentation on the plant, a research design was developed to investigate two aspects of production: (1) the water power supply system, and (2) the system of interchangeable parts and its impact on the labor process. This work has produced some surprising and intriguing results that remain the subject of continued inquiry (e.g., Nassaney and Abel 1998).

Excavations completely exposed the large steel penstock, waterwheel pit, and an associated raceway. At the base of the penstock we found what appeared to be the last turbine used at the cutlery probably abandoned as late as 1915. The turbine was likely produced in Turners Falls as local companies manufactured similar products. The use of water power technology well into the twentieth century was an unexpected result of our study; it may explain problems the firm had in meeting quotas long after competitors had turned to steam.

Another provocative find was a cache of several hundred cutlery wasters, discarded pieces of raw material, and cut-out metal fragments. These remains pose interesting questions regarding rates of industrial waste and their implication for the relationships between labor and management. The wasters, along with detailed insurance maps of the spatial organization of the workplace, clearly show how the labor process was segmented and deskilled (see Braverman 1974).

What emerged from the study of the Russell Cutlery is a clearer insight into the debate in the historical and anthropological literature concerning the linkage between technological innovation, deskilling, and the control of workers in industrial settings. Whereas an increase in fixed capital embodied in the forces of production undoubtedly led to increased efficiency, greater productivity, and the potential for larger profits in early industrial America, it is critical to recognize that technological changes had severe consequences for the relations of production. Mechanization and spatial reorganization in the work place served to create and reinforce relations of economic and social subordination. Interestingly, class relations were also reproduced beyond the workplace through a pervasive ideology of order and efficiency that permeated the home (e.g., Hayden 1981). Continued analysis suggests that technological innovations and subsequent physical changes brought about by industrialization were ultimately about social control; they were not politically neutral developments (Marglin 1974; Nassaney and Abel 1998). By placing the research on the Russell Cutlery in a broader context, the results have potential significance to an audience that extends beyond Turners Falls.

CONCLUSION

Unlike the American Bottom of west-central Illinois or the Four Corners region of the American Southwest, the archaeological record of the Turners Falls locality is not nationally or internationally renowned. For that matter, much of Northeastern archaeology has been marginalized, even in summaries of the prehistory of the Eastern Woodlands (Dincauze 1980b). Although many sites and locales achieve archaeological recognition for their "cultural superlatives," others are significant for the information that they can contribute to the broader fields of anthropology and history provided that they are investigated with these contexts in mind.

In some ways, the archaeology of the Turners Falls locality is not unlike other areas of the Northeast. It has benefited from a long history of discoveries, close interaction between amateurs and professionals concerned with archaeological remains, and legislation that has required the identification and evaluation of cultural resources. Despite these favorable conditions, few projects conducted in the area have helped to "center" New England archaeology, making notable the three exceptions discussed in this chapter.

Given the paucity of data on the earliest occupants of the Northeast, it is not surprising that any bona fide Paleoindian site should attract considerable attention. But mere descriptions of assemblages are likely to be relegated to a laundry list of sites in the absence of more integrated and regionally comparative research designs. The most significant contribution of the Hannemann site is what the site implies about other larger, spatially nonredundant sites in the Northeast as developed in Dincauze's (1993c) pioneering model.

Other rare and valuable resources are sites that exhibit relatively undisturbed vertical stratigraphy. The long history of land use, coupled with the superposition of distinct occupational strata, have made the Riverside Archaeological District an important place. Moreover, the preservation of recoverable animal remains led investigators to use an ecological model to understand seasonality, exploitation territories, and social dynamics at WMECO in a way that has potential implications for understanding hunter-gatherer-fishers elsewhere. Despite the important early contributions from investigations of sites like WMECO, very limited problem-oriented work has been conducted in the District since the 1970s. More refined techniques currently available for data recovery, analysis, and interpretation can be used profitably to ensure a wider appreciation of these resources by the profession and the public.

Sites associated with the modern world of the past four centuries may be the easiest to promote in the region. Historical or industrial archaeology in New England has been "centered" for some time now, perhaps beginning with Deetz's (1977) work at Plimoth Plantation and his even better-known gravestone studies. Moreover, New England is widely recognized as the birthplace of America's industrial revolution making places like the Russell Cutlery intrinsic sites of public curiosity and support. Industrial sites have the potential to be globally significant given that industrialization is an ongoing process that is not confined to New England or the Northeast. In so-called underdeveloped countries, entrepreneurs are challenged with effecting a successful economic transformation from an agrarian to an industrial order. Problem-oriented studies of the successes and failures of industrial enterprises can contribute to better understanding this process.

New England archaeologists should promote the anthropological relevance of their work and demonstrate how their archaeological data can have theoretical and practical application beyond the local context. When they regularly succeed in this endeavor, their work will be a welcome addition to reconstructions of prehistory and the histories of American archaeology.

ACKNOWLEDGMENTS

The University of Massachusetts Archaeological Services, under the direction of Mitch Mulholland, provided me with the opportunity to survey the historical and archaeological background of the Turners Falls locality and in so doing make a small contribution to our understanding of the past. I am indebted to earlier collaborators, Alan McArdle and Marjorie Able, who assisted in my studies of Turners Falls. This chapter has benefited from the constructive commentary of Mary Ann Levine, Bob Hasenstab, and Ken Sassaman. Figure 14.4 is reproduced through the courtesy of the *Greenfield Recorder*. I am proud to be among the fellowship of Dena Dincauze's intellectual progeny. Dena's logical rigor and commitment to the archaeology of the region have long been models worthy of emulation.

15

An Interdisciplinary Study of the John Alden Houses, 1627 and 1653, Duxbury, Massachusetts: Archaeology and Architecture

Mitchell T. Mulholland

This chapter describes an interdisciplinary study that employed archaeology, architectural history, and historic archival research to study two seventeenth-century houses once occupied by Mayflower passengers, John Alden and Priscilla Mullins. One house, apparently constructed in the 1620s or 1630s, is no longer standing, its remains reduced to an already excavated archaeological site (Figure 15.1). The second house, believed to have been built in 1653, survives today as a historic-house museum in Duxbury, Massachusetts. Much of the research summarized in this chapter focused on an assessment of the age and affiliation of this later house. Recent analysis of archaeological materials recovered from the site of the older house is reported here as well. Both efforts stemmed from the need to collect information about these important resources prior to construction of a new visitors' facility at the museum. The work illustrates the interpretive value of interdisciplinary research within cultural resource management.

1627/1632 JOHN ALDEN HOUSE

Operating seasonally out of Plymouth Colony, Mayflower cooper John Alden and his wife, Priscilla, built a small house on a low knoll immediately north of the Blue Fish River in Duxbury. The year of construction is not known, but local tradition places construction in 1627. Roland Wells Robbins (1969) places the construction at 1632. Tradition has it that Alden and his family lived in the first house until sometime before 1653, when some necessity (perhaps family size or perhaps weather) caused the family to build a new structure at a different location. No documentation related to the move to the new structure has been located at present.

Figure 15.1. Floor Plan of the 1627 Alden House Excavated by Roland Robbins (1969:44-45)

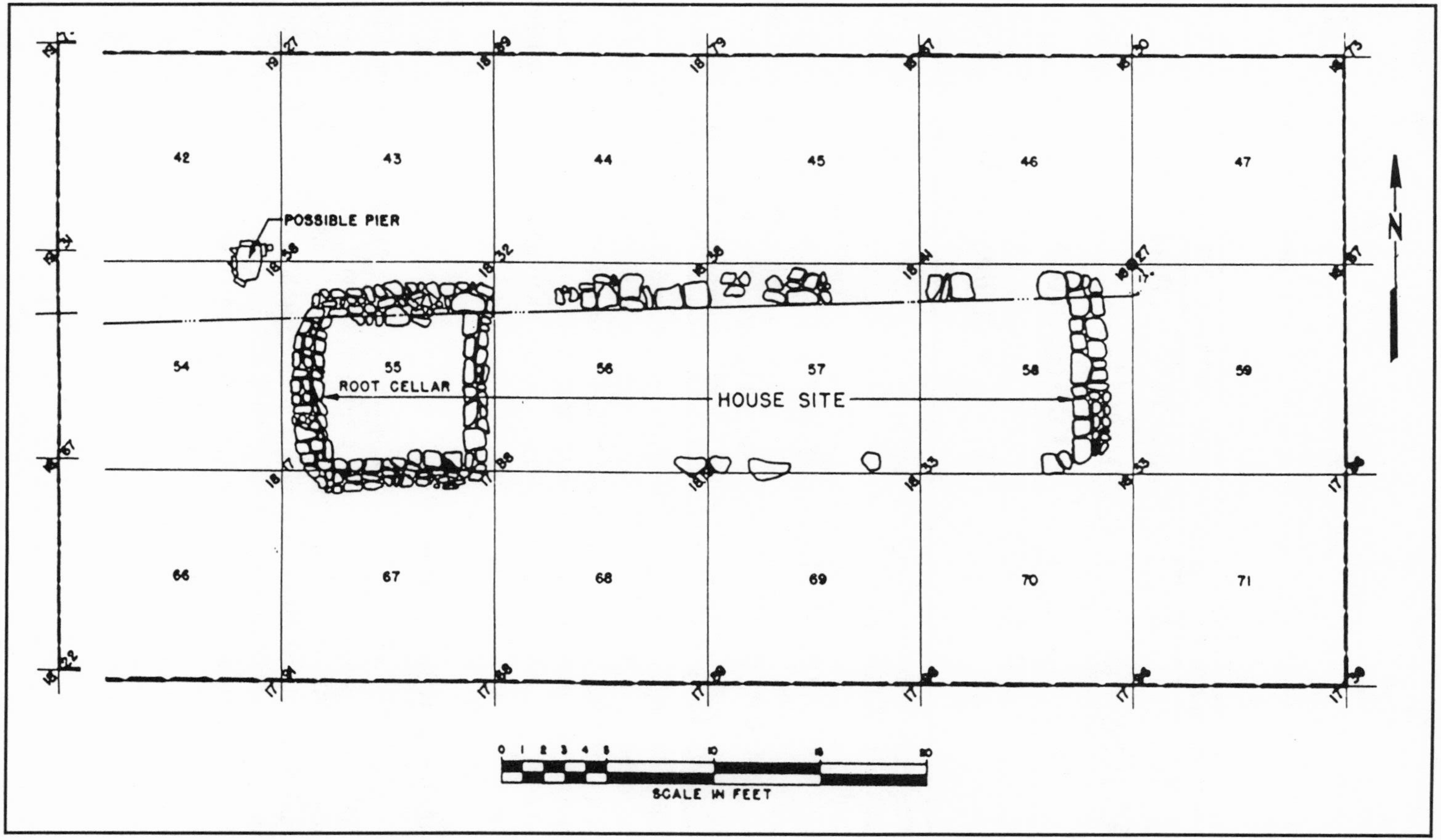

Stories concerning the disposition of the first house are varied. Some members of the Alden family believed that the original house was destroyed by fire, causing the move. Others believe that the elevation of the original house was too low and dangerously close to the water. Today, the museum docents tell the public that the 1627 house was moved intact to the location of the 1653 house and incorporated into its structure as the kitchen. Whatever the reason, a new house was constructed some 700 feet to the northwest of the older house on a knoll a few feet higher than the original and several hundred feet from the river.

On the basis of the results of a 1960 archaeological investigation (Robbins 1969), the first Alden house was long and narrow after an early English tradition (see Figure 15.1). More common in the Chesapeake Bay area, this impermanent early house form was found in low frequency throughout the northeast and perhaps can be traced to fourteenth-century England (Carson et al. 1981:138). The early Alden house has caught the attention of several New England scholars because it represents a type for which there are no known standing examples in the region. Citing Roland Robbins' (1969) work, James Deetz (1979:55) considered the narrow house type as an early structure, possible contemporary with post-hole structures. Deetz (1979:54–55) compared the early Alden house with the Miles Standish house in Duxbury, which was excavated in the 1860s, stating that there are no surviving examples in the region. Excavated in the 1860s by James Hall, one of the earliest historical archaeologists, the Standish structure was long and narrow with a small cellar at one end, measuring sixty by fifteen feet, a length-breadth ratio of 4:1 (Deetz 1979:55). Deetz noted the similarity in shape and ratio of the John Alden house which measures thirty-eight by ten feet. He also notes that similar buildings exist in Jamestown, Virginia, but are rare in New England.

1653 JOHN ALDEN HOUSE

There has been considerable interest in the identity of the builder of the "new" 1653 house, as well as the date of construction. John and Priscilla Alden's occupation of the new house in the seventeenth century and the great antiquity of the structure are part of a central theme in the historical significance of the house. Therefore the topics are important to the Alden Kindred of America, Inc., and to the visiting public. Oral tradition maintains that the existing Alden house was indeed the structure built and completed by John Alden Sr. in 1653. Wentworth (1980:20) notes that the idea of a 1653 construction date has been held (presumedly locally) for considerable time. She stated that "Everything about the house substantiates it (the date of 1653) making it even more reasonable to accept the traditional 1653." Other traditions include John Alden Sr.'s son Jonathan building the 1653 house, but Jonathan would only have been twenty-one years of age and unmarried in 1653. Regarding the move from the earlier house, Wentworth (1980:20) asserted that there may have been a spatial strain on the resources of the tiny first house, a hypothesis that is well taken. Between 1624 and 1647, the Aldens raised ten children (Wentworth 1980:100), and it is perhaps an unlikely feat for a family on a comparatively high social scale to suffer the noise and confusion in a narrow two-room house.

Precisely who built the house is a question that cannot be answered given the documents researched to date. The 1653 date of construction thus far cannot be substantiated through documentary records and remains problematical.

Architectural Evidence for Antiquity of the 1653 House

Little has been published on the architecture of the house (with the exception of Baxter [1921]) although the house is described or pictured in several architectural publications as an example of First Period standing architecture (e.g., Adams 1944–1949; Lathrop 1941; Long 1937; Wentworth 1973). Perhaps the most useful bit of information in Baxter's article is a floor plan showing the house as he saw it in ca. 1921 (Baxter 1921:400). The plan proves that the present configuration of the north part of the house is a twentieth-century product.

Wentworth's (1980) study of the Alden family provides the most complete discussion of the house, briefly describing the existing house plan, but focuses upon the occupants of the house from John Alden's construction to the present. Wentworth (1980:90) noted "The house structure cries for a skilled architectural examination. In the meantime, observation and speculations run wild."

Two independent structures appear to be present in the Alden House. They are a thirty-eight-by-eighteen-foot main house on the south side, and a thirty-eight-by-eleven-foot structure on the north. In this chapter the main house is referred to as the south block and the north section as the north block (Figure 15.2). It is traditionally believed that either the original (north) portion of the house was moved to the new location and was directly incorporated into the structure, or that it was dismantled and the materials reused in the construction of the new house. A popular theory espoused in the 1960s by Russell Edwards of the Alden Kindred and Roland Robbins (1969) was that the north rooms of the house were a part of the original structure that was moved to the site becoming the north section, and then a second story was added. Robbins noted that upon his inspection of the house, it appeared to him that the roof covered both the thirty-eight-by-eighteen-foot structure as well as the thirty-eight-by-eleven-foot structure. He suggested that with more inspection it may be evident that the roof once covered only the large structure (Robbins 1969:43). However, inspected in 1955 and 1976 by Abbott Lowell Cummings, the entire structure is interpreted as one-build (Cummings 1955–1956 and 1976). Cummings also has suggested the possibility of a lean-to on the north side that was abutted to the main structure (Abbott Cummings, personal communication 1995). He suggested that possible evidence for this may exist in the attic, access to which he was denied at the time. Other evidence could include changes in chimney flashing (evidence in flashing marks), or evidence of vestiges of an offset roof structure.

Figure 15.2
Floor Plan of the 1653 Alden House in 1980 (Wentworth 1980:87)

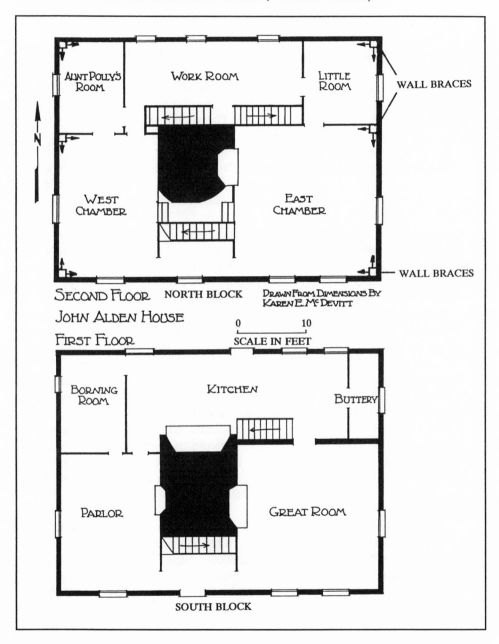

ALINT POLLY'S ROOM
WORK ROOM
LITTLE ROOM
WALL BRACES
N
WEST CHAMBER
EAST CHAMBER
WALL BRACES
SECOND FLOOR   NORTH BLOCK   DRAWN FROM DIMENSIONS BY KAREN E. MCDEVITT
JOHN ALDEN HOUSE
FIRST FLOOR
0   10
SCALE IN FEET
BORNING ROOM
KITCHEN
BUTTERY
PARLOR
GREAT ROOM
SOUTH BLOCK

These potential characteristics have been researched in this study and support a one-build construction. The roof as it exists today clearly covers the entire structure (north and south) and there is evidence of considerable reuse of materials from earlier structures. There is no evidence on the chimney for reconfiguration. However, the chimney stack has been grouted with clay.

Main Structure. Today the house appears to consist of two independent structures (see Figure 15.2). The southern part of the Alden house, which faces the Blue Fish River, is approximately thirty-eight by eighteen feet in size with the long (gable) end oriented in an east-west direction. The dimensions and main house plan are relatively consistent with houses constructed between 1637 and 1706 in the region (Cummings 1979:24). The interior of this section is a two-room plan, consisting of a great room on the east side of a central chimney and a parlor west of the chimney. The front door is more or less central, offset slightly to the west to allow room for the large size of the great room. Immediately beyond the front door is a narrow east-west hall, the opposite side of which is an east-west stairway providing access to the chambers in the second story.

The second story contains a large east chamber over the great room and the west chamber over the parlor (see Figure 15.2) and the large east or "best" chamber contains a fireplace with simple board paneling. The west chamber is narrower than the best chamber, and curiously has a thicker south wall (approximately eight inches), no doubt a nineteenth-century addition.

Typical of First Period (1625 to 1725) houses of plank construction, the east wall of the east (best) chamber reveals classic gunstock corner posts and diagonal wall braces that have not been plastered over. The posts and wall braces are evident on all four walls of the second floor of the main house (see Figure 15.2), further suggesting that the structure is independent from the northern structure. The north room has the braces only on the north corners also perhaps evidence of the independence of the north structure.

North Addition. A narrow, 38-by-11.5-foot structure appears to be attached to the north side of the main structure. Museum tradition has it that the north structure is the remains of the original 1627 Alden house, either moved or reassembled as an addition to the main house. Today the first floor consists of a narrow buttery on the east, a large kitchen with "walk-in" fireplace in the center, and a bed chamber in the west.

Evidence of the great antiquity of the north section of the house appears to be its layout with a central brick hearth and kitchen, and two end service rooms (see Figure 15.2), narrow floor plan identical to that excavated by Robbins, a chamfered summer beam, low ceiling, "walk-in" hearth, vertical wide-board feathered paneling on the walls, and a ten-by-thirteen-foot root cellar beneath the eastern buttery, reminiscent of the layout of the 1627 house. The buttery is misleading because it is not indicated in a 1921 house plan (Baxter 1921:400) and is a twentieth-century construction.

Attic. The attic reveals a roof that appears to have been built over both the main house and the addition. This was either constructed at the time the house was built or modified later to cover a lean-to. The structure is typical of late First Period construction with rafters widely spaced and common purlins trenched into the upper roof side. Rafters are mortised and tenoned and are joined together with single pegs and there is a ridge pole. Collar beams connect the rafters and are reused pieces from an earlier construction. Several of the collar beams including the gable-end collar beam have a coating of whitewash (a common early trait). The end collar beam has faint remnants of a green paint reminiscent of that now exposed on a corner post in the buttery, and on the beams on the first floor of the north structure. This collar beam and others also have evidence of hand sawing. The collar tie immediately west of the chimney stack has nail marks along its side indicating that it may have been used before as a wall stud.

The wide roof boards extend vertically from plate to ridge pole and show the even saw marks of an up-and-down sawmill. This is further evidence of construction popular in the latter part of the First Period or later. There is no evidence in the roof of anything but one construction event covering both the north and south blocks. There are no modifications in the flashing, roof boards, or timbers.

A dislodged floor board southeast of the chimney stack revealed evidence of the separate nature of the south and north blocks. The board was removed during recent construction. Ceiling joists span south to north the entire width of the south block, and their north ends rest on a large east-west timber that rests on the north wall plate of the south block. The joists rest on the east-west timber extending to the north wall of the north block. The joists are neither attached to each other nor to the east-west timber. Curiously they simply rest on the timber. A large eight-by-eight-inch timber spans both structures (south-north) in the approximate center of the house, which structurally ties the two outer walls. The outer boards of the north wall of the south block can be seen beneath the joists. The construction evident in this location suggests that the south block may be the oldest part of the house, with the joists above the north block shimmed to meet those of the south block. An alternative explanation may be the house was simply built in two sections during one construction event. The sill-to-sill wall boards may have been replaced (explaining why there is no apparent wear on the outer surface), or wear may be evident in areas that are not painted or wall-papered.

The gable ends are covered with vertical boards with 2.5 inch feathered molding. These are noted by Cummings as reused remnants of an early structure (Cummings 1976). The west-end collar beam is also evidence of reuse from another structure or another part of the Alden house. Unfortunately, the floor obscures the side boards of the second story walls on the east and west ends.

Archaeological Evidence for Antiquity of the 1653 House

In October 1995 an archaeological investigation was conducted on the two-acre parcel on which the 1653 house stands. The project was conducted in advance of the Alden Kindred's plans to build a barn/visitor's center on the site of a razed barn. Because federal and state funds are being considered for use in the new center, the Massachusetts Historical Commission recommended that a survey be conducted to ensure that significant archaeological resources would not be destroyed by the proposed construction. The study was conducted for the Alden Kindred by University of Massachusetts Archaeological Services (UMAS) under the direction of Paul Mullins and Mitchell Mulholland (1995). Surprisingly, during the archaeological investigation of the Alden house property, few seventeenth-century artifacts were found. The majority of materials were eighteenth and nineteenth century (the latter derived heavily from the area of the barn and outhouse).

Interestingly, there is little similarity in artifacts between the two houses. A tiny sherd of Westerwald pottery (1700–1783), once a part of a drinking vessel was recovered from the "new" house and is similar to fragments recovered from the "old." Westerwald is late for the period of John Alden Sr.'s first house and is probably related to postoccupational disturbances.

The full area of the roughly two-acre project area was investigated. Fifty-nine shovel test pits were excavated over the property. Soils in these test pits were undisturbed with the exception of the topsoil. No conclusively seventeenth-century artifacts were recovered. The few eighteenth-century artifacts with datable ranges included Westerwald stoneware (1700–1783), Nottingham stoneware (1700–1810), buff-white bodied earthenware with yellow glaze (1625–1730), and creamware (1762–1820). Two sherds of tin-enameled earthenware (delft 1640–1800) were found and could conceivably be of seventeenth-century manufacture because of the ware's wide date range. This thin distribution of materials was found on the south side of the house. All other historic artifacts postdate 1700. No archaeological features related to the seventeenth century were located. Evidence of Native American occupation was also found scattered over the property, notably a small prehistoric site dating to the Late Woodland period.

The house stands on a flat knoll which descends to the east and north. In the nineteenth century, a barn stood on this slope roughly 15 m northeast of the house, leaving a clear depression with occasional scattered stones in the vicinity. A dense quantity of mid-nineteenth- to early-twentieth-century artifacts was recovered in this area, particularly in and around the barn itself. The broad range of artifacts (e.g., food remains, plates, bottles, and buttons) suggests that household refuse was continually discarded on the slope immediately north of the house and around the barn during the late nineteenth century. A single test pit at the eastern end of the barn contained 1,093 artifacts alone (1,091 historic). The vast majority of the artifacts in the barn area dated from the mid-nineteenth century or later, but a small scatter of earlier artifacts was recovered, including a concentration of 39 creamware sherds in the test pit on the house's north end.

Eighteenth- and nineteenth-century datable materials include coal (probably 1850–1940), plain creamware (1762–1820), delftware (1640–1800), Jackfield earthenware (1740–1850), pearlware (1780–1820), and yelloware (1827–1900). Redware was found in abundance, evidence of dairying. The barn was studied in more detail in an excavation lead by Claire Carlson (1998).

In summary, a thin scatter of eighteenth-century artifacts was recovered around the house, particularly to the south. All of these artifacts were quite small and fragmentary, and clearly do not reflect eighteenth century occupation of the house. No conclusively seventeenth-century European artifacts were recovered. Artifacts recovered from the site suggest an occupation postdating 1700.

Deed Research

Deed research was conducted at the Plymouth County Registry of Deeds and the Plymouth County Commissioners' Office. The purpose of the deed research was to locate evidence of ownership of the 1653 house, detect any evidence of the early structure, determine the changes in values of the property over time, with a goal of determining which occupant or occupants were responsible for major renovation.

Deed research and probate inventories provided useful information concerning the development of the house. In the seventeenth and eighteenth centuries it was common to produce an inventory of all items within a house upon the death of its owner. John Alden died in 1687 intestate, but his probate inventory provided a meager list of tools and household goods. Unfortunately the inventory did not list the contents of each room. The value of the house, contents, and land was 100 pounds. At his son Jonathon's death (who also died intestate) a short inventory (Probate Records Vol. 1:255) was recorded in March 1697 and unfortunately does not include a room-by-room inventory. The value of the farm also was valued at 100-00-0 (pounds-shillings-pence). The inventory includes farming implements and animals, and a summary of very basic household items (e.g., beds, bedding and table linen, "one table Carpet and forme, Chairs and Cushions, Spinning wheels Cards hishel glas bottles, Earthen wear tubs pails" [*sic*]) (Wentworth 1980:111).

Jonathon granted his property to his son Colonel John Alden. John died in 1739 intestate, but settlement was made to his son Samuel. Samuel was left "the farme whereof deceased dwelt with all buildings and appurtenances as in inventory at 2000 pounds and wood lot at 160 pounds." Briggs's inventory includes an impressive amount of household and farm property and is listed in a room-by-room inventory. Rooms include "biggest lower room, biggest chamber, biggest westerly chamber, northwest chamber, northest [*sic*] chamber" (all with bed furniture) (Wentworth 1980:112–116). Interestingly, the first floor of the north block (kitchen and northwest bedroom first floor) is not mentioned, nor is the central room of the second floor of the north block. The westerly parlor also is not listed. The room description does mention the northeast and northwest chambers, both of which are in the north block, second floor. So it is clear that the north block was attached to the south block by 1739 and at least by this time was a two-story structure. The value of real estate at 2,000 pounds is impressive. This is approximately the value of $10,000, an enormous sum at the time. The probate inventory also reflects John's affluence. Clearly major modification occurred to the house and property during Colonel John Alden's tenure.

ARCHAEOLOGY OF THE 1627 HOUSE: THE ROBBINS COLLECTION

During the 1995 architectural study of the house, a large collection of artifacts was encountered in the attic in extremely perilous circumstances. The collection was that collected by Roland Wells Robbins in the 1960s and had been housed in the attic of the Alden house since the 1960s, when the town of Duxbury donated it to the Alden Kindred. Since the collection was discovered, a University Public Service Endowment Grant was obtained in part to analyze the collection, stabilize it, make arrangements for curation in a more suitable repository, and provide information for local schools. At the core of the project was modern identification of the ceramics, metal, glass, faunal material and small finds, and storage in archival-quality containers.

In 1960 the 1627 site was excavated by Roland Wells Robbins, who was engaged for the purpose by the Alden Kindred of America, Inc. Robbins, a window washer and house painter by trade, with very capable amateur skills in archaeology, was responsible for excavating several historic-period sites in the northeastern United States (Linebaugh 1996).

Robbins located the early structure first through probing and then through systematic excavation. The outline of the foundation measured 38 feet in length and 10.5 feet in width (Figure 15.1), then and now considered a rare First Period structure in New England. The house presumably faced south, the side facing the Blue Fish River, which was some 200 to 300 feet distant. Most, or all of the house rested upon a stone foundation. On the west end of the foundation, a seven-foot-deep, stone-lined root cellar was uncovered. While remains of a chimney were not found, a depression in the south-central portion of the house was believed by Robbins to have been the chimney base.

Numerous mid-seventeenth-century artifacts were recovered from the excavation including cutlery, spoons, hooks, buckles, North Devon pottery, a horseshoe, parts of a snaphaunce gun, and more. Window glass was diamond shaped with lead cames, typical of early First Period construction. More than 2,000 pounds of brick fragments were recovered from the house site, probably used as fill in the walls, and perhaps from the chimney. Hand-wrought square nails numbered 3,884, the great number interpreted by Robbins as evidence that the structure was dismantled. No evidence of fire was encountered (Robbins 1969).

More than 1,200 pieces of pottery were recovered, important because of their known manufacture dates. Curiously, Robbins spent little time discussing the ceramics (only two paragraphs are devoted to the subject) and he appears not to have analyzed the ceramics for dating purposes. On the other hand, the more robust ceramic typology that exists today was not available to him. Much time was given to the analysis of bore diameters of the 527 pipe stems recovered from the excavation. The pipe-stem bore analysis was used by Robbins to date the structure to the earlier half of the seventeenth century. Robbins's study does not indicate the time of abandonment of the house, but further analysis of the artifacts may assist in this. Robbins and his laboratory analysts sorted the materials by type, and carefully recorded their provenience.

Evidence in the 1627 Collection

In 1995, Paul Mullins of the University of Massachusetts and Constance Crosby of the Massachusetts Historical Commission, both analysts of historic material culture, conducted a brief review of the historic artifacts of the Robbins collection. While no field notes accompany the collection, the recording of provenience on all bags and boxes was very thorough. Several artifacts were also on display in the great room of the house. These were items of public interest pulled from the collection by Robbins for display purposes. Several large Native American ground stone tools were in use as door stops.

Thousands of nails were recovered from the 1627 house. Almost all nails from the site are hand-wrought. The majority of nails are rose head, which is a generic type used for many functions. A full range of penny sizes and nails is represented from tacks to spikes. Many nails are T heads and L heads commonly used in flooring. Point treatment varies with both flat-spatulated and fine points represented. Many lathe nails are in the collection and are the only indication of the use of lathe in the early house. Numerous horseshoe nails (and a horseshoe fragment) are represented. Several oxen shoes are in the collection as well as a horseshoe. A small number of nail fragments show evidence of burning, but there is no evidence of a widespread fire at the house. A few nails had wood attached, preserved by the association with the metal. Nails exhibit the whole range of uses typical in house construction.

What is curious is the great number of nails in the collection. Frugal reuse of wood was common throughout the seventeenth through nineteenth centuries, especially in coastal areas where the forests were denuded early. One would assume that nails would have been reused as well. The large number is suggestive of a structure that has rotted in place. Possible explanations are severe storms (there were several severe hurricanes in the eighteenth century), or long tenure resulting in deterioration of the structure.

Ceramics recovered from the site are predominantly lead-glaze, temporally nondiagnostic redwares. Redwares were produced locally, often by farmers or people also engaged in other careers. Redware vessels represented are utilitarian and not fine table wares. Their function is predominantly dairy and food storage. Vessel shapes were determined for only hollowware and include bowls, storage vessels, and jars. The largest fragments are "Iberian" or olive jars used for food storage (labeled at the Alden house as Indian pottery). Temporally diagnostic wares include North Devon (1650–1783), possibly a few fragments of Buckley (seventeenth century), and some red-bodied trailed slipwares. There is a very small quantity of delft wares which are temporally problematic ranging in age from 1640 to the nineteenth century. One small fragment of Rhenish/Westerwald (1650–1783) was also recovered. This is similar to the material found at the 1653 house during the archaeological survey.

The collection of glass artifacts contains a large amount of broad glass (made prior to crown glass), fitting the assumed time of occupation. Crown glass is present but in very small amounts. Much of the material is window glass. A few are fragments of diamond-paned windows. Lead cames from diamond pane windows were also recovered. Bottle glass included mostly dark wine/liquor bottles and at least one case bottle. All are consistent with seventeenth-century occupation.

Flatware in the collection consists of several fragments of cutlery, spoon handles, and spoon bowls. A strawberry-tipped spoon handle is one of the more interesting finds. A small brass spout of a teapot or other pouring container is also in the collection. One of the more curious items is a small finger ring engraved with what has been identified as an image of Saint Peter holding the keys to heaven. This is interesting, given the Puritan background of most of the Mayflower people, but it is possible that John Alden Sr. was not of that persuasion. After all, he was signed on as a tradesman and may have had a quite different background from the passengers.

Bones in the collection are disappointingly fragmentary. Many are difficult to identify beyond general categories. Included in the collection are bones of cow, medium-sized but unidentified mammals (either bovid or cervids), chickens, and other birds. Most species are domesticated animals. No horse bones were found. Several fish hooks were in the collection attesting to the importance of fish in the diet, although no fish bones were recovered.

Artifacts related to arms include several pieces of an English-made snaphaunce musket, a firearm common in the early seventeenth century. The piece has been evaluated by Richard Colton and determined to have been taken apart and stored. The gun may have been used for spare parts when later styles of flintlock muskets were introduced. Several parts would have been useable in both types of gun. Interestingly, John Alden Sr.'s probate inventory of 1687 lists "2 old guns" valued at 11 shillings." Obviously the old snaphaunce did not go with him to the new house. Other arms-related materials include a portion of a pike head. A halberd head from the early house is located in the Pilgrim Hall collection associated with the John Alden House. Halberds were often a mark of the rank of Sergeant (Richard Colton, personal communication 1997). It would be interesting if Alden's participation in a local militia could be corroborated. Robbins had the pike head identified by Ivor Noël Hume, who dated it to the early part of the seventeenth century. A gun fork, the only one of its kind in New England, was also found at the site. Robbins had this dated to 1550 to 1650 by military experts whom he does not identify (Robbins 1969:33). An iron buckle possibly associated with armor (a back and breast) is also in the collection. It is perhaps significant that these early seventeenth-century defensive items were relegated to trash as the years went by. Numerous fragments of shot sprue also have been identified. The latter would have been used to produce buckshot for hunting small animals and birds. The firearm, pike, and armor also are related to protection.

Items related to clothing include several brass buckles, an iron buckle, hooks, clasps, and buttons. Most of the buckles are associated with men's and women's girdles/belts. At least two clothing hooks once associated with a doublet is in the collection. Also present are a rusted scissors and awl possibly used in sewing, and a cock's head door hinge typical of the seventeenth century. Several straight pins are illustrated by Robbins (1969:33) but have not been located in the collection.

At least three coins are in the collection, one of which was not relocated by the UMAS analysts. Robbins describes a 1652 New England Oak Tree silver sixpence. This coin was produced well into the 1660s with no change of the date stamp (Richard Colton, personal communication 1997). Two copper farthings are also present, which probably date between 1625 and 1649 (Robbins 1969: 34). Coins thus date to the expected time period of pre–1653.

Originally thought to have been poorly fired bricks used as "nogging" for in-filling of the walls as insulation, most of the bricks in the collection are remnants of a fireplace and oven. One of the most interesting materials in the collection is clay "wattle" with impressions of round stalks of vegetation. This is believed to have been either infilling from the house's walls or possible chimney fill. Seventeenth-century chimneys often were made of clay with only the areas exposed to the weather and direct flame made of brick, or encased in wood. Dr. Abbott Cummings (personal communication 1996), indicated that it is unusual to find this type of material in the New World, being more common in England. Interestingly, when repair work was done on the chimney stack of the 1653 house in the 1950s, clay impressed with salt marsh hay was found in the structure (Russell Edwards, personal communication 1997).

Artifacts evaluated from the Robbins excavation place occupation of the house before 1650.

SUMMARY AND CONCLUSION

The archaeological and architectural studies and deed research have provided corroborating information concerning the development of the 1653 Alden house. At the time of Jonathan Alden's death the farm was only worth 100 pounds, not an exorbitant sum for the time. This value as well as the limited household inventory are suggestive of a simple house. Forty-two years later Jonathon's son Colonel John died leaving the property valued at 2,000 pounds with opulent and valuable interior furnishings. Colonel John's occupation of the house from 1697 to 1739 more clearly reflects most of the structural elements now evident in the house.

Deeds and probate inventories are consistent with permanent occupancy of the house beginning around the turn of the eighteenth century, further corroborating the results of the architectural and archaeological studies. While the structure is clearly a First Period house, it appears to have been constructed late in the period. This is an opinion expressed by Abbott Cummings (1955), the results of the archaeological investigation, and examination of visible features suggest the later construction date.

There are many wall boards, girts and timbers in the house than have early First Period characteristics. However, these features are used randomly throughout both sections of the house. There is no evidence that the north block was moved intact (it is of later plank construction than would be expected of an early English narrow house plan). There is no evidence that this structure was "flaked" or cut into pieces and moved. The timbers and many wall boards used in the construction of the north block are clearly datable to the early part of the First Period, but were rearranged at a later date. The 1627 house may have been dismantled and pieces reused throughout the newer structure, but these reused timbers could have come from another house. The volume of nails recovered from the site suggests that the 1627 house may have rotted in place, rather than having been razed or destroyed by fire. One hypothesis is that severe weather such as a hurricane could easily have caused major damage to the structure that might be undetectable in the archaeological record. In the seventeenth century, Governor Bradford mentions a severe hurricane causing damage to property.

Structurally, the north and south blocks appear to be separate structures, while the roof covering the structure is one-build. As suggested by Cummings and Robbins, the north structure could have originally formed a lean-to that received a full second story later than the original construction date.

The results of the entire study suggest that the "1653" Alden house may be of later construction than is traditionally believed. Architectural and archaeological evidence, and probate inventories suggest a late-seventeenth-/early-eighteenth-century date. The archaeological study revealed only a very faint presence of early European materials, none of which is conclusively dated to the seventeenth century.

References

Abercrombie, F. C.
1925 *The Turners Falls Power and Electric Company: A Public Utility since 1792.* Published by the author in Turners Falls, MA. On file at Northeast Utilities Northfield Mountain Facility, Northfield, MA.

Abrams, M. D.
1992 Fire and the Development of Oak Forests. *Bioscience* 42:346–353.

Adams, C. B.
1845 *Annual Report of the Geology of the State of Vermont.* Chauncy Goodrich, Burlington, VT.

Adams, J. T.
1944–1949 *Album of American History.* Scribner's, New York.

Anderson, D. G.
1990 The Paleoindian Colonization of Eastern North America: A View from the Southeastern United States. In *Early Paleoindian Economies of Eastern North America*, edited by K. B. Tankersley and B. L. Isaac, pp. 163–216. Research in Economic Anthropology, Supplement 5. JAI Press, Greenwich, CT.

Anderson, D. G., and M. K. Faught.
1998 The Distribution of Fluted Paleoindian Projectile Points: Update 1998. *Archaeology of Eastern North America* 26:163–187.

Anderson, M. K.
1991 Gardeners in Eden. *Wilderness Magazine* 195:27–30.
1995 *California Indian Basketry as a Model for the Reconstruction of Past Resource Management Systems in Wildlands of North America.* Unpublished ms. in possession of the author.

Anonymous.
1862 *The Visitor's Guide to the Public Rooms and Cabinets of Amherst College.*
1880a Nuggets. *Maine Mining Journal.* 28 May:357.
1880b Twin-Lead Mining Company. *Maine Mining Journal.* 16 April:231–233.
1881a Bagaduce. *Maine Mining Journal.* 23 September:185.

1881b Lodes, Leads and Veins. *Maine Mining Journal.* 29 July:56–57.

Ayers, H. G.

1976 *The Occupation of Ridgetop Sites in the Blue Ridge Mountains by Savannah River Archaic Peoples.* Paper presented at the annual meeting of the Southeastern Archaeological Conference, Tuscaloosa, AL.

Bagnall, C. T.

1875 Peske-ompsk-ut; or, the Falls Fight: A Series of Random Sketches Showing a Glimpse of the Early History of Turners Falls, which appeared in "The Turners Falls Reporter," during the months of January and February 1875. Printed at the "Reporter" Job Office, Turners Falls, MA.

Bailey, J. T.

1883 The Copper Deposits of Adams County, Pennsylvania. *The Engineering and Mining Journal* 35(7):88–89.

Bailey, L. W.

1899 *The Mineral Resources of the Province of New Brunswick.* Geological Survey of Canada, Annual Report, vol. 10, Ottawa, Ontario.

Balikci, A.

1970 *The Netsilik Eskimo.* The Natural History Press, Garden City, NY.

Barber, J. W.

1836 *Connecticut Historical Collections.* John W. Barber, New Haven, CT.

Barber, M. B.

1984 *Upland Archaeology in the East.* Cultural Resources Report No. 5, USDA/Forest Service, Region 8, Atlanta, GA.

Barber, R. J.

1977 *Phase I Assessment of Archaeological Potential, Green River Relief and Replacement Interceptor Project, Greenfield, Massachusetts.* On file at the Massachusetts Historical Commission, Office of the Secretary of State, Boston.

1980 Post-Pleistocene Anadromous Fish Exploitation at the Buswell Site, Northwestern Massachusetts. In *Early and Middle Archaic Cultures in the Northeast,* edited by D. R. Starbuck and C. E. Bolian, pp. 97–114. Occasional Publications in Northeastern Archaeology 7. Franklin Pierce College, Rindge, NH.

1982 *The Wheelers Site: A Specialized Shellfish Processing Station on the Merrimack River.* Peabody Museum Monograph 7. Harvard University, Cambridge, MA.

1983 Diversity in Shell Middens: The View from Morrill Point. *Man in the Northeast* 25:109–125.

Baron, W. R.

1988 Historical Climates of the Northeastern United States: Seventeenth through Nineteenth Centuries. In *Holocene Human Ecology in Northeastern North America,* edited by G. P. Nicholas, pp. 29–46. Plenum, New York.

Bartlett, F. L.

1880 The Bagaduce Mining District. *Maine Mining Journal.* 15 October: 246–247.

Bascom, F.

1896 The Ancient Volcanic Rocks of South Mountain, Pennsylvania. *Bulletin of the United States Geological Survey,* No. 136.

Bass, Q. R. II.

1977 *Prehistoric Settlement and Subsistence Patterns in the Great Smoky Mountains.* M.A. thesis, Department of Anthropology, University of Tennessee, Knoxville.

Bateman, A. M.
1923 Primary Chalcocite: Bristol Copper Mine, Connecticut. *Economic Geology* 18(2): 122–166.

Bawden, G.
1980 *Phase II Assessment of Archaeological Potential, Green River Relief and Replacement Interceptor Project, Greenfield, Massachusetts*. On file at the Massachusetts Historical Commission, Office of the Secretary of State, Boston.

Baxter, S.
1921 The Alden House at Duxbury, Massachusetts. *Architectural Record*, Volume XLIX, Number 5 (May 1921):399–407.

Beauchamp, W. M.
1902 *Metallic Implements of the New York Indians*. New York State Museum Bulletin 55. University of the State of New York, Albany, NY.

Beck, L. C.
1839 Notices of the Native Copper, Ores of Copper, and Other Minerals Found in the Vicinity of New Brunswick. *The American Journal of Science* 36:107–114.

Belcher, W. R.
1989 Prehistoric Fish Exploitation in East Penobscot Bay, Maine: The Knox Site and Sea-Level Rise. *Archaeology of Eastern North America* 17:175–191.

Bellantoni, N. F.
1987 *Faunal Resource Availability and Prehistoric Cultural Selection on Block Island, Rhode Island*. Ph.D. dissertation, Department of Anthropology, University of Connecticut, Storrs.

Bender, B.
1985 Emergent Tribal Formations in the American Midcontinent. *American Antiquity* 50:52–62.

Bender, S.
1986 *The Role of Mountain and Upland Archaeology in Regional Research*. Paper presented at the 26th annual meeting of the Northeastern Anthropological Association, Buffalo, NY.

Bendremer, J. C., E. A. Kellogg, and T. B. Largy.
1991 A Grass-Lined Maize Storage Pit and Early Maize Horticulture in Central Connecticut. *North American Archaeologist* 12:325–349.

Benedict, J. B.
1981 *Glacial Geology and Archaeology of the Timberline Ecotone*. Research Report No. 2. Center for Mountain Archaeology, Ward, CO.

Benge, E., and E. T. Wherry.
1908 Directory of the Mineral Localities in and around Philadelphia. *The Mineral Collector* 15:6–8.

Bennet, M. K.
1955 The Food Economy of the New England Indians, 1605–1675. *Journal of Political Economy* 63:369–395.

Bernstein, D. J.
1989a *An Archaeological Locational Survey for the Turners Falls Anadromous Fish Research Facility, Turners Falls, Massachusetts*. University of Massachusetts Archaeological Services Report, Amherst. On file at the Massachusetts Historical Commission, Office of the Secretary of State, Boston.

1989b *An Archaeological Locational Survey for the Turners Falls Water Pipeline Project, Turners Falls, Massachusetts*. University of Massachusetts Archaeological Services Report 100, Amherst. On file at the Massachusetts Historical Commission, Office of the Secretary of State, Boston.

1990 Trends in Prehistoric Subsistence on the Southern New England Coast: The View from Narragansett Bay. *North American Archaeologist* 11:321–352.

1993 *Prehistoric Subsistence on the Southern New England Coast: The Record from Narragansett Bay*. Academic Press, San Diego, CA.

Berry, G. S.

1898–99 The Great Shell Mounds of Damariscotta. *New England Magazine*, ns, 19:178–188.

Bettinger, R. L.

1991 *Hunter-Gatherers: Archaeological and Evolutionary Theory*. Plenum, New York.

Bettinger, R. L., and D. H. Thomas.

1984 *Aboriginal Occupation at Altitude: The Alpine Village Pattern in the Great Basin*. Ms. in possession of the author.

Beukens, R. P., L. A. Pavlish, R. G. V. Hancock, R. M. Farquhar, G. C. Wilson, P. L. Julig, and W. Ross.

1992 Radiocarbon Dating of Copper-Preserved Organics. *Radiocarbon* 34(3):890–897.

Bevier, G. M.

1914 The Present Status of the Copper Development in the South Mountain Region. In *Pennsylvania Geological Survey*, 3rd Series, Biennial Report, Appendix C, pp. 57–69.

Binford, L. R.

1978 *Nunamiut Ethnoarchaeology*. Academic Press, New York.

1980 Willow Smoke and Dogs' Tails: Hunter-Gatherer Settlement Systems and Archaeological Site Formation. *American Antiquity* 45:4–20.

Bishop, J. L.

1868 *A History of American Manufactures from 1608–1860*, vol. 1, 3rd ed. Edward Young & Co., Philadelphia.

Blake, W. P.

1888 *History of the Town of Hamden, Connecticut*. Price, Lee, & Co., New Haven, CT.

Blanton, D. B.

1985 Lithic Raw Material Procurement and Use During the Morrow Mountain Phase in South Carolina. In *Lithic Resource Procurement: Proceedings from the Second Conference on Prehistoric Chert Exploitation*, edited by S. C. Vehik, pp. 115–132. Center for Archaeological Investigations, Occasional Paper Number 4. Southern Illinois University, Carbondale.

Blanton, D. B., and K. E. Sassaman.

1989 Pattern and Process in the Middle Archaic Period of South Carolina. In *Studies in South Carolina Archaeology: Essays in Honor of Robert L. Stephenson*, edited by A. C. Goodyear III and G. T. Hanson, pp. 54–72. Anthropological Papers 9, Occasional Publications of the South Carolina Institute of Archaeology and Anthropology, Columbia, SC.

Bleed, P.

1986 The Optimal Design of Hunting Weapons: Maintainability or Reliability. *American Antiquity* 51:737–747.

Bloch, M.

1983 *Marxism and Anthropology*. Oxford University Press, New York.

Bonnichsen, R., D. Keenlyside, and K. Turnmire.

1991 Paleoindian Patterns in Maine and the Maritimes. In *Prehistoric Archaeology in the Maritime Provinces: Past and Present Research*, edited by M. Deal and S. Blair, pp. 1–36. Reports in Archaeology 8. The Council of Maritime Premiers, Maritime Committee on Archaeological Cooperation, Fredericton, ME.

Bonnichsen, R., and D. Sanger.

1977 Integrating Faunal Analysis. *Canadian Journal of Archaeology* 1:109–135.

Borstel, C.

1982 *Archaeological Investigations at the Young Site, Alton, Maine*. Occasional Publications in Maine Archaeology, No. 2. Maine Historic Preservation Commission, Augusta.

1984 Prehistoric Site Chronology: A Preliminary Report. In *Chapters in the Archaeology of Cape Cod: Results of the Cape Cod National Seashore Archaeological Survey 1979–1981, Vol. 1*, edited by F. P. McManamon, pp. 231–299. Cultural Resources Management Study No. 8, National Park Service, Boston.

Bouras, E. F., and P. M. Bock.

1997 Recent Paleoindian Discovery: The First People in the White Mountain Region of New Hampshire. *New Hampshire Archaeologist* 37(1):48–58.

Bourque, B. J.

1973 Aboriginal Settlement and Subsistence on the Maine Coast. *Man in the Northeast* 6:3–20.

1995 *Diversity and Complexity in Prehistoric Maritime Societies: A Gulf of Maine Perspective*. Plenum, New York.

Bourque, B. J., and S. L. Cox.

1981 1979 Maine State Museum Investigation of the Goddard Site. *Man in the Northeast* 22:3–27.

Bourque, B., K. Morris, and A. Spiess.

1978 Determining the Season of Death of Mammal Teeth from Archaeological Sites: A New Sectioning Technique. *Science* 199:530–531.

Bradford, W.

1912 *History of Plymouth Plantation 1620–1647*. 2 vols. Houghton Mifflin, Boston.

Bradford, W., and E. Winslow.

1841 Bradford and Winslow's Journal. In *Chronicles of the Pilgrim Fathers of the Colony of Plymouth*, edited by A. Young, pp. 109–252. Little, Brown, Boston. (orig. 1622)

Bragdon, K. J.

1996 *Native People of Southern New England, 1500–1650*. University of Oklahoma Press, Norman.

Brasser, T. J.

1978 Mahican. In *Northeast: Handbook of North American Indians, Vol. 15*, edited by B. Trigger, pp. 198–212. Smithsonian Institution Press, Washington, DC.

Braun, D. P.

1983 Pots as Tools. In *Archaeological Hammers and Theories*, edited by J. A. Moore and A. S. Keene, pp. 107–134. Academic Press, New York.

1987 Coevolution of Sedentism, Pottery Technology, and Horticulture in the Central Midwest, 200 B.C.–A.D. 600. In *Emergent Horticultural Economies of the Eastern*

Woodlands, edited by W. F. Keegan, pp. 153–216. Center for Archaeological Investigations, Occasional Paper No. 7. Southern Illinois University, Carbondale.

Braverman, H.
1974 *Labor and Monopoly Capital*. Monthly Review Press, New York.

Bridges, P.
1994 Prehistoric Diet and Health in a Coastal New York Skeletal Sample. *Northeastern Anthropology* 48:13–23.

Brigham-Grette, J., and D. U. Wise.
1988 Glacial and Deglacial Landforms of the Amherst Area, North-Central Massachusetts. In *Field Trip Guidebook, AMQUA 1988*, edited by J. Brigham-Grette. Contribution No. 63:209–244. Department of Geology and Geography, University of Massachusetts, Amherst.

Brooks, E.
1946 Pottery Types from Hampden County, Massachusetts. *Bulletin of the Massachusetts Archaeological Society* 7(4):78–79.

Brose, D. S.
1994 Archaeological Investigations at the PaleoCrossing Site, A Paleoindian Occupation in Medina County, Ohio. In *The First Discovery of America: Archaeological Evidence of the Early Inhabitants of the Ohio Area*, edited by W. S. Dancey, pp. 61–76. Ohio Archaeological Council, Columbus.

Broyles, B. J.
1966 Preliminary Report: The St. Albans Site (46 Ka 27), Kanawha County, West Virginia. *West Virginia Archaeologist* 19:1–43.
1971 *Second Preliminary Report: The St. Albans Site, Kanawha County, West Virginia*. West Virginia Geologic and Economic Survey, Report of Investigations No. 3. Morgantown.

Brumbach, H. J.
1975 "Iroquoian" Ceramics in "Algonkian" Territory. *Man in the Northeast* 10:17–28.
1986 Anadromous Fish and Fishing: A Synthesis of Data from the Hudson River Drainage. *Man in the Northeast* 32:35–66.

Buckley, G. P., editor.
1992 *Ecology and Management of Coppice Woodlands*. Chapman and Hall, London.

Bullen, R. P.
1940 The Dolly Bond Steatite Quarry. *Massachusetts Archaeological Society Bulletin* 2(1):14–22.
1942 Forts, Boundaries, or Ha-has? *Bulletin of the Massachusetts Archaeological Society* 4(1):1–11.
1972 The Orange Period of Peninsular Florida. In *Fiber-Tempered Pottery in Southeastern United States and Northern Colombia: Its Origins, Context, and Significance*, edited by R. P. Bullen and J. B. Stoltman, pp. 9–33. Florida Anthropological Society Publications, No. 6. *Florida Anthropologist* 25(2), Part 2.

Bullen, R. P., and H. B. Greene.
1970 Stratigraphic Tests at Stallings Island, Georgia. *Florida Anthropologist* 23:8–23.

Bunker, V.
1988 Eddy Site Research at Phillips Exeter Academy. *Conference on New England Archaeology Newsletter* 8(2):18.

Burden, E. T., J. H. McAndrews, and G. Norris.
1986 Geochemical Indicators in Lake Sediment of Upland Erosion Caused by Indian

and European Farming, Awenda Provincial Park, Ontario. *Canadian Journal of Earth Science* 23:55–65.

Butler, B. S., and W. S. Burbank.

1929 *The Copper Deposits of Michigan.* U.S. Geological Survey Professional Paper 144. U.S. Geological Survey, Washington, DC.

Butler, E. L.

1948 Algonkian Culture and Use of Maize in Southern New England. *Archaeological Society of Connecticut Bulletin* 22:3–39.

Butler, E., and W. S. Hadlock.

1949 Dogs of the Northeastern Woodland Indians. *Bulletin of the Massachusetts Archaeological Society* 10(2):17–35.

Butzer, K.

1971 *Environment and Archaeology.* Aldine, Chicago.

1992 The Americas before and after 1492: An Introduction to Current Geographical Research. *Annals of the Association of American Geographers* 82(3):345–368.

Byers, D. S.

1954 Bull Brook—A Fluted Point Site in Ipswich, Massachusetts. *American Antiquity* 4:343–351.

1959 Radiocarbon Dates for the Bull Brook Site, Massachusetts. *American Antiquity* 24(4):427–429.

Byers, D. S., and F. Johnson.

1940 *Two Sites on Martha's Vineyard.* Papers of the Robert S. Peabody Foundation for Archaeology 1(1), Andover, MA.

Byers, D. S., and I. Rouse.

1960 A Re-Examination of the Guida Farm. *Bulletin of the Archaeological Society of Connecticut* 30:5–39.

Callicott, J. B.

1995 Traditional American Indian and Western European Attitudes toward Nature: An Overview. In *Postmodern Environmental Ethics*, edited by M. Oelschlaeger, pp. 193–219. State University of New York Press, Albany.

Calloway, C. G.

1984 The Conquest of Vermont: Vermont's Indian Troubles in Context. *Vermont History* 52(3):161–179.

1990 *The Western Abenakis of Vermont, 1600–1800: War, Migration, and the Survival of an Indian People.* University of Oklahoma Press, Norman.

Canfield, F. A.

1889 *Catalogue of Minerals Found in New Jersey.* Geological Survey of New Jersey, Final Report of the State Geologist, vol. 2. John L. Murray, Trenton.

Carls, J.

1934 *Industrial Geography of Turners Falls, Massachusetts.* Unpublished master's thesis, Clark University, Worcester.

Carlson, C. C.

1980 *Report on the Analysis of the Fernald Point Site (43–24) Fish Remains.* Ms. on file, Department of Anthropology, University of Maine, Orono.

1981 *Report on the Analysis of the Frazer Point Site Fish Remains, Maine.* Ms. on file, Department of Anthropology, University of Maine, Orono.

1982 Report of the Faunal Analysis of the 1967 Excavations at the Smyth Site, New Hampshire. *New Hampshire Archaeologist* 23:91–102.

1983a *Summary Results on the Analysis of the Fish Bone from Fort Pentagöet (ME 084-3)*. Ms. on file, Department of Anthropology, University of Maine, Orono.

1983b *Summary Results of the Analysis of Fish Bone from the Damariscove Island Site (ME 046-1), Structure 23*. Ms. on file, Department of Anthropology, University of Maine, Orono.

1986a *Maritime Catchment Areas: An Analysis of Prehistoric Fishing Strategies in the Boothbay Region of Maine*. M.Sc. thesis, Institute for Quaternary Studies, University of Maine, Orono.

1986b *Report on the Faunal Analysis of the Sherbourn Site, New Hampshire*. New Hampshire Historical Society, Concord.

1986c *Report on the Fish Bone Analysis of the Long Island Site, Boston Harbor, MA*. Submitted to Barbara Luedtke, Department of Anthropology, University of Massachusetts, Boston.

1988a An Evaluation of Fish Growth Annuli for Seasonality Determination. In *Recent Developments in Environmental Analysis in Old and New World Archaeology*, edited by E. Webb, pp. 67-78. British Archaeological Reports, International Series 416. Oxford, England.

1988b Report on the Faunal Analysis (Fish and Shell) of the Boylston Street Fishweir, Boston. G. D. Hines Interests, Boston, and Timelines, Inc., Groton, MA.

1988c Where's the Salmon?: A Reevaluation of the Role of Anadromous Fisheries to Aboriginal New England. In *Holocene Human Ecology in Northeastern North America*, edited by G. P. Nicholas, pp. 47-80. Plenum, New York.

1989a *Report on the Faunal Analysis of the Historic Simons House Site, Mashpee, Massachusetts*. University of Massachusetts Archaeological Services Report 99. University of Massachusetts, Amherst.

1989b *Report on the Faunal Remains from the Ryder-Wood House Privy*. Ms. on file, Strawbery Bank Museum, New Hampshire.

1990a *The Hardy Site Faunal Remains, Salisbury, Connecticut*. Ms. on file, American Indian Archaeological Institute, Washington, Connecticut.

1990b *Report on the Faunal Analysis of the Eddy site, New Hampshire*. New Hampshire Archaeological Society, Concord.

1990c Seasonality of Fish Remains from Locus Q-6 of the Quidnet Site, Nantucket Island, Massachusetts. *Bulletin of the Massachusetts Archaeological Society* 51(1): 2-14.

1992 *The Atlantic Salmon in New England Prehistory and History*. Ph.D. dissertation, Department of Anthropology, University of Massachusetts, Amherst.

1995 The (In)Significance of Atlantic Salmon in New England. In *New England's Creatures: 1400-1900*, edited by P. Benes, pp. 1-10. Dublin Seminar for New England Folklife, Boston University Press, Boston. Reprinted 1996 in *Federal Archaeology* 8(3/4):22-30.

Carlson, Catherine C., G. J. Armelagos, and A. L. Magennis.

1992 Impact of Disease on the Precontact and Early Historic Populations of New England and the Maritimes. In *Disease and Demography in the Americas*, edited by J. W. Verano and D. H. Ubelaker, pp. 141-154. Smithsonian Institution Press, Washington, DC.

Carlson, Claire C.

1998 *Archaeological Site Examination/Data Recovery for the Barn Area of the John*

Alden House, Duxbury, Massachusetts. UMASS Archaeological Services Report 245. University of Massachusetts, Amherst.

Carr, C.
1993 Identifying Individual Vessels with X-Radiography. *American Antiquity* 58(1): 96–117.

Carson, C., N. Barka, W. Kelso, G. W. Stone, and D. Upton.
1981 Impermanent Architecture in the Southern Colonies. *Winterthur Portfolio* 16: 135–196.

Carter, W. E. H.
1904 The Mines of Ontario. *Journal of the Canadian Mining Institute* 7:114–167.

Casjens, L.
1978 *A Cultural Resource Overview of the Green Mountain National Forest, Vermont*. Report No. 72, Institute for Conservation Archaeology, Harvard University, Cambridge, MA.

Cassedy, D. F.
1983 *Middle Archaic Stemmed Points in Eastern North America*. On file, Department of Anthropology, State University of New York, Binghamton.
1984 *The Spatial Structure of Lithic Reduction: Analysis of a Multicomponent Prehistoric Site in the Lakes Region of New Hampshire*. M.A. thesis, Department of Anthropology, State University of New York, Binghamton.
1986 *Mt. Jasper to Moose Mountain: Volcanic Lithic Sources in the Uplands of New Hampshire*. Paper presented at the 26th annual meeting of the Northeastern Anthropological Association, Buffalo, NY.

Cassedy, D. F., P. Webb, A. Dowd, J. Jones, C. Cobb, S. Dillon, M. Reinbold, and T. Millis.
1993 *Iroquois Gas Transmission System, Phase III Archaeological Data Recovery Report, Vol. 2, The Hudson Valley Region*. Garrow and Associates, Inc., Atlanta Georgia. Report on file, New York State Office of Parks, Recreation, and Historic Preservation, Albany.

Ceci, L.
1975 Fish Fertilizer: A Native North American Practice? *Science* 188:26–30.
1979 Maize Cultivation in Coastal New York: The Archaeological, Agronomical, and Documentary Evidence. *North American Archaeologist* 1:45–74.
1982 Method and Theory in Coastal New York Archaeology: Paradigms of Settlement Pattern. *North American Archaeologist* 3(1):5–36.
1984 Shell Midden Deposits as Coastal Resources. *World Archaeology* 16:62–74.

Chamberlain, B. B.
1964 *These Fragile Outposts*. Parnassus Imprints, Yarmouth, MA.

Chapman, J.
1976 The Archaic Period in the Lower Little Tennessee River Valley: The Radiocarbon Dates. *Tennessee Anthropologist* 1(1):1–12.

Chase, T. H. P.
1988 *Shell Midden Seasonality Using Multiple Faunal Indicators: Applicatons to the Archaeology of Boothbay, Maine*. M.Sc. thesis, Institute for Quaternary Studies, University of Maine, Orono.

Chidester, A. H., A. E. J. Engle, and L. A. Wright.
1964 *Talc Resources of the United States*. Bulletin 1167. U.S. Geological Survey, Washington, DC.

Childs, S. T.
1984 Prehistoric Ceramic Analysis, Technology and Style. In *Chapters in the Archae-
      ology of Cape Cod, I: Results of the Cape Cod National Seashore Archeological
      Survey 1979–1981*, vol. 2, edited by F. P. McManamon, pp. 157–194. Division
      of Cultural Resources, North Atlantic Regional Office, National Park Service,
      Boston.
Chilton, E. S.
1994 *The Goat Island Rockshelter: New Light from Old Legacies*. Research Report 29,
      Department of Anthropology, University of Massachusetts, Amherst.
1996a *Embodiments of Choice: Native American Ceramic Diversity in the New England
      Interior*. Ph.D. dissertation, Department of Anthropology, University of Massa-
      chusetts, Amherst.
1996b New Evidence for Maize Horticulture in the New England Interior. Paper pre-
      sented at the New York Natural History Conference, Albany.
Cirmo, C. P., and C. T. Driscoll.
1993 Beaver Pond Biogeochemistry: Acid Neutralization Capacity Generation in a
      Headwater Wetland. *Wetlands* 13(4):277–292.
Claflin, W. H. Jr.
1931 *The Stalling's Island Mound, Columbia County, Georgia*. Papers of the Peabody
      Museum of Archaeology and Ethnology, vol. 14, no. 1. Harvard University,
      Cambridge, MA.
Clark, C. P.
1991 *Group Composition and the Role of Unique Raw Materials in the Terminal Wood-
      land Substage of the Lake Superior Basin*. Ph.D. dissertation, Depratment of
      Anthropology, Michigan State University, Lansing. University Microfilms, Ann
      Arbor, MI.
Clark, J. G. D.
1954 *Excavations at Star Carr*. Cambridge University Press, Cambridge.
Clarke, D.
1968 *Analytical Archaeology*. Methuen, London.
Cloues, R.
1974 *The Planning and Development of Turners Falls, Massachusetts 1864–1872*. Un-
      published seminar paper, Cornell University, on file at the Carnegie Public
      Library, Turners Falls, MA.
Cobb, C. R., and M. S. Nassaney.
1991 Introduction: Renewed Perspectives on Late Woodland Stability, Transformation,
      and Variation in the Southeastern United States. In *Stability, Transformation, and
      Variation: The Late Woodland Southeast*, edited by M. S. Nassaney and C. R.
      Cobb, pp. 1–10. Plenum, New York.
Cochrane, H.
1896 Rocks and Minerals of Connecticut. In *Report of the Board of Education of the
      State of Connecticut 1895/1896*, pp. 512–524. Case, Lockwood & Brainard Com-
      pany, Hartford.
Coe, J. L.
1964 *The Formative Cultures of the Carolina Piedmont*. Transactions of the American
      Philosophical Society 54(5). Philadelphia.

Coffin, C. C.
1947 Ancient Fish Weirs along the Housatonic River. *Archaeological Society of Connecticut Bulletin* 21:35–38.
Cole-Will, R., and R. Will.
1996 A Probable Middle Archaic Cemetery: The Richmond-Castle Site in Surry, Maine. *Archaeology of Eastern North America* 24: 149–158.
Coles, B., and J. Coles.
1986 *Sweet Track to Glastonbury: The Somerset Levels in Prehistory*. Thames and Hudson, New York.
Cook, T. G.
1976 Broadpoint: Culture, Phase, Horizon, Tradition, or Knife? *Journal of Anthropological Research* 32:337–357.
Cowie, E. R., J. B. Petersen, and N. A. Sidell.
1992 *The Contact Period in Central Maine: Archaeological Investigations at Ethnohistoric Norridgewock*. Paper presented at the 32nd annual meeting of the Northeastern Anthropological Association, Bridgewater, MA.
Cox, S. L.
1972 *A Reanalysis of the Shoop Site*. Smithsonian Institution, Washington, DC.
Cox, S. L., B. Bourque, R. Corey, R. Doyle, and R. Lewis.
1994 *Phase II Investigations of Site 39.1, Searsmont, Maine*. Maine State Museum, Augusta.
Crabtree, P.
1985 Historic Zooarchaeology: Some Methodological Considerations. *Historical Archaeology* 19(1):76–78.
Cronon, W.
1983 *Changes in the Land: Indians, Colonists, and the Ecology of New England*. Hill and Wang, New York.
Cross, D.
1941 *Archaeology of New Jersey*, vol. 1. New Jersey State Museum, Trenton.
Cross, J. R.
1990 *Specialized Production in Non-Stratified Society: An Example from the Late Archaic in the Northeast*. Ph.D. dissertation, Department of Anthropology, University of Massachusetts, Amherst. University Microfilms, Ann Arbor, MI.
Cross, J. R., and D. L. Doucette.
1994 *Middle Archaic Lithic Technology, Typology, and Classification: A View from Annasnappet Pond, Massachusetts*. Paper presented at the 61st annual meeting of the Eastern States Archaeological Federation, Albany, NY.
Cross, J. R., and L. C. Shaw.
1996 *An Overview of the Prehistory of the North Atlantic Region*. United States Department of the Interior, National Park Service, North Atlantic Region Office, Boston.
Crusoe, D. L., and C. B. DePratter.
1976 A New Look at the Georgia Coastal Shellmound Archaic. *Florida Anthropologist* 29:1–23.
Cummings, A. L.
1955–1956 Notes on the Alden House, Duxbury (June 26, 1955 and June 13, 1956).
1976 Notes on the Alden House, Duxbury (October 15, 1976).
1979 *The Framed Houses of Massachusetts Bay, 1625–1725*. Harvard University Press, Cambridge, MA.

Curran, M. L.

1984 The Whipple Site and Paleoindian Tool Assemblage Variation: A Comparison of Intrasite Structuring. *Archaeology of Eastern North America* 12:5–40.

1987 *The Spatial Organization of Paleoindian Populations in the Late Pleistocene of the Northeast.* Ph.D. dissertation, Department of Anthropology, University of Massachusetts, Amherst. University Microfilms, Ann Arbor, MI.

1994 New Hampshire Paleo-Indian Research and the Whipple Site. *The New Hampshire Archeologist* 33–34(1):29–52.

1996 Paleoindians in the Northeast: The Problem of Dating Fluted Point Sites. *The Review of Archaeology* 17(1):2–11.

Curran, M. L., and D. F. Dincauze.

1977 Paleoindians and Paleo-lakes: New Data from the Connecticut Drainage. In *Amerinds and Their Paleoenvironments in Northeastern North America*, edited by W. S. Newman and B. Salwen, pp. 333–348. *Annals of the New York Academy of Sciences* 288.

Curran, M. L., and J. R. Grimes.

1989 Ecological Implications for Paleoindian Lithic Procurement Economy in New England. In *Eastern Paleoindian Lithic Resource Use*, edited by C. J. Ellis and J. C. Lothrop, pp. 41–74. Westview Press, Boulder, CO.

Curran, M. L., and P. A. Thomas.

1979 *Phase III—Data Recovery: Wastewater Treatment System in the Riverside Archaeological District of Gill, Massachusetts.* Department of Anthropology Reports No. 19. University of Vermont, Burlington.

Currie, D. R.

1994 Micromorphology of a Native American Cornfield. *Archaeology of Eastern North America* 22:63–72.

Custer, J. F.

1984 *Delaware Prehistoric Archaeology: An Ecological Approach.* University of Delaware Press, Newark.

1987 Problems and Prospects in Northeastern Prehistoric Ceramic Studies. *North American Archaeologist* 8:97–123.

1988 Late Archaic Cultural Dynamics in the Central Middle Atlantic Region. *Journal of Middle Atlantic Archaeology* 4:39–59.

1989 *Prehistoric Cultures of the Delmarva Peninsula.* University of Delaware Press, Newark.

Custer, J. F., J. M. McNamara, and H. T. Ward.

1983 Woodland Ceramic Sequences of the Upper Delmarva Peninsula and Southeastern Pennsylvania. *Maryland Archaeology* 19(2):21–30.

Cwynar, L. C., and A. J. Levesque.

1995 Chironomid Evidence for Late-Glacial Climatic Reversals in Maine. *Quaternary Research* 43:405–413.

Dahlberg, R., editor.

1981 *Woman the Gatherer.* Yale University Press, New Haven.

Damas, D., editor.

1969 Contributions to Anthropology: Band Societies. *National Museums of Canada Bulletin* 228.

Dana, J. D.

1887 *Manual of Mineralogy and Petrography*, 4th ed. J. Wiley and Sons, New York.

Davis, S. A.
1991 Two Concentrations of Paleo-Indian Occupation in the Far Northeast. *Revista de Arqueologia Americana* 3:31–56.

Dawson, J. W.
1878 *Acadian Geology: The Geological Structure, Organic Remains, and Mineral Resources of Nova Scotia, New Brunswick, and Prince Edward Island*, 3rd ed. Macmillan and Co., London.

Day, G. M.
1953 The Indian as an Ecological Factor in the Northeastern Forest. *Ecology* 34:329–346.
1965 The Indian Occupation of Vermont. *Vermont History* 33:365–374.
1978 Western Abenaki. *In Northeast: Handbook of North American Indians*, vol. 15, edited by B. Trigger, pp. 148–159. Smithsonian Institution Press, Washington, DC.

DeBoer, W. R.
1988 Subterranean Storage and the Organization of Surplus: The View from Eastern North America. *Southeastern Archaeology* 7:1–20.

Décima, E. B., and D. F. Dincauze.
1998 The Boston Back Bay Fish Weirs. In *Hidden Dimensions: The Cultural Significance of Wetland Archaeology*, edited by K. Bernick, pp. 157–172. UBC Laboratory of Archaeology Occasional Publications, No. 1. University of British Columbia, Vancouver.

Deetz, J.
1977 *In Small Things Forgotten*. Anchor Press/Doubleday, Garden City, NY.
1979 Plymouth Colony Architecture: Archaeological Evidence from the Seventeenth Century. In *Architecture in Colonial Massachusetts*. The Colonial Society of Massachusetts, Boston. Distributed by the University Press of Virginia.

DeForest, J. W.
1964 *History of the Indians of Connecticut: From the Earliest Known Period to 1850*, reprinted. Archon Books, Hamden, CT. Originally published 1851, Wm. Jas. Hamersley, Hartford.

Delcourt, H. R., and P. A. Delcourt.
1991 *Quaternary Ecology: A Paleoecological Perspective*. Chapman and Hall, New York.

Deller, D. B., and C. Ellis.
1986 *Thedford II: A Paleo-Indian Site in the Ausable River Watershed of Southwestern Ontario*. Report on file, Ontario Ministry of Citizenship and Culture, Toronto.

Deloria, V. Jr.
1996 *Red Earth, White Lies: Native Americans and the Myth of Scientific Fact*. Scribner's, New York.

Denevan, W.
1992 The Pristine Myth: The Landscape of the Americas in 1492. *Annals of the Association of American Geographers* 82:369–385.

Dent, R. J. Jr.
1995 *Chesapeake Prehistory: Old Traditions, New Directions*. Plenum, New York.

Dewar, R. E.
1986 Discovering Settlement Systems of the Past in New England Site Distributions. *Man in the Northeast* 31:77–88.

Dillehay, T. D.
1996 *Monte Verde: A Late Pleistocene Settlement in Chile: the Archaeological Context. Vol. II.* Smithsonian Institution Press, Washington, DC.

Dincauze, D. F.
1968 *Cremation Cemeteries in Eastern Massachusetts.* Papers of the Peabody Museum of Archaeology and Ethnology, vol. 59, no. 1. Harvard University, Cambridge, MA.

1971 An Archaic Sequence for Southern New England. *American Antiquity* 36:194–198.

1972 The Atlantic Phase: A Late Archaic Culture in Massachusetts. *Man in the Northeast* 4:40–61.

1974 An Introduction to Archaeology in the Greater Boston Area. *Archaeology of Eastern North America* 2:39–67.

1975a Ceramic Sherds from the Charles River Basin. *Bulletin of the Archaeological Society of Connecticut* 39:5–17.

1975b The Late Archaic Period in Southern New England. *Arctic Anthropology* 12(2): 23–34.

1976 *The Neville Site: 8000 Years at Amoskeag Falls.* Peabody Museum Monographs 4. Harvard University, Cambridge, MA.

1978a The Case for Conservation Archaeology: Uniqueness and Universality, the Massachusetts Example. In *Conservation Archaeology in the Northeast: Toward a Research Orientation,* edited by A. E. Spiess, pp. 4–8. Peabody Museum Bulletin No. 3, Harvard University, Cambridge, MA.

1978b *Prehistoric Archaeological Resources in Hadley, Massachusetts: A 1978 Assessment with Recommendations for Protection.* Massachusetts Historic Commission, Office of the Secretary of State, Boston.

1980a *Excerpts from a Manuscript in Preparation: Archaeological Investigations at King Philip's Hill, Northfield, Massachusetts.* Ms. in possession of the author.

1980b Research Priorities in Northeastern Prehistory. In *Proceedings of the Conference on Northeastern Prehistory,* edited by J. A. Moore, pp. 29–48. Department of Anthropology Research Report 19. University of Massachusetts, Amherst.

1981 Paleoenvironmental Reconstruction in the Northeast: The Art of Multidisciplinary Science. In *Foundations of Northeast Archaeology,* edited by D. Snow, pp. 51–96. Academic Press, New York.

1985 Research Design. In *Reconnaissance Archaeological Study for the 500 Boylston Street Project,* pp. 17–26. Report submitted to G. D. Hines Interests, Inc., Boston.

1987 Strategies for Paleoenvironmental Reconstruction in Archaeology. In *Advances in Archaeological Method and Theory,* vol. 11, edited by M. B. Schiffer, pp. 255–336. Academic Press, Orlando.

1988a Archaeological Perspectives on Holocene Fluvial Rates and Processes in the Connecticut River Valley. In *Field Trip Guidebook, AMQUA 1988,* edited by J. Brigham-Grette. Contribution No. 63:182, Department of Geology and Geography, University of Massachusetts, Amherst.

1988b *Boylston Report.* Report submitted to Timelines Incorporated, Groton, MA.

1989 Geoarchaeology in New England: An Early Holocene Heat Spell? *Quarterly Review of Archaeology* 9(2):6–8.

1990 A Capsule Prehistory of Southern New England. In *The Pequots of Southern New England: The Fall and Rise of an American Indian Nation,* edited by L. M.

Hauptman and J. D. Wherry, pp. 19–32. University of Oklahoma Press, Norman.

1993a Centering. *Northeast Anthropology* 46:33–37.

1993b The Gardeners of Eden. In *Ela'Qua: Essays in Honor of Richard B. Woodbury*, edited by D. S. Krass, J. B. Thomas, and J. W. Cole, pp. 43–60. Department of Anthropology Research Report 28, University of Massachusetts, Amherst.

1993c Pioneering in the Pleistocene: Large Paleoindian Sites in the Northeast. In *Archaeology of Eastern North America: Papers in Honor of Stephen Williams*, edited by J. B. Stoltman, pp. 43–60. Archaeological Report No. 25. Mississippi Department of Archives and History, Jackson.

1997 Creating and Interpreting New England's Environments. *Conference on New England Archaeology Newsletter* 16:1–5.

Dincauze, D. F., and M. L. Curran.

1983 *Paleoindians as Generalists: An Ecological Perspective*. Paper presented at the annual meeting of the Society for American Archaeology, Pittsburgh.

Dincauze, D., and R. M. Gramly.

1973 Powissett Rockshelter: Alternative Behavior Patterns In a Simple Situation. *Pennsylvania Archaeologist* 43(1):43–61.

Dincauze, D. F., and D. M. Lacy.

1985 *Hardscrabble Archaeology: The Northeast Under Federal Mandate*. Paper presented at the 50th annual meeting of the Society for American Archaeology, Denver.

Dincauze, D. F., and M. Mulholland.

1977 Early and Middle Archaic Site Distributions and Habitats in Southern New England. In *Amerinds and Their Paleoenvironments in Northeastern North America*, edited by W. S. Newman and B. Salwen. *Annals of the New York Academy of Sciences* 288:439–456.

Dincauze, D. F., P. Thomas, M. Mulholland, and J. Wilson.

1976 *Cultural Resource Survey and Impact Evaluation Report, State Route 2 Extension: Corridor in Gill, Greenfield, Wendell, and Orange, Massachusetts*. On file at the Massachusetts Historical Commission, Office of the Secretary of State, Boston.

Dincauze, D. F., H. M. Wobst, R. J. Hasenstab, and D. M. Lacy.

1980 *Retrospective Assessment of Archaeological Survey Contracts in Massachusetts, 1970–1979*. Massachusetts Historical Commission, Boston.

Dixon, B.

1987 Surface Analysis of the Ochee Spring Steatite Quarry in Johnston, Rhode Island. *Man in the Northeast* 34:85–98.

Doucette, D. L., and J. R. Cross.

1998 *Archaeological Investigations within the Annasnappet Pond Archaeological District: Data Recovery Program for Loci 1, 2, 8, and 9, Carver, Massachusetts*. The Public Archaeology Laboratory, Inc. Report No. 580, submitted to the Massachusetts Highway Department. On file, Massachusetts Historical Commission, Boston.

Dunford, F. J.

1993 *Territory and Community: The Spatial Dimensions of Ceramic Design Variability on Cape Cod, Massachusetts (1000–400 Years B.P.)*. Ph.D. dissertation prospectus, Department of Anthropology, University of Massachusetts, Amherst.

Dunn, S. W.

1994 *The Mohicans and Their Land, 1609–1730*. Purple Mountain, Fleischmanns, NY.

Duns, D. D.

1880 On Stone Implements from Nova Scotia and Canada, and on the Use of Copper Implements by the Aborigines of Nova Scotia. *Proceedings of the Society of Antiquaries of Scotland, 1879–1880 New Series* 176–180.

Earl, K. M.

1950 *Investigation of Perkiomen Creek Copper Deposits, Montgomery County, PA.* Report of Investigations 4666. U.S. Department of the Interior, Bureau of Mines, Washington, DC.

Eaton, G.

1898 The Prehistoric Fauna of Block Island, as Indicated by Its Ancient Shell Heaps. *American Journal of Science* 6:137–159.

Egloff, K. T., M. E. Hodges, J. F. Custer, K. R. Doms, and L. D. McFaden.

1988 *Archaeological Investigations at Croaker Landing 44JC70 and 44JC71.* Division of Historic Landmarks, Richmond, VA.

Eisenberg, L.

1991 The Mohonk Rockshelter: A Major Neville Site in New York State. In *The Archaeology and Ethnohistory of the Lower Hudson Valley and Neighboring Regions: Essays in Honor of Louis A. Brennan*, edited by H. C. Kraft, pp. 159–176. Occasional Publications in Northeastern Anthropology, No. 11. Archaeological Services, Bethlehem, CT.

Eldridge, W., and J. Vaccaro.

1952 The Bull Brook Site, Ipswich, Mass. *Bulletin of the Massachusetts Archaeological Society* 13(4):39–43.

Elias, S. A.

1997 New Evidence of the Environments Encountered by Paleoindians in Central and Eastern Beringia. *Current Research in the Pleistocene* 14:123–125.

Elliott, D. T.

1989 *Falcon Field and Line Creek: Two Archaic and Woodland Period Sites in West Central Georgia.* Southeastern Archaeological Services, Athens, GA.

Elliott, D. T., R. J. Ledbetter, and E. A. Gordon.

1994 *Data Recovery at Lovers Lane, Phinizy Swamp and the Old Dike Sites Bobby Jones Expressway Extension Corridor Augusta, Georgia.* Occasional Papers in Cultural Resource Management 7. Georgia Department of Transportation, Atlanta.

Ellis, C. H.

1989 The Explanation of Northeastern Paleoindian Lithic Procurement Patterns. In *Eastern Paleoindian Lithic Resource Use*, edited by C. J. Ellis and J. C. Lothrop, pp. 139–164. Westview Press, Boulder, CO.

Ellis, C. H., and D. B. Deller.

1997 Variability in the Archaeological Record of Northeastern Early Paleoindians: A View from Southern Ontario. *Archaeology of Eastern North America* 25:1–30.

Ellis, C., and J. C. Lothrop, editors.

1989 *Eastern Paleoindian Lithic Resource Use.* Westview Press, Boulder, CO.

Ellis, C., A. C. Goodyear, D. F. Morse, and K. B. Tankersley.

1998 Archaeology of the Pleistocene-Holocene Transition in Eastern North America. *Quaternary International* 49/50:151–166.

Ells, R. W.

1904 *Bulletin on the Ores of Copper in the Provinces of Nova Scotia, New Brunswick and Quebec*. Geological Survey of Canada, Mineral Resources of Canada, Ottawa, Ontario.

Engelbrecht, W.
1972 The Reflection of Patterned Behavior in Iroquois Pottery. *Pennsylvania Archaeologist* 42(3):1–15.

Erlandson, J. M., and M. L. Moss.
1996 The Pleistocene-Holocene Transition along the Pacific Coast of North America. In *Humans at the End of the Ice Age: The Archaeology of the Pleistocene-Holocene Transition*, edited by L. G. Straus, B. V. Eriksen, J. M. M. Erlandson, and D. R. Yesner, pp. 277–301. Plenum, New York.

Erlandson, J. M., D. J. Kennett, B. L. Ingram, D. A. Guthrie, D. P. Morris, M. A. Tveskov, G. J. West, and P. L. Walker.
1996 An Archaeological and Paleontological Chronology for Daisy Cave (CA-SMI-261), San Miguel Island, California. *Radiocarbon* 38:355–373.

Evans, E. L.
1952 Native Copper Discoveries in the Seal Lake Area, Labrador. *Proceedings of the Geological Association of Canada* 5:111–116.

Fairbanks, C. F.
1942 The Taxonomic Position of Stallings Island, Georgia. *American Antiquity* 7: 223–231.

Faulkner, A.
1984 Archaeology of the Cod Fishery: Damariscove Island. *Historical Archaeology* 19(2).

Faulkner, A., and G. Faulkner.
1987 *The French at Pentagoet 1635–1674*. Special Publications of the New Brunswick Museum and Occasional Publications in Maine Archaeology, Maine Historic Preservation Commission, Augusta.

Fauth, J. L.
1978 *Geology and Mineral Resources of the Iron Springs Area, Adams and Franklin Counties, Pennsylvania*. Pennsylvania Geological Survey, Fourth Series, Atlas Series A129C, Harrisburg.

Fawcett-Sayett, M.
1988 Sociocultural Authority in Mohegan Society. *Artifacts* 16(3,4):28–29.

Feder, K. L.
1994 *A Village of Outcasts: Historical Archaeology and Documentary Research at the Lighthouse Site*. Mayfield, Mountain View, CA.

Fenton, W. N.
1978 Northern Iroquoian Culture Patterns. In *Handbook of the North American Indians, Vol. 15, The Northeast*, edited by B. G. Trigger, pp. 296–321. Smithsonian Institution, Washington, DC.

Filios, E.
1990 *Thresholds to Group Mobility among Hunter-gatherers: An Archaeological Example from Southern New England*. Ph.D. dissertation, Department of Anthropology, University of Massachusetts, Amherst.

Finlayson, W. D.
1977 The Saugeen Culture: A Middle Woodland Manifestation in Southwestern Ontario. *Archaeological Society of Canada Paper* 61. National Museum of Man, Ottawa.

Finn, M., and N. Goldman-Finn.
1997 *Steatite Exchange, Ceramics, and Mobility at the Archaic/Woodland Transition in the Midsouth.* Paper presented at the 62nd annual meeting of the Society for American Archaeology, Nashville, TN.

Fitting, J. E.
1968 Environmental Potential and the Postglacial Readaptation in Eastern North America. *American Antiquity* 33:441–445.

Fitzgerald, J.
1984 Floral and Faunal Archaeological Remains. In *Chapters in the Archaeology of Cape Cod, I*, vol. 2, edited by F. P. McManamon, pp. 43–82. Cultural Resources Managment Study 8, National Park Service, Boston.

Flegenheimer, N., and M. Zarate.
1997 Considerations on Radiocarbon and Calibrated Dates from Cerro La China and Cerro El Sombrere, Argentina. *Current Research in the Pleistocene* 14:27–28.

Forbes, A. B., editor.
1947 *Winthrop Papers. Vol. V, 1645–1649.* Massachusetts Historical Society, Boston.

Fowler, W. S.
1945 Motifs of Ceramic Design in Massachusetts: A Proposed Plan of Research. *Bulletin of the Massachusetts Archaeological Society* 6(4):64.
1946 The Hoe Complex of the Connecticut Valley. *American Antiquity* 12:29–34.
1948 Triangular Hoes of the Northeast and Their Diffusion. *Bulletin of the Massachusetts Archaeological Society* 9:83–88.
1954 Agricultural Tools and Techniques of the Northeast. *Bulletin of the Massachusetts Archaeological Society* 15:41–51.
1961 Was the Guida Farm Site the Center of Ceramic Influence? *Bulletin of the Massachusetts Archaeological Society* 23(1):20–21.
1963 Classification of Stone Implements of the Northeast. *Bulletin of the Massachusetts Archaeological Society* 25:1–29.
1966 Ceremonial and Domestic Products of Aboriginal New England. *Bulletin of the Massachusetts Archaeological Society* 27(3–4).
1973 Comparative Study of Hoe and Spade Blades. *Bulletin of the Massachusetts Archaeological Society* 35(1–2):1–8.

Frazer, P.
1877 The Copper Ores of Pennsylvania. *The Polytechnic Review* 3(16):158–159.
1880 *The Geology of Lancaster County.* Second Geological Survey of Pennsylvania. Harrisburg, PA.

Fried, M.
1967 *The Evolution of Political Society: An Essay in Political Anthropology.* Random House, New York.

Funk, R. E.
1976 *Recent Contributions to Hudson Valley Prehistory.* Memoir 22, New York State Museum, Albany.
1977 Early Cultures in the Hudson Drainage Basin. In *Amerinds and their Paleoenvironments in Northeastern North America*, edited by W. S. Newman and B. Salwen, pp. 316–332. *Annals of the New York Academy of Sciences* 288.
1991 The Middle Archaic in New York. *Journal of Middle Atlantic Archaeology* 7: 7–18.

1993   *Archaeological Investigations in the Upper Susquehanna Valley, New York State*, vol. 1. Persimmon Press, Buffalo, New York.

Galinat, W. C., and J. H. Gunnerson.

1963   Spread of Eight-Rowed Maize from the Prehistoric Southwest. *Harvard University Botanical Museum Leaflet* 20(5):117–160.

Gardener, L.

1897   Leift Lion Gardener His Relation of the Pequot Warres. In *History of the Pequot War*, edited by C. Orr, pp. 113–149. Helman-Taylor, Cleveland. (orig. 1736)

Gardner, W. M.

1975   Early Pottery in Eastern North America: A Viewpoint. In *Proceedings of the 1975 Middle Atlantic Conference*, edited by W. F. Kinsey, pp. 13–26. North Museum, Franklin and Marshall College, Lancaster, PA.

Gehring, C. T., translator.

1988   *New Netherland Project. Multiple volumes*. New York State Archives, Albany.

George, D. R.

1993   Final Report on the Analysis of Faunal Material Recovered from Archaeological Investigations of a Woodland Period Component at the Lambert Farm Site, Warwick, Rhode Island (Appendix C). In *Archaeological Investigations at the Lambert Farm Site, Warwick, Rhode Island: An Integrated Program of Research and Education by the Public Archaeology Laboratory,* vol. 1, edited by J. Kerber, pp. 167–183. The Public Archaeology Laboratory, Inc., Pawtucket, RI.

Gero, J. M.

1991   Who Experienced What in Prehistory? A Narrative Explanation from Queyash, Peru. In *Processual and Postprocessual Archaeologies: Multiple Ways of Knowing the Past*, edited by R. W. Preucel, pp. 126–139. Occasional Paper No. 10. Center for Archaeological Investigations, Southern Illinois University, Carbondale.

Gibson, J. L.

1996   Poverty Point and Greater Southeastern Prehistory: The Culture That Did Not Fit. In *Archaeology of the Mid-Holocene Southeast*, edited by K. E. Sassaman and D. G. Anderson, pp. 228–305. University Press of Florida, Gainesville.

Giddens, A.

1979   *Central Problems in Social Theory: Action, Structure and Contradiction in Social Analysis*. Macmillan Press, New York.

Gilman, A.

1981   The Development of Social Stratification in Bronze Age Europe. *Current Anthropology* 22(1):1–23.

Gilpin, E.

1880   *The Mines and Mineral Lands of Nova Scotia*. Robert T. Murray, Queen's Priner, Halifax.

Glock, W. S.

1935a Copper and Rare Types of Lost Stones in Glacial Tills. *Pan-American Geologist* 63:90–96.

1935b Native Copper Masses in Glacial Tills. *Pan-American Geologist* 63:24–26.

Goddard, I.

1978   Delaware. In *Northeast: Handbook of North American Indians*, vol. 15, edited by B. Trigger, pp. 213–239. Smithsonian Institution Press, Washington, DC.

Goebel, T., W. R. Powers, N. H. Bigelow, and A. S. Higgs.

1996   Walker Road. In *American Beginnings: The Prehistory and Paleoecology of*

Beringia, edited by F. H. West, pp. 356–363. University of Chicago Press, Chicago.

Goldthwait, R. P.

1935   The Damariscotta Shell Heaps and Coastal Stability. *American Journal of Science*, 5th series, 30 (175):1–13.

Goodby, R. G.

1992   *Diversity as a Typological Construct: Understanding Late Woodland Ceramics from Narragansett Bay*. Paper presented at the 32nd annual meeting of the Northeastern Anthropological Association, Bridgewater, MA.

1994   *Style, Meaning, and History: A Contextual Study of 17th Century Native American Ceramics From Southeastern New England*. Ph.D. dissertation, Department of Anthropology, Brown University, Providence, RI. University Microfilms, Ann Arbor, MI.

Gookin, D.

1970   *Historical Collections of the Indians of New England*, edited by J. H. Fiske, Towtaid, Worcester, MA. (orig. 1792)

Goudie, A.

1993   *The Human Impact on the Natural Environment*. Blackwell, New York.

Gramly, R. M.

1982   *The Vail Site: A Palaeo-Indian Encampment in Maine*. Bulletin of the Buffalo Society of Natural Sciences 30.

1988   *The Adkins Site: A Palaeo-Indian Habitation and Associated Stone Structure*. Persimmon Press Monographs in Archaeology, Buffalo, New York.

1998   *The Sugarloaf Site: Palaeo-Americans on the Connecticut River*. Persimmon Press Monographs in Archaeology, Buffalo, New York.

Gramly, R. M., and R. E. Funk.

1990   What is Known and Not Known about the Human Occupation of the Northeastern United States until 10,000 B.P. *Archaeology of Eastern North America* 18:5–31.

Gramly, R. M., and G. Summers.

1986   Nobles Pond: A Fluted Point Site in Northeastern Ohio. *Midcontinental Journal of Archaeology* 11:97–123.

Gray, N. H.

1982   Copper Occurrences in the Hartford Basin of Northern Connecticut. In *Guidebook for Fieldtrips in Connecticut and South Central Massachusetts*, edited by R. Joesten and S. S. Quarrier, pp. 195–208. New England Intercollegiate Geological Conference, Guidebook No. 5, Connecticut Geological and Natural Historical Survey, Hartford, CT.

Greenspan, R. L.

1990   The Rhode Island Sea Grant College Program Completion Report: Determination of Seasonality on *Mercenaria mercenaria* Shells from Archaeological Sites on Narragansett Bay, Rhode Island (Appendix D). In *Archaeological Investigations at the Lambert Farm Site, Warwick, Rhode Island: An Integrated Program of Research and Education by the Public Archaeology Laboratory*, vol. 1, edited by J. Kerber, pp. 184–193. The Public Archaeology Laboratory, Inc., Pawtucket, RI.

1993   Dog Burial: Lambert Farm Site (Appendix B). In *Archaeological Investigations at the Lambert Farm Site, Warwick, Rhode Island: An Integrated Program of Research and Education by the Public Archaeology Laboratory*, vol. 1, edited by J. Kerber, pp. 156–166. The Public Archaeology Laboratory, Inc., Pawtucket, RI.

Greenway, J. C. Jr.
1958 *Extinct and Vanishing Birds of the World*. American Committee for International Wild Life Protection, Special Publication 13, New York.

Grimes, J. R.
1979 A New Look at Bull Brook. *Anthropology* 3(1–2):109–130.

Grimes, J. R., W. Eldridge, B. L. Grimes, A. Vaccaro, F. Vaccaro, J. Vaccaro, N. Vaccaro, and A. Orsini.
1984 Bull Brook II. *Archaeology of Eastern North America* 12:159–183.

Grimes, J. R., and B. L. Grimes.
1985 Flakeshavers: Morphometric, Functional and Life-Cycle Analyses of a Paleoindian Unifacial Tool Class. *Archaeology of Eastern North America* 13:35–57.

Guilday, J. E.
1968 Archaeological Evidence of Caribou from New York and Massachusetts. *Journal of Mammalogy* 49(2):344–345.

Hadlock, W. S.
1939 The Taft's Point Shell Mound at West Gouldsboro, Maine. Robert Abbe Museum *Bulletin 5*.
1941 Three Shell Heaps on Frenchman's Bay. Robert Abbe Museum *Bulletin 6*.

Hall, R.
1967 Those Late Corn Dates: Isotopic Fractionation as a Source of Error in Carbon-14 Dating. *Michigan Archaeology* 13(4):171–180.

Hallowell, A. J.
1921 Indian Corn Hills. *American Anthropologist* 23:233.

Hamilton, H. D.
1985 *Maritime Adaptation in Western Maine: The Great Diamond Island Site*. Ph.D. dissertation, University of Pittsburgh.

Hamilton, N. D., and S. G. Pollock.
1996 The Munsungun Chert Utilization and Paleoindians in Southwestern Maine. *Current Research in the Pleistocene* 13:117–119.

Hamilton, S. H.
1904 *Geological Survey of New Jersey*. Annual Report of the State Geologist.

Hancock, M. E.
1982 The Determination of Archaeological Site Seasonality Using the Remains of *Mya arenaria*: Examples from the Central Maine Coast. M.Sc. thesis, Institute for Quaternary Studies, University of Maine, Orono.
1984 Analysis of Shellfish Remains: Seasonality Information. In *Chapters in the Archaeology of Cape Cod, I*, vol. 2, edited by F. P. McManamon, pp. 121–156. Cultural Resources Management Study 8, National Park Service, Boston.

Handley, B. M.
1996 Role of the Shark in Southern Rhode Island Prehistory: Diet or Dinner? *Bulletin of the Massachusetts Archaeological Society* 57(1):27–34.

Handsman, R. G.
1989 *The Fort Hill Project: Native Americans in Western Connecticut and an Archaeology of Living Traditions*. American Indian Archaeological Institute, Washington, CT.
1990 Corn and Culture, Pots and Politics: How to Listen to the Voices of Mohegan Women. Paper presented at the 23rd annual meeting of the Society for Historical Archaeology, Tucson, AZ.

Harrington, F.
1989   The Emergent Elite: Archaeology of the Joseph Sherburne House Lot. *Historical Archaeology* 23(1):2–18.
Harte, C. R.
1945   Connecticut's Iron and Copper. *Connecticut Society of Civil Engineers Proceedings* 12:131–166
Hartshorn, J. H.
1969   Geography and Geology of Glacial Lake Hitchcock. In *An Introduction to the Archaeology and History of the Connecticut Valley Indian*, edited by W. R. Young, pp. 19–27. Museum of Science Publication, New Series, vol. 1, no. 1. Springfield, MA.
Hasenstab, R. J.
1982   *Archaeological Background, Reconnaissance, and Intensive Survey for the Proposed Buckley Nursing Home in the Town of Greenfield, Franklin County, Massachusetts*. On file at the Massachusetts Historical Commission, Office of the Secretary of State, Boston.
1984   *An Analysis of the Use of Subsurface Shovel Probes in Assessing the Significance of Prehistoric Cultural Resources in the Northeast*. Paper presented at the annual meeting of Northeastern Anthropological Association, Hartford, CT.
1986a   *A Tentative Report on the Hannemann Paleo-Indian Site, Franklin County, Massachusetts*. Report on file with the Massachusetts Historical Commission, Boston.
1986b   *Windows on the World Beneath: Shovel Test Pits and Site Assessment in the Northeast*. Unpublished ms. on file at the Department of Anthropology, University of Massachusetts, Amherst.
1987   *Archaeological Locational Survey of the Turners Falls Airport, Franklin County, Massachusetts*. University of Massachusetts Archaeological Services Report 71. On file at the Massachusetts Historical Commission, Office of the Secretary of State, Boston.
1996   Aboriginal Settlement Patterns in Late Woodland Upper New York State. In *A Northeastern Millennium: History and Archaeology for Robert E. Funk*, edited by C. Lindner and E. Curtin. *Journal of Middle Atlantic Archaeology* 12:17–26.
1998   The Three Sisters: Staples of the Iroquois. In *Ethnobiology: Perspectives and Practices in the Northeastern United States and Eastern Canada*, edited by C. C. Bodner. Research Records No. 24. Rochester Museum and Science Center, Rochester.
Hasenstab, R. J., and R. D. Holmes.
1990   *Archaeological Site Locational Survey for the Proposed Randall Woods Housing Development, Montague, Massachusetts*. Report No. 106, UMass Archaeological Services, University of Massachusetts at Amherst.
Hasenstab, R. J., and D. M. Lacy.
1984   The Reporting of Small Scale Survey Results for Research Purposes: Suggestions for Improvement. *American Archaeology* 4(1):43–49.
Hasenstab, R. J., M. T. Mulholland, and R. D. Holmes.
1990   *Archaeological Investigations at Prehistoric Site 19-HD-109, Westfield, Massachusetts, for the Proposed Massachusetts Correctional Facility*. Report No. 107, UMass Archaeological Services, University of Massachusetts at Amherst.

Hatch, J. W.
1994 The Structure and Antiquity of Prehistoric Jasper Quarries in the Reading Prong, Pennsylvania. *Journal of Middle Atlantic Archaeology* 10:23–47.

Haviland, W. A., and M. W. Power.
1994 *The Original Vermonters: Native Inhabitants Past and Present.* University Press of New England. Hanover, New Hampshire.

Hayden, B.
1997 Observations on the Prehistoric Social and Economic Structure of the North American Plateau. *World Archaeology* 29(2):242–261.

Hayden, D.
1981 *The Grand Domestic Revolution.* MIT Press, Cambridge.

Hayes, C. F. III, D. Barber, and G. R. Hammell.
1978 *An Archaeological Survey of Gannagaro State Historic Site, Ontario County, New York.* Rochester Museum and Science Center. Report on file at the New York State Office of Parks, Recreation, and Historic Preservation, Albany.

Haynes, C. D., M. D. Ridpath, and M. A. J. Williams, editors.
1991 *Monsoonal Australia: Landscape, Ecology and Man in the Northern Lowlands.* A. A. Balkema, Rotterdam.

Haynes, G.
1991 *Mammoths, Mastodonts, and Elephants: Biology, Behavior, and the Fossil Record.* Cambridge University Press, New York.

Headland, T. N.
1997 Revisionism in Ecological Anthropology. *Current Anthropology* 38(4):605–630.

Heckenberger, M. J., J. B. Petersen, and N. A. Sidell.
1992 Early Evidence of Maize Agriculture in the Connecticut River Valley. *Archaeology of Eastern North America* 20:125–149.

Held, D.
1980 *Introduction to Critical Theory: Horkheimer to Habermas.* University of California Press, Berkeley.

Helm, J., E. S. Rogers, and J. G. E. Smith.
1981 Intercultural Relations and Cultural Change in the Shield and Mackenzie Borderlands. In *Subarctic: Handbook of North American Indians, Vol. 6,* edited by J. Helm, pp. 146–157. Smithsonian Institution Press, Washington, DC.

Henderson, H.
1884 The Copper Deposits of the South Mountain. *Transactions of the American Institute of Mining Engineers* 12:85–90.

Hight, S.
1978 *The Barton Collection.* Unpublished manuscript, Department of Anthropology, University of Massachusetts. On file at University of Massachusetts Archaeological Services, Amherst.
1979 *Riverside Archaeological District.* Draft of National Register District nomination. On file at the Department of Anthropology, University of Massachusetts, Amherst.
1980 *Fort Hill in Riverside, Gill, Massachusetts.* Unpublished manuscript, Department of Anthropology, University of Massachusetts. On file at University of Massachusetts Archaeological Services, Amherst.

Hill, J. N.
1970 *Broken K Pueblo: Prehistoric Social Organization in the American Southwest.*

Anthropological Papers of the Museum of Anthropology 18. University of Arizona, Tucson.

Hitchcock, E.

1823 *Sketch of the Geology, Mineralogy and Topography of the Connecticut.* S. Converse Publisher, New Haven, CT.

1841 *Final Report on the Geology of Massachusetts.* 2 vols. J. S. & C. Adams, Amherst, MA.

1844 Discovery of More Native Copper in the Town of Whately in Massachusetts, in the Valley of Connecticut River with Remarks upon its Origin. *American Journal of Science* 47:322–323.

Hodder, I.

1982 Theoretical Archaeology: A Reactionary View. In *Symbolic and Structural Archaeology*, edited by I. Hodder, pp. 1–16. Cambridge University Press, New York.

Hoffman, C.

1989 Figure and Ground: The Late Woodland Village Problem as Seen from the Uplands. *Bulletin of the Massachusetts Archaeological Society* 50(1):24–28.

1997 Pottery and Steatite in the Northeast: A Re-evaluation. Paper presented at the 62nd annual meeting of the Society for American Archaeology, Nashville.

Hoit, D. Jr.

1793 *Survey of Deerfield, Massachusetts.* Ms. on file at Memorial Hall Museum, Deerfield.

Holland, J. G.

1855 *History of Western Massachusetts.* Bowles, Springfield.

Holmes, C. E.

1996 Broken Mammoth. In *American Beginnings: The Prehistory and Palaeoecology of Beringia*, edited by F. H. West, pp.312–318. University of Chicago Press, Chicago.

Howe, D. E.

1988 The Beaver Meadow Brook Site: Prehistory on the West Bank at Sewall's Falls, Concord, New Hampshire. *The New Hampshire Archaeologist* 29(1):49–107.

Howley, J. P.

1882 List of Newfoundland Minerals. *The Mineralogical Magazine and Journal of the Mineralogical Society of Great Britain and Ireland* 4:36–41.

Hudson, T., and T. C. Blackburn.

1983 *The Material Culture of the Chumash Interaction Sphere. Vol. 2: Food Preparation and Shelter.* Ballenna Press, Menlo Park, CA.

Hulbert, E. M.

1897 Copper Mining in Connecticut. *The Connecticut Quarterly* 3:23–32.

Hunt, C. B.

1967 *Physiography of the United States.* W. H. Freeman & Co., San Francisco.

Huntington, F. W.

1982 Piscene Remains. In *Preliminary Report on the Excavation of Flagg Swamp Rockshelter. Institute for Conservation Archaeology.* Report 214. Peabody Museum, Harvard University, Cambridge, MA.

Inglis, J. T., editor.

1993 *Traditional Ecological Knowledge: Concepts and Cases.* Canadian Museum of Nature, Ottawa, Ontario.

Jackson, E. P.
1929 *Early Geography of the Champlain Valley.* Ph.D. dissertation, Department of Geography, University of Chicago.

Jahns, R. H.
1947 *Geological Features of the Connecticut Valley, Massachusetts, as Related to Recent Floods.* Paper 966. U.S. Geological Survey, Water Supply.
1966 Surficial Geological Map of the Greenfield Quadrangle, Franklin County, Massachusetts, to accompany Map GQ-474 Scale 1:24,000. United States Geological Survey, Washington, DC.

Jennings, F.
1975 *The Invasion of America: Indians, Colonialism, and the Cant of Conquest.* University of North Carolina Press, Chapel Hill. Reprinted 1976, W. W. Norton, New York.

Johnson, E. S.
1990 *Fort Hill Springfield: 1675/1895/1989.* Paper presented at the 30th annual meeting of the Northeastern Anthropological Association, Burlington, VT.
1992 *Community and Confederacy: A Protohistoric Political Geography of Southern New England.* Paper presented at the 32nd annual meeting of the Northeastern Anthropological Association, Bridgewater, MA.
1993 *"Some by Flatteries and Others by Threatenings": Political Strategies Among Native Americans of Seventeenth-Century Southern New England.* Ph.D. dissertation, Department of Anthropology, University of Massachusetts, Amherst. University Microfilms, Ann Arbor, MI.
1996 Uncas and the Politics of Contact. In *Northeastern Indian Lives, 1632–1816,* edited by R. S. Grumet, pp. 29–47. University of Massachusetts Press, Amherst.

Johnson, E. S., and J. W. Bradley.
1987 The Bark Wigwams Site: An Early Seventeenth-Century Component in Central Massachusetts. *Man in the Northeast* 33:1–26.

Johnson, E. S., and T. F. Mahlstedt.
1984 *Guide to Prehistoric Site Files and Artifact Classification System.* Massachusetts Historical Commission, Boston.

Johnson, F., editor.
1942 *The Boylston Street Fishweir: A Study on the Archaeology, Biology, and Geology of a Site on Boyltson Street in the Back Bay District of Boston, Massachusetts.* Papers of the Robert S. Peabody Foundation for Archaeology 2. Phillips Academy, Andover, MA.
1949 *The Boylston Street Fishweir II: A Study on the Archaeology, Biology, and Geology of a Site on Boyltson Street in the Back Bay District of Boston, Massachusetts.* Papers of the Robert S. Peabody Foundation for Archaeology 4(1). Phillips Academy, Andover, MA.

Johnson, J. K.
1979 Archaic Biface Manufacture: Production Failures, a Chronicle of the Misbegotten. *Lithic Technology* 8(2):25–35.

Johnson, R. W., and A. H. McArdle.
1986 *Archaeological Locational Survey of Cabot Woods, Turners Falls, Massachusetts: A Locational Survey for the Cabot Woods Fish Research Facility.* University of Massachusetts Archaeological Services Report 42. On file at the Massachusetts Historical Commission, Office of the Secretary of State, Boston.

1987 *Archaeological Locational Survey for G Street Extension, Turners Falls, Massa-chusetts*. University of Massachusetts Archaeological Services Report 77. On file at the Massachusetts Historical Commission, Office of the Secretary of State, Boston.

Johnston, C. A.
1994 Ecological Engineering of Wetlands by Beavers. In *Global Wetlands: Old World and New*, edited by W. J. Mitsch, pp. 379–383. Elsevier, New York.

Johnston, R. B., and K. A. Cassavoy.
1978 The Fishweirs at Atherley Narrows, Ontario. *American Antiquity* 43:697–709.

Josselyn, J.
1833 An Account of Two Voyages to New England. *Collections of the Massachusetts Historical Society*, 3rd series, vol. 3, pp. 211–354. E. W. Metcalf and Company, Boston. (orig. 1635)

Justice, N. D.
1987 *Stone Age Spear and Arrow Points of the Midcontinental and Eastern United States: A Modern Survey and Reference*. Indiana University Press, Bloomington.

Kaplan, L., M. B. Smith, and L. Sneddon.
1990 The Boylston Street Fishweir: Revisited. *Economic Botany* 44:516–528.

Kaye, C. A.
1962 Early Postglacial Beavers in Southeastern New England. *Science* 138:906–907.

Keene, A. S., and E. S. Chilton.
1995 *Toward an Archaeology of the Pocumtuck Homeland*. Paper presented at the 60th annual meeting of the Society for American Archaeology, Minneapolis, MN.

Keenlyside, D.
1991 Paleoindian Occupations of the Maritimes Region of Canada. In *Clovis: Origins and Adaptations*, edited by R. Bonnichsen and K. Turnside, pp. 163–173, Center for the Study of the First Americans, Oregon State University, Corvallis.

Kelly, R. L.
1995 *The Foraging Spectrum: Diversity in Hunter-Gatherer Lifeways*. Smithsonian Institution Press, Washington, DC.

Kenyon, V. B.
1979 A New Approach to the Analysis of New England Prehistoric Pottery. *Man in the Northeast* 18:81–84.

Kerber, J. E.
1985a Digging for Clams: Shell Midden Analysis in New England. *North American Archaeologist* 6:97–113.
1985b Potowomut Cores and Quahogs: Archaeology and the Environmental and Biological Sciences. *Bulletin of the Massachusetts Archaeological Society* 46(2):62–64.
1988a Where Are the Woodland Villages in the Narragansett Bay Region? *Bulletin of the Massachusetts Archaeological Society* 49(2):66–71.
1988b Where Are the Woodland Villages?: Preface. *Bulletin of the Massachusetts Archaeological Society* 49(2):44–45.
1994 *Archaeological Investigations at the Lambert Farm Site, Warwick, Rhode Island: An Integrated Program of Research and Education by the Public Archaeology Laboratory, Inc., Vol. I*. The Public Archaeology Laboratory, Inc., Pawtucket, RI.
1997 *Lambert Farm Public Archaeology and Canine Burials Along Narragansett Bay*. Harcourt Brace College Publishers, Fort Worth, TX.

Kerber, J. E., A. D. Leveillee, and R. L. Greenspan.
1989 An Unusual Dog Burial Feature at the Lambert Farm Site, Warwick, Rhode Island: Preliminary Observations. *Archaeology of Eastern North America* 17:165–174.

Kier, C. F. Jr., and F. Calverley.
1957 The Raccon Point Site, an Early Hunting and Fishing Station in the Lower Delaware Valley. *Pennsylvania Archaeologist* 27(2).

King, A., J. W. Hatch, and B. E. Scheetz.
1997 The Chemical Composition of Jasper Artefacts from New England and the Middle Atlantic: Implications for the Prehistoric Exchange of "Pennsylvania Jasper." *Journal of Archaeological Science* 24:793–812.

Kinsey, W. F. III.
1959 Recent Excavations on Bare Island in Pennsylvania: The Kent-Hally Site. *Pennsylvania Archaeologist* 29:109–133.
1972 *Archaeology in the Upper Delaware Valley*. Pennsylvania Historical and Museum Commission, Harrisburg, PA.

Klein, M. J.
1997 The Transition from Soapstone Bowls to Marcey Creek Ceramics in the Middle Atlantic Region: Vessel Technology, Ethnographic Data, and Regional Exchange. *Archaeology of Eastern North America* 25:143–158.

Knight, J. A.
1985 *Differential Preservation of Calcined Bone at the Hirundo Site, Alton, Maine.* M.Sc. thesis, Institute for Quaternary Studies, University of Maine, Orono.

Koteff, C., J. R. Stone, F. D. Larsen, G. M. Ashley, J. C. Boothroyd, and D. F. Dincauze.
1988 Glacial Lake Hitchcock, Postglacial Uplift, and Post-Lake Archaeology. In *Field Trip Guidebook, AMQUA 1988*, edited by J. Brigham-Grette. Contribution No. 63:169–208, Department of Geology and Geography, University of Massachusetts, Amherst.

Kraft, H. C.
1973 The Plenge Site: A Paleo-Indian Occupation Site in New Jersey. *Archaeology of Eastern North America* 1(1):56–117.
1977 Paleoindians in New Jersey. In *Amerinds and their Paleoenvironments in Northeastern North America*, edited by W. S. Newman and B. Salwen, pp. 264–281. *Annals of the New York Academy of Sciences* 288.

Krause, D. J.
1989 Testing a Tradition: Douglass Houghton and the Native Copper of Lake Superior. *Isis* 80:622–639.

Kristmanson, H., and M. Deal.
1993 The Identification and Interpretation of Finishing Marks on Prehistoric Nova Scotian Ceramics. *Canadian Journal of Archaeology* 17:74–84.

Kuhn, R. D., and R. E. Funk.
1994 The Mohawk Klock and Smith Sites. Ms. in possession of the authors.

Kulp, J. L., and L. E. Tryon.
1952 Carbon-14 Measurements on Geological Samples. *Geological Society of America Bulletin* 12:1274.

Lacy, D. M.
1985 *Expanding the Archaeology of the Original Vermonters*. Paper presented at the

25th annual meeting of the Northeastern Anthropological Association, Lake Placid, NY.

1986 *Peaks and Valleys in the Distribution of Archaeological Materials: The Green Mountains of Vermont*. Paper presented at the 26th annual meeting of the Northeastern Anthropological Association, Buffalo, NY.

1987 *Preliminary Report on the Homer Stone Quartzite Quarry*. Paper presented at the 27th annual meeting of the Northeastern Anthropological Association, Amherst, MA.

1988 Prospecting for Evidence of a Green Mountain Prehistory. In *The Archaeology of Rare and Unusual Events: Comparative Experiments In Field Archaeology*, edited by E. P. Morenon and P. A. Thomas. Occasional Papers in Archaeology, Number 50. Public Archaeology Program, Rhode Island College, Providence.

1989 *A "Human Remains Policy": Observations from the Green Mountain National Forest, Vermont*. Paper presented at the Annual Conference on New England Archaeology, Sturbridge, MA.

1991 Myth Busting and Green Mountain Prehistory. Paper presented at a joint meeting of the Vermont and New Hampshire Archaeological Societies, Enfield, NH.

1994 Prehistoric Land Use in the Green Mountains: A View from the National Forest. *Journal of Vermont Archaeology* 1:92–102.

1997 Rocks, Space and the Organization of Production at a Prehistoric Quartzite Quarry. *Journal of Vermont Archaeology* 2:37–42.

Lacy, D. M., and C. Bluto-Delvental.

1995 *Common Ground: Joint Stewardship of Abenaki Heritage Sites on the Green Mountain National Forest*. Paper presented at the 35th annual meeting of the Northeastern Anthropological Association, Lake Placid, NY.

Lacy, D. M., and R. J. Hasenstab.

1983 The Development of Least Effort Strategies in CRM: Competition for Scarce Resources in Massachusetts. In *The Socio-Politics of Archaeology*, edited by J. M. Gero, D. M. Lacy and M. L. Blakey, p. 31–50. Research Report Number 23. Department of Anthropology, University of Massachusetts, Amherst.

Lacy, D. M., J. Moody, and J. Bruchac.

1992 *Preliminary Heritage Resources Reconnaissance Report: Pico/Killington "Preferred" and "No Action" Alternatives*. Report submitted to the National Park Service Eastern Team, Applied Archaeology Center, Denver.

Lahti, E., A. Spiess, M. Hedden, R. Bradley, and A. Faulkner.

1981 Test Excavations at the Hodgdon Site. *Man in the Northeast* 21:19–36.

Lankton, L.

1991 *Cradle to Grave: Life, Work, and Death at the Lake Superior Copper Mines*. Oxford University Press, Oxford.

Lapham, D. M., and C. Gray.

1973 *Geology and Origin of the Triassic Magnetite Deposit and Diabase at Cornwall, Pennsylvania*. Bulletin M56, Pennsylvania Geological Survey, 4th Series, Harrisburg, PA.

Largy, T.

1995a Appendix II: Animal Species Identified at the Howland Orchard Shell Midden. In The Howland Orchard Shell Midden (M37s-26A), Duxbury, MA, by R. Holmes and B. Otto. *Bulletin of the Massachusetts Archaeological Society* 56(1).

1995b Bone from the Clamshell Bluff Site, Concord, Middlesex County, Massachusetts. *Bulletin of the Massachusetts Archaeological Society* 56(2):64–70.

Larsen, F. D.
1984 On the Relative Ages of Glacial Lake Hitchcock, Glacial Lake Winooski, and the Champlain Sea (abstract). *Geological Society of America Abstracts with Programs* 16(1):45.

Larson, G. J.
1982 Nonsynchronous Retreat of Ice Lobes from Southeastern Massachusetts. In *Late Wisconsinan Glaciation of New England*, edited by G. J. Larson and B. D. Stone, pp. 101–114. Kendall/Hunt, Dubuque, Iowa.

Lathrop, E.
1941 *Houses of Early America*. Tudor Publishing.

Laub, R. S., M. F. DeRemer, C. A. Dufort, and W. L. Parsons.
1988 The Hiscock Site: A Rich Late Quaternary Locality in Western New York State. In *Late Pleistocene and Early Holocene Paleoecology and Archaeology of the Eastern Great Lakes Region*, edited by R. S. Laub, N. G. Miller, and D. W. Steadman, pp. 67–81. Bulletin of the Buffalo Society of Natural Sciences, vol. 33. Buffalo.

Lavin, L.
1980 Analysis of Ceramic Vessels from the Ben Hollister Site, Glastonbury, Connecticut. *Bulletin of the Archaeological Society of Connecticut* 43:3–46.
1986 Pottery Classification and Cultural Models in Southern New England Prehistory. *North American Archaeologist* 7(1):1–14.
1988 The Morgan Site, Rocky Hill, Connecticut: A Late Woodland Farming Community in the Connecticut River Valley. *Bulletin of the Archaeological Society of Connecticut* 51:7–22.

Lavin, L., F. W. Gudrian, and L. Miroff.
1993 Prehistoric Pottery from the Morgan Site, Rocky Hill, Connecticut. *Bulletin of the Archaeological Society of Connecticut* 56:63–100.

Lavin, L., and R. Kra.
1994 Prehistoric Pottery Assemblages from Southern Connecticut: A Fresh Look at Ceramic Classification in Southern New England. *Bulletin of the Archaeological Society of Connecticut* 57:35–51.

Lavin, L., and L. Miroff.
1992 Aboriginal Pottery from the Indian Ridge Site, New Milford, Connecticut. *Bulletin of the Archaeological Society of Connecticut* 55:39–51.

Lechtman, H.
1977 Style in Technology—Some Early Thoughts. In *Material Culture: Style, Organization, and Dynamics of Technology*, edited by H. Lechtman and R. S. Merrill, pp. 3–20. West Publishing, St. Paul, MN.

Lee, R. B.
1979 *The !Kung San: Men, Women, and Work in a Foraging Society*. Cambridge University Press, New York.

Lee, R. B., and I. Devore, editors.
1968 *Man the Hunter*. Aldine, Hawthorn, NY.

Lemonnier, P.
1992 *Elements for an Anthropology of Technology*. Anthropological Papers 88. Museum of Anthropology, University of Michigan, Ann Arbor.

Lenig, D.
1965   The Oak Hill Horizon and Its Relation to the Development of Five Nations Iro-
       quois Culture. *Research and Transactions of the New York State Archaeological
       Association* 15(1): 1–114.
Leone, M. P., P. B. Potter Jr., and P. A. Shackel.
1987   Toward a Critical Archaeology. *Current Anthropology* 28(3):283–302.
Lescarbot, M.
1928   *Nova Francia, A Description of Acadia, 1606,* translated by Pierre Erondelle. A.
       Hebb, London. Reprinted 1928. Harper and Brothers, New York. (orig. 1609)
Lesley, J. P., and E. V. D'Invilliers.
1886   Report on the Cornwall Iron Ore Mines, Lebanon County. In *Annual Report of
       the Geological Survey of Pennsylvania for 1885,* pp. 491–570. Harrisburg.
Leveillee, A., and A. K. Davin.
1987   *Archaeological Investigations at the Oak Terrace and Red Leaf Sites, The Stone
       Ridge Development, Norwood, Massachusetts,* vols. 1 and 2. The Public Archaeol-
       ogy Laboratory, Inc. Report submitted to McNeil Associates. On file, Massachu-
       setts Historical Commission, Boston.
Leveillee, A., and B. Harrison.
1996   An Archaeological Landscape in Narragansett, Rhode Island: Point Judith Upper
       Pond. *Bulletin of the Massachusetts Archaeological Society* 57:58–63.
Levine, M. A.
1990   Accommodating Age: Radiocarbon Results and Fluted Point Sites in Northeastern
       North America. *Archaeology of Eastern North America* 18:33–63.
1996   *Native Copper, Hunter-Gatherers, and Northeastern Prehistory.* Ph.D. disserta-
       tion, Department of Anthropology, University of Massachusetts, Amherst.
Lewis, J. V.
1907a Copper Deposits of the New Jersey Triassic. *Economic Geology* 2(3):242–257.
1907b The Newark (Triassic) Copper Ores of New Jersey. *Geological Survey of New
       Jersey: Annual Report of the State Geologist,* pp. 131–164.
Lewis, H. T.
1982   Fire Technology and Resource Management in Aboriginal North America and
       Australia. In *Resource Managers: North American and Australian Hunter-
       Gatherers,* edited by N. M. Williams and E. S. Hunn, pp. 45–68. Westview
       Press, Boulder, CO.
Lindner, C. R.
1988   *Geoarchaeology of Culturally Induced Flood Impacts: Schoharie Valley, Eastern
       New York.* Ph.D. dissertation, Department of Anthropology, State University of
       New York, Albany.
Linebaugh, D. W.
1996   *The Road to Ruin and Restoration: Roland W. Robbins and the Professionalization
       of Historical Archaeology.* Ph.D. dissertation. American Studies Program, College
       of William and Mary, Williamsburg, VA.
Lininger, J.
1991   *Native Copper in the South Mountain of Pennsylvania: A Historical Perspective.*
       Paper presented to the Red Metal Retreat, Houghton, MI.
Little, E. A.
1993   Radiocarbon Age Calibration at Archaeological Sites of Coastal Massachusetts and
       Vicinity. *Journal of Archaeological Science* 20:457–471.

1994 Radiocarbon Ages of Shell and Charcoal in a Pit Feature at Myrick's Pond, Brewster, MA. *Bulletin of the Massachusetts Archaeological Society* 55:74–77.

1995 Apples and Oranges: Radiocarbon Dates on Shell and Charcoal at Dogan Point on the Lower Hudson River. In *Dogan Point: A Shell Matrix Site in the Lower Hudson Valley*, edited by C. Claassen, pp. 121–128. Occasional Publications in Northeastern Anthropology No. 14. Archaeological Services, Bethlehem, CT.

Little, E. A., and M. J. Schoeninger.

1995 The Late Woodland Diet on Nantucket Island and the Problem of Maize in Coastal New England. *American Antiquity* 60:351–368.

Little, R. D.

1984 *Dinosaurs, Dunes, and Drifting Continents*. Alley Geology Publications, Greenfield, MA.

Lizee, J. M.

1994a *Cross-mending Northeastern Ceramic Typologies*. Paper presented at the 34th annual meeting of the Northeastern Anthropological Association. Geneseo, NY.

1994b *Prehistoric Ceramic Sequences and Patterning in Southern New England: The Windsor Tradition*. Ph.D. dissertation, Department of Anthropology, University of Connecticut, Storrs. University Microfilms, Ann Arbor, MI.

Lizee, J. M., H. Neff, and M. D. Glascock.

1995 Clay Acquisition and Vessel Distribution Patterns: Neutron Activation Analysis of Late Windsor and Shantok Tradition Ceramics from Southern New England. *American Antiquity* 60:515–530.

Lockwood, J. H., editor.

1926 *Western Massachusetts, A History, 1636–1925*. Lewis Historical Publishing Co., New York.

Logan, Sir W. E.

1863 *Geology of Canada*. Geological Survey of Canada, Montreal, Québec.

Long, A., and B. Rippeteau.

1974 Testing Contemporaneity and Averaging Radiocarbon Dates. *American Antiquity* 39:205–215.

Long, E. W.

1937 *The Story of Duxbury 1637–1937*. The Duxbury Tercentenary Committee, Duxbury, MA.

Longacre, W. A.

1970 *Archaeology as Anthropology: A Case Study*. Anthropological Papers of the Museum of Anthropology 17. University of Arizona, Tucson.

Lord, A. C. Jr.

1962 The Hawes Site: A Burial Stone Bowl Complex. *Massachusetts Archaeological Society Bulletin* 23 (3–4):21–23.

Loring, S.

1978 Unpublished notes on the inventory of private archaeological collections in Vermont. On file at the Vermont Division for Historic Preservation, Montpelier.

1980 Paleo-Indian Hunters and the Champlain Sea: A Presumed Association. *Man in the Northeast* 19:15–42.

Luedtke, B. E.

1980 The Calf Island Site and the Late Prehistoric Period in Boston Harbor. *Man in the Northeast* 20:25–76.

1985   *The Camp at the Bend of the River*. Massachusetts Historical Commission Occasional Publications in Archaeology and History. Boston.
1986   Regional Variation in Massachusetts Ceramics. *North American Archaeologist* 7(2):113–135.
1987   The Pennsylvania Connection: Jasper at Massachusetts Sites. *Bulletin of the Massachusetts Archaeological Society* 48:37–47.
1988   Where are the Late Woodland Villages in Eastern Massachusetts? *Bulletin of the Massachusetts Archaeological Society* 49(2):58–65.
1992   *An Archaeologist's Guide to Chert and Flint*. Archaeological Research Tools 7. Institute of Archaeology, University of California, Los Angeles.
MacDonald, G. F.
1968   *Debert: A Palaeo-Indian Site in Central Nova Scotia*. Anthropology Papers No. 16. National Museums of Canada, Ottawa, Ontario.
MacNeish, R. S.
1952   *Iroquois Pottery Types: A Technique for the Study of Iroquois Pottery*. National Museum of Canada Bulletin 124. Minister of Resources and Development, Ottawa.
Mahlstedt, T.
1987   Prehistoric Overview. In *Historic and Archaeological Resources of Cape Cod and the Islands*, pp. 17–53. Massachusetts Historical Commission, Office of the Massachusetts Secretary of State, Boston.
Mandryk, C. A. S., H. Josenhans, D. W. Fedje, and R. W. Mathewes.
1998   Late Quaternary Paleoenvironments of Northwestern North America: Implications for Inland Versus Coastal Migration Routes. *Quaternary Science Reviews* (in press).
Manson, C.
1948   Marcey Creek Site: An Early Manifestation in the Potomac Valley. *American Antiquity* 13:223–226.
Marglin, S. A.
1974   What Do Bosses Do? The Origins and Functions of Hierarchy in Capitalist Production. *Review of Radical Political Economy* 6:60–112.
Mathis, M. A., and J. J. Crow, editors.
1983   *The Prehistory of North Carolina: An Archaeological Symposium*. Division of Archives and History, Department of Cultural Resources, Raleigh, NC.
Matson, R. G., and G. Coupland.
1995   *The Prehistory of the Northwest Coast*. Academic Press, San Diego, CA.
Maymon, J., and C. Bolian.
1992   The Wadleigh Falls Site: An Early and Middle Archaic Site in Southeastern New Hampshire. In *Early Holocene Occupation in Northern New England*, edited by B. S. Robinson, J. B. Petersen, and A. K. Robinson, pp. 117–134. Occasional Publications in Maine Archaeology No. 9. Maine Historic Preservation Commission, Augusta.
Mayr, E.
1982   *The Growth of Biological Thought*. Belknap Press of Harvard University, Cambridge, MA.
McAllister, D. E., S. L. Cumbaa, and C. R. Harington.
1981   Pleistocene Fishes (*Coregonus, Osmerus, Microgadus, Gasterosteus*) from Green Creek, Ontario, Canada. *Canadian Journal of Earth Sciences* 18:1356–1364.

McAndrews, J. H., and L. J. Jackson.
1988 Age and Environment of Late Pleistocene Mastodont and Mammoth in Southern Ontario. In *Late Pleistocene and Early Holocene Paleoecology and Archaeology of the Eastern Great Lakes Region*, edited by R. S. Laub, N. G. Miller, and D. W. Steadman, pp. 161–172. Bulletin of the Buffalo Society of Natural Sciences, vol. 33. Buffalo.

McBride, K. A.
1984 *Prehistory of the Lower Connecticut River Valley*. Ph.D. Dissertation, Department of Anthropology, University of Connecticut, Storrs.
1990 Archaeology of the Mashantucket Pequots. In *The Pequots in Southern New England: The Fall and Rise of an American Indian Nation*, edited by L. M. Hauptman and J. D. Wherry, pp. 96–116. University of Oklahoma Press, Norman.

McBride, K. A., and R. E. Dewar.
1981 Prehistoric Settlement in the Lower Connecticut River Valley. *Man in the Northeast* 22:37–66.
1987 Agriculture and Cultural Evolution: Causes and Effects in the Lower Connecticut River Valley. In *Emergent Horticultural Economies of the Eastern Woodlands*, edited by W. F. Keegan, pp. 305–328. Occasional Paper 7. Center for Archaeological Investigations, Southern Illinois University, Carbondale.

McCann, C.
1962 The Wilson Site, Bradford County, Pennsylvania. *Pennsylvania Archaeologist* 32(2).

McCary, B. C.
1975 The Williamson Paleo-Indian Site, Dinwiddie County, Virginia. *Chesopian* 13: 47–131.

McCormick, J. S.
1980 *Criteria in Archaeological Faunal Analysis: Four Passamaquoddy Bay Cases*. M.Sc. thesis, Institute for Quaternary Studies, University of Maine at Orono.

McGahan, J.
1989 *Vessel Lot Analysis: Indian Crossing Ceramics*. Prepared for a course on Analysis of Material Culture, University of Massachusetts. Ms. on file with the author.

McIntosh, R. P.
1991 *The Background of Ecology: Concept and Theory*. Cambridge University Press, Cambridge.

McLearen, D. C.
1991 Late Archaic and Early Woodland Material Culture in Virginia. In *Late Archaic and Early Woodland Research in Virginia: A Synthesis*, edited by T. R. Reinhart and M. E. Hodges, pp. 89–138. Council of Virginia Archaeologists, Richmond.

McManamon, F. P., editor.
1984 *Chapters in the Archaeology of Cape Cod*, vol. 2. Cultural Resources Management Study 8, National Park Service, Boston.

McNaughton, S. J., and L. L. Wolf.
1979 *General Ecology*, 2nd ed. Holt, Rinehart, Winston, New York.

McNett, C. W. Jr., B. A. McMillan, and S. B. Marshall.
1977 The Shawnee-Minisink Site. In *Amerinds and Their Paleoenvironments in Northeastern North America*, edited by W. S. Newman and B. Salwen, pp. 282–296. *Annals of the New York Academy of Sciences* 288.

McNichol, A. P., editor.
1996 ¹⁴C Cycling and the Oceans. *Radiocarbon* 38(3):387–602.

Meltzer, D. J.
1989 Why Don't We Know When the First People Came to North America? *American Antiquity* 54:471–490.

Merriam, R., R. Davis Jr., D. Brown, and M. Buerger.
1976 *The History of the John Russell Cutlery Company, 1833–1936.* Bete Press, Greenfield, MA.

Meyers, T. R., and G. W. Stewart.
1977 *The Geology of New Hampshire: Part III—Minerals and Mines.* Department of Resources and Economic Development, State of New Hampshire.

Moeller, R. W.
1984 The Ivory Pond Mastadon Project. *North American Archaeologist* 5(1):1–12.

Moore, J. A., editor.
1980 *Proceedings of the Conference on Northeastern Archaeology.* Research Reports No. 19. Department of Anthropology, University of Massachusetts, Amherst.

Moore, J. A.
1981 The Effects of Information Networks in Hunter-Gatherer Societies. In *Hunter-Gatherer Foraging Strategies: Ethnographic and Archaeological Analysis,* edited by B. Winterhalder and E. A. Smith, pp. 194–217. University of Chicago Press, Chicago.

Moore, J. A., and D. Root.
1979 Anadromous Fish, Stream Ranking, and Settlement. In *Ecological Anthropology of the Middle Connecticut River Valley,* edited by R. W. Paynter, pp. 27–44. Research Reports No. 18. Department of Anthropology, University of Massachusetts, Amherst.

Moore, O. K.
1957 Divination: A New Perspective. *American Anthropologist* 59:69–74.

Moorehead, W. K.
1922 *A Report of the Archaeology of Maine.* The Andover Press, Andover, MA.
1931 *The Merrimack Archaeological Survey.* Peabody Museum, Salem, MA.

Morenon, E. P.
1986 *Archaeological Sites at an Ecotone: Route 4 Extension, East Greenwich and North Kingston, Rhode Island.* Occasional Papers in Archaeology No. 14. Public Archaeology Program, Rhode Island College, Providence.

Morrill, P.
1960 *New Hampshire Mines and Mineral Localities,* 2nd ed. Montshire Museum, Hanover, NH.

Morse, D. F., D. G. Anderson, and A. C. Goodyear.
1996 The Pleistocene-Holocene Transition in the Eastern United States. In *Humans at the End of the Last Ice Age: The Archaeology of the Pleistocene-Holocene Transition,* edited by L. G. Strauss, B. V. Eriksen, J. M. Erlandson, and D. R. Yesner, pp. 319–338. Plenum, New York.

Morse, D. R.
1975 *Prehistoric Subsistence of Coastal Maine: A Zooarchaeological Study of the Turner Farm Site.* M.A. thesis, Ball State University, Muncie, IN.

Mouer, L. D.
1991 The Formative Transition in Virginia. In *Late Archaic and Early Woodland*

Research in Virginia: A Synthesis, edited by T. R. Reinhart and M. E. Hodges, pp. 1–88. Council of Virginia Archaeologists, Richmond.

Mrozowski, S. A.

1980 Aboriginal Ceramics. In *Burr's Hill: A 17th Century Wampanoag Burial Ground in Warren, Rhode Island*, edited by S. G. Gibson, pp. 84–87. Studies in Anthropology and Material Culture, vol. 2. Haffenreffer Museum of Anthropology, Brown University, Providence, RI.

1994 The Discovery of a Native American Cornfield on Cape Cod. *Archaeology of Eastern North America* 22:47–62.

Mulholland, M. T.

1988 Territoriality and Horticulture: A Perspective for Prehistoric Southern New England. In *Holocene Human Ecology in Northeastern North America*, edited by G. P. Nicholas, pp. 137–166. Plenum, New York.

Mulholland, M. T., R. W. Drinkwater, and S. Hight.

1983a *Archaeological Locational Survey of the Riverdale Area, West Springfield, Massachusetts*. Report No. 25–521 on file at the Massachusetts Historical Commission, Boston.

Mulholland, M. T., D. Lacy, R. Johnson, and R. Holmes.

1983b *Phase I Archaeological Survey for the Ainsworth Industrial Park, Greenfield, Massachusetts*. University of Massachusetts Archaeological Services Report 3. On file at the Massachusetts Historical Commission, Office of the Secretary of State, Boston.

Mulholland, M. T., A. S. McArdle, R. J. Hasenstab, and D. M. Lacy.

1982 *A Phase I Archaeological Survey of the Deerfield River Gorge Stillwater Bridge Hydroelectric Project*. Water Resources Research Center, University of Massachusetts, Amherst.

Mullins, P., and M. Mulholland.

1995 *Archaeological Investigations at the John Alden House, Duxbury, Massachusetts*. UMASS Archaeological Services Report 209. Submitted to the Alden Kindred of America.

Mundy, J.

1994 The Dancing Seeds of the Shinnecock Indians. In *Seed Savers: 1994 Harvest Edition*, edited by K. Whealy, pp. 79–82. Seed Savers Exchange, Decorah, Iowa.

Nader, L.

1996 *Naked Science: Anthropological Inquiry into Boundaries, Power, and Knowledge*. Routledge, New York.

Naiman, R. J., C. A. Johnston, and J. C. Kelley.

1988 Alteration of North American Streams by Beaver. *Bioscience* 38:753–762.

Naiman, R. J., T. Manning, and C. A. Johnson.

1991 Beaver Population Fluctuations and Tropospheric Methane Emissions in Boreal Wetlands. *Biogeochemistry* 12:1–15.

Nassaney, M. S.

1988 *Reconnaissance Background Study and Archaeological Locational Survey for the Proposed Turners Falls Heritage State Park, Turners Falls, Massachusetts*. University of Massachusetts Archaeological Services Report No. 92. On file at the Massachusetts Historical Commission, Office of the Secretary of State, Boston.

1989 An Epistemological Enquiry into Some Archaeological and Historical Interpretations of 17th Century Native American-European Relations. In *Archaeological*

Approaches to Cultural Identity, edited by S. J. Shennan, pp. 76–91. Unwin Hyman, London.

Nassaney, M. S., and M. R. Abel.

1993   The Social and Political Contexts of Cutlery Production in the Connecticut Valley. *Dialectical Anthropology* 18:247–289.

1998   *Urban Spaces, Labor Organization, and Social Control: Lessons from New England's Nineteenth-Century Cutlery Industry*. Ms. on file in the Department of Anthropology, Western Michigan University, Kalamazoo.

Nassaney, M. S., A. H. McArdle, and P. Stott.

1989   *Archaeological Locational Survey, Site Evaluation, and Data Recovery at the Russell-Harrington Cutlery Site, Turners Falls, Massachusetts*. University of Massachusetts Archaeological Services Report No. 68. On file at the Massachusetts Historical Commission, Office of the Secretary of State, Boston.

Nelson, B. A., editor.

1985   *Decoding Prehistoric Ceramic*. Southern Illinois University Press, Carbondale.

Nelson, C.

1975   Understanding Prehistoric Subsistence in New England: The Exemplary Soft-Shell Clam. In *Final Report of the Archaeological and Paleobotanical Resources of Twelve Islands in Boston Harbor*, edited by B. Luedtke, pp. 98–111. Department of Anthropology, University of Massachusetts, Boston.

Nelson, T. C.

1942   The Oysters. In *The Boylston Street Fishweir*, vol. 2, pp. 49–64. Papers of the Robert S. Peabody Foundation for Archaeology. Phillips Academy, Andover, MA.

Neusius, S. W., editor.

1986   *Foraging, Collecting, and Harvesting: Archaic Period Subsistence and Settlement in the Eastern Woodlands*. Occasional Paper No. 6. Center for Archaeological Investigations, Southern Illinois University, Carbondale.

Newby, P. E., and T. Webb III.

1994   Radiocarbon-dated Pollen and Sediment Records from Near the Boylston Street Fishweir Site in Boston, Massachusetts. *Quaternary Research* 41:214–224.

Nicholas, G. P.

1990   *The Archaeology of Early Place: Early Postglacial Land Use and Ecology at Robbins Swamp, Northwestern Connecticut*. Ph.D. dissertation, Department of Anthropology, University of Massachusetts, Amherst. University Microfilms, Ann Arbor, MI.

1991a   Places and Spaces: Changing Patterns of Wetland Use in Southern New England. *Man in the Northeast* 42:75–98.

1991b   Putting Wetlands into Perspective. *Man in the Northeast* 42:29–38.

1997   Education and Empowerment: Archaeology with, for, and by the Shuswap Nation. In *At a Crossroads: Archaeology and First Peoples in Canada*, edited by G. P. Nicholas and T. D. Andrews, pp. 85–105. Archaeology Press, Simon Fraser University, Burnaby, British Columbia.

1998   Hunter-Gatherers and Wetlands in North America. In *Hidden Dimensions: The Cultural Significance of Wetlands,* edited by K. Bernick, pp. 31–46. UBC Laboratory of Archaeology Occasional Publications, No. 1. University of British Columbia, Vancouver.

Nicholas, G. P., and T. D. Andrews.
1997   Indigenous Archaeology in the Postmodern World. In *At a Crossroads: Archaeology and First Peoples in Canada*, edited by G. P. Nicholas and T. D. Andrews, pp. 1–20. Archaeology Press, Simon Fraser University, Burnaby, British Columbia.

Oaks, R. Q. Jr., and D. R. Whitehead.
1979   Geologic Setting and Origin of the Dismal Swamp, Southeastern Virginia and Northeastern North Carolina. In *The Great Dismal Swamp*, edited by P. W. Kirks Jr., pp. 1–23. University Press of Virginia, Charlottesville.

Odell, G. H.
1996   Economizing Behavior and the Concept of "Curation." In *Stone Tools: Theoretical Insights into Human Prehistory*, edited by G. H. Odell, pp. 51–80. Plenum, New York.

Oldale, J. P., F. C. Whitmore Jr., and J. R. Grimes.
1987   Elephant Teeth from the Western Gulf of Maine, and Their Implications. *National Geographic Research* 3:439–446.

Oldale, R.
1989   Timing and Mechanism for the Deposition of the Glaciomarine Mud in and Around the Gulf of Maine: Alternative Models. *Maine Geological Survey Studies in Maine Geology* 5:1–10.
1992   *Cape Cod and the Islands: The Geologic Story*. Parnassus Imprints, East Orleans, MA.

Oliver, B. L.
1985   Tradition and Typology: Basic Elements of the Carolina Projectile Point Sequence. In *Structure and Process in Southeastern Archaeology*, edited by R. S. Dickens and H. T. Ward, pp. 195–211. University of Alabama Press, Tuscaloosa.

Osborn, A. J.
1977   Strandloopers, Mermaids, and Other Fairy Tales: Ecological Determinants of Marine Resource Utilization—The Peruvian Case. In *For Theory Building in Archaeology,* edited by L. R. Binford, pp. 157–205. Academic Press, New York.

Otis, L. D.
1949   The Stones of Stone Age New England. *Bulletin of the Massachusetts Archaeological Society* 11(2):45–47.

Owen-Smith, R. N.
1988   *Megaherbivores: The Influence of Very Large Body Size on Ecology*. Cambridge University Press, Cambridge, MA.

Painter, F.
1988   Two Terminal Archaic Cultures of S.E. Virginia and N.E. North Carolina. *Journal of Middle Atlantic Archaeology* 4:25–38.

Patterson, W. A. III, and K. E. Sassaman.
1988   Indian Fires in the Prehistory of New England. In *Holocene Human Ecology in Northeastern North America*, edited by G. P. Nicholas, pp. 107–135. Plenum, New York.

Paynter, R., editor.
1979   *Ecological Anthropology of the Middle Connecticut River Valley*. Research Reports No. 18. Department of Anthropology, University of Massachusetts, Amherst.

Paynter, R., and P. Thorbahn.
1975   *Prehistoric Archaeological Survey of the I-391 Project Corridor*. Report number

25-52 on file, Massachusetts Historical Commission, Boston.

Peacock, S. L., and N. J. Turner.
1998 *"Just Like a Garden": Traditional Resource Management and Biodiversity Conservation on the Interior Plateau of British Columbia.* In *Biodiversity and Native North America*, edited by P. Minnis and W. Elisens. University of Oklahoma Press, Norman (in press).

Pease, J. C., and J. M. Niles.
1819 *A Gazetteer of the States of Connecticut and Rhode Island.* William S. Marsh, Hartford.

Pendergast, J. F.
1973 The Roebuck Prehistoric Village Site Rim Sherds: An Attribute Analysis. *Archaeological Survey of Canada Paper* 8.

Perkins, G. H.
1900 *Report of the State Geologist on the Mineral Industries of Vermont.* Free Press, Burlington, VT.
1910 History and Condition of the State Cabinet. In *Report of the State Geologist on the Mineral Industries and Geology of Certain Areas of Vermont*, pp. 1–75. P. H. Gobie Press, Bellows Falls.
1921 Mineral Resources. In *Report of the State Geologist on the Mineral Industries and Geology of Vermont*, pp. 299–326. Free Press Printing Company, Burlington, VT.
1930 Minerals of Vermont. In *Report of the State Geologist on the Mineral Industries and Geology of Vermont*, pp. 253–259. Free Press Printing Company, Burlington, VT.

Petersen, J. B.
1980 *The Middle Woodland Ceramics of the Winooski Sites, A.D. 1–1000.* Vermont Archaeological Society New Series, Monograph 1.
1985 Ceramic Analysis in the Northeast: Resume and Prospect. In *Ceramic Analysis in the Northeast: Contributions to Methodology and Culture History.* Occasional Publications in Northeastern Anthropology 9:5–25.

Petersen, J. B., N. D. Hamilton, J. M. Adovasio, and A. L. McPherron.
1984 Netting Technology and the Antiquity of Fish Exploitation in Eastern North America. *Midcontinental Journal of Archaeology* 9(2):199–225.

Petersen, J. B., and D. E. Putnam.
1992 Early Holocene Occupation in the Central Gulf of Maine Region. In *Early Holocene Occupation in Northern New England*, edited by B. S. Robinson, J. B. Petersen and A. K. Robinson, pp. 13–61. Occasional Publications in Maine Archaeology No. 9. Maine Historic Preservation Commission, Augusta.

Petersen, J. B., B. S. Robinson, D. F. Belknap, J. Stark, and L. K. Kaplan.
1994 An Archaic and Woodland Period Fish Weir Complex in Central Maine. *Archaeology of Eastern North America* 22:197–222.

Phelps, D. S.
1983 Archaeology of the North Carolina Coast and Coastal Plain: Problems and Hypotheses. In *The Prehistory of North Carolina: An Archaeological Symposium*, edited by M. A. Mathis and J. J. Crow, pp. 1–51. North Carolina Division of Archives and History, Raleigh.

Pollock, S. G.
1987 Chert Formation in an Ordivician Volcanic Arc. *Journal of Sedimentary Petrology* 57:75–84.

Pollock, S., N. Hamilton, and R. Boisvert.

1996 The Mount Jasper Lithic Source, Berlin, New Hampshire. In *Guidebook to Field Trips in Northern New Hampshire and Adjacent Regions of Maine and Vermont*, edited by M. R. Van Baalen, pp. 245–253. NEIG C96, Department of Earth and Planetary Sciences, Harvard University, Cambridge, MA.

Pollock, S., N. Hamilton, and R. Bonnichsen.

n.d. Chert from the Munsungun Lake Formation (Maine) in Paleoamerican Archaeological Sites in Northeastern North America: Recognition of its Occurrence and Distribution. *Journal of Archaeological Sciences* (under review).

Pollock, S., N. Hamilton, and R. Doyle.

1995 Geology and Archaeology of Chert in the Munsungun Lake Formation. In *Guidebook to Field Trips in North-Central Maine*, edited by Lindley S. Hanson, pp. 159–181. NEIG C94. Maine Geological Survey, Augusta, ME.

Pope, G. D. Jr.

1953 The Pottery Types of Connecticut. *Bulletin of the Archaeological Society of Connecticut* 27:3–10.

Pratt, M. K., and P. P. Pratt.

1987 *Synopsis of Eligibility for the Crego Site, Town of Van Buren, Onondaga County, New York*. Pratt & Pratt Archaeological Consultants, Syracuse. Report on file, New York State Office of Parks, Recreation, and Historic Preservation, Albany.

Pressey, E. P.

1910 *History of Montague: A Typical Puritan Town*. New Clairvaux Press, Montague, MA.

Preucel, R. W.

1991a The Philosophy of Archaeology. In *Processual and Postprocessual Archaeologies: Multiple Ways of Knowing the Past*, edited by R. W. Preucel, pp. 17–29. Occasional Paper No. 10. Center for Archaeological Investigations, Southern Illinois University, Carbondale.

Preucel, R. W., editor.

1991b *Processual and Postprocessual Archaeologies: Multiple Ways of Knowing the Past*. Occasional Paper No. 10. Center for Archaeological Investigations, Southern Illinois University, Carbondale.

Prezzano, S. C.

1986 *Physical Properties of Ceramic Sherds from Five Middle and Late Woodland Sites in the Upper Susquehanna Drainage*. Master's thesis, Department of Anthropology, State University of New York, Binghamton.

Prime, F.

1878 *The Brown Hematite Reports of the Siluro-Cambrian Limestones of Lehigh County*. Second Geological Survey of Pennsylvania: Report of Progress 1875–6. Harrisburg, PA.

Pulsifer, D., editor.

1859 *Records of the Colony of New Plymouth in New England, Vol IX: Acts of the Commissioners of the United Colonies of New England, Vol. I, 1643–1651*. William White, Boston.

Putnam, F. W.

1882–1883 The Kitchen Midden of Maine. *Kansas Review* 6:523–526.

1883 Shell Heaps on the Coast of Maine. *Science* 1:319.

1887 Explorations of Shellheaps on the Coast of Maine. *Peabody Museum Reports*

20:531.

Pynchon, W.

1645–1650 Records of Accounts with Early Settlers and Indians. Microfilm of manuscript, Forbes Library, Northampton, MA.

Rainey, M. L., and D. Ritchie.

1994 *Final Report: Archaeological Site Examinations, Polpis Road Bicycle Path, Nantucket, Massachusetts*. Report No. 521. The Public Archaeology Laboratory, Inc., Pawtucket, RI.

Ramsden, P. G.

1977 Refinement of Some Aspects of Huron Ceramic Analysis. *Archaeological Survey of Canada Paper* 63.

Rapp, G., E. Henrickson, and J. Allert.

1990 Native Copper Sources of Artifact Copper in Pre-Columbian North America. In *Archaeological Geology of North America,* edited by N. P. Lasca and J. Donahue, pp. 479–498. Centennial Special Volume 4. Geological Society of America, Boulder, CO.

Reice, S. R.

1984 Nonequilibrium Determinants of Biological Community Structure. *American Scientist* 82:424–435.

Rhodin, A. J., and T. Largy.

1984 Prehistoric Occurrence of the Redbelly Turtle (*Pseudemys rubriventris*) at Concord, Middlesex County, Massachusetts. *Herpetological Review* 15(4):107.

Rice, P. M.

1987 *Pottery Analysis: A Sourcebook*. University of Chicago Press, Chicago.

Rickard, T. A.

1932 *A History of American Mining*. McGraw-Hill, New York.

Ritchie, W. A.

1944 *The Pre-Iroquoian Occupation of New York State*. Rochester Museum of Arts and Science, Memoir 1. Rochester, NY.

1957 *Traces of Early Man in the Northeast*. Bulletin 358. New York State Museum and Science Service, University of the State of New York, Albany.

1959 *The Stony Brook Site and Its Relation to Archaic and Transitional Cultures on Long Island*. Bulletin 372. New York State Museum and Science Service, University of the State of New York, State Education Department, Albany.

1965 *The Archaeology of New York State*. Natural History Press, Garden City, NY.

1969a *The Archaeology of Martha's Vineyard*. Natural History Press, New York.

1969b *The Archaeology of New York State*, 2nd ed. Natural History Press, Garden City, NY.

1971 *Typology and Nomenclature for New York Projectile Points*. New York State Museum and Science Service Bulletin No. 384. Rev. ed. Albany.

1980 *The Archaeology of New York State*, Rev. ed. Harbor Hill, Harrison, NY.

Ritchie, W. A., and R. E. Funk.

1973 *Aboriginal Settlement Patterns in the Northeast*. Memoir 20. New York State Museum and Science Service, University of the State of New York, Albany.

Robbins, M.

1968 *An Archaic Ceremonial Complex at Assawompsett*. Massachusetts Archaeological Society.

1980 *Wapanucket: An Archaeological Report*. Massachusetts Archaeological Society.

Robbins, R. W.
1969 *Pilgrim John Alden's Progress: Archaeological Excavations in Duxbury.* The Pilgrim Society, Plymouth, MA.

Robinson, B. C.
1985 *The Nelson Island and Seabrook Marsh Sites, Part 1.* Occasional Publications in Northeastern Anthropology No. 9. Maine Historic Preservation Commission, Augusta.

Robinson, B. S.
1992 Early and Middle Archaic Period Occupation in the Gulf of Maine Region: Mortuary and Technological Patterning. In *Early Holocene Occupation in Northern New England,* edited by B. S. Robinson, J. B. Petersen, and A. K. Robinson, pp. 63–116. Occasional Publications in Maine Archaeology No. 9. Augusta.
1996 A Regional Analysis of the Moorehead Burial Tradition: 8500–3700 B.P. *Archaeology of Eastern North America* 24:95–147.

Rodimon, W. S.
1963 *W. S. Rodimon Collection of Indian Objects.* Pioneer Valley Press, Westfield, MA.

Roger, E. H.
1943 The Indian River Village Site. *Bulletin of the Archaeological Society of Connecticut* 14.

Rogers, E. S.
1963 *The Hunting Group-Hunting Territory Complex among the Mistassini Indians.* Bulletin 195. National Museum of Canada, Ottawa, Ontario.

Rojo, A.
1987 Excavated Fish Vertebrae as Predictors in Bioarchaeological Research. *North American Archaeologist* 8(3):209–226.

Roosevelt, A. C., M. Lima da Costa, C. Lopes Machado, M. Michab, N. Mercier, H. Valladas, J. Feathers, W. Barnett, M. Imazio da Silviera, A. Henderson, J. Sliva, B. Chernoff, D. S. Reese, J. A. Holman, N. Toth, and K. Schick.
1996 Paleoindian Cave Dwellers in the Amazon: The Peopling of the Americas. *Science* 272:373–384.

Root, D.
1984 *Material Dimensions of Social Inequality in Non-stratified Societies: An Archaeological Perspective.* Ph.D. dissertation, Department of Anthropology, University of Massachusetts, Amherst.

Rose, A. W.
1970 *Atlas of Pennsylvania's Mineral Resources.* Part 3: Metal Mines and Occurrences in Pennsylvania. Pennsylvania Geological Survey, 4th series, Bulletin M50, Harrisburg, PA.

Rosier, J.
1843 A True Relation of the Most Prosperous Voyage Made This Present Year, 1605, By Captain George Waymouth, in the Discovery of the Land of Virginia. *Collections of the Massachusetts Historical Society,* 3rd series, vol. VIII, pp. 125–157. Charles C. Little and James Brown, Boston. (orig. 1605)

Rouse, I.
1945 Styles of Pottery in Connecticut. *Bulletin of the Massachusetts Archaeological Society* 7(1):108.
1947 Ceramic Traditions and Sequences in Connecticut. *Bulletin of the Archaeological*

Society of Connecticut 21:10–25.

Ruffin, E.

1844   An Essay on Calcareous Manures, 4th ed. Laurens Wallazz, Philadelphia.

Sahlins, M.

1995   How "Natives" Think: About Captain Cook, for Example. University of Chicago Press, Chicago.

Sainsbury, J.

1975   Indian Labor in Early Rhode Island. Rhode Island History 30:378–393.

Salisbury, N.

1982   Manitou and Providence: Indians, Europeans, and the Making of New England 1500–1643. Oxford University Press, New York.

Salisbury, R. D.

1885   Notes on the Dispersion of Drift Copper. Transactions of the Wisconsin Academy of Sciences, Arts, and Letters 6:42–50.

Salwen, B.

1966   European Trade Goods and the Chronology of the Fort Shantok Site. Bulletin of the Archaeological Society of Connecticut 34:5–39.

1969   A Tentative "in situ" Solution to the Mohegan-Pequot Problem. In An Introduction to the Archaeology and History of the Connecticut Valley Indian, edited by W. R. Young, pp. 81–88. Springfield Museum of Science Publications New Series 1(1). Springfield, MA.

1978   Indians of Southern New England and Long Island: Early Period. In Northeast: Handbook of North American Indians, vol. 15, edited by B. Trigger, pp. 160–176. Smithsonian Institution Press, Washington, DC.

Sandweiss, D. H., H. McInnis, R. L. Burger, A. Cano, B. Ojeda, R. Paredes, M. del Carmen Sandweiss, and M. D. Glascock.

1998   Quebrada Jaguay: Early South American Maritime Adaptations. Science 281: 1830–1832.

Sanger, D.

1979   Introduction. In Discovering Maine's Archaeological Heritage. The Maine Historic Preservation Commission, Augusta.

1980   Archaeological Salvage and Test Excavations, Fernald Point, Acadia National Park, Maine. Report to the U.S. National Park Service, contract 6-0022-77-01, U.S. Department of the Interior, National Park Service, Denver, CO.

1981   Unscrambling Messages in the Midden. Archaeology of Eastern North America 9:37–42.

1982   Changing Views of Aboriginal Seasonality and Settlement in the Gulf of Maine. Canadian Journal of Anthropology 2(2):195–203.

1986   An Introduction to the Prehistory of the Passamaquoddy Bay Region. The American Review of Canadian Studies 16(2):139–159.

1996   Gilman Falls Site: Implications for the Early and Middle Archaic of the Maritime Peninsula. Canadian Journal of Archaeology 20:7–28.

Sanger, D., R. B. Davis, R. G. MacKay, and H. W. Borns Jr.

1977   The Hirundo Archaeological Project—An Interdisciplinary Approach to Central Maine Prehistory. In Amerinds and Their Paleoenvironments in Northeastern North America, edited by W. S. Newman and B. Salwen, pp. 457–471. Annals of the New York Academy of Sciences 288.

Sassaman, K. E.
1986 *Upland Lithic Scatters and Middle Archaic Settlement in the South Carolina Piedmont*. Paper presented at the 26th annual meeting of the Northeastern Anthropological Association, Buffalo, NY.
1993a *Early Pottery in the Southeast: Tradition and Innovation in Cooking Technology*. University of Alabama Press, Tuscaloosa.
1993b *Mims Point 1992: Archaeological Investigations at a Prehistoric Habitation Site in the Sumter National Forest, South Carolina*. Savannah River Archaeological Research Papers 4. South Carolina Institute of Archaeology and Anthropology, Columbia.
1996 Technological Innovations in Economic and Social Contexts. In *Archaeology of the Mid-Holocene Southeast*, edited by K. E. Sassaman and D. G. Anderson, pp. 37–74. University Press of Florida, Gainesville.
1997 Refining Soapstone Vessel Chronology in the Southeast. *Early Georgia* 25(1): 1–20.
1998 Distribution, Timing, and Technology of Early Pottery in the Southeastern United States. *Revista de Arquelolgia Americana* (in press).
Sassaman, K. E., and W. Rudolphi.
1995 The Handedness of Stallings Potters and Its Implications for Social Organization. Paper presented at the annual meeting of the Southeastern Archaeological Conference, Knoxville, TN.
Saville, F. H.
1920 A Montauk Cemetery at Easthampton, Long Island. *Indian Notes and Monographs* 2(3):59–102. Museum of the American Indian, Heye Foundation, New York.
Savulis, E. R., and C. C. Carlson.
1989 *An Archaeological Excavation at the Historic Simons House Site, Mashpee, Massachusetts*. University of Massachusetts Archaeological Serives, Report 89-B. University of Massachusetts, Amherst.
Schiffer, M. B.
1976 *Behavioral Archaeology*. Academic Press, New York.
Schiffer, M. B., J. M. Skibo, T. C. Boelke, M. A. Neupert, and M. Aronson.
1994 New Perspectives on Experimental Archaeology: Surface Treatments and Thermal Response of the Clay Cooking Pot. *American Antiquity* 59:197–217.
Sears, P. B.
1932 The Archaeology of Environment in Eastern North America. *American Anthropologist* 34:610–622.
Seeman, M., G. Summers, E. Dowd, and L. Morris.
1994 Fluted Point Characteristics of Three Large Sites: The Implications for Modeling Early Paleoindian Settlement Patterns in Ohio. In *The First Discovery of America*, edited by W. S. Dancey, pp. 77–94. Ohio Archaeological Council, Columbus.
Shaw, L.
1990 *The Fox 3 (Willowbend) Site: Woodland Period Adaptations on Cape Cod*. University of Massachusetts Archaeological Services Report. University of Massachusetts, Amherst.
Sheldon, G.
1895 *History of Deerfield*, vol. 1. E. H. Hall and Co., Greenfield, MA.
1920 A Guide to the Museum of the Pocumtuck Valley Memorial Association. Deerfield, MA.

1972 *A History of Deerfield, Massachusetts.* A facsimile of the 1895–96 edition, published by the Pocumtuck Valley Memorial Association, E. H. Hall and Co., MA.

Shepard, C. U.

1837 *Report on the Geological Survey of Connecticut.* B. L. Hamlen, New Haven, CT.

Silliman, B.

1810 Mineralogical and Geological Observations on New Haven and Its Vicinity. *American Mineralogical Journal* 1(3):139–149.

1818 Native Copper. *The American Journal of Science* 1:55–56.

Simmons, I. G.

1989 *Changing the Face of the Earth: Culture, Environment, History.* Basil Blackwell, New York.

Simmons, W. S.

1970 *Cautantowwit's House: An Indian Burial Ground on the Island of Conanicut in Narragansett Bay.* Brown University Press, Providence, RI.

Simmons, W. S., and G. F. Aubin.

1975 Narragansett Kinship. *Man in the Northeast* 9:21–31.

Singer, D. A.

1985 The Use of Fish Remains as a Socio-Economic Measure: An Example from 19th Century New England. *Historical Archaeology* 19(2):110–113.

Slattery, R. G.

1946 A Prehistoric Indian Site on Seldon Island, Montgomery County, Maryland. *Journal of the Washington Academy of Sciences* 36:262–266.

Smith, B. D.

1986 The Archaeology of the Southeastern United States: From Dalton to DeSoto, 10,500–500 B.P. *Advances in World Archaeology* 5:1–88.

1995 Seed Plant Domestication in Eastern North America. In *Last Hunters, First Farmers*, edited by T. D. Price and A. B. Gebauer, pp. 193–213. School of American Research, Santa Fe, NM.

Smith, C.

1944 Clues to the Chronology of Coastal New York. *American Antiquity* 1:87–98.

1947 An Outline of the Archaeology of Coastal New York. *Bulletin of the Archaeological Society of Connecticut* 21:3–9.

1950 *The Archaeology of Coastal New York.* Anthropological Papers of the American Museum of Natural History, vol. 43(2), New York.

Smith, R.

1980 *Ecology and Field Biology.* Harper and Row, New York.

Smith, W. B.

1929 *The Jones Cove Shell-Heap at West Gouldsboro, Maine.* Lafayette National Park Museum Bulletin 1. Bar Harbor, ME.

Snow, D. R.

1968 Wabanaki "Family Hunting Territories." *American Anthropologist* 70(6):1143–1151.

1978 Eastern Abenaki. In *Northeast: Handbook of North American Indians*, vol. 15, edited by B. Trigger, pp. 138–147. Smithsonian Institution Press, Washington, DC.

1980 *The Archaeology of New England.* Academic Press, New York.

1992 *Discussants Comments for the Symposium "Correlating Archaeology and Linguistics: Algonquians and Iroquoians."* Presented at the 57th annual meeting of the

Society for American Archaeology, Pittsburgh, PA.

1992 Disease and Population Decline in the Northeast. In *Disease and Demography in the Americas*, edited by J. W. Verano and D. H. Ubelaker, pp. 177–186. Smithsonian Institution Press, Washington, DC.

Solecki, R.

1950 The Archaeological Position of Historic Fort Corchaug, Long Island and its Relation to Contemporary Forts. *Bulletin of the Archaeological Society of Connecticut* 24:3–40.

Southon, J. R., D. E. Nelson, and J. S. Vogel.

1990 A Record of Past Ocean-Atmosphere Radiocarbon Differences from the Northeast Pacific. *Paleoceanography* 5:197–206.

Speck, F.

1977 *Naskapi: Savage Hunters of the Labrador Peninsula*. University of Oklahoma Press, Norman.

Spiess, A. E.

1984 Arctic Garbage and New England Paleo-Indians: The Single Occupation Option. *Archaeology of Eastern North America* 12:280–285.

1990 Deer Tooth Sectioning, Eruption, and Seasonality of Deer Hunting in Prehistoric Maine. *Man in the Northeast* 39:29–44.

1992 Archaic Period Subsistence in New England and the Atlantic Provinces. In *Early Holocene Occupation in Northern New England*, edited by B. S. Robinson, J. B. Petersen and A. K. Robinson, pp. 163–185. Occasional Publications in Maine Archaeology No. 9. Maine Historic Preservation Commission, Augusta.

Spiess, A. E., M. L. Curran, and J. R. Grimes.

1984-1985 Caribou (*Rangifer tarandus* L.) Bones from New England Paleoindian Sites. *North American Archaeologist* 6(2):145–159.

Spiess, A. E., and M. Hedden.

1983 *Kidder Point and Sears Island in Prehistory*. Occasional Publications in Maine Archaeology No. 3. Maine Historic Preservation Commission, Augusta.

Spiess, A. E., and R. A. Lewis.

1995 Features and Activity Areas: The Spatial Analysis of Faunal Remains (Appendix 8). In *Diversity and Complexity in Prehistoric Maritime Societies: A Gulf of Maine Perspective,* by B. J. Bourque, pp. 337-373. Plenum, New York

Spiess, A. E., and J. Mosher.

1994 Hedden: A Paleoindian Site on the Kennebunk Plains. *Maine Archaeological Society Bulletin* 34(2):25–54.

Spiess, A. E., J. Mosher, K. Callum, and N. Asch Sidell.

1995 Fire on the Plains: Paleoenvironmental Data from the Hedden Site. *Maine Archaeological Society Bulletin* 35(1):13–52.

Spiess, A., and D. B. Wilson.

1987 *Michaud: A Paleoindian Site in the New England-Maritimes Region*. Occasional Publication in Maine Archaeology No. 6.

Spiess, A., D. B. Wilson, and J. Bradley.

1998 Paleoindian Occupation in the New England-Maritime Region: Beyond Cultural Ecology. *Archaeology of Eastern North America* 26:188–196.

Squier, E. G.

1851 *Antiquities of the State of New York*. George H. Derby, Buffalo, NY.

Stanner, W. E. H.
1987 The Dreaming. In *Traditional Aboriginal Society: A Reader*, edited by W. H.
      Edwards, pp. 225–236. Macmillan Australia, South Melbourne.
Stanyard, W. F.
1997 *The Big Haynes Reservoir Archaeological Project: A Perspective on the Native
      American History of North-Central Georgia between 8,000 B.C. and A.D. 1838.*
      Report submitted to Conyers-Rockdale-Big Haynes Impoundment Authority by
      Garrow and Associates, Atlanta, GA.
Starbuck, D. R.
1980 The Middle Archaic in Central Connecticut: The Excavation of the Lewis-Walpole
      Site (6-HT-15). In *Early and Middle Archaic Cultures in the Northeast*, edited by
      D. R. Starbuck and C. E. Bolian, pp. 5–37. Occasional Publications in North-
      eastern Anthropology, No. 7. George's Mill, NH.
1982 *A Middle Archaic Site in Belmont, New Hampshire.* New Hampshire Department
      of Public Works and Highways, Concord.
Starbuck, D. R., and C. E. Bolian, editors.
1980 *Early and Middle Archaic Cultures in the Northeast.* Occasional Publications in
      Northeastern Anthropology, No. 7. George's Mill, NH.
Stark, M. T., editor.
1998 *The Archaeology of Social Boundaries.* Smithsonian Institution Press, Washing-
      ton, DC.
Steadman, D. W., T. W. Stafford Jr., and R. E. Funk.
1997 Nonassociation of Paleoindians with AMS-Dated Late Pleistocene Mammals from
      the Dutchess Quarry Caves, New York. *Quaternary Research* 47:105–116.
Stephenson, R. L., and A. L. L. Ferguson.
1963 *The Accokeek Creek Site: A Middle Atlantic Seaboard Culture Sequence.* Anthro-
      pological Papers 20. Museum of Anthropology, University of Michigan, Ann
      Arbor.
Steward, J.
1969 Postscript to Bands: On Taxonomy, Processes, and Causes. In Contributions to
      Anthropology: Band Societies, edited by D. Damas. *National Museums of Canada
      Bulletin* 228:288–295.
Stewart, R. M.
1989 Trade and Exchange in Middle Atlantic Region Prehistory. *Archaeology of East-
      ern North America* 17:47–78.
Stiles, E.
1916 *Extracts from the Itineraries and other Miscellanies of Ezra Stiles, D.D., LL.D.
      1755–1794 with a Selection from His Correspondence*, edited by F. Bowditch
      Dexter. Yale University Press, New Haven, CT.
Stone, O. L.
1930 *History of Massachusetts Industries.* S. J. Clarke Publishing, Boston.
Storck, P. L.
1988 The Early Palaeo-Indian Occupation of Ontario: Colonization or Diffusion? In
      *Late Pleistocene and Early Holocene Paleoecology and Archeology of the Eastern
      Great Lakes Region*, edited by R. S. Laub. *Bulletin of the Buffalo Society of
      Natural Sciences* 33:243–250.
Storck, P. L., and J. Tomenchuk.
1990 An Early Paleoindian Cache of Informal Tools at the Udora Site, Ontario. *Re-*

search in Economic Anthropology, Supplement 5:45–93. JAI Press, Greenwich, CT.

Storck, P. L., and P. H. von Bitter.

1989 The Geological Age and Occurrence of Fossil Hill Formation Chert: Implications for Early Paleoindian Settlement Patterns. In *Eastern Paleoindian Lithic Resource Use*, edited by C. J. Ellis and J. C. Lothrop, pp. 165–190. Westview Press, Boulder, CO.

Stose, G. W.

1910 The Copper Deposits of South Mountain in Southern Pennsylvania. *Bulletin of the United States Geological Survey*, No. 430, pp. 122–131.

1932 *Geology and Mineral Resources of Adams County Pennsylvania*. Pennsylvania Geological Survey, 4th series, County Reports C1, Harrisburg, PA.

Stose, G. W., and F. Bascom.

1929 *Geological Atlas of the United States: Fairfield-Gettysburg Folio*. U.S. Geological Survey, Washington, DC.

Stothers, D. M.

1977 The Princess Point Complex. *Archaeological Survey of Canada Paper 58*.

1996 Resource Procurement and Band Territories: A Model for Lower Great Lakes Paleoindian and Early Archaic Settlement Systems. *Archaeology of Eastern North America* 24:173–216.

Stoughton, R. M.

1978 *History of the Town of Gill, Franklin County, Massachusetts: 1793–1943*. E. A. Hall, Greenfield, MA.

Strauss, A. E.

1979 *A Study of Prehistoric Swordfishing by Members of the Moorehead Burial Tradition Between 4500 and 3700 B.P.: The Exploitation of a Dangerous Resource and its Effects on Social Status and Religion*. M.A. thesis, Department of Anthropology, State University of New York, Binghamton.

1994 *Intensive Archaeological Survey and Excavation of a Prehistoric Shell Pit Feature at Houselot 37 Bates Lane in Brewster, Massachusetts*. Report prepared for Massachusetts Historical Commission, Boston.

Stuiver, M., and T. F. Braziunas.

1993 Modeling Atmospheric ^{14}C Influences and ^{14}C Ages of Marine Samples to 10,000 BC. *Radiocarbon* 35(1): 137–189.

Stuiver, M., and G. W. Pearson.

1993 High Precision Bidecadal Calibration of the Radiocarbon Time Scale, A.D. 1950–500 B.C. and 2500–6000 B.C. *Radiocarbon* 35(1):1–23.

Stuiver, M., G. W. Pearson, and T. Braziunas.

1986 Radiocarbon Age Calibration of Marine Samples back to 9000 Cal Yr B.P. *Radiocarbon* 28(2B):980–1021.

Stuiver, M., and H. A. Polach.

1977 Discussion: Reporting of ^{14}C Data. *Radiocarbon* 19:355–363.

Stuiver, M., and P. J. Reimer.

1993 Extended ^{14}C Data Base and Revised CALIB 3.03 Age Calibration Program. *Radiocarbon* 35:215–230.

Swigart, N.

1987 The Woodruff Rock Shelter Site 6LF125. An Interim Report: Faunal Remains as a Means to Evaluate Environment and Culture. *Bulletin of the Archaeological*

Society of Connecticut 50:43-65.
Taber, M. A.
1955 A History of the Cutlery Industry in the Connecticut Valley. Smith College Studies in History, vol. 41. Northampton, MA.
Tankersley, K. B.
1991 A Geoarchaeological Investigation of Distribution and Exchange in the Raw Material Economies of Clovis Groups in Eastern North America. In Raw Material Economies among Prehistoric Hunter-Gatherers, edited by A. Montet-White and S. Holen, pp. 285-303. Publications in Anthropology 19. Department of Anthropology, University of Kansas, Lawrence.
1994 Was Clovis a Colonizing Population in Eastern North America? In The First Discovery of America: Archaeological Evidence of the Early Inhabitants of the Ohio Area, edited by W. S. Dancey, pp. 1-15. The Ohio Archaeological Council, Columbus.
Tankersley, K. B., and J. D. Holland.
1994 Lithic Procurement Patterns at the PaleoCrossing Site, Medina County, Ohio. Current Research in the Pleistocene 11:61-63.
Tankersley, K. B., S. Vanderlaan, J. D. Holland, and S. Bland.
1997 Geochronology of the Arc Site: A Paleoindian Habitation in the Great Lakes Region. Archaeology of Eastern North America 25:31-44.
Taylor, R. E.
1987 Radiocarbon Dating: An Archaeological Perspective. Academic Press, New York.
Taylor, R. E., A. Long, and R. S. Kra, editors.
1992 Radiocarbon After Four Decades: An Interdisciplinary Perspective. Springer-Verlag, New York.
Temple, J. H.
1887 History of North Brookfield. Town of North Brookfield, MA.
Temple, J. H., and G. Sheldon.
1875 History of the Town of Northfield. Joel Munsell, Albany, NY.
Terry, R. D., and G. V. Chilingar.
1955 Data Sheet 6. Geotimes. Available from the American Geological Institute, Washington, DC. Reprinted from the Journal of Sedimentary Petrology 25: 229-234.
Thelfall, M. E., and J. Bowen.
1981 Faunal Analysis of a Coastal Midden in Rhode Island: Greenwich Cove. Paper presented at the 21st annual meeting of the Northeastern Anthropological Association, Saratoga Springs, NY.
Thomas, M. M.
1993 Preliminary Report of Investigations: Prehistoric and Historic Native Copper Mining in Northwestern Wisconsin. Unpublished Honors Student Research, Department of Anthropology, University of Minnesota, Duluth.
Thomas, P. A.
1976 Contrastive Subsistence Strategies and Land Use as Factors for Understanding Indian-White Relations in New England. Ethnohistory 23(1):1-18.
1979a In the Maelstrom of Change: The Indian Trade and Culture Process in the Middle Connecticut River Valley, 1635-1665. Ph.D. dissertation, Department of Anthropology, University of Massachusetts, Amherst.
1979b The Wills Hill Site: A Middle Woodland Hunting-Gathering Camp. Massachusetts Archaeological Society Bulletin 40(2):39-54.

1980 The Riverside District, the WMECO Site, and Suggestions for Archaeological Modelling. In *Early and Middle Archaic Cultures in the Northeast*, edited by D. R. Starbuck and C. E. Bolian, pp. 73–96. Occasional Publications in Northeastern Anthropology No. 7.

1986 Discerning Some Spatial Characteristics of Small, Short-term, Single Occupation Sites: Implications for New England Archaeology. *Man in the Northeast* 31: 99–121.

Thomas, P. A., P. Doherty, and E. J. Warren.

1982 *Cultural Resource Management Study, Ball Mountain Lake, Jamaica and Londonderry, Vermont.* Report No. 39, Department of Anthropology, University of Vermont, Burlington.

Thorbahn, P. F.

1984 *Depositional Mosaics.* Paper presented at the 24th annual meeting of the Northeastern Anthropological Association, Hartford, CT.

1988 Where Are the Late Woodland Villages in Southern New England? *Bulletin of the Massachusetts Archaeological Society* 49(2):46–57.

Thurman, M. D.

1985 A Cultural Synthesis of the Middle Atlantic Coastal Plain. Part I: " Culture Area" and Regional Sequence. *Journal of Middle Atlantic Archaeology* 1:7–32.

Traill, R. J.

1970 *A Catalogue of Canadian Minerals.* Department of Energy, Mines and Resources, Geological Survey of Canada Paper 69–45.

Trigger, B. G.

1966 Sir Daniel Wilson: Canada's First Anthropologist. *Anthropologica* 8:3–28.

1981 Giants and Pygmies: The Professionalization of Canadian Archaeology. In *Towards a History of Archaeology,* edited by G. Daniel, pp. 69–84. Thames and Hudson, London.

1989 *A History of Archaeological Thought.* Cambridge University Press, New York.

Trumbull, B. D. D.

1818 *A Complete History of Connecticut,* 2 vols. Malty, Goldsmith and Co. and Samuel Wadsworth, New Haven.

Trumbull, J. H.

1850 *Public Records of the Colony of Connecticut, 1636–1776,* 15 vols. Brown and Parsons, Hartford.

Trumbull, J. Russel.

1898 *History of Northampton, Massachusetts, from its Settlement in 1654,* 2 vols. Gazette Printing Co., Northampton, MA.

Truncer, J.

1991 Current Research on Soapstone Vessels. *Bulletin of the Archaeological Society of New Jersey* 46:49–53.

1997 *Steatite Vessel Function.* Paper presented at the 62nd annual meeting of the Society for American Archaeology, Nashville, TN.

Truncer, J., M. D. Glascock, and H. Neff.

1998 Steatite Source Characterization in Eastern North America: New Results Using Instrumental Neutron Activation Analysis. *Archaeometry* 40:23–44.

Tuck, J. A.

1978 Northern Iroquoian Prehistory. In *Handbook of the North American Indians, Vol.*

15, *The Northeast*, edited by B. G. Trigger, pp. 322–333. Smithsonian Institution Press, Washington, DC.

Turnbaugh, W. A.

1975 Toward an Explanation of the Broadpoint Dispersal in Eastern North America. *Journal of Anthropological Research* 31:51–68.

Turner, B. L. III, W. C. Clark, R. W. Kates, J. F. Richards, J. T. Mathews, and W. B. Myer.

1990 *The Earth as Transformed by Human Action: Global and Regional Changes in the Biosphere over the Past 300 Years*. Cambridge University Press, Cambridge.

Turner, N. J.

1991 Burning Mountain Sides for Better Crops: Aboriginal Landscape Burning in British Columbia. In *Archaeology in Montana*, edited by K. P. Cannon. Montana Archaeological Society, Bozeman.

Tyzzer, E. E.

1943 Animal Tooth Implements from the Shell Heaps of Maine. *American Antiquity* 8: 354–362.

Tzedakis, P. C.

1987 A 10,000-Year Record of Environmental Change from Cape Cod, Massachusetts. *Current Research in the Pleistocene* 4.

Uchupi, E., D. Aubrey, G. S. Giese, and D. J. Kim.

1997 *The Late Quaternary Construction of Cape Cod Massachusetts: A Reconsideration of the W. M. Davis Model*. Geological Society of America Special Paper 309.

Ulrich, T. G.

1979a *An Archaeological Survey of the Deerfield Industrial Park*. Report to the Deerfield Economic Development and Industrial Corporation (DEDIC), South Deerfield, Massachusetts.

1979b Subsistence, Horticulture, and Ecosystems: A Modeling Approach to Cultural Resource Management. In *Ecological Anthropology of the Middle Connecticut River Valley*, edited by R. W. Paynter, pp. 57–63. Research Report No. 18. Department of Anthropology, University of Massachusetts, Amherst.

Vogel, J. C., A. Fuls, E. Visser, and B. Becker.

1993 Pretoria Calibration Curve for Short-Lived Samples, 1930 BC–3350 BC. *Radiocarbon* 33(1):73–86.

Walker, D.

1970 Direction and Rate in Some British Post-Glacial Hydroseres. In *Studies in the Vegetational History of the British Isles*, edited by D. Walker and R. G. West, pp. 117–139. Cambridge University Press, Cambridge.

Waring, A. J. Jr.

1968 The Bilbo Site, Chatham County, Georgia (orig. 1940). In *The Waring Papers: The Collected Works of Antonio J. Waring, Jr.*, edited by S. Williams, pp. 152–197. Papers of the Peabody Museum of Archaeology and Ethnology, vol. 58. Harvard University, Cambridge, MA.

Waselkov, G. A.

1982 *Shellfish Gathering and Shell Midden Archaeology*. Ph.D. Dissertation, Department of Anthropology, University of North Carolina, Chapel Hill.

Waters, J. H.

1965 Animal Remains from Some New England Woodland Sites. *Bulletin of the Archaeological Society of Connecticut* 33:5–12.

1967 Fish Remains from Southern New England Archaeological Sites. *Copeia* 1: 244–245.

Watters, D. R., J. Donahue, and R. Stuckenrath.
1992 Paleoshorelines and the Prehistory of Barbuda, West Indies. In *Paleoshorelines and Prehistory: An Investigation of Method*, edited by L. L. Johnson, pp. 15–52. CRC Press, Boca Raton, FL.

Webb, R. S., and P. Newby.
1987 Evidence for Changes in Lake Levels in the Northeastern United States during the Holocene. *International Union for Quaternary Research Programme with Abstracts*, p. 286. 12th International Congress, Ottawa, Ontario.

Webb, W. S.
1946 *Indian Knoll, Site Oh2, Ohio County, Kentucky*. Reports in Anthropology, Pt. 1, Vol. 4, No. 3. Department of Anthropology, University of Kentucky, Lexington.
1957 *The Development of the Spearthrower*. Occasional Papers in Anthropology 2. Department of Anthropology, University of Kentucky, Lexington.

Webb, W. S., and W. G. Haag.
1939 *The Chiggerville Site, Site 1, Ohio County, Kentucky*. Reports in Anthropology and Archaeology, Vol. 4, No. 1. Department of Anthropology, University of Kentucky, Lexington.

Weed, W. H.
1911 *Copper Deposits of the Appalachian States*. U.S. Geological Survey Bulletin 455. Washington, DC.

Weeks, J. M.
1971a *Report of the Archaeological Survey Between the French King Bridge and the Western End of the Proposed Route 2 Extension*. Unpublished manuscript, Massachusetts Archaeological Society. On file at the University of Massachusetts Archaeological Services, Amherst.
1971b Steatite-Tempered Pottery in New England. *Man in the Northeast* 2:103–104.

Wentworth, D.
1973 *The Settlement and Growth of Duxbury, 1628–1870*. The Duxbury and Rural Historical Society Duxbury, MA.
1980 *The Alden Family in the Alden House*. The Duxbury and Rural Historical Society, Duxbury, MA.

West, F. H.
1996 Beringia and New World Origins: The Archaeological Evidence. In *American Beginnings: The Prehistory and Palaeoecology of Beringia*, edited by F. H. West, pp. 537–559. University of Chicago Press, Chicago.

Wherry, E. T.
1909 The Newark Copper Deposits of South-Eastern Pennsylvania. *Economic Geology* 3:726–738.

White, M. E.
1963 Settlement Pattern Change and the Development of Horticulture in the New York-Ontario Area. *Pennsylvania Archaeologist* 33:1–12.

Whitman, W.
1927 Song for All Seas, All Ships. In *Leaves of Grass* [1855], edited by E. Holloway, p. 222. Doubleday, Page, and Company, Garden City, NY.

Wiessner, P.
1982 Risk, Reciprocity and Social Influences on !Kung San Economics. In *Politics and*

History in Band Societies, edited by E. Leacock and R. Lee, pp. 61–84. Cambridge University Press, New York.

1983   Style and Social Information in Kalahari San Projectile Points. *American Antiquity* 48:253–276.

1990   Is There a Unity to Style? In *The Uses of Style in Archaeology*, edited by M. Conkey and C. Hastorf, pp. 105–112. Cambridge University Press, Cambridge.

Wilder, H. H., and E. B. Delabarre.

1920   Indian Corn-hills in Massachusetts. *American Anthropologist* 22:203–225.

Willey, G. R., and P. Phillips.

1958   *Method and Theory in American Archaeology*. University of Chicago Press, Chicago.

Willey, G. R., and J. A. Sabloff.

1993   *A History of American Archaeology*, 3rd ed. W. H. Freeman and Company, New York.

Williams, L. E.

1972   *Fort Shantock and Fort Corchaug: A Comparative Study of Seventeenth Century Culture Change in the Long Island Sound Area*. Ph.D. dissertation, New York University. University Microfilms, Ann Arbor, MI.

Williams, N. M., and E. S. Hunn, editors.

1982   *Resource Managers: North American and Australian Hunter-Gatherers*. Westview Press, Boulder, CO.

Williams, R.

1963   *The Complete Writings of Roger Williams*, vol. 6, edited by J. R. Bartlett. Russell and Russell, New York.

1973   *A Key into the Language of America*, edited by J. J. Teunissen and E. J. Hinz, Wayne State University Press, Detroit, MI. (orig. 1643)

Willoughby, C. C.

1927   An Ancient Indian Fish-Weir. *American Anthropologist* 29:105–108.

1935   *Antiquities of the New England Indians*. Peabody Museum of American Archaeology and Ethnology, Harvard University, Cambridge, MA.

Wilson, D., and A. Spiess.

1990   Study Unit 1: Fluted Point Paleoindian. *Maine Archaeological Society Bulletin* 30(1):15–31.

Wilson, M. L., and S. J. Dyl II.

1992   The Michigan Copper Country. *The Mineralogical Record* 23(2).

Wilson, Sir D.

1855   Antiquities of the Copper Region of the North American Lakes. *Proceedings of the Antiquaries of Scotland* 2:203–212.

1856   The Ancient Miners of Lake Superior. *The Canadian Journal* 1(3):225–237.

Winkler, M. G.

1985   A 12,000-Year History of Vegetation and Climate for Cape Cod, Massachusetts. *Quaternary Research* 23.

Winkler, M. G., and P. Sanford.

1995   Coastal Massachusetts Pond Development: Edaphic, Climatic, and Sea Level Impacts Since Deglaciation. *Journal of Paleolimnology* 14:311–336.

Winslow, E.

1841   Good News from New England. In *Chronicles of the Pilgrim Fathers of the*

Colony of Plymouth, edited by A. Young, pp. 269–375. Charles C. Little and James Brown, Boston. (orig. 1624)

Wise, C. L.
1975 A Proposed Early to Middle Woodland Ceramic Sequence for the Delmarva Peninsula. *Maryland Archaeology* 11:21–29.

Witthoft, J.
1952 A Paleo-Indian Site in Eastern Pennsylvania: An Early Hunting Culture. *Proceedings of the American Philosophical Society* 96(4):464–495.
1953 Broad Spearpoints and the Transitional Period Cultures. *Pennsylvania Archaeologist* 23(1):4–31.

Wobst, H. M.
1974 Boundary Conditions for Paleolithic Social Systems: A Simulation Approach. *American Antiquity* 39:147–178.
1977 Stylistic Behavior and Information Exchange. In *Papers for the Director: Research Essays in Honor of James B. Griffin*, edited by C. E. Cleland, pp. 317–342. Anthropology Papers, Museum of Anthropology, vol. 61, University of Michigan, Ann Arbor.
1978 The Archaeo-Ethnology of Hunter-Gatherers or the Tyranny of the Ethnographic Record in Archaeology. *American Antiquity* 43(2):303–309.
1983 We Can't See the Forest for the Trees: Sampling and the Shapes of Archaeological Distributions. In *Archaeological Hammers and Theories*, edited by J. A. Moore and A. S. Keene, pp. 37–85. Academic Press, New York.

Wood, W.
1977 *New England's Prospect*, edited by A. T. Vaughan. The Commonwealth Series, W. E. A. Bernhard, general editor. University of Massachusetts Press, Amherst. (orig. 1634)

Woodward, H. P.
1944 *Copper Mines and Mining in New Jersey*. Geological Series, Bulletin 57, Department of Conservation and Development. State of New Jersey, Trenton.

Wright, G. A., S. Bender, and S. Reeve.
1980 High Country Adaptation. *Plains Anthropologist* 25:181–198.

Wright, H. A.
1897 Discovery of Aboriginal Remains near Springfield, Massachusetts. *Scientific American* 76(11):170.

Wright, J. V.
1978 The Implications of Probable Early and Middle Archaic Projectile Points from Southern Ontario. *Canadian Journal of Archaeology* 2:59–78.
1980 The Role of Attribute Analysis in the Study of Iroquoian Culture Prehistory. In *Proceedings of the 1979 Iroquois Pottery Conferences*, edited by C. F. Hayes III, pp. 21–26. Rochester Museum and Science Center, Research Records 13, Rochester, New York.

Wylie, A.
1989 Matters of Fact and Matters of Interest. In *Archaeological Approaches to Cultural Identity*, edited by S. J. Shennan, pp. 94–109. Unwin Hyman, London.

Wyman, J.
1868 An Account of Some Kjoekken, Moeddings, or Shell-heaps, in Maine and Massachusetts. *American Naturalist* 1:561–584.

Yellen, J.
1977 *Archaeological Approaches to the Present: Models for Reconstructing the Past.*
      Academic Press, New York.
Yesner, D. R.
1984 The Evolution of Aboriginal Fishing Strategies in Southwestern Maine. *Récherches Amerindiennes au Québec* 14(1):34–44.
Yesner, D. R., N. Hamilton, and R. Doyle Jr.
1983 Landlocked Salmon and Early Holocene Lacustrine Adaptations in Southwestern Maine. *North American Archaeologist* 4(4):307–333.
Zeolli, G. D.
1978 Two Grooved Axe Associations from the South Shore. *Bulletin of the Massachusetts Archaeological Society* 39(2):41–46.

Index

About the Editors and Contributors

CATHERINE C. CARLSON is an associate professor in the Department of Social and Environmental Studies at the University College of the Cariboo, Kamloops, British Columbia, where she teaches archaeology and ethnography.

ELIZABETH S. CHILTON is an assistant professor in the Department of Anthropology at Harvard University. Her research interests include New England prehistory, hunter-gatherers, the origins of agriculture, small-scale horticultural societies, ceramic studies, and the epistemology of classification.

JOHN R. CROSS served recently as the archaeologist for the Portland Natural Gas Transmission Survey Project in Maine. His research interests include lithic technologies and the Archaic occupation of New England.

MARY LOU CURRAN is an associate curator in the Archaeology Department, Peabody-Essex Museum, Salem, Massachusetts, and is associate editor of *The Review of Archaeology*. As a member of the Tangle Lakes project, she assisted in editing a recent volume on Siberian and Alaskan early sites research (Frederick H. West, editor). Current research in Paleoindian studies includes ongoing work on the Bull Brook and Whipple site collections.

FREDERICK J. DUNFORD is resident archaeologist at the Cape Cod Museum of Natural History and a research associate at the R. S. Peabody Museum of Archaeology in Andover, Massachusetts. Dunford and Greg O'Brien are authors of *Secrets in the Sand: The Archaeology of Cape Cod* (1997).

ELENA FILIOS is adjunct assistant professor at Central Connecticut State University, New Britain, Connecticut, and at Holyoke Community College, Holyoke, Massachusetts. Her interests include the social dimensions of hunter-gatherer mobility and public education. She is the regional coordinator of the

Southern New England Archaeology Program at Central Connecticut State University and Massachusetts Coordinator of the Society for American Archaeology's Public Education Network.

ROBERT J. HASENSTAB is project archaeologist for the Central Artery/Tunnel Project in Boston, Massachusetts. His research interests include Late Woodland archaeology, aboriginal settlement, and horticulture.

ERIC S. JOHNSON is a preservation planner at the Massachusetts Historical Commission. Among his most recent publication is "Uncas and the Politics of Contact" (in *Northeastern Indian Lives, 1632-1861*, edited by Robert S. Grument, Norman: University of Oklahoma Press, 1996), an account of the life and times of the seventeenth-century Mohegan sachem.

ALICE B. KEHOE is professor of anthropology at Marquette University. Her research interests include the archaeology and ethnology of North American Indians, the history of archaeology, and gender studies in archaeology. She is author of numerous publications including such books as *North American Indians* and *The Ghost Dance: Ethnohistory and Revitalization*. Her articles have appeared in many journals including *American Antiquity, Current Anthropology,* and *Plains Anthropologist.*

DAVID M. LACY has been the archaeologist for the Green Mountain and Finger Lakes National Forest since 1986, and has served on Vermont's Advisory Council on Historic Preservation since 1991. In these capacities, he maintains an interest in and familiarity with the culture histories and research issues of all the region's occupations, from Paleoindians to the Civilian Conservation Corps.

MARY ANN LEVINE is an assistant professor in the Department of Anthropology at Franklin and Marshall College in Lancaster, Pennsylvania. Her research interests include Northeastern prehistory, hunter-gatherers, and women in archaeology.

ELIZABETH A. LITTLE is a research fellow at the Nantucket Historical Association and research associate at the R. S. Peabody Museum of Archaeology, Andover, Massachusetts. A student of ethnohistory, isotopes, and radiocarbon dating in the northeast, she coauthored in 1995 an article in *American Antiquity* with Margaret Schoeninger titled "The Late Woodland Diet on Nantucket Island and the Problem of Maize in Coastal New England."

MITCHELL T. MULHOLLAND is director of University of Massachusetts Archaeological Services. His research interests include cultural resource management, culture and paleoclimate, archaeological survey methods, computer applications, and New England archaeology. He is the author of numerous reports, articles, and book chapters.

MICHAEL S. NASSANEY is an associate professor of anthropology at Western Michigan University. His research interests include social archaeology, political economy, and the ways in which social relations are created and reproduced through material culture, especially in North America.

GEORGE P. NICHOLAS is Archaeology Program Director for the Simon Fraser University/Secwepemc Cultural Education Society in British Columbia, Canada. His research interests include the Paleoindian and Archaic occupations of New England, paleoenvironmental reconstruction, and the relationship of archaeology to indigenous peoples. He has published numerous articles on New England archaeology and edited the volume *Holocene Human Ecology in Northeastern North America* (1988).

KENNETH E. SASSAMAN recently joined the Anthropology Department of the University of Florida after eleven years with the Savannah River Archaeological Research Program of the South Carolina Institute of Archaeology and Anthropology, University of South Carolina. His research centers on the hunter-gatherer prehistory of the American Southeast, technological change, and social theory.